Royal Collections IV

The Grand Ducal House of Hesse

By Arturo E. Beéche & Ilana D. Miller

ISBN: 978-1-944207-08-3

EUROHISTORY.COM

Aerial view of Darmstadt before its destruction during World War II.

EUROHISTORY.COM

Eurohistory & Kensington House Books
6300 Kensington Avenue
East Richmond Heights, CA 94805
USA
Email: eurohistory@comcast.net or aebeeche@mac.com
Phone: 510.236.1730

Arturo E. Beéche & Ilana D. Miller
The Grand Ducal House of Hesse
ISBN: 978-1-944207-08-3

Cover artwork by David W. Higdon

Disclaimer

Cover: Grand Duke Ludwig IV and his family.
Back cover: Grand Duke Ernst Ludwig of Hesse and by Rhine; Irène, Princess Henry of Prussia;
Grand Duke Paul Alexandrovich of Russia; Princess Alix of Hesse and by Rhine; Prince Waldemar
of Prussia; Grand Duke Serge Alexandrovich of Russia; Grand Duchess Elisabeth Feodorovna of Russia.

To the memory of Lu and Peg …

"Don't forget …
Think deeply, speak gently,
love much, laugh often,
work hard, give freely,
pay promptly, pray earnestly…"

✶✶✶✶✶

Acknowledgements

The authors would like to express their deep appreciation to several people whose contributions and permissions deeply enriched this book. Among them are:

HM Queen Elizabeth II
The late Landgraf Moritz of Hesse
The late Prince Alfred of Prussia
Archduchess Helen of Austria
The Margrave and Margravine of Baden
Prince Ludwig and Princess Marianne of Baden
Prince Andreas of Saxe-Coburg and Gotha
Duke Borwin of Mecklenburg
Duchess Donata of Mecklenburg-Schwerin
The late Fürst Kraft of Hohenlohe-Langenburg
Fürst Philipp and Fürstin Saskia of Hohenlohe-Langenburg
The Dowager Fürstin Irma of Hohenlohe-Langenburg
Fürstin Katharina of Hohenlohe-Oehringen
Prince Andreas and Princess Luise of Hohenlohe-Langenburg
Count Hans-Veit zu Toerring-Jettenbach
Hereditary Count Ignaz zu Toerring-Jettenbach
The late Countess Mountbatten of Burma

Many thanks to our friend Larry Russell for his support
toward the publication of the book!

Special appreciation to The Beéche Trust for once again
contributing to another Eurohistory project.

Ilana would like to add, "During this strange time, it has been a pleasure to do an endeavor with an enthusiastic partner, so first let me thank my fellow author, Arturo Beéche for his expertise and encouragement. As always, the support of family is very important so I want to thank my husband, Tom Heller and as always my parents, Gloria and Sherman Miller for their never-ending presence in my life. Thanks also to Katrina Warne for her constant encouragement and to Dave Higdon for his editing."

The authors would also like to thank the following friends for their
suggestions, advise, guidance, resources, and ideas:

Seth B. Leonard, Annet Bakker, Mary E. Houck, M.D.
Jan Dirk van der Nyet, Hilde Vieveen, Albert Nieboer, Marianne van Dam,
Katie Tice, Geoff Teeter, and the late William M. Lalor,

Contents

Grand Duke Ludwig IV and Grand Duchess Alice of Hesse and by Rhine with their children. From the left: Victoria, Ludwig IV holding Marie, Ernst Ludwig, Alice holding Alix, and Elisabeth with her hand on Irène.

Author's Note

When Arturo E. Beéche founded Eurohistory in 1997, he envisioned the creation of a library of royal books encompassing all of Europe's ruling and formerly ruling dynasties. Two decades later, and after more than 30 books and over 120 issues of Eurohistory, the royalty journal he founded in 1997, we bring you The Grand Ducal House of Hesse. This is the third German dynasty that Eurohistory publishes a book about, the first two being the Ducal House of Saxe-Coburg and Gotha and the Royal House of Bavaria (Volume I). Most other Eurohistory books have focused on various royal personalities, as well as other dynasties, among them: the Romanovs, the Greek Royal House, the Danish Royal House, the Bourbons of the Two Sicilies, the Braganzas of Portugal, and the Nassaus of Luxembourg.

This project is the culmination of more than two decades of research conducted by Arturo E. Beéche and Ilana D. Miller. Having already cooperated on several books and articles with Ms. Miller, a regular contributor to Eurohistory, pairing for another collaborative project was seamless. The Hesse and by Rhine Dynasty is one which Ms. Miller, better-known for her extensive work on the four daughters of Grand Duchess Alice of Hesse and by Rhine, with particular interest on Victoria Milford Haven, also feels passionately about. The result of years of research in Europe allowed Ms. Miller a unique insight into the lives of these four tragic sisters.

Initially, the authors had hoped that they could start the story of the Hessians at the very beginning of their dynasty, back in the XIII century. However, space constraints caused by the abundant pictographic material contained in this work forced the authors to rethink the structure of the book. Instead of bringing the reader to the historical start of the House of Hesse from within the confines of the ancient House of Brabant, they realized that it would be easier to begin the storyline in 1567. This was the year when the sons of Landgrave Philipp "the Magnanimous" divided his vast lands among them. All branches of the Hessian dynasty stem from this territorial division. The chapter that was taken out will be used when a book on the branch of Hesse-Kassel is written.

The Grand Ducal House of Hesse and by Rhine is among the most important German dynasties. Its members form a kaleidoscope of unique human beings: military and religious leaders, peculiar and heroic figures, talented artists and scientists, patrons of the arts and music, visionary and romantic architects, lucky and tragic people, dilettantes more interested in passing by than making a mark. They simply had it all. Their mark, not only in Darmstadt, but also throughout the Rhineland, is palpable in nearly every aspect of the region's history, arts, letters, music, and architecture.

The authors were inspired by having had the opportunity to meet members of this extended family. They profited from the reminiscences shared by royalty who knew the last three generations of the House of Hesse and by Rhine. We wish to thank them for access to rare primary sources and family vignettes. Throughout their research, no other Hessian impacted them as much as Victoria Milford Haven, born Princess Victoria of Hesse and by Rhine. A woman of immense conviction and unmeasurable integrity, self-facing and matter-of-fact, she served as guide and inspiration to the authors. She was as an inspiration, a source of strength, a path to emulate when life's vagaries make one think that there is no tomorrow. She never gave up...she composed herself, picked up the shattered pieces around her, and continued onward, ready for tragedy, but emboldened to overcome it....

The Grand Duchy of Hesse in German Empire

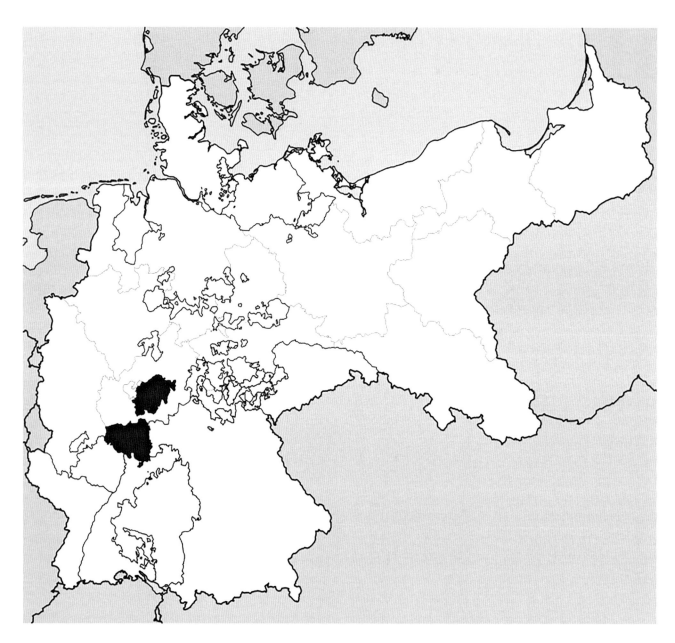

Established as an independent landgraviate in 1567, after the death of Landgrave Philipp "the Magnanimous," the lands encompassing Hesse-Darmstadt shifted several times due to partitions, losses, acquisitions, and political expediency. In 1806, the Landgraviate of Hesse-Darmstadt was elevated to a Grand Duchy by the grace of Emperor Napoléon. The name Hesse-Darmstadt was later superseded by that of "Hesse and by Rhine," the country eventually becoming widely known as the "Grand Duchy of Hesse." This map of the German Empire, prior to the Great War, shows the territories, colored in black, that formed the Grand Duchy of Hesse in 1914.

Prologue

Hesse, a sizeable modern-day German state, is probably best known for the large city of Frankfurt as well as for being the home of the pharmaceutical company, Merck, found outside the bustling town of Darmstadt. Both of these are situated on the left side of the Rhine River, which runs through the area. What is less well-known save to aficionados, is that it is also the home of a quaint old Grand Duchy, and it existed before the Second Reich as well as during it.

The attractive green hills and valleys that are all a part of its lovely landscape are nestled snuggly in the Rhine River Valley. The countryside is dotted with charming and picturesque hamlets, villages, and towns. In keeping with its Grimm's fairy tale quality, mysterious mists and fogs hover over its woods and forests as well as lovely castles and palaces that easily set off a fertile and fanciful imagination. Visions of its Royal and Imperial past shimmer over the blue-green hills.

There are the ghosts of four young girls in white dresses, satin sashes with hair ribbons flying, playing at Heiligenberg; the shade of an Empress, ill and disappointed with her husband's infidelities; the sweet sounds of a little girl playing in her life-sized play house at Wolfsgarten; the horrible murders in a far-off cellar; and the mourning crowds lining the town for the funeral of the entire Grand Ducal Family, save one ill-fated little girl and her devastated uncle.

The life and death of one family, horrible and sad as it was, coincided with the real and difficult birth of another branch of the family. Named for a small village with an extinct title, they had a patriarch who succumbed to love and a mother who was quietly ambitious for her four handsome sons. They presented a united front that held steadfast, one for the other. The family extended its reach to Great Britain by achieving great success as well as experiencing unbelievable tragedy.

To say that tragedy followed the Hesse and by Rhines, Battenbergs, and Mountbattens, though, is an oversimplification and a disservice to the accomplishments of these family members. It implies helplessness, which was certainly not the case. Ultimately, through prejudice and slights, they evolved into a modern aristocratic family: successful, hardworking, and non-complacent...

****

The Last Division of the Vast Landgraviate of Hesse
1567

The line of the Landgraves of Hesse-Darmstadt emanated from the division of his properties by Landgrave Philipp "the Magnanimous" of Hesse. He owned vast territories in the Rhineland and modern-day Westphalia. These realms extended from Kassel to Frankfurt and surrounding areas. Following Germanic inheritance tradition, Landgrave Philipp divided his realm among all his surviving sons: Hesse-Kassel went to his eldest son Wilhelm; Ludwig received Hesse-Marburg; Philipp became Landgrave of Hesse-

Landgrave Philipp "the Magnanimous" and his wife Christina of Saxony, founders of the six lines of the House of Hesse.

Rheinfels; and Georg succeeded as Landgrave of Hesse-Darmstadt. In total landmass, Wilhelm received half of their father's inheritance, while Ludwig received one fourth, and Philipp and Georg one eighth each. These initial divisions were later traded, exchanged, and inherited by various lines of Hessian princes. Every time a line would die out, reshuffling of territories ensued. Consequently, the lands under the rule of the House of Hesse constructed a kaleidoscope of ever-changing borders, oftentimes redrawn by the fortunes, or misfortunes, of the local landgrave.

Just to provide an example regarding this penchant for constantly shifting borders – In 1604, Landgrave Ludwig of Hesse-Marburg died without issue. Two years before, Ludwig exchanged parts of his realm with his nephew Moritz, Landgrave of Hesse-Kassel. Three years later, Moritz inherited the remainder of Marburg and incorporated the lands into his own landgraviate. In 1606, he acquired the right to administer the vast holdings of the Abbey of Hersfeld, and thirteen years later, he exchanged some of his Hessian landholdings for Saxon-held territories. All this trading and territorial reshaping in a lifetime. Upon his death in 1632, the borders of his landgraviate moved yet again when his realm was divided among three of his sons. This latest partitioning created three new Landgraviates of Hesse: Hesse-Kassel (Electors); Hesse-Eschwege, and Hesse-Rheinfels-Rotenburg. It was not going to be the last territorial reshuffling caused by death, exchange, or the sale of land.

By the 19th century, six Hessian lines remained: the Electors of Hesse-Kassel, the Landgraves of Hesse-Philippstahl, the Landgraves of Hesse-Philippstahl-Barchfeld, the Landgraves of Hesse-Rotenburg, the Landgraves of Hesse-Darmstadt (who in 1806 became Grand Dukes of Hesse, and later changed their title to Grand Dukes of Hesse and by Rhine, although their realm continued being officially known by its initial grand ducal name) and the Landgraves of Hesse-Homburg.

Chapter I

The Landgraves of Hesse- Darmstadt 1567-1790

Landgrave Georg I of Hesse-Darmstadt (1547-1596)

Georg, future first Landgrave of Hesse-Darmstadt, was born in Kassel on September 10, 1547.[1] When Landgravine Christine gave birth to her sixth child Georg, his father Philipp had already been in imperial captivity for three months. With the death of Christine, a year and a half later, caring for her minor children became a matter of grave concern. Hence, responsibility over the young Hessians fell to their barely 17-year-old brother Wilhelm, who sent them to the Electoral Court in Dresden, where their older sister Agnes cared for them. The Hessian guests remained in Saxony until Landgrave Philipp returned from custody in 1552.

Landgrave Georg I of Hesse-Darmstadt.

In order to enable his education far away from the court, Georg was sent to the fortress of Ziegenhain.[2] There, he was under the supervision of the tutor Guntram Schenck von Schweinsberg. Along with young Georg were sons of various knights who served under his father. Five years later, in 1561, Georg attended the University of Marburg, a venerable institution founded by his august father. Georg's political future was also settled by his father through Landgrave Phillip's Testamentary Modification of 1560, which granted the young Hessian his own realm centered around Katzenelnbogen and Darmstadt. However, in the years before the division of Hesse after Philip's death in 1567, and the subsequent "fraternal contract" among his sons, Georg was considered as governor of Darmstadt. The town was due for rehabilitation after the damage suffered during the of the Schmalkaldic wars. Darmstadt was in shambles and the ramshackle old Residenzschloß (main residence) was derelict and desolate. There were plans for a new government building that would include the Town Hall, as well as the very important office that administered fish farming on the Rhein and water supply for the region.

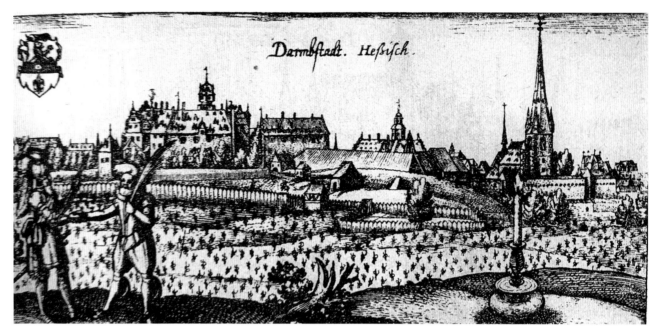

Darmstadt around the year 1624.

The origins of the castle lie in the time of the ancient Counts of Katzenelnbogen. In the middle of the 13th century they erected a moated castle in Darmstadt, the town having received city rights in 1330. A year later the castle was first mentioned. Over the next two centuries, the Counts of Katzenelnbogen kept building and adding to the castle. By the middle of the 15th century, the moat was drained, and the structure updated. The only two remaining traces of the old moated castle are the shape of the central church yard and the outer walls of the Lords' Room. When the last Count of Katzenelnbogen died in 1479, Darmstadt fell to Landgrave Heinrich III of Hesse. During the reign of Landgrave Philipp "the Magnanimous" the Residenzschloß was destroyed twice when Darmstadt was sacked and burnt. Landgrave Georg I of Hesse-Darmstadt extended the castle considerably to a Renaissance complex and secured it with ditches and bastions.

A new gatehouse in the north of the castle, was built in 1627 by Jakob Müller. The bell building was built between 1663 to 1671 to plans by the architect Johann Wilhelm Pfannmüller. In 1693, Darmstadt was attacked by French troops. The castle keep was destroyed. In 1715, Landgrave Ernst Ludwig commissioned the French architect Louis Remy de la Fosse to plan a new baroque palace with four large wings, after the chancellery had burned down. This would have completely replaced the old castle. Due to lack of money, however, only two wings were completed by 1726. This therefore was the last major structural change made to the castle. When Hesse-Darmstadt joined the Confederation of the Rhine in 1806, the castle became the seat of the Grand Dukes in Darmstadt. However, just as soon as possible, plans to build a newer palace were started.

On September 11, 1944, the Residenzschloß burned down to the outer walls. Reconstruction took two decades before the external condition of the prewar period was largely restored to detail. Work on restoring the inside was a costly and painstakingly slow process. Today, the Residenzschloß houses important museums, archives, and offices.

Barely 20-years-old when he took over the government of his inheritance in 1567, Landgrave Georg was able to build on the reforms and reconstruction initiated by his brother Landgrave Ludwig, which included renewed efforts to provide assistance to the crafts to help restart the battered economy. Georg seems to have been, *"a serious-minded, pious young man, who developed into a wise and strong ruler."*[3] Furthermore, Lord Mountbatten described him as someone who, *"examined all questions affecting the welfare of his state personally and then laid down his policy so clearly that it is said nothing happened in Hesse-Darmstadt that was not in accordance with his wishes."*[4] Georg supported agriculture and led efforts to improve farms and orchards, while also building a canal, *"to drain a swamp and turn it into fertile land."*[5] Furthermore, Georg sought to continue improving his realm by creating schools, starting a silk industry, and introducing the use of the Gregorian calendar. He was an effective administrator of the feebled inheritance he received and ran his court

Landgravine Magdalena of Hesse-Darmstadt (née Lippe).

in an *"orderly and economical way."*[6] Determined to leave his children a clean exchequer and a debt-free legacy, he succeeded in increasing his country's treasury. In spite of his efforts to be judicious about money management, Georg was also able to repair many of his residences, while also acquiring new estates, among them Schloß Kranichstein. This allowed him, *"to live in different parts of his country and watch over the welfare of all parts personally."*[7]

Five years into his reign, on August 17, 1572, Georg married Countess Magdalena of Lippe, a daughter of Count Bernhard VIII of Lippe and his wife, the

former Countess Catharina of Waldeck-Eisenberg.[8] Magdalena was raised at the court of Landgrave Wilhelm of Hesse, Georg's elder brother, where she was considered naturally beautiful. She and Georg met at his brother's court and became very fond of each other, their attraction leading them to the marriage altar. Magdalena, who was pious, virtuous and benevolent, gave her beloved husband ten offspring. In 1576, Magdalena gave birth to their first child, Philipp Wilhelm, who died soon after birth. The following year, her second son, Ludwig V (1577-1626), was born in Darmstadt. Christina and Elisabeth followed in 1578 and 1579, respectively.[9] Christina married Count Friedrich Magnus of Erbach in 1595 but died in childbirth the following year. Elisabeth married in 1601 Count Johann-Casimir of Nassau-Saarbrücken-Weilburg. Her husband died in 1602, before the couple celebrated their first wedding anniversary. Elisabeth's luck in marriage did not improve for in 1611 tragedy struck once again as she was about to marry Count Palatine Johann August of Veldenz-Lützelstein (b. 1575). The groom had been previously married to Countess Anna Elisabeth of Palatinate-Simmern, widow of Elisabeth's uncle Landgrave Wilhelm of Hesse-Rheinfels. Johann August died at Schloß Lemberg while on his way to marry Elisabeth. She lived a long life dying in 1655, the last surviving child of her parents.[10]

In 1580, Landgravine Magdalena gave birth to a third daughter, Marie Hedwig, who died two years later.[11] Georg and Magdalena's third son,

Philipp III (1581-1643), succeeded to his own realm, Hesse-Butzbach. Although married twice, Philipp III died childless and his lands reverted to Hesse-Darmstadt.[12] Countess Anna, Georg and Magdalena's seventh child, was born in 1583. She married Count Albrecht Otto of Solms-Laubach (1576-1610) and died in 1631.[13] In 1585, Magdalena gave birth to Friedrich, who received his own Landgraviate of Hesse-Homburg, and died in 1638.[14] Friedrich's descendants ruled over his domains until 1866, when their line became extinct. Briefly, Hesse-Homburg reverted to Hesse and by Rhine, before Prussia annexed the landgraviate after the Seven Weeks' War.

Schloß Kranichstein.

as a hunting lodge and retreat. Landgrave Georg I had the three-winged Renaissance building constructed between 1578-1580 by his master builder Jakob Kesselhuth. His descendants, the hunting enthusiasts Landgraves Ernst Ludwig and Ludwig VIII organized large hunting festivals in the form of par force hunts. For this purpose, the still functional building was adapted to the baroque notions of representation, elegance, and luxury. Schloß Kranichstein had the express purpose of conveying to the landgrave's guests his importance, prominence, and power. In the surrounding forests the landgraves built other hunting structures, including the Dianaburg, a baroque hunting lodge built by Ludwig VIII in 1765. Over 350 years, the forests of Kranichstein were used by the landgraves and the later Grand Dukes of Hesse and by Rhine for hunting.

Magdalena's last two pregnancies were troublesome as both babies died soon after birth. Exhausted by what seemed a constant state of pregnancy, Magdalena suffered the fate of many other contemporary women and died as a result of childbirth. In fact, Magdalena did not recover from the birth of her son Johann in 1587.[15] She was buried in the choir of the City Church (Stadtkirche) in Darmstadt.

Back in 1572, Landgrave Georg initiated the first stages of the construction of the Darmstadt Residenzschloß, which stands in the center of the town to this day. He also designated Schloß Lichtenberg as a dower house, while acquiring Schloß Kranichstein, as previously mentioned,

From June 1863, Schloß Kranichstein housed future Grand Duke Ludwig IV and his wife Alice until the completion of the Neues Palais in 1866. On June 2, 1863 Alice wrote to her mother, Queen Victoria: *"If I return now, I have to unpack and pack for Kranichstein and the house there, which has been uninhabited for no more than eighty years."*[16] In the following years, until Alice's death in 1878, Schloß Kranichstein was used as a summer residence. In a letter dated June 27, 1863, she wrote to her mother: *"I bathe every morning and swim around, there is*

Landgrave Georg I of Hesse-Darmstadt.

a beautiful little bathhouse there."[17] She also describes how her husband had a skating accident in 1875 when the ice broke and he fell through: *"Louis put me in terrible terror last week, breaking in a very deep spot on the ice. Since it was in Kranichstein, he dressed and rubbed himself in front of the stove in the steward's room, in whose clothes he also came home, he looked very funny."*[18]

In 1917, Schloß Kranichstein became a museum when Grand Duke Ernst Ludwig had all hunting equipment and corresponding accessories from his castles and hunting lodges collected. Court Marshal Count Kuno von Hardenberg set up the hunting museum. The Hessian Hunting Foundation acquired the facility after the Second World War and finally reopened the museum in 1952 with a focus on the baroque era. From 1988 to 1996, the castle was comprehensively renovated by the state of Hesse, the city of Darmstadt, and the Hessian Hunting Foundation. The original Renaissance version was restored on the ground floor. Since the end of the late 1990s, Kranichstein has served as a popular and picturesque wedding venue.

Landgrave Georg's zeal for rebuilding was not restricted to architectural projects, in fact, he also put in place reforms designed to accelerate the economic recovery of his realm. Darmstadt had suffered greatly in the multiple wars Landgrave Philipp was involved, and it was to his young son to lead the recovery. He gave priority to the improvement of the administration and economy of the landgraviate. For the reorganization of the judiciary and the official governmental structure, Georg relied on the assistance and good work of Johann Milchling von Schönstadt and Chancellor Johan Fischwer, who had served his brothers in Kassel and Marburg. The economic reforms were sustainable, particularly in the areas of agriculture, water supply, fisheries' management, and the reforestation of neglected deciduous forests with coniferous trees. In 1569, Georg traveled to Italy, where he was introduced to the silk industry.[19] Consequently, he brought silkworms to Darmstadt and started

Epitaph of Landgrave Georg I and Landgravine Magdalena, Darmstadt Stadtkirche.

an industry around silk. Undoubtedly, Georg succeeded in *"raising the standard of living and repairing the ravishes of war in a most remarkable way."*[20]

Unlike his father, Georg reduced military expenditures to a minimum. His most prominent military adventure was getting involved in the liquidation of the county of Diez, which his father had set aside for the children from his bigamous marriage to Margarethe von der Saale. The sudden death of most of the Counts of Diez between 1568-69, led to the Landgrave Philipp's legitimate sons moving quickly to undo their father's decision to provide revenue sources for his second family.

In matters of faith, he was a Protestant zealot. Imbued with a heightened sense of righteousness, Georg's religious reforms persecuted suspected "witches," which caused serious differences with his brothers. His nickname "the Pious" most likely refers to his strict adherence to pure Lutheran lore.

Two years after his wife's death, Landgrave Georg married Eleonore of Württemberg (1552-1618).[21] She was the widow of Fürst Joachim Ernst of Anhalt (1538-1586), her parents being Duke Christoph of Württemberg and his wife, the former Margravine Anna Maria of Brandenburg-Ansbach.[22] They had one son, Heinrich, who was born in 1590, but died in 1601.[23] Georg and Elenore had no other children. Georg died in 1596 and was succeeded as Landgrave of Hesse-Darmstadt by his eldest son Ludwig V.

Landgrave Ludwig V of Hesse-Darmstadt (1577-1626)

Born in Darmstadt on September 24, 1577, Ludwig was the second son of Landgrave Georg I and his first wife.[24] He had an older brother Philipp Wilhelm, born and died in 1576. Ludwig V was known as "the steadfast" for his unquestioned loyalty to three succeeding Habsburg Emperors in spite of the political and financial sacrifices this course of action entailed.

Landgrave Ludwig V of Hesse-Darmstadt.

Since Ludwig V had to take over the government of the landgraviate at the age of eighteen, he was unable to embark on the lengthy educational journeys that had become the norm for young men of his standing. In 1595, he had embarked on a four-month tour of France and Italy.[25] In 1597 and 1598, he visited Berlin, both journeys with the purpose of settling on a wife. His choice had landed on Magdalena of Brandenburg, daughter of Elector Johan Georg I and his third wife Elisabeth of Anhalt-Zerbst. In his bride and her family, Ludwig found as strict Lutherans as he was. His wedding had to be rescheduled as Magdalena's father died in early 1598, forcing the couple to marry later that summer. Given that the court in Berlin was in mourning, the actual wedding celebrations, against custom, took place in Darmstadt, the groom's hometown.

Ludwig V and Magdalena were prolific parents, having twelve offspring between 1600 and 1616. The children were: Magdalena (1600-1624), who married Duke Ludwig Friedrich of Württemberg-

Montbéliard; Anna-Eleonore (1601-1659), married to Duke Georg of Brunswick-Lüneburg; Marie (1602-1610); Sophie Agnes (1604-1664), who married Count Palatine Johann Friedrich of Hippolstein; Landgrave Georg II; Juliana (1606-1659), who married Ulrich II, Count of East Frisia; Amalia (1607-1627); Johann, Landgrave of Hesse-Braubach (1609-1651); Heinrich (1612-1629); Hedwig (1613-1614); Ludwig (b./d. 1614); and Friedrich (1616-1682).[26]

Two of the younger sons of Landgrave Ludwig V, Johann and Friedrich, were also significant. Johann was an army commander in Austria, then served under the Swedish flag, and finally returned to imperial service. A few years before his death, he retired to Braubach, which his father had appropriated for him as an independent landgraviate. Since there were no children from his marriage to Countess Johannetta of Sayn-Wittgenstein, upon Johann's death in 1651, Braubach returned to Darmstadt. Johannetta survived her husband for half a century.[27] In 1661, still a young woman, she married Duke Johann Georg I of Saxe-Weimar-Eisenach. As for Friedrich, he converted to Catholicism while in Italy, was Grand Master of the Order of St John, and finally attained the office of Prince-Bishop and Cardinal of Breslau.

Ludwig's youngest son, Friedrich, is considered by historians to be among the most remarkable characters of the Hessian dynasty. Before his tenth birthday, Friedrich matriculated at the University of Marburg. In 1628, he was elected rector in

SERENISSIMVS & EMINENTISSIMVS PRINCEPS ac DOMINVS DOMINVS FRIDERICVS S R E CARDINALIS, LANDGRAVIVS HASSIÆ EQVESTRIS MELITENSIVM ORDL. S. Ioannis Baptistæ Magn, per Germaniam Prior, Com.inCatzenelenbogen, Dietz, Ziegenheim, Nidda, Isenburg & Budingen; etc.

Friedrich, Cardinal Hesse.

succession to his brother Heinrich. The following year he traveled to Italy, where he matriculated at the University of Sienna, and came under strong Catholic influence *"for he was converted to that faith on 9th January 1637 in Rome, and two days later entered the Order of St John as a Knight of Malta."*[28] The next few years saw Friedrich serving the Maltese with distinction, even commanding the *"galleys which defeated the Turks when they were besieging Malta."*[29]

In 1642, Friedrich entered the service of King Felipe IV. He not only served as Captain-General of Minorca, but also commanded the East Indies Fleet before transferring to become Commander-in-Chief of the Spanish Cavalry and Infantry forces in the Netherlands. Five years after entering Spanish service, Friedrich became Grand Prior of the Order of St John in Germany. In 1652, Landgrave Friedrich was appointed Cardinal-Deacon, the first of many high offices he received, including being elected Bishop of Breslau in 1671.[30]

Emperor Leopold I held Landgrave Friedrich in high esteem and loaded him with honors. He was named Protector of the Kingdoms of Aragon and Sicily, Imperial Ambassador. Even as he served as Bishop of Breslau, Leopold named Friedrich Commander-in-Chief of Silesia.

Friedrich of Hesse-Darmstadt died at Breslau on February 19, 1682.[31] His life was one filled with remarkable achievements. He was *"an outstanding scholar, administrator, Admiral, General and*

Cardinal."[32] He was buried in the St Elisabeth's Chapel in the Cathedral of Breslau. His heart was brought to the Presbytery of the Church of Neisse.

The first years of the reign of Ludwig V were a continuation of the expansion plans started by his father for the Darmstadt Residenzschloß. He also invested considerable resources in planning the expansion and modernization of the old suburb around Darmstadt's Balonplatz.

With the death in the fall of 1604 of Landgrave Ludwig of Hesse-Marburg, the last of the sons of "magnanimous" Philipp, the dispute over his valuable heritage became the dominant theme. The testament of the Landgrave of Hesse-Marburg had made the keeping of his nephews in the pure doctrine of Lutheranism a precondition for the division of his territories. Ludwig's nephews began a long dispute over the spoils that required many years to be settled. While most civil, imperial, and religious authorities sided with Darmstadt, the Landgrave of Hesse was relentless in his quest to obtain the lion's share of the Marburg inheritance.

As his vassal, Emperor Rudolf II confirmed Ludwig V's succession of Hesse-Darmstadt in feudal tenure. His two younger brothers, Philipp and Friedrich, were also named co-rulers. However, Ludwig was able to make financial and territorial arrangements with his brothers that allowed him to retain the bulk of his lands. In 1609 Ludwig

An allegory showing Habsburg Emperor Rudolf II and his Hessian ally, Landgrave Ludwig V.

gave Butzbach to Philipp, while in 1622 Friedrich received Homburg. Butzbach returned to Hesse-Darmstadt in 1643 upon the death of its first landgrave since Philipp died childless.

Regardless of the heated political-denominational tensions in the Empire exacerbated by the founding of the Protestant "Union" and Catholic "League," Landgrave Ludwig, after his wife died in 1616 needed an escape. The respite he sought from his travails was found in embarking on a great pilgrimage that was to lead him through Spain to Palestine via Malta. However, the journey was aborted in Malta on the advice of the Grand Master of the Knights of St John because of the pirate threat in the eastern Mediterranean. Instead, Landgrave Ludwig, who later became known as the faithful (fidelis) for his strict adherence to the Lutheran faith, decided to pay a visit to the Pope in Rome. Concerned with possible rumors about him returning to the fold of Catholicism, Ludwig V wrote to his subjects, *"I have made deep impression on the pope, but I have not kissed his slippers, because I said before our meeting that I will not do such a thing ... in my religion I have been well known everywhere..."*[33] Thankful for the welcome he received from the Knights of St John, he sent them a cast bronze shield with the Hesse coat of arms, which stands today in front of the cathedral in la Valetta.

In the meantime, war ignited across Germany, a devastating conflict known as the Thirty Years War.

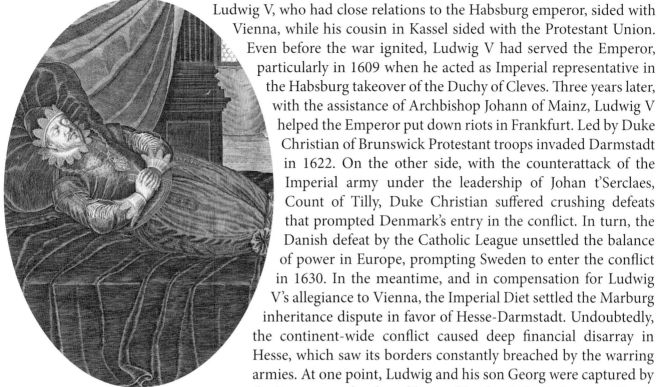

Deathbed of Landgrave Ludwig V.

Ludwig V, who had close relations to the Habsburg emperor, sided with Vienna, while his cousin in Kassel sided with the Protestant Union. Even before the war ignited, Ludwig V had served the Emperor, particularly in 1609 when he acted as Imperial representative in the Habsburg takeover of the Duchy of Cleves. Three years later, with the assistance of Archbishop Johann of Mainz, Ludwig V helped the Emperor put down riots in Frankfurt. Led by Duke Christian of Brunswick Protestant troops invaded Darmstadt in 1622. On the other side, with the counterattack of the Imperial army under the leadership of Johan t'Serclaes, Count of Tilly, Duke Christian suffered crushing defeats that prompted Denmark's entry in the conflict. In turn, the Danish defeat by the Catholic League unsettled the balance of power in Europe, prompting Sweden to enter the conflict in 1630. In the meantime, and in compensation for Ludwig V's allegiance to Vienna, the Imperial Diet settled the Marburg inheritance dispute in favor of Hesse-Darmstadt. Undoubtedly, the continent-wide conflict caused deep financial disarray in Hesse, which saw its borders constantly breached by the warring armies. At one point, Ludwig and his son Georg were captured by the Protestants, but later liberated by the Catholic League. Hence, as long as the Emperor was victorious in Germany, conditions were favorable for Hesse-Darmstadt.

Rivalry between Ludwig V and his Kassel cousin Moritz had led to intellectual and educational disputes. One of the implications of this rivalry was the founding in 1605 and the opening of a university in Gießen. This was a reaction to the granting of imperial privileges in 1607. This was a Lutheran counter-university to Marburg with professors who did not follow the dictates of Landgrave Moritz of Hesse-Kassel. Controversial Lutheran orthodoxy determined from the beginning, and throughout the 17th century, the character of the "Ludoviciana," as the University of Gießen was called.[34] Since Ludwig V gained the Marburg region in 1625, he reunited the two universities in Marburg. However, in 1650, they were again and finally separated as self-standing institutions.

Through the adoption of primogeniture among his descendants, Ludwig V ensured that his lands were not further divided. Exceptions were made only if the second-born could not be compensated with money, as was the case with his brothers Landgrave Philipp of Hesse-Butzbach (1609) or Friedrich of Hesse-Homburg (1622). Apart from Homburg, these areas, which were independent for a short time, eventually returned to Darmstadt once the title-holder died without male heirs. Ludwig V expanded

Landgravine Magdalena (née Brandenburg).

his country by buying various areas, such as the lordship of Kelsterbach and the acquisition of half of the Marburg heritage, especially Gießen and Nidda. He had previously acquired the towns of Schotten and Stornfels.

Landgraf Ludwig V died on July 27, 1626, two months short of his 49th birthday. He rests inside the Darmstadt City Church, immortalized by an artistic memorial. There is a small epitaph that records the merits of the Landgrave. In the representation of the Last Judgment on the ceiling of the crypt, Ludwig is portrayed resurrected, the heads of his father and his wife behind him floating in the clouds.

****

Landgrave Georg II of Hesse-Darmstadt (1605-1661)

Following his devotion to Lutheranism and conservative thought, Ludwig V stipulated that his eldest son had to be instructed in theology, as well as in languages and mathematics. Georg had read the Bible seven times before the age of 18, and 28 times before the end of his life. He was particularly concerned about religious education through churches and schools. In his early years, emphasis was also given to physical exercise, while music played an important part in young Georg's educational plan. He was fluent in French and could give speeches in Latin. In the summer of 1621, accompanied by Count Johan Casimir of Erbach, the 16-year-old went on the usual "Grand Tour" – he visited the Netherlands and continued on through France, Spain, and

Landgrave Georg II.

ended in Portugal. From Lisbon he traveled by sea to Marseille.[36] On the news of the attack by Count Mansfeld, who had occupied Darmstadt and caused great destruction and panic, Georg traveled to Dresden to gain the support of the Elector of Saxony. There the young Hessian heir began a relationship with the daughter of his host. An engagement with Sophie Eleonora of Saxony (1609-1671) soon ensued. Starting in the fall of 1624, Georg traveled twice to Italy for educational purposes. The wedding planned for the summer of 1626 was postponed due to the death of Landgrave Ludwig V.

Eventually, Georg II and Sophie Eleonora were married at Torgau on April 1, 1627.[37] The newlyweds had fifteen children. They were: Landgrave Ludwig VI; Magdalena-Sybilla (1631-1651); Georg (1632-1676), firstly married to Dorothea Augusta of Schleswig-Holstein-Sonderburg, and secondly to Julianna-Alexandrina of Leiningen-Dachsburg; Sophie Eleonora (1634-1663), married to Wilhelm-Christof of Hesse-Homburg; Elisabeth Amalia (1635-1709), married to Philipp-Wilhelm, Elector Palatine; Louisa (1636-1697), married to Count Christof-Ludwig of Stolberg; Anna Maria (b./d. 1637); Anna Sophia (1638-1683), Abbess of Quedlinburg; Amalia Julianna (b./d. 1639);

a stillborn in 1640; Henrietta Dorothea (1641-1672), married to Johann II, Count of Waldeck u. Pyrmont; Johann (1642-1643); Augusta Philippina (1643-1672); Agnes (b./d. 1645); and Maria Hedwig (1647-1680).[38]

Landgrave Georg II inherited a difficult legacy. While not warrior of great distinction, he was a noted scholar. In the disputes with Kassel for the Marburg inheritance, there were still some successes. Georg II managed to conquer Rheinfels, which his father had been unable to do. This conflict, known as the "Hessenkrieg" (Hessian War), consumed resources and was greatly responsible for the further reduction in population of Kassel and Darmstadt. War played a major role during the reign of Georg II. During the first years of his reign, he could not prevent Sweden and France conquering some of Hesse-Darmstadt's territories and giving them to Hesse-Kassel. When in 1631, King Gustav Adolf of Sweden marched through the Rhineland, Georg II demanded neutrality, but it cost him the fortress of Rüsselheim. However, the disorderly withdrawal of Swedish troops in 1634 brought new devastation to Hesse-Darmstadt. Lord Mountbatten described his ancestor's quandary arguing that Georg, *"did his best to preserve peace and follow his father's policy of keeping out of the Thirty Years War, whilst remaining an adherent of Emperor Ferdinand II."*[39] Furthermore, he *"had the good of his people at heart and carried out many improvements, new works and schemes in the country."*[40]

Landgrave Georg II and Landgravine Sophie Eleonora.

After the ostracism suffered by his cousin Landgrave Wilhelm V of Hesse-Kassel, due to his alliance with France against the Emperor, Georg was appointed in 1636 to serve as administrator of all Hesse. In the interim, before a longer-lasting solution could be found, Wilhelm V died in Leer, East Frisia, on September 21, 1637.[41] As his successor Wilhelm VI was a child of eight, his widow Amalia Elisabeth (née Hanau-Münzenberg) served as regent for their son. She was a skillful negotiator and effective regent and settled her line's disputes with their Darmstadt cousins.

With the end of the Thirty Years War, the Hessenkrieg came to an end as well, and it concluded with treaties signed in 1648. The Marburg area remained under Kassel; the Gießen area became part of Darmstadt, together with parts of Itter, the so-called Hessian hinterland. A reconstituted landgraviate was thus able to begin its long recovery from the bleeding it suffered during the Thirty Years War. Landgrave Georg, who had held court at Schloß Lichtenberg in 1630-1632, then in Gießen until 1649, because it was safer there, returned to Darmstadt.

To alleviate the landgraviate's continued financial problems, the estates approved the Landgrave's income. This included new taxes on parcels, livestock, and fruit to pay off the large mountain of debt left behind by three decades of war. Georg also made great efforts to attract inhabitants who had fled during the conflict. He understood that by repopulating the landgraviate, there would be a

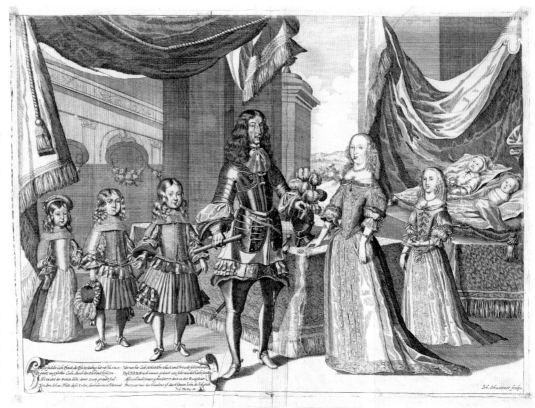

Landgrave Georg II and Landgravine Sophie Eleonora of Hesse-Darmstadt with some of their children. From the left: Sophie Eleonora (married to Wilhelm-Christof of Hesse-Homburg); Georg; Ludwig VI, Georg II and Sophie Eleonora; Magdalena-Sybilla; Elisabeth (married to Philipp Wilhelm, Elector Palatine); and Louisa (married to Christof-Ludwig of Stolberg). The print represents the Landgrave of Hesse-Darmstadt's family in the late 1630s.

noted rise in public revenue. He also hoped that the development of Rüsselheim would create a major trading city with a port and connection to the commercial centers on the Main, Rhine, and Neckar This dream had to be buried due to its exorbitant cost.

As if the suffering caused by war was not enough, Hesse-Darmstadt was also ravaged by the plague. In 1635, for example, thousands of people died of the dreaded illness in five months. Between war and plague, the Rhineland was devastated, and it would take decades for the region to recover.

Bright spots in this dire time were provided by Landgrave Georg II's interest in education. In 1628, there was general church visitation and land survey for the whole country to take stock of the conditions in local churches and schools. The following year, Georg II led the way in establishing the Darmstadt Pedagogy.[42] These reforms are still present in Darmstadt today, where the Ludwig-Georg-Gymnasium, a renowned school, keeps the memories and principles of the princely founders alive.

The establishment of this pedagogy, for which Marburg served as the example, was a measure within a comprehensive reform of the school system. The new schools in Darmstadt, St Goar, Gießen, Schmalkalden, and Alsfeld, served as the feeder schools for centers of higher education.[43] Also, the elementary schools, divided into three classes, were made compulsory. At that time, the benefits of education were already taking effect – the list of those admitted to the Marburg Scholarship Institute clearly shows not all students came from privileged families. This, to say the least, was a very advanced educational system, decades ahead of what was offered in most of Europe!

Yet, the verdict on Georg II is ambiguous. Some historians argue that he was a failed landgrave, *"perhaps the saddest among the sad appearances of the princes at that time."* Others, like Wilhelm Diehl, author of his biography saw in him something completely different, *"the best who ever sat on the Hessian-Darmstadt throne."*[44]

Georg II inherited the throne of Hesse-Darmstadt at an extremely difficult time. For most of his reign, the country was ravaged by war. The plague took a tremendous toll, as did financial and social dislocation. Yet, even while facing all these challenges, his educational reforms were not only forward-looking, but also long-lasting. Lord Mountbatten described his ancestor was, *"a statesman and energetic and competent patriot,"* whose real greatness, *"emerged when he had to face the appalling situation in his country."*[45] One of his epitaphs best describes his view of what a ruler ought to be, *"for neither wealth nor power of faith, but fidelity and faith, establish a dominion."*[46]

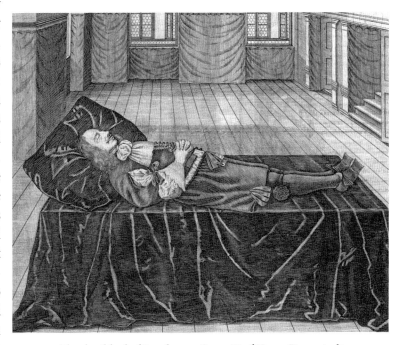

The deathbed of Landgrave Georg II of Hesse-Darmstadt.

****

Landgrave Ludwig VI of Hesse-Darmstadt (1630-1678)

After the death of Georg II, his son succeeded him as Landgrave Ludwig VI. He was born in Darmstadt on January 25, 1630.[47] As youths, Ludwig and his brother Georg attended the University of Marburg. However, when that part of Upper Hesse fell to the Hesse-Kassel troops commanded by Major General Geyso, the young counts transferred to Gießen, where they continued their studies.

It was while a student, that Ludwig made a lifelong friendship with a fellow student, Georg Ernst of Erbach. Later both young men embarked on educational journeys that took them to Holstein, Denmark, and Sweden. A visit to the Duke of Holstein-Gottorp had an eventful meaning for Ludwig as it led to his 1650 marriage to his host's daughter, Maria Elisabeth.[48]

Ludwig and Maria Elisabeth had ten children: Magdalena-Sybilla (1652-1712), married to Duke Wilhelm Ludwig of Württemberg; Sophia Eleonora (b./d. 1653); Georg (1654-1655); Maria Elisabeth (1656-1715), who married Duke Heinrich of Saxe-Römhild; Augusta Magdalena (1657-1674); Ludwig VII; Friedrich (1659-1676); Sophia Maria (1661-1712), married to Duke Christian of Saxe-Eisenberg; and two stillborn children in 1662 and 1665. This last pregnancy cost Maria Elisabeth's life. Ludwig VI is said to have been desolate by the loss of his wife. Of course, that did not prevent him finding a second wife in 1666: Elisabeth Dorothea of Saxe-Gotha (1640-1709), with whom he also had nine children. This second brood included: Ernst Ludwig; Georg (1669-1705); Sophia Louisa (1670-1758), married to Prince Albrecht Ernst zu Oettingen; and her stillborn twin; Philipp (1671-1736); Johann (1672-1673); Heinrich (1674-1741); Elisabeth Dorothea (1676-1721), married to Friedrich III of Hesse-Homburg; and Friedrich (1677-1708).[49]

An important relationship of Landgrave Ludwig VI's was his friendship with Veit Ludwig von

Seckendorff, a prominent court officer of the Duke of Saxe-Gotha. Author of an important book titled *"Teutonic Princely States,"* Seckendorff was one of the leading state theorists of the time. In Darmstadt, he became chief adviser to Ludwig concerning the takeover, in 1661, of the landgraviate's finances, which had been shattered by the aftermath of the Thirty Years War. Seckendorff reorganized the government but was only partly successful for soon enough Hesse-Darmstadt was at war once again.[50]

As early as 1661-62, Landgrave Ludwig succeeded in purchasing the castle and village of Eberstadt from the Baron von Frankenstein, who relocated to Franconia. Ludwig's plans also included major infrastructure projects, most prominent among them the construction of star-shaped fortress ring surrounding Darmstadt. These plans had to be archived when in 1663 Emperor Leopold I requested troops from Darmstadt to fight against the invading Turks. Soon after, Darmstadt also participated in the "Dutch War" against King Louis XIV of France. Hesse-Darmstadt was again in the middle of the theater of war and suffered devastation at the hands of both the French Marshal Viscount de Turenne

Landgrave Ludwig VI of Hesse-Darmstadt.

and passing Imperial armies. Ludwig VI finally actively joined the conflict after Schloß Auerbach was destroyed by the invading French forces.

A lasting legacy Ludwig VI gave Darmstadt was its carillon, one of the oldest in Germany. A carillon is a musical instrument that is typically housed in the bell tower of a church or municipal building. Darmstadt's carillon Ludwig VI acquired during a visit to the Netherlands. He visited Maastricht in 1669 and was impressed by the city's carillon, which is said to have inspired the one installed in Mainz cathedral. The landgrave hired carillon-maker Salomon Verbeck from Amsterdam, and Peter Hemony to cast the bells. The intricate clockwork was created by Peter Call of Nijmegen. According to Ludwig's wishes, the carillon was to *"hourly play spiritual songs as an inanimate creature proclaimed the praise of the Almighty."*[51] A special inauguration ceremony did not take place, but by the end of 1671 the carillon was in use. It remained an unavoidable part of Darmstadt until the tragic evening of September 11, 1944, when Darmstadt was firebombed by the Allies. A new carillon was built in 1951 thanks to a citizens' initiative.

Ludwig VI's interest in art and science was shown in his promotion of the court library, and many historians consider him to be its true founder. Ludwig was also a member of the "Palmenorden," an organization founded in Weimar in 1617, considered the first and most important language society. Princes, aristocrats, great scholars, and writers belonged to it.[52] The Palmenorden worked toward the, *"care and purification of the native language, translation of foreign masterpieces, refinement of patriotic feeling and customs."*[53]

During the second half of Ludwig's reign Darmstadt became a center of music. This development was encouraged by Landgravine Elisabeth Dorothea, whose hometown of Gotha was a leading musical center. On her way from Gotha to Darmstadt, Elisabeth Dorothea was welcomed by musicians as she passed through Gießen, Butzbach, and Frankfurt. Once she arrived in Darmstadt, she was celebrated for several days at the Residenzschloß Darmstadt. The highlight of the festivities was the *"Congratulatory Spectacle"* written by Johannes Mylius and presented by members of the court society and school pupils.

This was the prelude to annual birthday celebrations and games at court, which were partly devised or written by the Landgravine and stimulated the development of the Darmstadt theater. Such was the Ludwig VI and Elisabeth Dorothea's fascination with music and theater, that in 1670 they rebuilt the old riding school into a theater

Landgravine Maria Elisabeth (née Schleswig-Holstein).

In 1671, Elisabeth Dorothea was able to hire her old music teacher Carl Wolfgang Briegel, Chapel Master to her father. Briegel was responsible for the introduction of the opera to Darmstadt. He was a notable composer of secular and sacred music that can still be found inside hymnals in many Protestant churches around the world. Briegel's most important work was the *"Darmstadt hymn book."*[54]

Landgrave Ludwig VI died in Darmstadt on April 24, 1678.[55] He was succeeded by his eldest son, Ludwig VII, from his first marriage. The new Landgrave of Hesse-Darmstadt, however, did not live long enough to make much of a mark.

It is worth mentioning that Landgrave Ludwig VI's younger sons had colorful careers. Georg (1669-1705) entered the military as a soldier of fortune after a "grand tour" of Flanders, France, and Switzerland. He participated in the great Austrian war against the Turks and commanded a Venetian regiment that fought in the Peloponnese. In 1691, Georg fought under King William III of England to suppress a Jacobite uprising in Ireland. Following this adventure, Georg returned to Imperial service commanding a cuirassier regiment that bore the name "Hesse-Darmstadt" until his death. Around 1694, Georg converted to Catholicism, a decision that benefitted his career in the Austrian military. He was also, at one point, thinking of marrying his cousin Sophia Dorothea of Palatinate-Neuburg, a sister of the second wife of King Carlos II of Spain, who had recently become the widow of Odoardo Farnese, Hereditary Prince

Landgrave Georg.   *Landgrave Philipp.*   *Landgrave Heinrich.*

of Parma. Her only daughter, Isabella, later married King Felipe V of Spain, becoming the real power behind the Spanish throne. In 1697, Georg entered the service of the Habsburg Spanish monarch and was stationed in Catalonia, granted both a Spanish grandeeship and the order of the Golden Fleece, and made Viceroy of Catalonia.[56]

Georg's position in Catalonia ended with the arrival of King Felipe V. In 1701, he traveled to Vienna and later wintered in Darmstadt. The following year, Georg traveled to London to represent the interests of the Habsburgs to King William III, who died in the interim. Georg, onboard an English frigate as observer, then traveled to Cadiz. At the beginning of 1704, the Habsburg claimant to the Spanish throne reinstated Georg as Spanish commander. Later that summer, as captain general of the army of "King Carlos III" and General Vicar of Aragon, he led the successful capture of the fortress of Gibraltar, defending it against a French siege. In the course of his planned campaign to recapture Barcelona, Georg fell in the fight for Fort Montjuich on September 14, 1705. His grave in the church of San Pedro de Gava was destroyed; a brass container, which arrived in Darmstadt via France in 1711, with his heart, rests in Darmstadt's City Church.[57]

Ludwig VI's next son, Philipp (1671-1736), also entered military service. His supervised education concluded in 1688 with the end of his mother's regency. The following year he joined, as a cadet, the army formed by Willem of Orange as it gathered in the Netherlands to defend against France. In 1691, Philipp was appointed commander of a cavalry regiment. There were plans to marry Philipp to Albertina of Waldeck, but this project was unrealized. Instead, in 1692, Philipp announced that he intended to marry Princess Marie Thérèse of Croÿ Havré, a Catholic and francophone aristocrat two-years his junior.[58] Upon hearing news of her son's marriage plans, Dowager Landgravine Elisabeth Dorothea expressed her opposition and sent Court Marshal von Oeynhausen to Brussels to talk some sense to her son. It was all to no avail for on March 24, 1693, the young couple not only married, but Philipp converted to Catholicism as well. The couple had six children: a stillborn in 1696; Joseph (1699-1768), Bishop of Augsburg; Wilhelm Ludwig (b./d. 1704); Theodora (1706-1784), married to Antonio-Ferdinando

Joseph, Bishop of Augsburg.

Gonzaga, Duke of Guastalla; Leopold (1708-1764), married Enrichetta Maria d'Este, Princess of Modena, widow of the last Farnese Duke of Parma, Antonio; and Karl (b./d. 1710).[59] None of Philipp and Marie Thérèse's children left offspring.

Philipp remained in Austrian service the remainder of his life. He served the Habsburgs in Flanders, Hungary, Italy, and Vienna, and also fought against the Turks. In 1714, he was appointed Governor of Mantua. Marie Thérèse died in Bologna that spring. Four years later, there were discussions to arrange his marriage to Eleonora Luise Gonzaga, widow of Francesco Maria de Medici, but the proposed marriage never took place. He died in Vienna on August 11, 1736.[60] His body was buried in St Stephen's, while his heart was sent in an urn for burial in the Landgrave's Crypt in Darmstadt's City Church.

Heinrich, the next to youngest child of Ludwig VI and Elisabeth Dorothea, was born in Darmstadt on September 29, 1674.[61] The seventh child his mother gave birth to in as many years, not surprisingly, Heinrich had a weak constitution responsible for delaying his entry into the path already set by his older brothers: the military. In 1695, he volunteered to serve with the Imperial troops under the command of Margrave Ludwig of Baden, stationed in the Upper Rhine. Some years late Dowager Landgravine Elisabeth Dorothea was unsuccessful in obtaining for Heinrich a post in the Spanish army. In 1700, he was in Venice and momentarily thought he would receive an appointment to the Dutch East Indies. Instead, he served for a short while in the Swedish army. In 1703, Heinrich went to London, where he embarked on the expedition to Spain that conquered Gibraltar. At this time, Heinrich also converted to Catholicism. In 1705, he not only served as his brother Georg's representative as interim governor of Gibraltar, but after Georg's death in battle, Heinrich received a commission as colonel of the royal guard and served as commandant of the fortress of Lérida. By the time he left Spain in 1710 to settle at Schloß Butzbach, vacant since his mother's death, Heinrich had attained the rank of Lieutenant-Field Marshal. He remained unmarried and died on January 31, 1741, having returned to the Reformed church on his last Christmas day.[62]

The youngest sibling, Friedrich, was born in Darmstadt on September 18, 1677, just months before his father's death.[63] Destined to an ecclesiastical career, Friedrich converted to Catholicism in 1697. After receiving several appointments and getting a tonsure (the practice of shaving some or all of the hair in the scalp as a sign of religious devotion) in Rome, Friedrich realized he lacked vocation. The reason, as in most such cases, was a young lady by the name of Maria Petronella Stockmans, who had also opted to enter an abbey without possessing the necessary disposition for such a path. They were quietly, and secretly, married in Styria in 1704. Three years later, Friedrich went to Russia, where he received a commission from Peter the Great to serve in a dragoon regiment. He died in the Battle of Lesnaya, Lithuania, on October 13, 1708.[64] Friedrich was buried in a Roman Catholic Church in Smolensk. As for his widow, who had given birth to their daughter (Maria Anna Friederike) in Vienna in 1705, she remained in the service of Princess Charlotte Amalia Rakoczi (née Hesse-Rheinfels-Wanfried) for several years. Maria Petronella died in Vienna in 1751. Although Friedrich's marriage was arguably invalid due to his spiritual status, his daughter always called herself *"a princess of Hesse-Darmstadt."*[65]

Landgrave Ludwig VII of Hesse-Darmstadt (1658-1678)

The only surviving son of Landgrave Ludwig VI and his first wife, Maria Elisabeth, Ludwig VII was born in Darmstadt on June 22, 1658.[66] He attended university in Gießen and embarked on several journeys that took him to Magdeburg, Hamburg, and Holstein. He also visited Silesia twice, where he stayed with his great uncle Cardinal Friedrich of Breslau. Later, Ludwig VII traveled to Vienna, Venice, and Rome. In 1676, he became engaged to his cousin Princess Erdmuthe Dorothea of Saxe-Zeitz. The death of Landgrave Ludwig VI delayed the wedding, which was rescheduled for later in the year. Landgrave Ludwig VII died on his trip to marry Erdmuthe Dorothea. He was taken seriously ill upon arriving at Schloß Friedenstein, residence of his stepmother's family. His illness lasted eighteen days and he died on August 31, 1678.[67] He was Landgrave of Hesse-Darmstadt for a total of eighteen weeks and four days. Ludwig VII's bride, sixteen-years-old at the time of his death outlived him until 1720. In 1679, Erdmuthe Dorothea married Duke Christian II of Saxe-Merseburg, by whom she had seven children.[68] Her line of descendants did not survive as her only grandchild was born and died on June 23, 1720.[69]

****

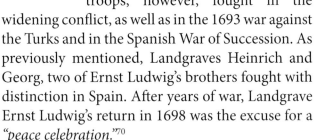

Landgrave Ludwig VII.

Landgrave Ernst Ludwig of Hesse-Darmstadt (1667-1739)

Ernst Ludwig's government began under dismal circumstances. The armies of Louis XIV of France had invaded the Rhine after they conquered and partly burned Speyer, Worms, and Heidelberg. Twice, in 1691 and 1693, Darmstadt was invaded and charged with heavy wartime reparations. To protect some of Darmstadt's most notable treasures, the authorities had gone as far as burying them as the French armies approached. The carillon, for example, was dismantled and taken to Frankfurt for safety. It remained buried there from 1693-1698. Even the ruling family departed seeking refuge in safer areas away from the conflict. Hessian troops, however, fought in the widening conflict, as well as in the 1693 war against the Turks and in the Spanish War of Succession. As previously mentioned, Landgraves Heinrich and Georg, two of Ernst Ludwig's brothers fought with distinction in Spain. After years of war, Landgrave Ernst Ludwig's return in 1698 was the excuse for a *"peace celebration."*[70]

This was the era of absolute monarchy, and Ernst Ludwig lost little time in adopting Louis XIV as his role model for governing. Along with this new self-image of a landgrave who did not have to render accounts to anyone, came a massive expenditure in infrastructure designed to elevate the image of the ruler. That was the reason behind the building of a new castle, a task for which Ernst Ludwig hired a renowned master builder named Louis Remy de la Fosse, whom he had met during a visit to Hannover. De la Fosse came to Darmstadt in 1714, where he worked until his death in 1725. Furnished

Landgrave Ernst Ludwig.

with great powers of autonomy and the enormous sum of 300,000 gulden granted by the estates, De la Fosse was able to start his magnificent plans for the new castle in Darmstadt. The vast construction project was not completed until decades after the architect and his master's deaths. Emperor Joseph II is said to have called the castle *"a perfect place."*[71]

In addition to the castle's imposing market plaza façade, De la Fosse also worked on other projects, among them the Orangerie building in Bessungen (which later served known as the emergency home for the Landestheater from 1945-1972), the Prettlack Haus with the Prinz-Georg garden, and the portal of the castle church. Since plans to build an entirely new opera met with resistance due to excessive costs, Ernst Ludwig had to be satisfied with a less costly option mandating the renovation of the riding hall into a theater. The theater had room for 350 spectators and had good proportions. It was was destroyed during the devastating firebombing of Darmstadt in 1944. Its site is now occupied by buildings of the Technical University of Darmstadt.

Landgrave Ernst Ludwig's building activity was not confined to Darmstadt as the princely builder needed a hunting lodge. He was a passionate hunter. To satisfy his great passion, Ernst Ludwig created hunting grounds in Mönchbruch near Groß Gerau, and built Wolfsgarten near Langen. In these pleasure properties he hosted par force hunts, a type of hunt practiced since antiquity and in the Middle Ages, consisting of hunting stags with the help of dogs over long stretches. A third hunting property, Schloß Kranichstein was also acquired.[72] He, as well as his son Ludwig VIII, practiced this type of hunting with a passion that caused the participants the highest pleasure. The effects of the hunt, however, were extremely bad for the area residents as oftentimes their crops were trampled. Compensation to local farmers and peasants, not surprisingly, was never forthcoming.

During Ernst Ludwig's long reign new religious conflicts arose in Hesse-

Schloß Wolfsgarten, built by Landgrave Ernst Ludwig in the 1720s.

Darmstadt. This problem was caused by the large number of French Huguenots who requested asylum after being expelled from their country. The presence of these "Protestants" who practiced and worshipped differently tipped religious balance and caused considerable angst among the Lutheran hierarchy. The matter was settled after a report by the University of Gießen. In it, refugees were granted confessional safety, as long as they swore an oath of loyalty to the sovereign and promised not to challenge the ruling confession. This is how Huguenot communities, which exist until today, came to be in Rohrbach, Wembach, Hahn, and Walldorf. Ernst Ludwig's tolerance was not only directed to the benefit of other Protestants. In 1695, the landgrave granted the Jews of Hesse-Darmstadt free exercise of their religion.

Landgrave Ernst Ludwig of Hesse-Darmstadt.

this great heyday of the opera of the High Baroque era lasted until financial circumstances almost completely stopped this work. For Graupner, this meant refocusing to writing music and to the composition of church cantatas. He was a prolific writer of music, his personal legacy including: 1418 church and 24 secular cantatas, 113 symphonies, 84 orchestral suites, 50 concerts, among much else. A 1728 book containing a large number of his music catalogue is still preserved in Darmstadt.

Other areas in which Ernst Ludwig brought i m p r o v e m e n t s included the judiciary and the press. In 1724, Ernst Ludwig issued the Rules of Procedure for the benefit of his subjects and in 1726 published a new judicial code. Furthermore, Ernst Ludwig also incentivized the creation of newspapers in Darmstadt. One of them being the *Darmstädter Zeitung*, later becoming the *Darmstädter Tagblatt*, one of the oldest in Germany.[74] The newspapers were initially used to publish official announcements, sentences, and orders.

A princely builder and hunting enthusiast, Ernst Ludwig was also a friend and patron of the opera. He owned a house in Hamburg, where he liked to visit the opera performances. At this time, Georg Friedrich Händel was engaged as a violinist in the Hamburg Opera. Also, since 1706, the talented Christoph Graupner played the klaver, a keyboard musical instrument similar to the piano. Three years later, Ernst Ludwig convinced Graupner to commit to playing in Darmstadt. Graupner initially played for several years under Briegel as Vice Chapel Music Master, until he could succeed him.[73] With Graupner in Darmstadt there was a revival of opera music in the town. For ten years,

When it came to settling on a wife, Ernst Ludwig chose a lady six years his senior – Margravine Dorothea Charlotte of Brandenburg (1661-1705), was the daughter of Margrave Albrecht V and his wife Countess Sophia Margaretha of Oettingen-Oettingen.[75] From this marriage, Ernst Ludwig had five children. They were: Dorothea Sophia (1689-1723), married to Count Johann Friedrich of Hohenlohe-Oehringen; Ludwig VIII; Karl Wilhelm (1693-1707); Franz Ernst (1695-1716);

and Friederike Charlotte (1698-1777), who married Landgrave Maximilian of Hesse-Kassel.[76]

Landgravine Dorothea Charlotte died in Darmstadt on November 15, 1705.[77] Her husband remained a widower for over two decades, which is not to mean that his bed and private quarters remained forbidden to fair ladies. In fact, Ernst Ludwig was romantically involved with several court ladies, as well as women from less illustrious backgrounds. The good landgrave was not one who would discriminate. It was not until 1727 that he married again. His second wife was Baroness Louise von Spiegel zu Desenberg (1690-1751), the widow of Count Franz Christoph von Freyen-Seyboldsdorff. The bride not belonging to a family of equal rank to that of her second

Landgrave Ludwig VIII.

husband's, the marriage was morganatic. They had two daughters who received the title of Countesses of Eppstein, Louise (1727-1753) and Friederike (1730-1770).[78]

While he was a beacon in many areas, such as culture, architecture, the judiciary, and the arts, as a responsible administrator of his realm's public finances, Ernst Ludwig was a total failure. Public debt doubled during his long reign. The large construction projects in the Residenzschloß, as well as in the new hunting grounds, high expenditures for territorial extensions, funds for the settlement of territorial disputes, monies spent on opera and court music, as well as war costs nearly bankrupted Hesse-Darmstadt. At one point, Landgrave Ernst

Ludwig was so desperate for revenue that he even hired an alchemist who convinced him that he could make gold. Hesse-Darmstadt's debt burden rose from two million gulden in 1688 to four million by the time of the Landgrave's death.

Landgrave Ernst Ludwig, the sixth holder of the title, died at Schloß Jägersburg near Darmstadt on September 12, 1739.[79]

****

Landgrave Ludwig VIII of Hesse-Darmstadt (1691-1768)

Landgrave Ludwig VIII was born in Darmstadt on April 5, 1690. His childhood was marked by the upheavals caused by war along the Rhineland, which caused the repeated relocation of his father's court to the Upper Hessian fortress town of Gießen. Even after his parents returned to Darmstadt's Residenzschloß in 1698, with a prematurely fêted *"peace celebration,"* Ludwig remained in Gießen with his tutor at least temporarily.[80] The planned "Grand Tour" was postponed after his mother's death and he had to wait a year before embarking on a trip to Switzerland. The second part of the journey, partly in the company of his brother Franz Ernst, took place in the spring of 1709. On this trip Ludwig visited Holland and the Spanish Netherlands. He also visited the English court, where he stayed for several weeks. A planned visit to France in 1716 was cancelled due to its considerable cost.

During Christmas 1716, Ludwig became engaged to Charlotte, daughter and heir of Count Johann Reinhard of Hanau-Lichtenberg, who had married Margravine Dorothea Friederike of Brandenburg-Ansbach. Ludwig and Charlotte were married at Philippsruhe, her father's magnificent palace, on the groom's 26th birthday. In 1717, Ludwig made a first inspection to Buchsweiler as the city and area were to pass from his father-in-law to the House of Hesse-Darmstadt. Also, the town of Babenhausen would be inherited by Charlotte's offspring.[81]

Ludwig and Charlotte were the parents of six children: Ludwig IX; Charlotte Wilhelmina (1720-1721); Georg Wilhelm (1722-1782); Karoline Luise (1723-1783), who married Karl Friedrich, Margrave of Baden-Durlach; Louisa Augusta (1725-1742); and Johann Friedrich (1726-1746).[82] Unfortunately, Charlotte never recovered from giving birth to her sixth child. She died on July 1, 1726.[83] Her father died a decade later, at which time the bulk of his estate passed to Charlotte's children. Ludwig VIII took possession of Hanau-Lichtenberg after Count Johan Reinhard's death, taking advantage of the journey to finally visit Paris and Strasbourg.

Landgrave Ludwig VIII has gone down in history as the greatest hunter among the Landgraves of Hesse-Darmstadt. His favorite country residence was Schloß Kranichstein, which provided him with a fitting setting to hunt to his heart's delight. Along with his father or friends, Ludwig VIII participated in countless par force hunts. Kranichstein, as well as his other country estates, were handsomely decorated with paintings depicting hunts, as well as with hunting trophies and all sorts of paraphernalia related to hunting. As a memento for his hunting guests, as well as a reward and an incentive for the hunting staff, Ludwig VIII had his own medals minted – golden "deer ducats" with the inscription *"money connects, makes and finds."*[84]

Landgravine Charlotte Christine (née Hanau).

Because of his humor, his affability, and generosity, the Landgrave was popular with his hunting companions. Ludwig VIII's hunts sometimes included as many as one-hundred mounted hunters galloping along the countryside without a worry other than catching the stag. The inhabitants of the territories through which the hunts were usually terrorized by the entire experience.

Ludwig VIII kept close relationships with many of the leading political figures of his time, most prominently among them Empress Maria Theresa. He supported her claims and was a loyal ally to the Habsburgs. The Empress described him as, *"a most faithful friend and vassal and last grand seigneur."*[85] As her father had only two daughters, Emperor Karl VI attempted, not with complete success, to have the other powers agree to the Pragmatic Sanction, a change in the law that would allow female succession. This path would thus open the road for his eldest daughter Archduchess Maria Theresa to succeed the Emperor. Many of Europe's monarchs were appeased with concessions; a few continued to oppose the Habsburg offer in the hope that once Karl VI died, they would easily attack and take as much as they could grab.

Some monarchs who were related to the Habsburgs, asserted their claims to the Imperial throne as soon as news of Karl VI's death reached them. Most prominent among them was the Elector of Bavaria, who managed to get elected as Emperor Karl VII.[86] The ensuing conflict, the Habsburg fight for survival and retention of the Imperial throne is known as the War of Austrian Succession. Rising as Maria Theresa's most vicious enemy was King Friedrich II "the Great" of Prussia. He took large areas of Silesia from the Habsburgs and quickly abandoned Karl VII to his doomed fate. In every conflict that Maria Theresa fought in her lifetime, Ludwig VIII was a loyal ally and contributed Hessian troops. He proved his affection for Maria Theresa by always being ready to give her cause military support, whether during the War of Austrian Succession (1740-1748), or during the Seven Years' War (1756-1763). The Empress recognized Ludwig VIII's friendship and loyalty by granting him several sinecures, among them the rank of Austrian General Field Marshal. More importantly, Maria Theresa interceded on Ludwig VIII's behalf to assist in the restructuring of his country's enormous debts. Truth be told, Maria Theresa saved Ludwig VIII of Hesse-Darmstadt from bankruptcy.

While Ludwig VIII supported the Habsburgs, his son, the later Landgrave Ludwig IX, was a close friend of Friedrich the Great. As such, Ludwig IX served in the Prussian military, reaching the rank of General. It was only due to paternal pressure that the Hessian heir finally left Prussian service in 1756. The Seven Years' War had started and Ludwig VIII, as usual, sided with the Habsburgs.

He wanted his son to join him in his support for Vienna. Ludwig IX, a dutiful son, did not hesitate and returned to Darmstadt.

The attachment of Ludwig VIII to Maria Theresa and her family was again demonstrated during a meeting at Heusenstamm on March 29, 1764.[87] On the way to Frankfurt am Main to be crowned as King of the Romans, the title given to the Imperial heir, Joseph II and his father Emperor Franz met with Landgrave Ludwig VIII. Surely, they must have reminisced that in 1745, it was Ludwig VIII who brought the news to Archduke Franz (né Lorraine) that the Electors had chosen him as the new Holy Roman Emperor. In appreciation, at the coronation Ludwig VIII received a diamond ring with the image of Maria Theresa and a sword valued at 7,000 gulden.

Landgrave Ludwig IX.

Ludwig VIII died in October 1768.[88] His death was caused by a head injury he received during a performance of George Lillo's piece *"The Merchant of London"* at the de la Fosse Opera House in Darmstadt.

****

Landgrave Ludwig IX of Hesse-Darmstadt (1719-1790)

Ludwig IX, Landgrave of Hesse-Darmstadt, was born in Darmstadt on December 15, 1719.[89] Ludwig IX came to govern early, unlike his father. From his earliest years, Ludwig was engaged in a careful educational plan in which his maternal grandfather played an important role. As Johann

Reinhard of Hanau-Lichtenberg had named his grandson Ludwig of Hesse-Darmstadt as heir to his realm, the old count wished to have the youngster prepared to assume his inheritance when the time came. As both heir to Hesse-Darmstadt and Hanau-Lichtenberg, Ludwig stood to become one of the leading German rulers of his time. In 1733, his Hessian grandfather, Ernst Ludwig, named him the titular colonel of the Darmstadt Life Regiment. Ludwig was fourteen years old. This was followed by his Hanau grandfather commanding Ludwig, along with his younger brother Georg Wilhelm, to settle at Schloß Buchsweiler, a vast residence in Alsace. There, the boys were taught by private tutors and later attended the University of Strasbourg. They lived in a large city palace initially known as the Hôtel de Hanau, but later referred to as the Hôtel Hesse-Darmstadt.

The Hanau-Lichtenberg inheritance was a sizeable and rich legacy, although a complicated one as it was located along the border between France and Germany. It was formed by various estates under different sovereignty: nine estates were in Upper Alsace under French sovereignty, while four were on the German side of the border. Other estates belonging to the inheritance included: Pirmasens, Lichtenau and Willstädt in Lower Alsace.

At that time, Buchsweiler must have been a delightful residence for it and the surrounding gardens were commonly referred to the "Little Versailles." Johann Wolfgang von Goethe, who was a student in Strasbourg was deeply impressed by

Landgravine Karoline
(née Zweibrücken-Birkenfeld).

the estate and remembered it thus,

"This town was the main place of the Counts Hanau-Lichtenberg, a title held by the Landgrave of Hesse-Darmstadt under French sovereignty. A government and chamber of staff made the place an important centerpiece of a very beautiful and desirable princely possession. We easily forgot the uneven streets, the irregular shape of the place, when we went out to look at the old castle and the splendidly landscaped gardens on a hill. Many pleasure groves, tame and wild flocks of pheasants, and the scattered old ruins showed how pleasant this little residence once must have been."[90]

During the French Revolution, the castle was confiscated by the state. A revolutionary mob invaded the property and pillaged Buchsweiler in November 1793. Today, only a few monuments in Buchsweiler (Bouxwiller) are reminiscent of this significant period. Recognizable still are the palace square, some remainders of the stables, as well as parts of the once vast palace gardens. In the Protestant church one can still see a count's chair bearing the coats of arms of the Hanau and Hesse-Darmstadt. Otherwise Buchsweiler is today a typical small Alsatian town with angular streets and many beautiful old half-timbered houses.

While living in Buchsweiler, Ludwig often visited Countess Karoline of Zweibrücken-Birkenfeld, whose husband Count Christian III had died in 1735.[91] From her marriage, Karoline gave birth to four children: Caroline (1721-1774); Christian IV (1722-1775), Count and Duke

Palatine of Zweibrücken; Count Friedrich Michael of Birkenfeld (1724-1767), whose youngest son became King Maximilian I of Bavaria; and Christiane Henriette (1725-1816). These social interactions led to the engagement of Ludwig with the countess's eldest daughter. Yet, before the couple's scheduled wedding, Ludwig traveled to France, where he visited Louis XV's court at Versailles. Upon returning to Hanau, Ludwig officially ascended his throne and celebrated his wedding to Karoline at Zweibrücken on August 12, 1741.[92]

The year following their wedding, Ludwig and Karoline had a stillborn child. Four years later, the Countess of Hanau-Lichtenberg gave birth to a daughter, Karoline (1746-1821), who married Friedrich Ludwig, Landgrave of Hesse-Homburg. The couple's third child, Friederike, was born in 1751, and went on to marry King Friedrich Wilhelm II of Prussia. The first son and heir, Ludwig, was born in Prenzlau on June 14, 1753. One year later, Karoline gave birth to Amalie (1754-1832), who married Hereditary Prince Karl of Baden. In 1755, Wilhelmine was born also at Prenzlau. She married Tsesarevich Paul Petrovich of Russia and died in 1776 in childbirth. Louise (1757-1830) was born next. She married Carl August of Saxe-Weimar-Eisenach. She was followed by two boys, Friedrich (1759-1802) and Christian (1763-1830), who remained unmarried and left no descendants.[93]

At the time of his marriage, Ludwig resided at Buchsweiler in Alsace. He began his military career in the service of his father, but later entered French service (1742). In the same year he joined

his regiment, the "Royal Allemand," stationed in Prague. He was with his soldiers when an unusually cold December caused the death of many. The French army retreated from there to Cheb. In 1743, he left French service and entered the Prussian army with the rank of colonel of the Selchow Regiment, garrisoned in Prenzlau. His brother, Georg Wilhelm, also entered service in the army of Friedrich the Great. Due to his Habsburg sympathies, their father opposed his sons' service under the Prussian banner He demanded them back from the King of Prussia. However, his request was not granted and both princes fought for Prussia, then France's ally, during the Silesian campaign of 1744-1745. In fact, Ludwig's Prussian service earned him the friendship of King Friedrich the Great, who respected the Hessian's military prowess. As for Ludwig's wife, the Prussian monarch enjoyed her company because she was a wonderful hostess and conversationalist.

Landgrave Ludwig IX.

After the end of the Austrian War of Succession, Hereditary Prince Ludwig returned to Pirmasens in Hanau, but remained in Prussian service. In 1750, he resumed command of his regiment and moved with his wife to Prenzlau, where he resided until 1757. In Prenzlau, Karoline found life stifling, writing that *"My stay here is very lonesome ...one talks of war, and training for war, and of soldiers and such like matters. My life is monotonous and simple; all I can do isto ensure that I do not let boredom get me down."*[94] Consequently, three of his children were born there. As for Karoline, at the end of 1756, after the outbreak of the Seven Years' War, she settled in Berlin for almost a year. Appointed

Lieutenant-General at the outbreak of the Seven Years' War, Ludwig commanded a corps of 10,000 men, with whom he invaded Silesia. At the urgent request of his father, who offered the valid reason that the French would take part in the war against Prussia and treat Ludwig as an enemy because of Hanau being under French sovereignty, Ludwig resigned Prussian service and returned in 1757 to Pirmasens. He resided there, while his wife set up her court in Buchsweiler and later in Darmstadt. The marriage, which had been arranged by her mother, was prolific, yet unhappy. While Ludwig was only interested in military matters, his wife was a known intellectual.

Schloß Buschweiler, favored home of the "Great Landgravine" Caroline.

Johann Wolfgang von Goethe, who participated in Karoline's salon, referred to her as *"the Great Landgravine."*[95] At Buchsweiler, she surrounded herself with artists and, writers and philosophers. Friedrich the Great respected her so much, that he used to refer to her as, *"the Glory and Wonder of our century."*[96] After her death in 1774, the Prussian king sent an urn to Darmstadt decorated with the text *"femina sexo, ingenio vir"* (A woman by sex, a man by spirit!).[97]

In 1768, after the death of his father, Ludwig IX assumed the government of his Hessian lands. A thoroughly military man, he presided over the expansion of his forces. In fact, he devoted most of his time to caring for his soldiers. Military exercises constituted his chief occupation, and at the same time his most agreeable object of conversation. In order not to be interrupted by the weather as he engaged in his passionate soldier-playing, he built a large exercise house, inside which his entire regiment could exercise in bad weather. His entourage consisted almost exclusively of officers of the garrison. He ignored all the courtiers and the nobility, with just a few exceptions. Ludwig IX was lucky in counting with the assistance of Minister Friedrich Carl von Moser, who had taken on the task of restoring and sanitizing the neglected pecuniary conditions of the house and the country. This was a gigantic task, bearing in mind that the Landgrave claimed the revenues of his military in such a manner that the family was constantly in financial trouble. Landgravine Karoline, it is said, had difficulty finding the funds to even purchase proper clothing for her children, as well as paying the salaries of their tutors. At one point, she was forced to pawn her personal jewelry so she could raise enough money to finance her household.

Even before succeeding his father, Ludwig IX was aware of the ominous condition of the finances of Hesse-Darmstadt. To avoid the complete financial collapse of his realm, the Ludwig IX prepared reforms that would include austerity measures aimed at remedying the desolate state finances. These included the cancellation of the hunts organized by his father, as well as drastic restriction of the theater and music business. The county's finances were in such a troubling state, that even Vienna became involved an ordered Minister von Moser to implement immediate reforms. Moser also tried to implement budgetary reductions to the military budget, but the Landgrave objected every time he could.

Upon realizing the impecuniousness of the Landgravine, Minister von Moser expressed his opposition to the Landgrave's extravagant military expenditures. At Pirmasens, from where he conducted most of his administrative duties, Ludwig IX surrounded himself with an intimate cabinet of sycophants, who steered him in the wrong direction. This corrupted clique of whisperers tried their best to seed discord between the Landgrave and his government, but whenever von Moser was received in audience by Ludwig IX, he won the day. After all, Ludwig's clear, penetrating mind decided in favor of the minister in most cases, and only where his master's grenadiers were concerned, did he find Moser sometimes obstinate.

As Ludwig IX and Karoline lived separately for the last ten years of her life, the Landgrave of Hesse-Darmstadt found enjoyment and distraction in the embrace of several women. He had a multi-year relationship with the young Ernestine Flachsland, who bore his son Ludwig Ernst von Hessenzweig (1761-1774).[98] However, none captivated him more than one Marie Adelaide Cheirouze (b. 1752). He married her at Bad Ems in 1775 and granted Marie Adelaide the title of Countess of Lemberg.[99] She died at Diez ten years later.

Landgrave Ludwig IX died at Pirmasens on April 6, 1790.[100] He was spared witnessing the direst abuses of the French Revolution, which included

Landgrave Ludwig IX.

the loss of most of Hanau-Lichtenberg, including Schloß Buchsweiler.

Before moving on to the next generation, it is necessary to take the time to discuss the life of Georg Wilhelm of Hesse-Darmstadt, Ludwig IX's brother. Born in Darmstadt on July 11, 1722, he married at Shloß Heidesheim in 1748 Countess Luise of Leiningen-Dachsburg (1729-1818), daughter of Count Christian Carl and his wife, the former Countess Catharina Polyxena of Solms-Rödelheim.[101] Nine children were fathered by Georg Wilhelm with his wife: Ludwig (1749-1823), married morganatically to Friederike Schmidt, created Baroness von Hessenheim; Wilhelm (b./d. 1750); Friederike (1752-1782), married to the future Grand Duke Karl II of Mecklenburg-Strelitz, and mother of several children, among them: Duchess Charlotte of Saxe-Altenburg, Fürstin Therese of Thurn und Taxis, Queen Luise of Prussia, Queen Friederike of Hannover, and Grand Duke Georg of Mecklenburg-Strelitz; Georg (1754-1830); Charlotte (1755-1785), married to her widowed brother-in-law later Grand Duke Karl II of Mecklenburg-Strelitz; Friedrich (1759-1808), married morganatically to Caroline Seitz; Louise Henriette (1761-1829), who married her first cousin Landgrave Ludwig X of Hesse-Darmstadt; and Augusta (1765-1796), who married the future King Maximilian I of Bavaria.[102]

As a young man, Georg Wilhelm received a command position with a regiment in Darmstadt. This followed entry into the Prussian military, where he served for several years. In 1740-1741, he accompanied his brother Ludwig on a visit to France, where they were received by King Louis XV at Versailles. This was followed by subsequent visits to Dresden and Berlin, as well representing his father at the coronation ceremony of Emperor Karl VII, held in Frankfurt in February 1742. Then, Georg Wilhelm returned to Prussian service and fought against Austria during the Silesian campaigns.

Shortly after the sudden death of their younger brother Johann Friedrich, who had joined the Austrian military to compensate for his brothers serving under the Prussian banner, Georg Wilhelm was appointed as Sergeant-General in a Hessian regiment. The Prussians, not to be outdone, gave him the rank of Lieutenant General.

At one point, Georg Wilhelm was seriously considered as a possible husband for Empress Elisabeth of Russia (1709-1762), Peter the Great's daughter. This was a diplomatic plot to build a bridge between Germany and the rising Russian Empire.[103] This plan, however, failed to materialize, in no small measure due to the fact that the bride would have been thirteen-years the groom's senior. Landgrave Ludwig VIII, however, preferred that his son marry locally. Anyhow, Georg Wilhelm's marriage to Luise Albertine put an end to any other matrimonial projects.

Georg Wilhelm and his wife lived in Darmstadt, a decision that provided him with an excuse to remain away from military service for some time. While at home, he served as commanding general of the entire Hessian infantry. After briefly fighting for Prussia during the Seven Years' War, he returned permanently to Darmstadt. There, he also served as governor of the fortresses of Gießen and Philippsburg.[104] By 1771, he had risen to the rank of General Field Marshal. It is worth mentioning that after his father's death in 1768, Georg Wilhelm, along with Landgravine Karoline, represented his brother Ludwig IX in Darmstadt as the Landgrave rarely left

Landgrave Georg Wilhelm and Landgravine Luise Albertine of Hesse-Darmstadt.

Pirmasens. Later, after Karoline's death in 1774, Georg Wilhelm assisted his nephew Ludwig in the same role as representative of the absent Landgrave Ludwig IX.

Georg Wilhelm of Hesse-Darmstadt died on June 21, 1782.[105] He was three weeks away from celebrating his 60th birthday. His widow, 53-years-old at the time of his death survived Georg Wilhelm for thirty-six years. Luise Albertine died at Neustrelitz, Mecklenburg, on March 11, 1818.[106] By then she was a venerable old lady of 89-years.

Chapter II

A New Grand Duchy – Ludwig I and Ludwig II 1790–(1806)–1848

Grand Duke Ludwig I of Hesse and by Rhine (1753-1830)

On June 14, 1753[1], the man who would succeed as Ludwig X of Hesse-Darmstadt was born in Prenzlau, a Prussian military garrison town located on the Ucker River, in Brandenburg, about 62 miles northeast of Berlin. There is where his father, Landgrave Ludwig IX was stationed for several years of service under the Prussian banner. From an early age, young Ludwig was torn between two opposing poles: Ludwig IX and his independent-minded estranged wife, Landgravine Caroline. Each parent tried to influence their son to be more in tune with their contrasting views of the world. This dichotomy was observed during most of Ludwig's life as Europe transitioned from enlightened late absolutism to a bourgeois authoritarian state that toyed with minimal democratic principles. Thus, the education of young Ludwig was a sampling of the clashes between these two worlds. His father, a military officer, appointed his eldest son a colonel in 1756. Pirmasens, the paternal home, was an enclave of latent militarism and when staying with his father, Ludwig was expected to be completely involved in his father's endless soldiering. The complete opposite took place when Ludwig transferred to Buchsweiler or Darmstadt under his mother's aegis and watchful eye. In her shadow, the young man was exposed to the leading thinkers of his time and interacted with artists, philosophers, writers, and the like. While Ludwig IX ordered the military training if his son to begin, young Ludwig was also sent to study at the University of Leiden in the Netherlands. While there, he received a nominal commission in a Dutch regiment. During his years in university, Ludwig took educational trips to London and Paris. The visit to the French capital brought the young man into closer contact with leading figures of the Enlightenment, among them Denis Diderot, Melchior Grimm, and d'Alembert, devotees of his mother.[2] They were to become life-long friends of Ludwig's as well. In fact, they (Diderot and Grimm) came along to Russia with Ludwig and spent a winter in St Petersburg with him at the time of his sister's wedding.

The Hesse-Darmstadt dynasty was to develop a long relationship with the Romanovs, a connection that began with a marriage and was solidified by several others over the course of more than a century. In 1773, Ludwig accompanied his mother and sisters on a journey from Berlin to St Petersburg. The visit to Russia centered around the wedding of his sister Wilhelmine to Tsesarevich Paul Petrovich, Catherine the Great's heir. Upon arriving, the Hessian princesses were examined by Paul Petrovich, who chose Wilhelmine. His mother recalled the experience when she wrote, *"My son from the first minute fell in love with Princess Wilhelmine, I gave him three days to see if he was hesitating, and since this princess is superior in all aspects to her sisters...the eldest is very meek; the youngest seems to be very clever; in average, we all have the desired qualities: her face is charming, the features are correct, she is gentle, smart; I am very pleased with her, and my son is in love..."*[3] In Russia, Wilhelmine adopted Russian Orthodoxy and received the name Natalia Alexeievna. While on this visit, Ludwig participated as an observer in the successful Turkish campaign led by Count Pyotor Alexandrovich Rumyantsev. This adventure gained Ludwig the rank of Lieutenant General in the Russian army.

In March 1776, Ludwig of Hesse-Darmstadt became engaged to Sophie Dorothea of Württemberg.[4] The announcement came from Mömpelgard, an exquisite property her family had owned since the 14th century. However, no sooner had enthusiasm began taking over the hearts of the young couple that ominous news arrived from Russia. Natalia Alexeievna was dead. Desperate to procure an heir to her empire, Catherine the Great demanded that Ludwig give up Sophie Dorothea (Maria Feodorovna), thus allowing Paul Petrovich to marry her. Catherine had initially wanted Paul Petrovich to marry the Württemberger, but she was deemed too young at the time. Hence, and since the Russians had expressed an interest in her a few years before, Ludwig felt compelled to agree to their request. Not wanting to cause offense, Catherine the Great softened Ludwig's disappointment by agreeing to a financial compensation for his sacrifice. Ludwig, notwithstanding the Russian compensation, was deeply slighted.[5]

In the meantime, Ludwig traveled to Weimar at the invitation of his brother-in-law Duke Carl August, who had married Ludwig's youngest sister Louise. He was the son of another enlightened royal lady, Anna Amalia of Brunswick-Wolfenbüttel, whose friendship with the Landgravine of Hesse-Darmstadt was based on their shared intellectual pursuits. As Luise and her new husband were experiencing marital difficulties due to their discordant personalities and the overwhelming presence of her mother-in-law, Ludwig's visit was a much-welcome respite. For Ludwig, the visit to Weimar provided a truly unique opportunity to participate in the nascent, vibrant intellectual atmosphere at court. Among Anna Amalia's circle of learned men was none other than Goethe.

Grand Duke Ludwig I ruled as Landgrave of Hesse-Darmstadt Ludwig X until 1806, when he became Grand Duke.

While disappointed by having to give up his bride, Ludwig could not afford to play morose, forlorn love bird for long. The dynasty needed an heir and the responsibility to provide one rested on his shoulders. Back in Darmstadt, Ludwig realized that the solution to his quandary was right under his nose. His new bride basically lived under the same roof and was someone he had known all her life. She was Luise Henriette, one of the daughters of Ludwig's uncle Georg Wilhelm.[6] The couple married in Darmstadt on February 19, 1777.[7]

Ludwig and Luise Henriette were the parents of eight children: Ludwig II; Luise (1779-1811), married to Prince Ludwig of Anhalt-Cöthen; Georg (1780-1856), who converted to Catholicism and married morganatically Charlotte Török de Szendrö, created Princess of Nidda; Friedrich (1788-1867), who also converted to Catholicism and remained unmarried; stillborn twins in 1789; Emil (1790-1856); and Gustav (1791-1806).[8]

Since his father lived permanently in Pirmasens, Ludwig settled in Darmstadt, where in addition to military duties as Inspector General and Director of the War College, he represented his father's interests. It was to him that fell the reactivation of

Landgravine Luise Henriette.

the court theater and musical life in Darmstadt, as well as court life. In many of these responsibilities, Ludwig was assisted by his uncle and father-in-law Landgrave Georg Wilhelm.

When the young couple did not stay in Darmstadt, they usually moved to the beautiful Auerbach on the Bergstrasse.[9] Ludwig remained in constant contact with the Weimar court and the local intellectual personalities. Friedrich Schiller, who was in Mannheim at that time, also received invitations to Ludwig's court several times. Communication between them continued for many years. Ludwig eagerly maintained the court's support of music.[10] There were musical performances that Ludwig himself conducted. While he dedicated considerable time to intellectual pursuits, Ludwig did not forget his military duties. In all, for nearly thirteen years he led a quiet life in Darmstadt dedicated to his duties and a growing family.

The will to reform his country, which was announced shortly after his accession to the throne in 1790, began with a "Freedom Letter" for Catholics, allowing them the free practice of their confession.[11] Unfortunately, just as Ludwig X embarked on his reign, the effects of the revolution began spreading over the French borders. The country's political instability reached the gates of Buchsweiler and the government of Hanau-Lichtenberg evacuated across the Rhine seeking safer ground. Suddenly, war and revolution were all around and the next quarter of a century witnessed one of the most tumultuous historical periods Europe had ever experienced.

Although hardly any state wished for a violent revolution in Germany, the mood of the burgeoning middle classes was directed everywhere against the privileges of the nobility and the clergy. It seemed to a successful merchant and entrepreneur that the stakes were stacked against their own success by centuries of governmental abuse and socio-economic inequality. The system, undoubtedly, was disproportionately in favor of the existing hierarchy. Something had to change.

Socio-economic discontent was not restricted to within France's borders. In fact, it was present, fueled by the new ideas espoused by the Enlightenment, in Hesse-Darmstadt. However, both the character of the populace and their Landgrave served to soften the people's willingness to fall prey to extremes. Landgrave Ludwig X, by his firm guidance, as well as by his benevolent conduct, had gained such general love and respect that to an extent violent disturbances never showed themselves in his country. His subjects remained immutable toward their prince, even when the French invaded Germany and preached revolutionary ideas to the Germans. The French tried to convey to the Germans that due to princely abuse, they had a right to rise against oppression and obliterate their surroundings, much like it was done by revolutionary zealots in France. Destruction was necessary, a requirement, for rebuilding to be truly successful. Destruction for its sake, however, was anathema to most Germans. Man's freedom was an attractive idea but attaining it at the expense of absolute mayhem did not gain much footing among the Germanic people. Their psyche and culture, their inner being, rejected such an approach.

Landgravine Luise Henriette.

In April 1792, war broke out between France and the Holy Roman Empire.[12] On both sides of the Rhine preparations began in earnest for what promised to be a monumental conflict. Landgrave Ludwig X now proved his loyalty. He sent a much stronger contingent against the French than might be expected in proportion to the population and strength of his country. However, success initially leaned on the side of the French. Mainz and Frankfurt fell to the advancing armies of General Count Adam de Custine, an able military leader who led successful campaigns in the Upper Rhine region. Ludwig X lost the part of the county of Hanau-Lichtenberg lying on the left bank of the Rhine. Already, and before the outbreak of hostilities, revolutionary hordes had wrested many of his possessions in Alsace. The French National Assembly had specifically legislated against the Hesse, treating them as foreigners in France.

The Hessian troops first fought on the side of the Prussians, then – after the separate peace of Basel – on the side of the Austrians, and partly also under English leadership in Holland. As long as there was still hope of effective resistance to the advances of the French revolutionaries, Ludwig held fast his support for the Habsburg Emperor and the Empire's interests. But when, through the peace of Campo Formio (in 1797), Mainz and the whole left bank of the Rhine fell into the hands of the French and their power came dangerously near his country, Ludwig X accepted reality. He signed a neutrality convention with France presented to him by General Jean-Baptiste Bernadotte. Suddenly, and after years of fighting, this action seemed the only option available to him to retain his country's independence.

A new Europe had finally arrived, settled, and taken hold of the future. France, under the leadership of Napoleon Bonaparte seemed an unstoppable force. War between Paris and Vienna came to an end with the signing of the Treaty of Lunéville. At the Battle of Marengo, Napoleon had inflicted a devastating defeat on Emperor Franz II and the Habsburgs' allies. Forcing upon them immediate negotiations to restore peace, the Austrians and their German allies agreed to sign the treaty that demanded, *"there shall be, henceforth and forever, peace, amity, and good understanding"* between France and her former enemies.[13] As a result of territorial concessions, Austria relinquished certain holdings within the Holy Roman Empire, while France gained the left bank of the Rhine. Hereditary Count Ignaz zu Toerring-Jettenbach described the deep and tragic repercussions of this treaty,

"Apart from the enormous change of ownership of territories, it was one of the biggest cultural changes that happened in the Reich as most of the abbeys were dissolved. Some of these abbeys had existed for nearly 1,000 years. Through the abbeys not only Christianization, but also the whole roots of our culture had been founded. They were centers of study, language, science, moral guidance, and often the first settlement in uncivilized areas. They also set guidelines in art through music, architecture, paintings, wood carving, and many more areas of artistic expression. In their libraries, history, science, and art were recorded."[14]

Lunéville granted France control over a vast land area, as well as gaining the country several million new inhabitants. By the end of negotiations, a massive 45,000 sq/km had changed hands and over 5 million received new sovereigns. In total, *"two electorates, 9 dioceses, 44 abbeys, and the independence of over 40 free cities were dissolved,"*[15] and these lands were used to compensate rulers who had lost landholdings on the left bank of the Rhine. This compensation agreement, known as the "Reichsdeputationshauptschluss," was the last substantial law passed by the Holy Roman Empire in a diet gathered in Regensburg in February 1803.

Landgrave Ludwig X's landgraviate experienced considerable territorial shifts. The losses included: a) the county of Hanau-Lichtenberg's holding on the left side of the Rhine to France; b) Lichtenberg and Willstädt to Baden; c) Braubach, Katzenelnbogen, Ems, Kleeberg, Eppstein, and the village of Weiperfelden to

Ludwig X of Hesse-Darmstadt before his elevation to grand duke.

Nassau. His losses also included nearly 100,000 subjects and some 40 sq/mi.[16] He also waived his right to protect Wetzlar and received for this all the Palatine areas of Lindenfels, Umstadt, Otzberg and the remains of Oppenheim and Alzey, the Mainz areas of Gernsheim, Bensheim, Heppenheim, Lorsch, Fürth, Steinheim, Alzenau, Vilbel, Rockenburg, Haßlach, Astheim and Hirschhorn. Archbishopric of Mainz possessions on the Darmstadt side of the Main River were gained, as was the rest of the Bishopric of Worms, the imperial city of Friedberg, the abbeys of Seligenstadt and Marienschloss, the provost of Wimpfen, and the duchy of Westphalia. His gains included some 103 sq/mi with 218,000 inhabitants. On the other hand, the landgrave took on a million gulden of new debt for the newly acquired lands. He also accepted the obligation to increase the income of the Hesse-Homburg line by a quarter and to pay the Prince zu Sayn-Wittgenstein 15,000 gulden annually.

Arguably, the "Reichsdeputationhauptschluss" brought sizeable territorial gains in what was to become the future southern province of Starkenburg, in the Weterau, and Westphalia. Once the redistribution was settled, these gains provided the impetus for comprehensive administrative reforms. Ludwig X, in a way, was better prepared to piece a more cohesive administrative unit, one that clearly laid strong foundations for the grand ducal title he was about to be granted.

The peace restored by the Treaty of Lunéville was, however, fleeting. In 1805, war between Austria and France broke out anew. While the Landgrave Ludwig X of Hesse-Darmstadt, faithful to his earlier policy and long-standing allegiances, would have joined Austria, Napoleon's quick and decisive victories put a quick end to any such decisions. Nevertheless, Ludwig X initially rejected an offer of alliance with the French by declaring that his duty bound him to the German Reich and Emperor Franz II. However, when in the autumn of 1805 the call for a French alliance was repeated under threat, Ludwig X decided to negotiate. Napoleon's blistering defeat of Austria and Prussia in the Battle of Austerlitz made Ludwig's choices very clear. Consequently, and given the political realities of the time, on July 12, 1806, Hesse-Darmstadt joined other German states in an alliance under Napoleon's protectorate.[17] Thus, the Confederation of the Rhine came to be. It was the death sentence of the Holy Roman Empire of the German Nation, which following an ultimatum from Napoleon, Emperor Franz II dissolved on August 6.

Hesse-Darmstadt became a French client state and was asked to contribute soldiers and resources toward Napoleon's increasing military adventures. Hessian troops participated in French campaigns in Spain and Russia. In return Ludwig X was compensated by receiving a new title and given higher status. He now became Grand Duke Ludwig I. The newly created Grand Duchy of Hesse was enlarged with the assimilation of territories of Imperial counts and knights, abbeys, and cities. Little did Ludwig X and the other signatories of the Confederation of the Rhine know that under Napoleon they would find themselves more subordinated than under any previous Habsburg ruler. In the end, most of Germany joined, the remaining holdouts being Austria, Prussia, Danish Holstein, and Swedish Pomerania.

Grand Duke Ludwig I's statue towering over Darmstadt's Luisenplatz.

Prior to the elevation of Hesse-Darmstadt to a grand duchy, its landholdings had been dispersed over a very large area. They lacked political cohesion and resembled a hodgepodge of estates loosely pieced together. The redistribution forced upon the new grand duchy was vast and complicated. However, it created a consistent territorial unit that provided for better administration and governance. Hence, in 1806, the following territorial exchanges and acquisitions were placed under the sovereignty of the Grand Duchy of Hesse: 1) the Landgraviate of Hesse-Homburg; 2) the Burgraviate of Friedberg; 3) the lordships of Breuberg, Heubach, ands Habitzheim; 4) the county of Erbach; 5) the lordship of Ibenstadtt; 6) the possessions of the House of Solms in Weterau, with the exception of the bailiwicks of Hohensolms, Braunfels, and Greifenstein; 7) the county of Sayn-Wittgenstein; 8) the part of the county of Königstein owned by the counts of Stolberg-Gedern; 9) the county of Schlitz owned by the Counts of Schlitz gennant Görz; 10) the lands of the von Riedesel family; 11) 1/3 of the village of Burggäfenrode owned by the Counts von und zu Eltz; 12) Staten; 13) the possessions of the Order of Malta in Nieder-Wiesel.[18] Further exchanges, cessions, and acquisitions took place with neighboring states, all geared toward constructing a more uniform administrative unit that could be better governed.

Also, at this time, Ludwig began construction on a new city palace since the Residenzschloß was no longer safe to serve as a permanent residence. Known as the Old Palace, this was the new city residence of the Landgraves of Hesse-Darmstadt, later serving as the official residence of the Grand Dukes of Hesse and by Rhine. It was located on the Luisenplatz.

Initially, the new palace was called the "Palais." Another structure was then known as the Old Palace – this was the city residence of Landgrave Georg Wilhelm, located on the market square opposite the medieval Residenzschloß. This medieval and rambling building had been the residence of the ancient Counts of Katzenelnbogen, whose extinction in the 15th century brought Darmstadt to the Hessian dynasty. After the sale of Georg Wilhelm's Old Palace in 1822, the new palace built on the Luisenplatz inherited the name.

The guarded main entrance of the new Old Palace was directly in the direction of Luisenplatz. Opposite was the Alexander Palais. It was the first large city residence specifically built for the landgraves of Hesse-Darmstadt. Previously, on the site stood the former horse barracks of the old post office. Initially, the space was intended as the site of the public Darmstadt orphanage, but this was built farther away toward the Bessungen Tor (Gate). The area in front of the palace was still a parade ground. The palace was built between 1802 and 1804, presumably by Michael Mittermeyer (1758-1816), during the planned expansion of Darmstadt under Landgrave Ludwig X of Hesse-Darmstadt. In 1832, according to plans by Georg Moller, the hall in the direction of the courtyard was connected to the front of the building.[19] This was necessary because the Residenzschloß's Kaisersaal, which had been used for court balls and festivities, as well as the rest of the ancient castle, was in poor structural condition. The renovation was never

The Residenzschloss in Darmstadt.

fully completed as the parliament reduced the funds that Grand Duke Ludwig II had requested to finish the project.

The Old Palace continued being used by various members of the dynasty as it contained apartments that were always ready to use. In fact, in 1892 Princess Victoria of Battenberg gave birth there to her son George at one of them.[20] In 1903, the Old Palace hosted the civil wedding of Princess Alice of Battenberg, Victoria's eldest daughter, and Prince Andreas of Greece.[21]

After the fall of the monarchy, the Old Palace became the seat of the Hessian tax office. The building was later the home of the Hessian Ministry of Labor and Economics. In 1935, it also became the seat of the Land Settlement Office. Nine years later, the Old Palace was almost completely destroyed during the bombing of Darmstadt. It was finally demolished at the beginning of the 1950s in the redesign of the center of Darmstadt. Today, the site is occupied by a multi-use building called "Luisencenter."

The Confederation of the Rhine served its purposed until Napoleon overreached and marched into Russia. In 1812, Imperial France invaded Mother Russia and by doing so made a fatal tactical error. No sooner that news of Napoleon's defeat in Russia reached the chancelleries of Europe than his enemies, and many supposed allies, joined forces to free themselves of the French yoke. Many of the client states that had unwillingly joined the

Confederation of the Rhine saw an opportunity for freedom and immediately sided with Austria, Prussia, Russia, and England. At the Battle of Leipzig in 1813 (also known as Battle of the Nations), Napoleon suffered a crippling defeat. Hessian troops fought on the side of the French. In all, it involved 600,000 soldiers and had nearly 130,000 casualties. It was the largest battle Europe had witnessed to date. Napoleon retreated to France as the Confederation of the Rhine collapsed. France's enemies readied to invade

The Old Palace in Darmstadt.

and bring war to Napoleon's own doorstep. The French Emperor realized the precariousness of his situation when he realized that the previous year all had joined him, but now they had turned on him.[22]

The Allies, led by Austrian Chancellor Prince Clemens von Metternich, offered Napoleon a peace settlement known as the Frankfurt Proposals. In this memorandum, which contained moderate terms, the Allies offered that Napoleon could remain on the throne as "Emperor of France." Furthermore, in exchange, France would be required to return to what French revolutionaries had claimed as the country's "Natural borders." These were the Pyrenees, the Alps, and the Rhine River. France would be allowed to retain early revolutionary conquests: Belgium, Savoy and the Rhineland (the west bank of the Rhine). In exchange, Napoleon was required to forfeit all other conquests, including Spain, Poland, the Netherlands, and most of Italy and Germany east of the Rhine. Surprisingly, Napoleon believed he could meet the Allies in the battlefield one more time and extract better conditions. His generals did not believe that the Grand Armée could stop the country's enemies. Hence, after wasting precious months that could have saved his throne, Napoleon I abdicated on April 4, 1814, in favor of his son with his Habsburg wife Marie Louise as regent. Lacking political support for this option, Napoleon was forced to announce his unconditional abdication two days later.

After the defeat suffered by Napoleon in the Battle of Leipzig, Grand Duke Ludwig, abandoned the Confederation of the Rhine and joined the Allies. Hessian troops now changed sides and fused into the very large military machine formed by Austria, Prussia, Russia, England, and Napoleon's former client states. On November 5, 1813, Ludwig announced that the Grand Duchy of Hesse had agreed to join the grand coalition forming against the French.[23] The Grand Duke then ordered his troops to be reequipped and to begin training for the new campaign against their former ally. Leading the Hessians was Prince Emil, Ludwig's son, who had commanded the Hessian contingent in Russia.

The various peace conferences organized by the Allies, gave the opportunity for Ludwig I to further benefit his realm. The task of the Congress of Vienna was to give Europe's political conditions a firm shape, provide a balance of power, and, as far as possible, to harmonize the new states of the Napoleonic period with the old ones that had fallen in the previous two decades. If the Grand Duchy of Hesse did not gain considerable increase of its surface area, it certainly improved territorial and administrative cohesion. Furthermore, the majority of the lands it gained were fertile and prosperous. As a result of the resolutions of the Congress of Vienna and the other treaties concluded with neighboring states in 1815 and 1816, the Grand Duke relinquished: 1) to Prussia went the Duchy of Westphalia and the sovereignty over the County of Wittgenstein; 2) to Bavaria the sovereignty over the bailiwicks of Miltenberg, Amorbach, Alzenau, and Heubach; 3) to Hesse-Kassel some smaller districts villages and bailiwicks; and 4) to the Landgrave of Hesse-Homburg restored sovereignty. On the other hand, the Grand Duchy received ample compensation: 1) the greater part of the former department of Donnersberg with the cities of Mainz, Bingen, Alzey, and Worms, together with the salt flats of Kreuznach, the present province of Hessian Rhine; 2) the sovereignty over the greater part of the counties of Isenburg, the Solms-Rödelheim; 3) portions of the County of Ingelheim; and 4) from the Electorate of Hesse all territories ceded to Hesse in 1810.[24] The acreage of the newly pieced state, which had yet again been redrawn, covered nearly 3,000 sq/mi, with (in 1817) 629,000 inhabitants.

Grand Duke Ludwig I.

In recognition of the acquisition of the province of Hessian Rhineland, Mainz being its largest city, Ludwig I modified the name of his realm to be the Grand Duchy of Hesse and by Rhine.

No small task now landed on the shoulders of Ludwig I. His newly constituted country, many of its parts having changed lords frequently over the previous two decades, now had to be shaped into a single administrative unit. Upper Hesse with a more North Germanic character was to be merged with Rhine Hesse, which was half French due to the long French rule – smaller ruling possessions had to be inserted into the larger whole. The prosperity of the Grand Duchy's inhabitants had been shaken due to more than two decades of constant warfare, while the state was seriously indebted.

If, in spite of all the challenges he faced, Ludwig I left a well-ordered state at the time of his death, if the wounds of the war scarred as quickly as it happened, and prosperity and happiness soon reigned, this is chiefly the personal merit of the Grand Duke. Ludwig I immediately after the conclusion of peace, energetically embarked on an extensive program of reform and rebuilding. At first, he endeavored to introduce financial prudence into all branches of grand ducal administration. He limited the expenses of his court, as much as his dignity permitted. If, nonetheless, he began several public works projects, such as the construction of a new theater in 1816, the bigger impetus behind them was providing employment to the poorer classes by building public structures.

Much more important and incisive were the improvements and changes experienced by the administration of the country. The separation of administration from the judiciary duties was implemented, giving Hesse and by Rhine citizens further legal recourse. A new law code, modeled on Austrian law, was introduced. All state sinecures were abolished and in the year 1816 – the first such action in Germany – he ordered the abolishment of tithes. That same year, on May 25, serfdom was abolished. The Grand Ducal Edict promulgated to address this ill literally reads: *"We find serfdom neither appropriate to the spirit of the age nor to the dignity which we have desired to recognize among our beloved subjects as citizens."*[25] Farming, and especially livestock, had been greatly improved by instruction and by adopting modern, more productive methods. The dams and riverbeds, which the government built at great expense and with considerable care, gave the villages along the river banks more security and increased land ownership. The expansion and improvement of the roads facilitated traffic and thereby increased trade and commerce.

Finally, Ludwig I crowned his life's work by giving his people a modern constitution in 1820. He had already agreed to the introduction of a constitution at the Congress of Vienna. The Hesse State Ministry issued a notice on February 16, 1819, announcing the promise of the Grand Duke to hold the first legislative assembly in May 1820, and before that time have in place an actual constitution. This document was published by the Edict of March 18, 1820.[26] However, since this constitution was not agreed to by the estates, it often aroused dissatisfaction. To solve this impasse, Ludwig, through his ministry, announced that the present constitutional edict, was by no means the charter that the estates had to adopt – by no means the promised constitution itself. In fact, sensing growing opposition to it, Ludwig asked for consultation with the estates. On June 27, 1820, he inaugurated the assembly of the estates convened on the basis of the Constitutional Edict. His speech from the throne, concluded memorably: *"I hope that the premises that I make for you will serve you satisfactorily. I will gladly listen to your wishes and suggestions and help you wherever you need help. I have ordered my authorities to meet you with confidence and openness. Do the same, then we will all be happy and have a good pattern to follow."*[27]

Following this olive branch extended by Ludwig I, the estates were in consultation with the government to oversee the new constitution. On December 21, 1820, after the new chart was completed, it was proclaimed and solemnly handed over to the Estates.[28] The contents of the constitutional document do not differ significantly from all the others issued in Germany in the first half of this century. Certain citizenship rights were stipulated, and the bicameral system introduced. Ludwig I recognized that the constitutional charter was far from perfect. In fact, he believed that the best such document was the constitution of the United States. Yet as long as the meritorious old Grand Duke was in office, hardly anyone dared publicly criticize him. Only one particular aspect deserves to be clearly stated, emphasized, because it demonstrates the magnanimity of Ludwig I – the Grand Duke granted one third of his domains for the government to use judiciously to gradually reduce the national debt. The other two thirds were destined to remain forever a debt-free, inalienable property of the Grand Ducal family. The income raised from the grand ducal domains flowed into the treasury and from it, revenue was used to fund the civil list and the appanages granted to members of the dynasty.

As important as the establishment of a constitution was for Hesse, no less important was another are of work sponsored by Ludwig. To many scholars, this is still regarded as one of the foundational stones of the modern-day German state. The Grand Duchy of Hesse and by Rhine was the first German state to sign a customs settlement with Prussia. The agreement of both states, which came into force on January 1, 1828, contained many of the chief provisions which we find in the later customs union treaties existing throughout Germany.[29] Hesse had suggested this treaty to increase trade, commerce, road building. The

Prussian-Hessian customs union was later joined by Electoral Hesse, which led the way for many other states to join it.

Furthermore, and in addition to this successful and versatile work in the field of politics and administration, Ludwig continued to promote the arts and sciences. The construction of a new theater was already mentioned. Other public works included the building of a new museum. In a book on art and science in the Rhine, Goethe hailed this new institution as, *"extraordinarily wealthy, excellently arranged and assembled; here you will find masterpieces of art from all centuries and times."*[30] Darmstadt was indeed the depository of invaluable treasures. Landgrave Ludwig VI was an avid book collector. He planted the seed of what became one of the most important court libraries in Germany. His descendants constantly added volumes to it as their collecting never abated. Darmstadt, the grand ducal, was considerably embellished and enlarged; the number of its inhabitants increased from 9,000 to 16,000. So much of the development of the state was headed by Ludwig personally, that his person and the state of Hesse are so intricately interwoven – one cannot be described without mention of the other.

Finally, Ludwig I was deeply concerned with the education of his subjects. He believed that good citizens could only be so if they were educated. Hence, the betterment of the citizenry was an important motive behind the cultural policies supported by the grand duke. This view of citizenship and education was also supported by one his longest serving cabinet members, Ernst Schleiermacher (1755-1844). These programs included: the opening of the court library and museum, a comprehensive scholarship program for artists and musicians and the construction of the Court Theater (1819) with 1800 seats. Such was the imprint Ludwig I left on his grand duchy, that in 1844 he was immortalized by the construction in the middle of the Luisenplatz of a tall column topped with his statue. Known as the long Ludwig, it still presides over the landscape of Darmstadt.

Grand Duke Ludwig I died in Darmstadt on April 6, 1830[31], exactly 40 years after he succeeded his father Landgrave Ludwig IX. His wife, Grand Duchess Luise, with whom he had lived happily for 53 years, had predeceased him on October 24, 1829.[32]

Grand Duke Ludwig I and Grand Duchess Luise.

****

Grand Duke Ludwig II of Hesse and by Rhine – A Grand Ducal Scandal (1777-1848)

The eldest son of the first Grand Duke of Hesse and by Rhine, Ludwig II stood all his life in the overpowering shadow of his father. Born in Darmstadt on December 16, 1777[33], he was a talented, honorable, and educated man, yet he lacked the pronounced cultural interests of his erudite parents.

Ludwig's youth took place during a relatively peaceful period until in 1790, the full effects of the French revolution reached Germany. Educationally, this was a time in which, under the protection of the princes, arts and sciences flourished in Germany. It was in vogue to be an erudite, intellectual, enlightened despot. As he approached his late teens, Ludwig was under the guidance of Privy Councilor Friedrich von Petersen (1753-1827), the brother of the Darmstadt court preacher.[34] Petersen not only accompanied Ludwig during his studies in Leipzig 1795-1798, but he also directed the youngster's moral and religious upbringing. He was not amply successful in either endeavor....

As the late 1790s approached, war spread across Germany. French troops poured across the Rhein and forced Ludwig's parents to flee Darmstadt twice. The first time in the fall of 1795 to Eisenach and soon afterwards in July 1796 to Kleinzschocher near Leipzig, where the prince met his parents.[35] Before returning to Darmstadt after completing his studies in 1799, Ludwig had traveled in the company of Baron v. Baumbach to visit his indolent Prussian uncle, King Friedrich Wilhelm II of Prussia.

In 1794, Ludwig started military service under the Hessian banner. That year he received the rank of colonel and was made chief of his own infantry regiment. Further advancements ensued: in 1801 he rose to Major General; in 1806 Lieutenant General; and 1813 Infantry General. However, Ludwig never saw frontline action. Instead, and to keep his son safe, Grand Duke Ludwig preferred to send his heir on diplomatic missions. Ludwig represented his father in Paris at Napoleon's coronation in 1804; in 1808 at the Prince's Congress in Erfurt; and 1818 at the coronation of King Louis XVIII.[36] In 1806, when Hesse became a grand duchy, Ludwig's new title became Hereditary Prince of Hesse.

By the beginning of the new century, finding young Ludwig a spouse was indispensable. The next generation of Hessians was required and the hereditary prince, already 25-years old, needed to settle down and fulfill his dynastic obligations. In December 1802, Ambassador August von Pappenheim, reported from Paris to Darmstadt that Napoleon was also in search of a bride. Newly crowned as Emperor of the French, he wished to divorce his wife Joséphine, by whom he had been unable to produce offspring, and find a nubile young princess. The new empire needed an heir – Napoleon was obligated to produce one. French diplomats suggested Wilhelmine of Baden, the youngest daughter of the Hereditary Prince of Baden and his wife Amalie of Hesse-Darmstadt, a daughter of Landgrave Ludwig IX. Shortly after, news of the collapse of this plan were reported by British ambassador Lord Whitworth and Prussia's representative Marchese Lucchesini. Pappenheim confirmed that the project had failed due to Empress Josephine's tears. Darmstadt then moved rapidly to secure Wilhelmine's hand for Ludwig II. The fact that the young princess was but 14-years-old did not seem to bother anyone. Nor did it cause pause with anyone that bride and groom were grandchildren of Landgrave Ludwig IX. It was hardly surprising that the wedding, celebrated in Karlsruhe in the summer of 1804, even before the bride's sixteenth birthday, failed to produce much happiness for either groom or bride.[37]

Ten days before celebrating her second wedding anniversary, Wilhelmine gave birth to their first child, a son named Ludwig in honor of both his father and grandfather.[38] The new mother was only 17-years-old. She had a stillborn in 1807. Nearly two years later, a second son, Karl, was also born in Darmstadt on April 23.[39] Soon after, Ludwig and Wilhelmine began living in separate establishments. She had tired of her husband's many liaisons and given up on their marriage. In fact, Karl was the hereditary couple's last child together, although Ludwig would be a gentleman in later years by recognizing his wife's second set of children as his own.

The Hessian heir was apparently minimally involved in governmental affairs as his father preferred to be the one in charge. However, Hereditary Prince Ludwig was called to participate in several governmental committees dealing with land issues. Constitutionally, he was a member of the First Chamber, whose sittings he regularly attended and often took part in discussions. Later, in 1823 he joined the State Council. Otherwise he always kept away from immediate interaction with the government, yet in his seclusion he was a diligent and thoughtful observer of affairs of state.

In personal domestic matters, Ludwig tried to keep a cordial relationship with his estranged wife. Wilhelmine felt that having provided the dynasty with an heir and a spare, she could then begin constructing a life that suited her best.

Grand Duchess Wilhelmine (née Baden).

Ludwig was not to be a part of that life. She was keen on gardening and architecture. In 1810, with the assistance of gardening master Johann Michael Zeyher, Wilhelmine created a new garden on the eastern edge of town.[40] Named Rosenhöhe, this new leisure park was to provide her with much enjoyment. She even had a small house built there to spend time surrounded by nature.

Five years after work on the Rosenhöhe started, Wilhelmine had a chance encounter that changed her life. In 1815, she visited in Karlsruhe her sister Friederike, the divorced ex-Queen of Sweden (1781-1826). Since the former Swedish queen visited Switzerland frequently, she had hired, as a riding instructor, Captain August von Senarclens de Grancy (1794-1871).[41] A young Swiss from the canton of Vaud, he was born at his family home, Château d'Etoy, ancestral seat of his maternal relations. Wilhelmine, upon meeting the dashing young officer, offered him employment in her own

household. From the day he accept the offer, until Wilhelmine's death, August was to be the main male presence in her life.[42] It had been tradition in Hesse for the Landgrave to have mistresses and the wife silently accept it as a "fait acompli." Now, for the first time, the roles had turned. The Grand Duchess challenged tradition and moral norms and established her own household with the man who made her happy, the same man who would father her second set of children.

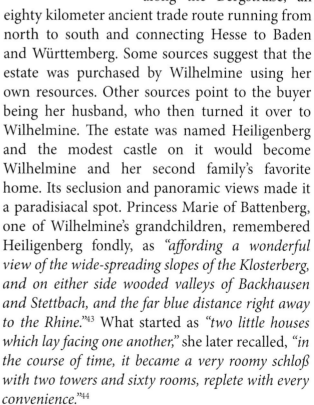

In the late 1820s, Wilhelmine came into possession of an estate in the hills east of Jugenheim, a hamlet then, situated some twelve kilometers south of Darmstadt. Jugenheim was one of countless villages located along the Bergstraße, an eighty kilometer ancient trade route running from north to south and connecting Hesse to Baden and Württemberg. Some sources suggest that the estate was purchased by Wilhelmine using her own resources. Other sources point to the buyer being her husband, who then turned it over to Wilhelmine. The estate was named Heiligenberg and the modest castle on it would become Wilhelmine and her second family's favorite home. Its seclusion and panoramic views made it a paradisiacal spot. Princess Marie of Battenberg, one of Wilhelmine's grandchildren, remembered Heiligenberg fondly, as *"affording a wonderful view of the wide-spreading slopes of the Klosterberg, and on either side wooded valleys of Backhausen and Stettbach, and the far blue distance right away to the Rhine."*[43] What started as *"two little houses which lay facing one another,"* she later recalled, *"in the course of time, it became a very roomy schloß with two towers and sixty rooms, replete with every convenience."*[44]

After the secularization of church and monastic property in 1803, the estate of Heiligenberg became the property of Hessian Court officer Baron August Konrad von Hofmann, who built an agricultural estate there. It is possible that the architect was the famed Georg Moller, who had received many commissions for grand ducal buildings. Hofmann later sold the estate to the grand ducal family, Wilhelmine using Heiligenberg as a summer residence for the remainder of her life. When her husband Ludwig came into his inheritance

Schloß Heiligenberg.

which increased his available resources he asked Georg Moller for assistance expanding the existing castle. Later, Heiligenberg was inherited by the third-born son of the Grand Ducal couple, Prince Alexander of Hesse and by Rhine. He, along with his morganatic wife Princess Julie of Battenberg and their children, moved there in 1862. During his life, Alexander continued expanding the castle every time finances allowed. The plans he always returned to were designed by Georg Moller in 1846.

Until 1914, due to the extensive dynastic connections of the Battenberg family, Heiligenberg was the center of regular visits by the Romanovs, as well as a meeting place of kings, princes, and diplomats. Alexander and Julie's daughter, Princess Marie of Erbach-Schönberg left vivid memories of growing up at there.

It is not clear, and perhaps we will never know, when Hereditary Prince Ludwig became aware, or was informed, of his wife's liaison with August. What we

do know is that Ludwig seemed not to have much of an issue with his wife's unorthodox relationship with the young Swiss baron. Ludwig made him his stable master, later elevating him to the rank of major general in the Hessian army. Then as if by magic, a second set of children started making their appearance. In May 1821, Wilhelmine gave birth to Elisabeth, who died in Switzerland five years later of scarlet fever.[45] Elisabeth's body was later laid to rest inside a new mausoleum built for the gran ducal family in the Rosenhöhe. The famous sculptor Christian Rauch created a life-sized marble tomb depicting a young child laying on the floor. Her death was devastating to her mother, who donated funds for the creation of a relief institution called the "Elisabethenstift."[46] It still functions as an institution of social welfare today.

Children continued arriving in the grand ducal nursery with some degree of regularity. In 1822, Wilhelmine had a stillborn.[47] This was followed the next year by a healthy baby boy, Alexander.[48] Lastly, on August 8, 1824, Wilhelmine gave birth to her last child, Marie.[49] Hereditary Prince Ludwig did not make much fuss about the arrival of these children his estranged wife kept giving birth to. Indeed, he did not raise a whisper in protest and recognized them all as his own.

Years later, after Wilhelmine's death, her family still revered her. There is a famous engraving designed by Moritz von Schind with a model of the proposed statue of Ludwig I that was to sit atop a column in the middle of Darmstadt's Luisenplatz. Members of the grand ducal family stand around the statue, while from the rear wall hangs an imposing portrait, at the very center of the engraving, of Grand Duchess Wilhelmine still keeping an eye on both sets of her children.

Grand Duchess Wilhelmine died at her house in the Rosenhöhe on January 27, 1836.[50] Senarclens retained his position at the court, and he even advanced to become the Colonel and Major General à la suite. He did not marry until later in the year Wilhelmine died. His wife was Countess Luise

The Palais Rosenhöhe, Wilhelmine's Darmstadt home.

von Otting-Fünfstetten, by whom he had several children. They all retained their Darmstadt roots, one of them, Baroness Wilhelmine Senarclens de Grancy (1837-1912), served as lady-in-waiting and court-lady steward of the two last Grand Dukes of Hesse and by Rhine. August Senarclens de Grancy died in Jugenheim in 1871.[51]

Back in 1829, Ludwig and Wilhelmine celebrated their 25th wedding anniversary. Soon thereafter, on April 6, 1830, he succeeded to the grand ducal throne on the passing of his father. The beginning of his reign, as well as the end, witnessed revolutionary riots that never extended over the entire Grand Duchy, but were still concerning. Shortly after his accession, the Grand Duke returned from a trip to Upper Hesse, which he had made in order to get to know this province. He was very satisfied with the reception he received, and then riots broke out in the same province. These disturbances soon assumed a threatening character. Armed gangs, consisting largely of non-Hessians, traversed the country, preaching revolution and inciting riots

and, in particular, demanding the firing of grand ducal officials. Revolution had toppled King Charles X in Paris and suddenly it seemed headed to threaten peaceful Germany. The energetic intervention of the troops under the command of Prince Emil, Ludwig II's brother, however, succeeded in suppressing the revolt. The uprising had found little support among the rural population, and in some cases even open resistance. It was not a difficult task for Prince Emil to restore order. However, the embers of unrest continued thriving in the country, especially in Upper Hesse and among the students of the University of Gießen. The seeds for the unrest of 1848 were planted.

In the internal administration of the Grand Duchy, Ludwig, assisted by Minister of State Carl du Bos du Thil, continued his father's reforms.[52] To be sure, it was not great new institutions, such as the granting of a constitution or the founding of the customs union, which his father had created or to which he had lent his assistance. The administrative mechanism had been partially redesigned and thereby simplified. The two Christian confessions represented in the country were given special attention by the government of Ludwig II. By Edict of March 21, 1837, a Protestant seminary was built in Friedberg. Previously by a document signed on June 22, 1830, *"for the glory of God, for the welfare of the Catholic Church and for the benefit of the State University"* a Catholic-theological educational institution was built and attached as a faculty to the University of Gießen.[53] Catholic faculty were granted equal rights with the

Protestant faculty. Public instruction was supported by the establishment of several secondary schools throughout the grand duchy. Significant improvements took place in the judiciary. The forest and police criminal matters were transferred to the ordinary courts. A new penal code was introduced.

The grand duchy's economy also experienced some challenging times. National debt caused a reduction in the civil list. Some architectural projects concerning the grand ducal palace were stopped, while others reduced in size and scope. The Court Theater, at one point closed due to budgetary pressures, was later reopened as Hereditary Princess Mathilde was a theater enthusiast and became its patron.

The family of Grand Duke Ludwig II. Standing, from left: Prince Carl, Prince Georg, Prince Friedrich, Grand Duke Ludwig II, Hereditary Grand Duke Ludwig, Prince Alexander, Tsarevna Marie Alexandrovna, Tsesarevich Alexander Nikolaevich. At front: Princess Carl with her sons Ludwig (IV) and Heinrich, Hereditary Grand Duchess Mathilde. Hanging from the rear wall, keeping guard over her family, is a painting of Grand Duchess Wilhelmine; her husband is depicted in a statue model for the one used on top the Luisenplatz column.

In the area of industry there was considerable progress during the reign of Ludwig II. Crafts schools were founded all over the country, and important trade exhibitions were organized. One of these exhibitions took place at Mainz in 1842 and welcomed industry from all German states. It was the first general German trade exhibition and it displayed the wares of 715 exhibitors.[54] Likewise, the first railroads in Hesse were built under the government of Ludwig II. Many still important rail lines were deployed, among them: the Main-Neckar-Bahn between Frankfurt and Heidelberg-Mannheim via Darmstadt and the Main-Weser-Bahn between Frankfurt and Kassel, the latter cutting through the province of Upper Hesse from south to north. Both lines were state railways and administered by the states of Hesse and by Rhine, Electoral Hesse and Baden.

Ludwig II was not an innovator. He was sage enough to see the good of his father's reforms and wished to invest his energy in making them even better. State Minister du Thil was instrumental, as he had been for Ludwig I, in assisting the new grand duke cleanse and expand the economy. He once wrote that, *"the arrows that had been forged during the reign of Ludwig I were saved to use against his son."*[55] Opponents of the grand duke falsely claimed that Hesse, *"had become the most reactionary and most depraved area in Germany."*[56] Nothing could be farther from the truth as Ludwig II was a decent, although perhaps unimaginative, man. He was a dedicated ruler who tried to provide a stable development for his realm, one that would secure people's well-being, even if democracy had to be set aside. Ludwig, one can argue, was an enlightened despot at a time when such an approach to governance was seen as politically reactionary.

Hesse and by Rhine had suffered from mismanagement and excessive public debts for generations. Both Ludwig I and his son tried their best to correct these endemic structural problems by cleansing the economy and reforming administrative institutions. Successful economic policy included: expansion of the German Customs Union (Zollverein), roads and railway construction, new agricultural and trade associations, more vocational schools. However, to achieve these goals, Ludwig II and du Thil supported a government that tended to side with the conservatives. The people viewed them as champions of domestic repression. When revolution toppled King Louis Philippe in Paris in early 1848, its fires soon reached Darmstadt. Shocked by the unrest, Ludwig II agreed to the

Grand Duke Ludwig II.

dismissal of du Thil. On March 5, the grand duke consented to sharing his governmental role with the Hereditary Prince Ludwig. A Hessian guilder minted for the occasion showed the young co-regent's profile and the inscription: *"Free press, People's Army, Circuit Courts, Religious Freedom, German Parliament – 6 March 1848."*

The second Grand Duke of Hesse and by Rhine retired to the privacy of his home and quietly passed away on June 16, 1848.[57] For the previous five years he had been in declining health. His death went mostly unnoticed by his subjects.

At the time of his death, only four of Ludwig II's children remained: Ludwig III, Karl, Alexander, and Marie. Two from the time when he and Wilhelmine lived under the same roof; two from the time when she had her own, and separate, establishment with August Senarclens de Grancy.

Chapter III

Grand Duke Ludwig III and Prince Karl
1806-1877

Ludwig III, Grand Duke of Hesse and by Rhine, was born in Darmstadt on June 9, 1806.[1] He grew to become a giant physically, his great-niece Victoria remembering him as,

"immensely tall and stooped very much... He had two little stiff curls to his ears. Uncle Louis and my grandfather were most severely brought up. When as children they refused spinach and if it was not all eaten up for dinner it was served for supper cold, and if some remained, te reappeared at breakfast the next day."[2] Furthermore, there was a degree of sadism involved in their upbringing since, *"To get to their rooms at night they had to walk unaccompanied down a long unlit passage and suffered agonies of terror from a tame raven which sometimes popped out on them."*[3]

Grand Duke Ludwig III.

A peculiar man in many odd ways, Ludwig III liked spending time away from the public, preferring the company of his personal attendants. Once at a lunch, he kept sniffling and refused his niece Marie Battenberg's offer of a handkerchief. He had left his at home. He would only use his own, he replied to his hostess. *"He continued sniffling until his valet...came and produced one of the Grand Duke's own, the size of a small tablecloth,"* Princess Victoria recollected.[4] In every one of his many residences, with the exception of Schloß Auerbach, he had a room identically decorated in *"dark green wallpaper, mahogany furniture upholstered in green rep."*[5] Not one family member was allowed to occupy the grand duke's green room whenever they stayed at one of the many palaces and hunting lodges. These rooms were his inner sanctum.

Grand Duke Ludwig III did not play a meddling role in the life of his extended family. He left everyone alone. He was courteous and welcoming when required. Some Sundays he would host family dinners in which the fare was as boring as the conversation. The youngsters in the family dreaded these gatherings as they would rob them of free time. *"We often had to appear at the end of them, beautifully got up and were presented with finger biscuits by the old gentleman, my mother having protested against free distribution of sweets,"* Princess Victoria wrote.[6]

These were the heady, difficult days of Napoleonic Era, as the first-born of the Hereditary Grand Ducal couple made his entry into a fast-changing and quite unstable world. He received his first lessons from Dr. Johann Philipp Dieffenbach, as well as the court preacher Dr. Ernst Zimmermann. In the summer of 1819, the young Ludwig went to Lausanne, where he spent nearly two years studying. Ludwig's travel master was none other than August Senarclens de Grancy, his mother's favorite.[7]

After returning from Switzerland, his military studies began in earnest. In 1821, Ludwig was appointed as captain of the Life Guards Regiment. In the fall of 1823, Ludwig attended the University of Leipzig, where he devoted himself to two years of higher scientific education.[8] The study of history, philosophy, and law occupied most of his time in Leipzig, the same university his father attended. Meanwhile, his military career continued. In 1825, he was promoted to colonel; in 1830 to Major General and commander of the Life Guards Regiment (later Infantry regiment No. 115); in 1833 Lieutenant General; and 1843 General of the Infantry.[9] Ludwig, who had never seen battle, was nonetheless a passionate military enthusiast, who devoted himself meticulously to the uniform-related regulations and organization of his army.

Grand Duchess Mathilde.

This study period in Leipzig was followed by educational trips, starting in the spring of 1827, which the prince embarked on with his younger brother Karl. They visited Bavaria, Austria, Upper and Central Italy. Other important destinations, Rome and Naples, had to be given up because of a life-threatening illness Ludwig contracted while in Florence.[10] This trip was followed by a longer stay in France and Belgium.

In April 1830, Grand Duke Ludwig II ascended the Hessian throne. At the time, young Ludwig seems to have been involved in a worrisome liaison with a young woman named Elisabeth Müller, daughter of a Darmstadt coachman.[11] After massive pressure from his parents, Ludwig gave her up and searched for a suitable wife. In an effort to increase his son's responsibilities, on December 25, 1833, Ludwig II assigned him an official position within the government dealing with medical issues, an area for which the future Ludwig III had true passion. On that same day the Hereditary Grand Duke Ludwig married Princess Mathilde, eldest daughter of King Ludwig I of Bavaria and his long-suffering wife Therese (née Saxe-Hildburghausen). The ceremony took place in Munich. It was customary then to celebrate most royal weddings in the bride's ancestral home.

Born in Augsburg on August 30, 1813, Mathilde was the first daughter of then Crown Prince Ludwig and Crown Princess Therese.[12] She was one of many children, among them King Maximilian II and Prince Regent Luitpold of Bavaria, King Otto of Greece, and Duchess Adelgunde of Modena.[13] Mathilde received a careful education that included science, foreign languages, drama, painting and drawing, in addition to later receiving instruction in religion by Bishop Oettl from Eichstätt. Her marriage prospects as the eldest daughter of the Bavarian monarch were excellent. Hence, from an early age several candidates were shuffled for her hand in marriage. As early as 1828, the widowed Emperor dom Pedro I of Brazil made inquiries.[14] He eventually married her first cousin Princess Amélie of Leuchtenberg. Then, King Louis Philippe made inquiries about allying his revolutionary monarchy to the respected Royal House of Bavaria. Crown Prince Ferdinand of the

Grand Duke Ludwig III.   *Grand Duchess Mathilde.*

Two-Sicilies was interested in Mathilde, as was the somewhat older Grand Duke Leopold II of Tuscany. A visit by Mathilde's Hessian cousin Ludwig, who was accompanied by his brother Karl in February–March 1833, quickly led to a betrothal.[15] Both sets of parents actively worked to spark romantic embers between Mathilde and Ludwig. It was a good choice, everyone thought, particularly since both groom and bride were also closely related: Mathilde's paternal grandmother was Augusta, a daughter of Prince Georg Wilhelm and Princess Luise Albertine of Hesse-Darmstadt; Ludwig III was also this couple's great-grandson through their daughter Luise.

In spite of the enthusiasm demonstrated by both sets of parents, there were serious concerns regarding the couple's engagement. These issues centered on religious matters: Ludwig was Lutheran, Mathilde Catholic. Back in those days, such confessional issues mattered a great deal. While matrimonial alliances between Protestants and Catholics did happen, they caused intense negotiations and had detailed rules, particularly concerning the religious education of any children had by the couple. Consequently, the marriage contract negotiations between Munich and Darmstadt, complicated due to the identity of the groom and bride, also included a religious aspect. The Hessian delegation to the marriage negotiations was led by the Fürst zu Sayn-Wittgenstein and Baron von Riedesel, whose family served the House of Hesse and by Rhine for generations.[16]

The confessional problem was solved elegantly – first a Protestant (December 25), then a Catholic wedding, as happened on December 26, 1833.[17] Since Ludwig was the heir to his house, the religion of the children would be that of their dynasty, Lutheranism. Once the marriage contract was agreed upon, preparations continued in earnest. The bridal gifts were arranged to allow public viewing, as were the couple's future apartments in Darmstadt.

Ludwig and Mathilde made their entry into the Grand Duchy of Hesse and by Rhine on January 10, 1834. Welcoming them at the border was a beautiful triumphal arch built just for the occasion. The wedding gift given to Mathilde by the city of Darmstadt was a summer house built by prominent architect Georg Moller. It was built on the future site of the artists' colony we now know as "Mathildenhöhe," located on one of the highest spots in Darmstadt, as well as a few hundred meters away from the Rosenhöhe. Although Darmstadt was from then onward her home, Mathilde retained very close contact with her relatives in Munich and Athens.

Above all, Darmstadt benefited from the artistic interests of Mathilde of Bavaria. She was committed to the Court Theater, music, and fine arts. Mathilde also provided assistance and support for training trips of Hessian artists to Munich or Greece. With the death of her mother-in-law Wilhelmine in 1836, she took over the representational duties at the court and the continuation of Wilhelmine's patronage of countless social endeavors. For example, Mathilde was actively involved in the creation of educational centers for children of the poorer classes. She also provided patronage for a women's association (founded in 1849) for the rescue of morally-at-risk children, which was later named "Mathilde Society."[18] She also lent her patronage to an older *"Association for the support of poor patients from the countryside,"* as well as what became the *"Mathilde Hospital,"* which tended to the needy in Hesse and by Rhine. She recognized that to reduce poverty, the lesser classes had to be able to obtain loans to finance enterprises or small farms. With

Grand Duchess Mathilde earlier in her youth.

this in mind, Mathilde supported the foundation of savings and loan institutions in Friedberg and Nidda. At the national level, Mathilde, with her husband's support, created in 1858 the *Ludwig and Mathilde Foundation,* which supported social causes, particularly the plight of widows and orphans of civil servants.[19] This organization remained active until 1933. Mathilde, who remained childless, included her sister-in-law Princess Elisabeth, wife of Prince Karl, in many of her charities.

After her death in 1862, Grand Duchess Mathilde was buried in a special crypt in St Ludwig's Church.[20] A funeral service was also held in the Darmstadt City Church. The Bishop of Mainz, Baron Wilhelm von Ketteler, delivered the commemorative speech during the laying of the funerary marble monument donated by her father in 1865 – the Munich artist Max von Widmann depicted the dormant Mathilde lying with a cross in her hands. St Ludwig's was destroyed during the Second World War. Mathilde's coffin was reburied on the ground floor. The funerary monument had to be removed because it was too severely damaged. In addition to Grand Duchess Mathilde, Prince Friedrich (1788-1867), the son of Grand Duke Ludwig I, was also be buried in St Ludwig's. He was a benefactor of the parish and had donated one of the church bells.

As revolution spilled over the French border in March 1848, Grand Duke Ludwig II fired Minister du Thil and asked his eldest son to take over the government as co-ruler. The aging father, who was ill, thought he found in his popular son the man capable of effectively countering the 1848 revolutionary movement. Hence, on March 5, 1848, he created a constitutionally-sanctioned co-regency.[21] He was not wrong. The people of Darmstadt received the news with loud cheers and hoped for a more liberal future. Hereditary Grand Duke Ludwig lost little time in implementing rapid, liberal but firm measures. These included the appointment of Heinrich von Gagern as chief minister, thus robbing the incipient revolutionary movement of any further success. While in neighboring Baden the revolution was victorious over the Grand Duke and the government, even if only for a short time, Hesse and by Rhine remained, if not entirely unaffected, at least comparatively at peace. The co-regency lasted until June 16, 1848, when Grand Duke Ludwig II passed away.[22]

The first German parliament gathered in Frankfurt's Paulskirche in 1848. Heinrich von Gagern served as its president. The "democratic" experiment bitterly disappointed the high expectations held by those supporting political reform. The Parliament was unable to come to constructive decisions to reconcile democratic popular sentiment and dynastic interests. The rivalry of the leading powers, Prussia and Austria, became apparent in the daily working of the body. All these disappointments weighed heavily on the political climate. The supporters of Austria, who feared Prussia's ambitions gathered in the "Darmstadt Conference." Prussia laid the foundation of what would become an association of client states named the North German Confederation.

The Grand Duke of Hesse and by Rhine was not a reactionary. Yet, as much as Ludwig III was

Grand Duke Ludwig III.

inclined to leniency, and as much as it suited his character to meet the legitimate wishes of his people for reforming the country's institutions, he resolutely opposed the violent tendencies of those seeking to overthrow the government. The province of Rhineland Hesse experienced widespread disturbances as it was more industrialized than the grand duchy's other two provinces, Upper Hesse and Starkenburg. When disturbances invaded the streets, Hessian troops were displayed on the ground and order was restored, thus avoiding the more violent protests that were witnessed in other areas of the Rhineland Palatinate, Baden, Munich, and even regions under Prussian control.

Like many of his ancestors, Ludwig III was interested in Hessian history and art promotion. During his reign, the opera and ballet company could claim European-quality levels. The Darmstadt Court Theater stood as an equal to the first stages of Europe. He also patroned numerous historical studies, committed himself to securing Protestant and Catholic rights, dedicated himself to the study of medieval castles, and sponsored a compilation of the history of the Hessian regiments. His interest in historical sites related to his family prompted him to buy back Schloß Braunshardt, built as a country residence of Prince Georg Wilhelm, the brother of Ludwig IX.[23] His granddaughter, Queen Luise of Prussia, had spent part of her youth there. Princess Alix, the future Russian Empress Alexandra Feodorovna, also spent part of her youth in the castle.

In 1857, Ludwig III gave the order that each locality had to create a "chronicle" (registry) and

In the early 1860s, political uncertainty affected Germany due to Prussia's ambitions. In order to discuss solutions, Grand Duke Ludwig III joined other fellow German sovereigns and Emperor Franz Joseph at the "Princes' Congress" in Frankfurt 1863. The Hessian grand duke is second-to-last on the right side of the photo. Emperor Franz Joseph, on the first step, is surrounded by the Kings of Hannover, Bavaria, and Saxony. In the end, the conflict led to war between Prussia and Austria in 1866.

manage it in a conscientious manner, a task he entrusted to local pastors. Inside these chronicles site-specific, and menial, practices (confessionals, births, baptisms, weddings, deaths) were to be preserved. They allowed the authorities of the grand duchy to manage population growth, culture, population movement. These registries acted as an early type of census. Grand Duke Ludwig's passion for cataloguing and documenting was not restricted to the creation of these registries. One of his particular interests was to create uniforms for as many professional groups as possible, making the person wearing one easily identified with a profession. Not only should soldiers be recognized by their uniforms, but also railroaders, lawyers, theater supervisors, pastors, etc... From this time comes, for example, the "Luther skirt" for Protestant pastors and the long frock coat, buttoned up to the top, just like the Catholic priests.

Ludwig's love of history made him support the construction of an impressive monument to Luther and the Protestant Reformation. The inauguration of the Luther monument in Worms was held on June 25, 1868.[24] It was an event of historical proportions. Almost all sites connected with Luther had been destroyed in 1689 when war took a heavy toll on Worms. Efforts for the construction of this monument were led by the Lutheran Dean of Worms Herr Keim and by Dr. Eich, a high school teacher. These men wanted to erect a memorial appropriate to the reformer. The monument, with a price-tag of more than 250,000 marks, had a 3.30 meters-high figure of Luther standing on a five-meter-high pedestal. Surrounding it were four pre-Reformers: Savonarola, Petrus Waldus, John Wyclif, and Johannes Hus. The princes who most fostered Luther's cause, Saxon Friedrich "the Wise," and Landgrave Philipp "the Magnanimous" of Hesse, were also included in the monument. The inauguration ceremony, which was attended by the Grand Duke, King Wilhelm I and Crown Prince Friedrich of Prussia, and King Karl of Württemberg, was a powerful depiction of a self-confident Protestantism. To all, it seemed as if a nationalist and strong Germany was ready for the arrival of a new Reich under the leadership of a Protestant emperor. The country was about to get what it hoped for.

It was during Ludwig's reign that Bismarck's anti-Catholic "Kulturkampf," a government-sponsored discrimination against the church was implemented. Church policies and laws passed had the hoped effect of a program of contrasts, announcing the separation of the hitherto close ties between church and state. The emergence and growing influence of the center as a Catholic party truly concerned Bismarck. The few lean results (for example: the civil status legislation – that is, the state taking over the registration of births, marriages, and deaths, which was previously done by the churches), hardly justified the political toll and ideological effort. Hesse initially let itself be pushed to adopt the Kulturkampf. The Hessian government, wanting to exert some degree of control over organized churches, did adopt a church tax in 1876.

The reactionary movement that prevailed in Germany at the beginning of the 1850s naturally did not remain without influence on the Grand Duke's government. Baron Reinhard von Dalwigk was called to head a new ministry, inaugurating for the grand duchy a period of conservative government. Many of the concessions initially granted by the government in 1848 were eventually rescinded and the status-quo was restored. How little Grand Duke Ludwig III was personally inclined to implement some of these reactionary measures is the fact that, although he had approved the reintroduction of the death penalty, he never confirmed a single death sentence. It cannot be denied that Baron von Dalwigk's government was repressive. However, its ability to bring peace and restore order allowed Hesse and by Rhine to focus on governmental

policies geared toward continuing economic expansion. Doing so served to uplift the prosperity of the people. Ludwig III, undoubtedly, was also extremely open to economic development in the Grand Duchy at the time of early industrialization. Trade and commerce, agriculture, and all branches of industry found lively governmental promotion. Advancement in communication infrastructure, for example, was exemplary. Numerous railways were built; the foundation of credit institutes was promoted. It seemed for a long while as if Hesse and by Rhine's progress was unstoppable.

Then came war….

The year 1866 began with somewhat good news for the expansion of Hesse and by Rhine. On March 24[25], news arrived of the long-awaited death of Landgrave Ferdinand of Hesse-Homburg, last male of his line. The Hesse-Homburg line sprang from the Landgrave Georg I of Hesse-Darmstadt, whose youngest son, Friedrich I, received Homburg and other territories as his inheritance. His descendants successfully ruled this landgraviate for several centuries. No one could have imagined that in one generation of siblings that included several males not one surviving male heir would be produced. These landgraves were the sons of Friedrich Ludwig (1748-1820), who in 1768 married his distant cousin Landgravine Karoline, daughter of Landgrave Ludwig IX of Hesse-Darmstadt.[26] They produced an astounding number of children, 15 in fact: eight sons, five daughters, and two stillborn. Four of the sons (Friedrich, Ludwig, Philipp, Gustav) married, yet only one produced a child.

Landgrave Ferdinand of Hesse-Homburg.

Grand Duke Ludwig III.

Between 1820-1866 these five brothers succeeded their older brother as Landgrave of Hesse-Homburg: Friedrich r. 1820-1829, Ludwig r. 1829-1839, Philipp r. 1839-1846; Gustav r. 1846-1848, and Ferdinand r. 1848-1866.[27] The only one of these Landgraves of Hesse-Homburg to produce a son was Gustav, who was the father of Hereditary Prince Friedrich. Unfortunately, the young heir died in Bonn on April 1, 1848.[28] His early death robbed the Hesse-Homburg line of its only direct heir for the next generation since Landgrave Gustav's only immediate surviving male heir was his bachelor brother Ferdinand, an old man nearly 65-years-old. Hence, when he succeeded his brother later in 1848, Ferdinand's landgraviate would revert to the senior branch of Hesse and by Rhine unless he produced an heir. He never did…

As Darmstadt dealt with the political changes mandated by Ludwig III inheriting the Landgraviate of Hesse-Homburg, the seeds of war were about to spring with deadly force across Germany. These were planted when in 1863-1864, Prussia and Austria went to war with Denmark over the provinces of Schleswig-Holstein. In spite of the brave defense offered by the numerically inferior Danish army, the outcome of the war was a foregone conclusion: Denmark lost Schleswig-Holstein, the Dukes of Augustenburg and Glücksburg were robbed of their realms, Austria and Prussia unsuccessfully attempted to co-administer the duchies. By 1866 war was on the horizon as Prussian Chief Minister Otto von Bismarck followed a policy designed to extricate Austria from German affairs, while implementing Prussian hegemony over the country. The Schleswig-Holstein conflict became the spark needed to engage Austria in the battlefield.

Since he was strongly focused on the protection of his own dynasty and did not want to see the sovereignty of his country diminished by revolutionary upheaval, Ludwig III became closer to both Austria and France. These powers seemed to him guarantors of the existence of the German middle states, which he saw threatened by Prussia's insatiable hunger for land and power. This fear and suspicion had led Ludwig III to pursue, with Minister von Dalwigk, the termination of the customs agreement between Darmstadt and Berlin.[29] Therefore, when Berlin and Vienna went to wear in 1866, Ludwig III sided with the Austrians. It was a disastrous choice.

In the Austro-Prussian War of 1866, which ignited on June 14, Ludwig III stood firmly by the side of Emperor Franz Joseph and the Austrian Empire.[30] Also, on Austria's side were: Bavaria, Hannover, Saxony, Württemberg, Electoral Hesse, Baden, Nassau, Saxe-Meiningen, Reuß, Schaumburg-Lippe, and the Free City of Frankfurt. In a matter of a month, Prussia and its allies inflicted fatal blows on Austria and her allies. The smaller battles won by the Austrian side achieved little to derail the Prussian juggernaut. It did not help Vienna one bit that Italy declared war in an effort to gain Austrian-controlled regions in Northern Italy. By July 24, the last battle was fought, and peace negotiations began. Prussia inflicted devastating reparations on her enemies: Austria surrendered Venice to France, but Emperor Napoleon III handed it to Italy as secretly agreed with Prussia, and also lost all official influence over members of the German Confederation, pushing Vienna to become a Danube-basin empire; Schleswig-Holstein became Prussian; Hesse and by Rhine lost not only Hesse-Homburg, but also other territories it had controlled for generations; the King of Hannover, the Elector of Hesse (Kassel), the Duke of Nassau lost their throne; Frankfurt was annexed by Prussia; Saxony, Saxe-Meiningen, Reuß, Schaumburg-Lippe were spared, but joined the Prussian-controlled North German Confederation.

Emperor Franz Joseph of Austria.

The unfortunate, but necessary, fratricidal war also cost the grand duchy an old Hessian district, the so-called Hinterland (the districts of Vöhl, Biedenkopf, and Battenberg). Although Darmstadt was taxed with a devastating compensatory payment of three million gulden to Prussia, the grand ducal family's web of dynastic relationships prevented a more onerous fate. The loss of Upper Hesse, which Bismarck wanted to annex to the new Prussian province of Hesse-Nassau, was only prevented by the intervention of Tsar Alexander II, who was married to Marie, Grand Duke Ludwig III's sister. The connection established by Prince Ludwig when he married Princess Alice, Queen Victoria's daughter, also put pressure on Prussia not to annex Hesse and by Rhine. Alice's older sister Victoria was married to Crown Prince Friedrich of Prussia and this link

was also used to Darmstadt's benefit. Militarily, the entire Hessian army was subordinated to the Supreme Command of Prussia.

Initially, Grand Duke Ludwig III did not have much sympathy for German unification, and at least between 1866-1870, along with Minister von Dalwigk, maintained close ties with Austria and France. Then, the dispute of 1866 was soon forgotten when Bismarck tricked France into a major military conflict. Not only were the French defeated and their Emperor captured and dethroned, but Prussia's victory allowed Bismarck the political strength to proclaim the new German Reich with King Wilhelm I of Prussia as German Emperor. The Hessians, without hesitation, supported Bismarck and the Hohenzollerns.

It was obvious that Minister-President von Dalwigk, who for decades had fought so passionately against Prussia's leadership in Germany, was leaving the political scene. With his dismissal, forced by Bismarck after the founding of the empire in 1871, the personal rule of Ludwig III basically came to an end. He withdrew increasingly into private life with his second wife Magdalena Appel, a former dancer at the Darmstadt Hoftheater, and relinquished his representative duties to his nephew and successor Ludwig and his wife Alice. Ludwig III had married Frau Appel secretly and morganatically in 1868.[31] He was four decades her senior. Quietly, he created her Baroness von Hochstädten.[32] *"In his latter years he married his housemaid, who was kept discreetly out of sight. She was an unassuming, kindly body and my mother befriended her after his death.*

I remember her coming to tea to our mother and speaking of him as Der gute Herr," Princess Victoria Battenberg recalled.[33] The baroness was never included in any court functions and was kept away from public sight.

By the time his end came, *"Ludwig III was popular in the country and a good honest Constitutional Sovereign."*[34] The Grand Duke died of erysipelas at his summer residence in Seeheim on June 13, 1877.[35] He died still holding on to his peculiar belief, among them, *"Kaspar Hauser being the lost Prince of Baden."* Baroness von Hochstädten survived her husband until her death in Wiesbaden in 1917.[36]

Grand Duke Ludwig III's image would be incomplete if one wanted to forget his personal qualities. The gentleness and kindness of his nature won the hearts of his people. Significant knowledge, supported by an eminent memory, quick comprehension, and keen judgment also raised him in this respect over the crowd. His love for the arts, especially for music, was particularly evident in the care of his court theater.

Grand Duke Ludwig III.

****

Prince Karl of Hesse and by Rhine (1809-1877)

Prince Karl, born in Darmstadt on April 23, 1809, was the second son of Grand Duke Ludwig II and Grand Duchess Wilhelmine.[37]

Unlike his brother Ludwig, who was the very image of health and physical strength, Karl was, *"delicate, suffering all his life from bronchitis and frequent migraines. He was very much of an invalid,"* recalled his granddaughter Victoria.[38] *"My grandmother took the greatest of care of him. They were a very devoted couple. He was a gentle person, lived a retired life and was very old fashioned in his habits. He was a good-looking man with a clean shaven face framed by side whiskers. He wore high cravats like stocks and fancy waistcoats and generally a frock coat. Out of doors in winter he always wore a black silk "respirator" over his mouth,"* Victoria wrote.[39] Much like his older brother, Karl had his own peculiarities, his granddaughter recalling that, *"He had a passion for collecting all kinds of odds and ends. He had a cabinet in his dressing room which was filled with all sorts of collections: in one drawer were seals cut off from envelopes (in old days most letters were sealed) – When enough seals were collected they were melted down for a new stick of sealing wax. In another drawer were used postage stamps and I was told that the missionaries employed them in China – the Chinese were supposed to paper the walls with them. In a further drawer were old capsules from wine bottles and silver paper off chocolates. From this lead spoons for orphanages were cast. He had also a number of small bon-bonnieres which contained rolled bread crumbs with which he fed the goldfish in his garden pond. When in his little house in the Rosenhöhe, he used to walk down a certain avenue after lunch sucking a caramel, the coloured paper wrapper of which was always thrust into the same hole in an old tree. He was devoted to birds and had several cages with exotic birds in his room. In the winter evenings, he and my grandmother sat at a round table under the Holbein Madonna. He cut out pictures for scrap books. – It was a great honour when one was allowed to assist him, - and my grandmother knitted or read aloud. He was very kind to us little girls and we were fond of him.*[40]

As a child and adolescent, Karl was his older brother Ludwig's school and traveling companion. The brothers remained close their entire life. With him Karl studied in Leipzig in 1824-1825, where he took the same lessons as his brother, besides learning the flute and Italian.[41] In March 1825, Austrian Chancellor Prince Clemens von Metternich offered young Karl a position in the Imperial & Royal Hussar Regiment nr. 5, also known as the "King of England Regiment."

Prince Karl of Hesse and by Rhine.

In March 1827, he traveled to Vienna, from where accompanied by his brother Ludwig, he continued to Italy and on to Paris.[42] In May 1828, Karl began a five-year service with his Hussars, who, as the father wrote, *"should bring to him the experience, the world and the knowledge of human nature that a young man of his class needed."*[43] Appointed colonel in 1832, Prince Karl would be dismissed the year after with the honorary rank of Lieutenant Field Marshal. Having returned to continue military service in Darmstadt as a major general, from 1836 he was the commander of the four infantry regiments stationed in Offenbach and Friedberg, which until then were named after Grand Duchess Wilhelmine, his mother. In years later, these regiments would be renamed after Prince Karl. Although he was promoted to Lieutenant General (1840) and General of the Infantry (1848), Karl did not see military service in the revolutionary years of 1848-49 or in the wars of the 1860s.

Princess Karl of Hesse and by Rhine (née Prussia).

In Darmstadt, the famed architect Georg Moller was charged with building a classical-style residence for Prince Karl in 1834-1836. The Prince Karl Palais was located on the Wilhelminenstraße (at Nr. 34 in 1900).[44] The elegant building was just a few meters from the new city palace that was built as a substitute to the medieval Residenzschloß. Both palaces faced the Luisenplatz, where the statue of Grand Duke Ludwig I was erected in the 1840s. Originally, the palace was a three-story, nine-axle building with

Princess Karl of Hesse and by Rhine (née Prussia).

stepped attic, and therein contained small slightly oval skylights and a hipped roof. The attic was later expanded as a fourth floor and a new roof was added. The original structure was later connected to the right-angled building in the crossing area to today's Annastraße by a single-story porch with balustrade. The most famous room of the palace was the so-called "Blue Room of Princess Elisabeth," decorated in Biedermeier style and walls covered blue wallpaper. Rebuilt several times, the last major change was implemented in 1927 by architect Peter Müller.

Just as his new home was nearing completion, Prince Karl married. His bride was Princess Elisabeth, daughter of Prince Wilhelm of Prussia and his wife, the former Landgravine Maria Anne of Hesse-Homburg.[45] Both Elisabeth's grandmothers belonged to the House of Hesse-Darmstadt, as they were daughters of Landgrave Ludwig IX. Her paternal grandmother was Landgravine Friederike who married King Friedrich Wilhelm II of Prussia. Elisabeth's maternal grandmother was Landgravine Karoline, who had married Landgrave Friedrich Ludwig of Hesse-Homburg. This not only made Elisabeth's parents first cousins, but also made them first cousins of her future parents-in-law, Ludwig II and Wilhelmine of Hesse and by Rhine, who were first cousins themselves. Interestingly for genealogists, Karl and Elisabeth's children thus had four great-grandparents who were all siblings, and instead of having 16 different great-grandparents, the couple's offspring only had 10.

June 18, 1815 – On the day of the decisive Battle of Waterloo, in which Prince Wilhelm of Prussia commanded a Prussian cavalry brigade, his daughter Elisabeth was born in faraway Berlin. To the baby's baptismal names Marie Elisabeth Karoline was added that of "Victoria." Her sponsors were the victorious Prince von Blücher and the Duke of Wellington. Elisabeth's childhood years, in Berlin and Schönhausen, were more peaceful. Holiday destinations would take her family to Homburg von der Höhe and, after 1822, Schloß Fischbach in Silesia.[46] Later when her father was made Governor-General of the Rhine Province, the family lived in Mainz and Cologne. Although her parents had nine children, only four survived into adulthood: Adalbert (1811-1873), married morganatically to a Viennese dancer, Therese Elssler, later created Baroness von Barnim; Waldemar (1817-1849), unmarried; and Marie (1825-1889), who married King Maximilian II of Bavaria, and was the mother of King Ludwig II and King Otto.[47] Marie was also a sister-in-law of Grand Duchess Mathilde, Elisabeth's own sister-in-law.

After the engagement during a pre-Christmas 1835 visit by Prince Karl to Schloß Fischbach, the couple had to postpone their wedding due to the unexpected death of Grand Duchess Wilhelmine. Elisabeth, years later, inherited Fischbach from her father's estate. Yet, as Elisabeth's parents lived in Mainz, Darmstadt was not far. Karl could visit his bride frequently, which made the wait bearable until a new wedding date could be set.

Prince Karl and Princess Elisabeth were married in Berlin on October 22, 1836.[48] Soon after, they made their official entry into Darmstadt, where they were able to move into the newly built Prinz Karl Palais. Elisabeth's dowry included a famous painting of the Madonna, which from then onward graced one of the walls in her new, elegant, yet unostentatious home. The couple's welcoming celebrations included opera performances, as well as a masked ball for 2500 people from all classes at the Darmstadt Court Theater.

While in Darmstadt, the Karls of Hesse resided in their palais, but also spent summers at his late mother's small palace on the Rosenhöhe, which was located just a few miles away. When not in Darmstadt, Karl and Elisabeth lived in a grand ducal hunting lodge in Bessungen, which was then south of the capital. Today, Bessungen is a suburb of Darmstadt. It was in Bessungen where on September 1, 1837, Elisabeth gave birth to her first child, a baby boy baptized with the traditional Hessian name Ludwig.[49] As his uncle and namesake, then Hereditary Grand Duke Ludwig, was childless,

Prince Karl of Hesse and by Rhine.

the baby prince was third-in-line to succeed to the grand ducal throne. A little over a year later, on November 28, 1838, a second son, Heinrich, was also born at Bessungen.[50] A five-year gap ensued, and it was not until 1843 that Elisabeth gave birth again. This time the new arrival, a baby girl named Anna, was born in Darmstadt.[51] Lastly, a third son, Wilhelm, was born at Bessungen on November 16, 1845.[52]

Once he settled down to build a family, Karl's life focused on his local military obligations and assisting his brother as counselor. He also served as a member of the First Chamber of the Hesse Parliament. The rest of his time, Prince Karl dedicated to his family life and private endeavors. As for his wife, motherhood seemed to be her calling. Princess Elisabeth simply cherished her children and took particular care participating in raising them. Even Crown Princess Victoria of Prussia later described her as, *"happier in her own family,"* even if she was, *"quite negative."*[53]

Prince Karl and Princess Elisabeth of Hesse and by Rhine with their family. From the left: Prince Wilhelm, Princess Alice, Prince Heinrich, Princess Anna, Prince Ludwig holding his daughter Princess Victoria, Prince Karl, and Princess Elisabeth.

This photograph, dating from late 1863, is quite possibly the last showing the family together. Six months later, Princess Anna married Grand Duke Friedrich Franz II of Mecklenburg-Schwerin and moved to away. She died in Schwerin in April 1865 while giving birth to her first child.

An ambitious royal matron, Princess Elisabeth desperately tried to find suitable spouses for her sons Wilhelm and Heinrich. Ultimately, she failed and both married morganatically. Had they married equally and fathered sons, they could have saved the dynasty from extinction.

Along with her cousin Grand Duchess Mathilde, Elisabeth embarked on many social welfare commitments in Darmstadt. One of the projects closest to her heart was providing assistance to poor and dislocated families. One of these endeavors included the foundation of an organization that created a safe home for abused women housed in the former monastery at Arnsburg. A second rescue house was opened in Hähnlein on the Bergstraße. More importantly, in 1858 on the name day of St Elisabeth in Darmstadt, Princess Karl inaugurated the main deaconess house of the Elisabeth Foundation, which today serves as a hospital.[54]

Since Ludwig III and Mathilde were childless, the succession would fall to the line of Prince Karl. By the late 1850s, it was a foregone conclusion that Ludwig, Karl and Elisabeth's eldest son, would one day become Grand Duke of Hesse and By Rhine. Finding him a proper spouse was a matter of national importance. The first machinations concerning Ludwig's matrimonial prospects came from a letter Crown Princess Victoria of Prussia sent to her mother Queen Victoria in November 1859. In the letter, Victoria tells her mother that her husband Friedrich told his cousin Adalbert of Prussia, Princess Karl's brother, *"I hope he* (Ludwig) *will not marry before having looked at different Princesses my four sisters-in-law for instance, they are none of them engaged."*[55] Toward this suggestion, Victoria confirmed to her mother the Hessians, were susceptible, *"that would be grist to Elisabeth's mill,"* she said, as Adalbert, *"knew his sister wished it very much."*[56] After also receiving positive reports from her uncle King Leopold of the Belgians, Queen Victoria invited Prince Ludwig and his brother Heinrich to visit her family during Ascot in the summer of 1860. Two years later Ludwig of Hesse and by Rhine married Alice of Great Britain. Theirs was to become a complicated marriage, yet one that ultimately turned into a solid union.

Princess Elisabeth's success in the royal marriage market continued in 1864, when her daughter Anna was married to Grand Duke Friedrich Franz II of Mecklenburg-Schwerin.[57] She was his second wife but would not be his last. Anna was attractive and well-educated, she had excellent connections and seemed healthy. At one point, Queen Victoria instructed her daughter the Prussian crown princess to look into Anna as a candidate to marry the Prince of Wales. Anna's prospects were put to an end to when the Prince Consort met her, one of his reasons being not wanting two of his children married into House Hesse and by Rhine. Crown Princess Victoria also had reservations about Anna, whom she believed had a troubling *"twitch."*[58]

Anna's childhood ended with her confirmation in 1859. Soon afterward, Princess Elisabeth began training Anna to become involved in her many charities and social work organizations, including the Elisabeth Foundation. It was very sad for the grand ducal family to lose Grand Duchess Mathilde while she was still an arguably young woman. It was particularly painful for her niece as Mathilde died on Anna's nineteenth birthday. Shortly thereafter, the family traveled to England for the wedding of Prince Ludwig and also took advantage of the journey to pay a visit to Napoleon III's Paris. Anna was one of Princess Alice's bridesmaids, the other three were her sisters Helena, Louise, and Beatrice.

In August 1863, Anna met Grand Duke Friedrich

Franz II of Mecklenburg-Schwerin while he was attending the "Princes' Congress" in Frankfurt.[59] His wife Augusta (née Reuß-Schleiz-Köstritz) had died the previous year, leaving behind four children. One of these motherless children was to become the famed Grand Duchess Vladimir of Russia. A visit by the 40-year-old ruler to Darmstadt, followed by a trip to common relatives in Bad Homburg, allowed Anna to get to know her future husband. After the official engagement on December 19, it was in early 1864 that Anna traveled to Altenburg in Thüringen where she first met her indomitable future mother-in-law Alexandrine (née Prussia) and Friedrich Franz's children. After the return of her bridegroom and brother Heinrich from the Danish War, the wedding was celebrated in Darmstadt on May 12, 1864.[60] The couple's ceremonial entry into the Mecklenburg-Schwerin summer residence Schloß Ludwigslust followed numerous tours around the grand duchy. Anna was well-liked and her future in Schwerin seemed secure. Unfortunately, life had other plans.

A few months after her wedding, Anna realized she was pregnant. It was a normal pregnancy, and everything seemed to be going accordingly. On April 5, 1865, she gave birth to a baby girl at Schloß Schwerin.[61] Apparently, Anna caught an infection after her daughter's birth, which had gone well. The infection was not cared for properly and her condition worsened overnight. Grand Duchess Anna died on April 7.

Grand Duchess Anna of Mecklenburg-Schwerin.

Princess Alice was devastated by Anna's death as both had become very close since Alice settled in Darmstadt. To the Queen Alice wrote, *"Oh it is sad, very sad! – Life indeed is but a short journey, on which we have our duty to do, and in which joy and sorrow alternatively prevail."*[62] To Ludwig, who had departed to Schwerin upon receiving news of his sister's death, Alice wrote, *"When one of us dies, it will be terribly hard for the other, when all contact is cut off – and when the fearful silence of the grave intervenes. May the dear Lord preserve us for each other and let us die together."*[63] The Queen, still in deep mourning years after the death of the Prince Consort echoed Alice's despondency when she wrote about her own worries and what *"anxiety it is to be a mother to have married daughters with these events happening often – it is always such a risk and such an uncertain thing."*[64]

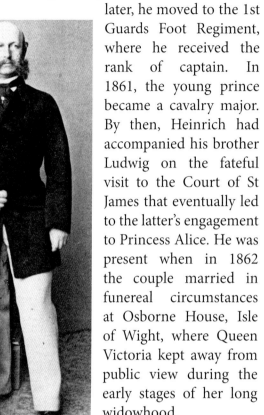

Grand Duke Friedrich Franz II and Grand Duchess Anna of Mecklenburg-Schwerin.

Grand Duchess Anna's daughter survived her mother and was baptized Anna Alexandrine, after her mother and her paternal grandmother, Alexandrine of Prussia. Unfortunately, she died in Schwerin on February 8, 1882.[65]

Prince Heinrich was the second son of Karl and Elisabeth of Hesse and by Rhine. As was the case with his older brother, Heinrich was born at Bessungen. His birth took place on November 28, 1838.[66] Ludwig and Heinrich were study partners and spent much of their early years together as they were one year apart. In 1856, both completed a year of study in Göttingen, later Heinrich enrolling

for a summer course in Gießen. Concurrently with his studies, Heinrich also started military service. In 1854, Heinrich was made an officer in the 1st Hessian Infantry regiment, but he did not begin active service probably until 1857. Two years later, he moved to the 1st Guards Foot Regiment, where he received the rank of captain. In 1861, the young prince became a cavalry major. By then, Heinrich had accompanied his brother Ludwig on the fateful visit to the Court of St James that eventually led to the latter's engagement to Princess Alice. He was present when in 1862 the couple married in funereal circumstances at Osborne House, Isle of Wight, where Queen Victoria kept away from public view during the early stages of her long widowhood.

Once returned from England, Heinrich resumed his service in Darmstadt. He was a staff officer in the cavalry division during the Danish War in 1864, where his future brother-in-law Friedrich Franz of Mecklenburg-Schwerin also saw service. In the Seven Weeks' War, Heinrich saw action in the Battle of Königgrätz as commander of the Prussian 2nd Ulan Guard Regiment. During the Franco-Prussian War, he became a brigade commander. Afterward, he continued his military career by serving as commander in Dusseldorf and Trier. Then in 1879, he was appointed commander of the 25th Grand Ducal Hessian Division. Eight years later, Heinrich attained the rank of cavalry general.

While he demonstrated great reverence for

his military duties, Heinrich was lackadaisical concerning his dynastic ones. His mother tried desperately to pair her handsome second son to many an eligible princess, yet Heinrich would not fall for any such trap. Focus on his military career provided him a cover for conducting liaisons with women he could have never married dynastically. Finally, Heinrich fell under the spell of Caroline Willich genant von Pöllnitz, daughter of an army officer. She was born in Butzbach in 1848, and even though her parents belonged to the lower ranks of the Hessian aristocracy, Caroline lacked the quarterings for the marriage to be recognized as equal. Therefore, Heinrich and Caroline married morganatically in Darmstadt on February 28, 1878.[67] Heinrich's brother, Grand Duke Ludwig IV, created Caroline Baroness von Nidda. She gave birth to a son the following January but died two days later. Her son, Baron Karl von Nidda lived until 1920.[68] He never married.

In 1892, Prince Heinrich remarried, morganatically. His second wife was Milena (Emilie) Hrzic de Topuska, of Croatian extraction.[69] She was a singer in the Darmstadt Court Opera. She received the title Baroness von Dornberg. The next summer, she gave birth in Munich to a son, Elimar, who later entered the military and was killed during the Great War. Both of Prince Heinrich's sons died unmarried and childless.

By the turn of the century, Prince Heinrich's health was faltering. Death came to him on September 16, 1900, while living in Munich.[70] Six years later, his widow remarried Baron Maximilian von Bassus, an official at the Bavarian court. Milena died in Munich in 1961, one of the last nearly forgotten remnants of a bygone era.

Prince Wilhelm of Hesse and by Rhine.

The family's youngest brother, Prince Wilhelm, was under less pressure to start a military career, yet as was tradition within the family, he received his first commission while still a teenager. Unlike his older brothers, Wilhelm was allowed to follow a more literary and artistic path when attending university, which he did in Edinburgh and Bonn during several terms in 1863-1865. During some of these terms, Heinrich was a classmate of Prince Ludwig's brother-in-law, Prince Alfred, later Duke of Edinburgh and Saxe-Coburg and Gotha. Another close friend of Wilhelm's was his first cousin King Ludwig II of Bavaria, with whom he kept a voluminous correspondence.

Wilhelm's first military commission came in 1862 when he received the rank of lieutenant in his father's regiment, the "Prinz Karl." During the Seven Weeks' War, Wilhelm was attached as a captain to the headquarters of the 8th German Federal Army Corps under the command of his uncle Prince Alexander. In the Franco-Prussian War, Wilhelm served in the staff of the 25th Grand Ducal Hessian Division. From them onward, promotions arrived with some degree of regularity: colonel in 1873, major general in 1875, and infantry general in 1890. However, Wilhelm

Prince Heinrich, Princess Anna, and Prince Wilhelm of Hesse and by Rhine.

led a dilettantish life in Darmstadt without any specific military functions. His niece Victoria, not one to ever mince words, described Wilhelm as, *"a passionate Wagnerian, did nothing, and was the spoilt child of my grandmother."*[71]

Since 1872, Wilhelm sat in the First Chamber of the Parliament in Darmstadt as a member of the dynasty. He maintained close relations with his brother Ludwig IV and his sister-in-law Princess Alice, as well as their uncle Prince Alexander. He traveled to Italy and was a frequent visitor to England, where he maintained many friendships, not just with members of the Royal Family.

Much like his brother Heinrich, Wilhelm avoided getting trapped in his mother's matrimonial match-making. In fact, in the second half of the 1870s, he began a liaison with a Josephine Bender, a ballet dancer in the Darmstadt Court Theater. The relationship produced a son in 1877.[72] The baby was named Gottfried, but it was not until he was seven-years-old that his parents married. There was no doubt that given Josephine's background, nothing short of a morganatic marriage would do. This ceremony took place near Metz, France, on February 24, 1884.[73] Josephine was created "Frau von Lichtenberg," while her son was legitimated and given the last name von Lichtenberg.

The Palais Rosenhöhe served as the home of Prince Wilhelm. The small palace was located some two hundred meters away from Darmstadt's eastern railway station. The building and park's history are closely related to Grand Duchess Wilhelmine, who in 1810 purchased the property and commissioned architect Johann Michael Zeyher to build a large garden in "modern style." Zeyher, a master at creating English landscape gardens, designed a vast park-like area with winding paths and countless rare trees and shrubs. Pavilions and a tea house (which stands still today), completed the park, along with a modest residence designed by Georg Moller. This last

Prince Heinrich of Hesse and by Rhine.

building, which Wilhelmine used as a summer residence became known as the Palais Rosenhöhe. Like no other, this corner of earth, Wilhelmine found it irresistible. It was her retreat, a private world in which court life played no role. In 1826, after the tragic death of her daughter Elisabeth, Wilhelmine ordered the building of a mausoleum. It was from then onward that the Rosenhöhe became the traditional burial ground for the grand ducal family.

After Wilhelmine's death, the park came to her son Karl as an inheritance. He, along with his wife, continued the tradition of using the Rosenhöhe as a summer residence. During this time, the construction of the still existing smaller summer house began. After Princess Elisabeth's death, the Rosenhöhe became the property of two of her sons – Grand Duke Ludwig IV and Wilhelm. The brothers divided the complex and manifested this division through a wall leading through the park. After Wilhelm's death, his share passed to his nephew Grand Duke Ernst Ludwig, who had a new mausoleum built for his parents and siblings. Designed by renowned architect Karl Hofmann, the building was inspired by the tomb of the Empress Placidia in Ravenna, both inside and out. The heart of the park – the Rosarium – was created by garden master Ludwig Dittmann at the beginning of the 20th century. The aim was to create a *"garden that Germany did not know yet."* For this purpose, the architectural rigor of Italian gardens was combined with the diversity of plants and flowers of English garden art. Lastly and created in 1914 by Albin Müller (1871-1941) and Bernhard Hoetger (1874-1949), the Löwentor (Lower Gate), was built for the last exhibition of the Darmstadt artists' colony on the Mathildenhöhe. It was given its place at the entrance of the park in 1926 with clinker pillars redesigned for this purpose with a lion placed on top of each column. The Rosenhöhe remains one Darmstadt's most beautiful sights.

Prince Heinrich with Prince Alfred, Duke of Edinburgh.

Prince Wilhelm died at the Palais Rosenhöhe on May 24, 1900.[74] As his death caused his share of the park to revert to his nephew Ernst Ludwig, Frau von Lichtenberg and her son had to vacate their home and settled in Darmstadt. In 1901, Gottfried von Lichtenberg married Elisabeth Müller, their ceremony taking place in his hometown.[75] We do not know if any members of the grand ducal family were in attendance, since the Lichtenbergs seem to have disappeared from the public realm. Gottfried entered military service and was a casualty in the early stages of the Great War. He had one son, Gottfried (1902-1958), born in Mainz, who left one daughter, Alexandra, from his marriage to Traute-Irmgard Knispel.[76] As for Frau von Lichtenberg, she remained a widow and died in Darmstadt in 1942.[77]

Grand Duke Ludwig IV.

Chapter IV

Darmstadt and Windsor
Ludwig IV and the English Connections –
tragedy and single parenthood

In 1862, in the midst of great tragedy and a very grief-laden and funereal atmosphere, the second daughter of the bereaved Queen Victoria, Princess Alice, married Prince Friedrich Wilhelm Ludwig of Hesse and by Rhine. The couple was married at Osborne House on the Isle of Wight and the Queen could not stop weeping during the entire service. This could hardly be called encouraging to the newlyweds. However, through the lamentations, the Queen was at least happy that she would not be losing an extremely useful daughter, as they say, but gaining a son.

But Alice, though she enjoyed being useful, also wanted to marry and have a family of her own. She was born at Buckingham Palace on April 23, 1843, the third child and second daughter of Queen Victoria and Prince Albert, the Prince Consort.[1] She was christened Alice Maud Mary having been preceded by Albert Edward ("Bertie") and the Queen's first born, Victoria ("Vicky"). The brood that eventually numbered nine was raised under the supervision of their father. The Queen, as has often been noted, had little interest in infants and babies, though she took much more interest in her children later in life. Their father, however, paid a great deal of attention to all aspects of their lives and most especially their education and their childhood was a happy one. He charged that Baron von Stockmar, who had supervised his own education to do the same for his children.

Alice was an incredibly bright child, though she was overshadowed by her brilliant older sister, and eagerly learned her lessons. As she got older, she became very close to her elder brother "Bertie," the Prince of Wales. It was she that could draw him out, it was she that helped him through his lessons, and was so much kinder to him then the brilliant and mercurial Vicky. The two elder daughters would soon become "roommates" and companions in the school room where they learned a full program of reading, writing, geography, poetry, art, dancing and of course, bible lessons. Indeed, had Vicky not been her sister, Alice with her intellect, her gentleness and humility, her questioning, her deeply spiritual nature and well-developed social conscience would have been the shining light of the family. It is important to note that Alice contracted scarlet fever in 1855 and this had the impact of permanently weakening her constitution and may have been a cause of her ill-health and delicacy as she grew older.

For the compassionate and empathetic daughter, childhood ended quickly. Vicky, married and Alice became the oldest daughter at home, though she was only fifteen. In that fateful year of 1861, she nursed not only her grandmother, the Duchess of Kent during her last illness, but more important, her father. Seeing her father failing and her mother grieving and, frankly, unhelpful, must have been very difficult for her, but nevertheless she soldiered on. During Albert's last illness, Alice's mind focused completely on nursing her father, and acting as his confident. Although it was tragic that a daughter was nursing her own father on his deathbed, Alice found the work deeply satisfying. Despite the love and care, the Prince

Prince Ludwig of Hesse and by Rhine.

quickly succumbed to typhoid, no doubt weakened by worry and over-work. Alice vowed afterward that she would honor his memory in word and deed as faithfully as did her mother. Alice immediately moved into the bedroom next to her mother's and was put "in charge" of her. She, though, herself, in the throes of grief, would take her mother's orders, convey messages between the Queen and her ministers and *"she was still the sole channel for the nation's official business, and still the main prop for her mother."*[2]

After these deaths, the Queen relied heavily on Alice for support. Alice, being of a somewhat melancholy disposition, could doubtless have used a great deal of support herself, but this was not forthcoming in the winter of 1861-62. Her only solace was that her late father had very much wished her to marry and after rejecting several suitors, including the Prince of Orange and Prince Albrecht of Prussia, Alice accepted the proposal of Prince Ludwig of Hesse (as he was called in the family) and by Rhine.

Alice's courtship with Prince Ludwig began in the summer of 1860. Other princes had danced before Queen Victoria's second daughter including the troublesome Prince of Orange, also known as the "Orange Boy." However, in his case it was that she was not quite right for the Princess being a rather dissolute young man. Later events would prove this to be correct. Prince Ludwig, by no means dissolute, was judged to be a far more worthy contender.

In June of 1860, Queen Victoria invited Prince Ludwig and his brother Prince Heinrich to accompany her and her family to Ascot. As mentioned before, since the Grand Duke's first marriage to Princess Mathilde of Bavaria was unfortunately childless, Ludwig was destined to inherit the grand ducal throne.

Princess Alice of Great Britain and Ireland.

It was obvious that week at Ascot that Ludwig and Alice were attracted to one another. Such happenings were eagerly remarked upon when a presentable young prince was in the company of one of the Queen's unmarried daughters. Usually, the Queen was not receptive, and in some cases, downright resistant to courting and romances. She was never very comfortable with romance or, indeed, anything that might mean that one of her daughters might be taken from her.

Ludwig, possibly out of fear, but more probably of shyness, did not approach the Queen and the Prince Consort during that first visit. Perhaps he was intimidated by the fact that he could not, at present, offer Alice anywhere near the standard of living she was currently enjoying. Certainly, it would have been a coup for the Hessian Family to capture the hand of the second daughter of the Queen, who was considered the doyenne of monarchs. But it was all the more puzzling since Ludwig left before anything was settled. Albert had actually hoped for and expected the Prince's addresses to their daughter.

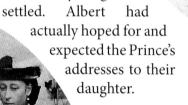

Princess Alice in her wedding dress.

Six months later, the young suitor was invited once again to Windsor with more felicitous results. He and Alice were left alone in a room and, more emboldened than before, Ludwig quickly proposed. He was accepted though Alice promptly went to her mother to ask if this was all right.

"Certainly," the Queen was said to reply, and continued to crochet furiously, since she was at least as agitated as the now successful suitor.[3]

However, all would be arranged to suit the Queen, of course, and not the engaged couple. For one, they would have to wait at least a year, due to the immaturity of the bride. The delay was more likely so that the Queen could get used to losing another daughter to marriage. Next, she envisioned that the couple, who, at present, had no pressing duties or obligations at the Hessian Court, would naturally spend most of their year attending on herself. The Queen was of a mindset, somewhat prevalent of the time, that

Prince Ludwig and Princess Alice.

Osborne House, July 1, 1862 – The Queen "tossed fretfully" as daylight made its arrival. Princess Alice kept her company throughout the night. The Queen gave her daughter a blessing and a Prayer Book, just as her own mother had done when she married Prince Albert of Saxe-Coburg and Gotha in 1840. It was a dull day and the wind was strong, as grey clouds rolled in from the sea. The Queen and all of her children were present. A large number of royals had traveled to the island to witness and partake in the somber wedding festivities. Besides a bevy of Hessians, other guests included: the Duchess of Cambridge and her children: the Duke of Cambridge, Grand Duchess Augusta of Mecklenburg-Strelitz and Princess Mary Adelaide of Cambridge; Crown Prince Friedrich of Prussia and his wife Victoria; Duke Ernst of Saxe-Coburg and Gotha, the Duke de Nemours and his sister Princess Clementine, with her husband August of Saxe-Coburg and Gotha; Dowager Fürstin Feodore of Hohenlohe-Langenburg, Queen' Victoria's half-sister, along with her son Prince Viktor; and Prince Edward of Saxe-Weimar-Eisenach.

middle and upper-class daughters should exist as unpaid secretaries, companions and even maids. Were they to marry heirs to kingdoms, such as did Alice's eldest sister, Vicky, then she could understand that they must go there to live and their first allegiances would be to their new homes (except, of course when it came to childbirth, when it was understood that English physicians, nurses and nannies were unquestionably a must). However, if this was not the case, then, they were to be nearly as much at their Mama's disposal as they had before their marriages. Queen Victoria described Ludwig as *"so good, and kind an so quiet."*[4] Above all, he was unassuming. The Queen felt that she would not have any problems convincing the couple of the efficacy of her plan.

An ideal "stay-at-home" daughter though she was proving, it had been Albert's wish that Alice should marry. As the weeks went by, the Queen came slightly and most reluctantly back to herself, and the wishes of her beloved Albert became paramount. She was, therefore, determined that this wedding would be made to happen as soon as possible. The date was set for July 1, 1862. Nevertheless, the months leading up to the ceremony continued to be full of sadness. Grand Duke Ludwig III's first wife, the Grand Duchess Mathilde, died in May of that year, and Queen Victoria commented that the *"Angel of Death still follows us....*[N]*ow Alice's marriage will be even more gloomy."*[5]

The wedding took place July 1, 1862, with the Queen and her family shedding copious tears.[6] Ludwig's brothers and father were present as well as Ernst II, Duke of Saxe-Coburg and Gotha, who gave the bride away. One can only imagine what they were thinking during this tear-drenched ceremony.

During her long widowhood, Queen Victoria turned the memory of her beloved Albert into a family cult. His early and unexpected death, turned him into a near-perfect being in his widow's mind. Their descendants were expected to follow suit. Not only were they all made mindful of her loss, but everyone had to mind his memory. In this image, The Queen sits by a portait of the Prince Consort with her daughters Louise and Alice.

After the "festivities" Alice and her groom had their honeymoon at St Clare, Springfield near Ryde. The Queen was busily making her plans for the couple during that time. Alice would have all her children in England since Victoria did not quite trust German physicians or midwives and the couple would continue to keep her company while little Hessians arrived at suitable intervals. This is not precisely how things turned out.

After their honeymoon, Alice and Ludwig took up residence in the village of Bessungen in Upper Wilhelminenstrasse. Ludwig was not overburdened with wealth and they settled in what would have been considered a comparatively modest "gentlemen's" residence and set to the business of having a family. Very soon afterward, the babies came: Victoria (1863-1950), Elisabeth (1864-1918), Irène (1866-

A family gathering in England. Standing in back, from the left: Princess Louise (Duchess of Argyll), Prince Ludwig, and Princess Alice of Hesse and by Rhine, Prince Alfred (Duke of Edinburgh and Saxe-Coburg and Gotha), the Prince of Wales, Crown Princess Victoria of Prussia, and Duke Ernst II of Saxe-Coburg and Gotha. At front, same order: Prince Arthur (Duke of Connaught), the Princess of Wales, Princess Beatrice, Crown Friedrich of Prussia, Prince Leopold (Duke of Albany), and Princess Helena (Princess Christian of Schleswig-Holstein-Sonderburg-Augustenburg.

1953), Ernst Ludwig (1868-1937), Friedrich Wilhelm (1870-1873) Alix (1872-1918) and Marie (1874-1878).[7] As the family increased, luckily their fortunes began to do so as well. With the substantial dowry that Alice received from Parliament, and a generous contribution from her mother, they could build a larger residence in Darmstadt that would, when it was completed, be called the Neues Palais.[8]

The Neues Palais, the home Alice and Ludwig built in Darmstadt.

From 1866 onward, the family lived in this lovely palace during their sojourns in Darmstadt but during their holidays, they might be anywhere from Balmoral in Scotland, to middle class lodgings by the seaside in Blankenberghe, Belgium. Another favorite palace to visit was Heiligenberg, the home of Prince Alexander of Hesse and by Rhine and his wife, Princess Julia von Battenberg. It was at this house that the Hessian children came into frequent contact with their Russian Aunt, Marie, Empress of Russia but also their cousins,

Nicholas, Alexander, Vladimir, Alexei, Marie, Serge and Paul. Most of the older cousins were too old to be interested in the much younger Hessian children, but Serge and Paul were close playmates and friends.

Another favored home in Hesse was their hunting lodge, Kranichstein. This home was especially beautiful during the summer when they could ride horses and ponies, run with their dogs, row in the beautiful lake, and hunt. It was called by some Sleeping Beauty's castle, and it did, indeed, go to sleep when a tragic event, one of the many tragedies that plagued the Hessian family, occurred, but that is for later.

Prince Ludwig in Garter robes, while Princess Alice wears court dress and the famed Hessian tiara.

Alice had also become heavily involved in the duchy becoming what they called a true *Landesmütter*, carrying on social work, organizing hospitals, orphanages and a women's union later called the *Alice Frauen Verein*. The chief emphasis of the Union was the training of Red Cross Nurses. However, there were many auxiliary branches that reached into the areas of education for women, a home for unwed mothers and an insane asylum. Alice was a great follower of Florence Nightingale and believed fervently in her *Notes on Nursing*.[9] In addition, there is little doubt that she would also be aware of the work of Dorothea Dix. She was an American progressive, who in the early 1840's investigated the care of the insane, prisoners and indigent in the state of Massachusetts. It was through this kind of investigation that conditions for the socially neglected began to improve. Alice was a strong feminist, imbued with a profound social conscience and deep reformer instincts. She managed to pass these laudatory qualities on to her children.[10]

Princess Victoria.   *Princess Elisabeth.*   *Princess Irène.*

Though Alice was something of a melancholy person, she nevertheless loved Darmstadt. For a small town it had a great deal of culture. Its rulers and later its Grand Dukes had ever encouraged endeavors in art, literature, music, architecture and theater. It had a most impressive opera house and the famous singers of their day sang there including Jenny Lind. Alice happily continued to invigorate art and culture in her Grand Duchy. She was friendly with the great romantic composer, Johannes Brahms with whom she played piano duets and had lengthy religious and philosophical conversations with the well-known philosopher and theologian, David Strauss . She was very much the sensitive and introspective intellectual and found as time went on that this did not exactly mesh with her husband's bluff and hearty disposition.

While a devoted couple the two were in many ways mismatched. Ludwig, as mentioned was a hale and robust soul who was happiest outdoors stalking in the woods with a British-style Norfolk jacket and a gun in hand. Alice, on the other hand was a much more complex individual. Beside her cultural and philanthropic pursuits, she had a much more curious and questioning nature. Her queries into the profundities of life that she discussed with Herr Strauss made her husband and more importantly, her mother, extremely uncomfortable. The Queen expressed her disapproval in a letter where she warned that trying to find out the reasons and *"explanation of everything…*[will make you]*…miserable."*[11]

Princess Alice was unusual among royal mothers in that she spent a great deal of time with her children. They were not just trotted out for their parents for an hour after tea, cleaned and dressed

Princess Marie.

Prince Ernst Ludwig.

Prince Friedrich.

Princess Alix.

– Alice was very interested in their diet, their studies, their activities and all that they did. For a royal Princess, she was quite a "hands on" mother.

Prince Ludwig, on the other hand, when not preoccupied with military matters, was usually out hunting and shooting. Certainly, this was understandable when Hesse was involved in the Second Schleswig-Holstein war in February – August 1864. Also called The Schleswig Holstein Question, this was a conflict that broke out several times in the 19th century. It seemed to be essentially a tug of war over the Duchies of Schleswig and Holstein by what would be the new Prussian-dominated Germany and Denmark. But truly, it was about the leadership of the Germanic peoples – Prussia and Austria.

The second of the two conflicts began in 1863 when the Danish King Frederik VII died without issue. Christian IX came to the throne and claimed that he was the rightful heir of both Duchies. The Prussian Prime Minister, Chancellor Otto von Bismarck with his forces and Austria declared war on Denmark and triumphed. The Duchies of Schleswig-Holstein was annexed to what would eventually be the German Empire. This naturally caused considerable bad blood between the Danes and Prussians and, of course, their rulers as well. Alexandra ("Alix"), eldest daughter of Christian IX, wife of the Prince of Wales, detested the Germans and there would always be a strain between her and her sister-in-law Vicky, who was married to the future German Kaiser Friedrich III.

Princess Alice holding her first child, Victoria.

Princess Alix, Prince Ernst Ludwig, Princess Marie.

Princess Victoria, Prince Friedrich, Princess Elisabeth.

Princess Irène, Princess Victoria, and Princess Elisabeth.

Nothing really seemed settled and in June 1866, a critical political crisis occurred. Chancellor von Bismarck decided the time was at last ripe to challenge the Austrians and Southern Germans for hegemony of all the Germanic peoples and thereby form a Second Reich. To this end, he instigated a war between Austria and Prussia ostensibly over violations of the Schleswig-Holstein Treaty. The Austro-Prussian War began on June 16, 1866 and continued for seven bloody weeks. The Germanic peoples lined up behind each side, with Hesse and by Rhine[12] and Hesse-Kassel fighting with Austria as many of the Southern German entities did. However, ten days after hostilities started, the Austrians were defeated decisively at the Battle of Sadowa (Königrättz) in Bohemia. Though the war dragged on for weeks more, the Prussians triumphed because their military machine was far more modern and efficient. When Austria and her forces were defeated in September of that year the two sides signed what was called the Peace of Prague. Hesse and by Rhine was assessed a devastating indemnity of three million florins, a huge sum which took years to pay.[13] Along with the indemnity, there were other revenues and lands which the treaty entitled the Prussians to appropriate. Those lands included parts of the Hessian Grand Duchy proper: Hesse Homburg and Frankfurt. The good news for Hesse was that they were to endure a short occupation of six weeks, and eventually, looting which had been going on for several months, was curbed. The other good news was due to Vicky's intercession with her husband and father-in-law, Ludwig III would not lose his throne and remain the Grand Duke of Hesse and by Rhine.

During this time, Alice had just given birth to her third child, Irène, but nevertheless was much occupied with the nursing of the sick and wounded. Unsurprisingly, her health was compromised in her unceasing efforts. The best part of the peace for Alice that that Victoria and Ella, whom she had sent to the safety of their grandmother, Queen Victoria, could now return home.

Grand Duchess Alice, at center, surrounded by her children. Clockwise from the top: Victoria, Irène, Ernst Ludwig, Marie, Alix, and Elisabeth.

Afterward, though considerably financially crippled, the family was able to take up its normal life once again. It was also at this point where Queen Victoria and Alice began to repair their relationship[14] and the Hessian Family renewed its lengthy visits to England. There was much visiting back and forth between the English and Hessian Aunts, Uncles and Cousins.

It was in November 25, 1868 when Alice gave birth for a fourth time to the long-awaited heir. He was called Ernst Ludwig, named after some past forbears, and, his eldest sister Victoria in fact wished for another sister and was most disappointed, but that would come later.

In 1870, though things in the family continued on an even keel, the Franco-Prussian War broke out and Ludwig and his Hessian troops were once again away now fighting *with* the Prussians. Alice, as was her wont, plunged back into feverish nursing with almost a fanatical zeal. This time, she took her eldest children, Victoria and Ella, along with her to soup kitchens and hospitals in order that they should understand what was going on and its unfortunate consequences. It was no doubt these scenes from their early childhood that inspired Victoria's radical ideas and charitable impulses later in life as well as Ella's profound service to the poor when she was an adult. It was unfortunate that while Ludwig was away, Alice once again gave birth — this time to another little boy, Friedrich Wilhelm (Frittie). Preliminary peace negotiations only came to pass in the beginning of 1871 and Ludwig was away from his family until May 1871.

During the intervening years, Alice's health was never strong. She was the sort of person who drove herself mercilessly at whatever task she had allotted herself and never thought of her own physical well-being. In this, she was much like her father, Prince Albert. A contributor to her low spirits had to have been the discovery of much bruising on her little boy Frittie the following year. Alice had, of course, been aware of her brother, Leopold's hemophilia, but probably did not expect to see it in her own son.

Grand Duchess Alice of Hesse and by Rhine.

point of exhaustion and kept an extensive travel schedule with her family moving from house to house or visiting relatives in other parts of Germany, France, and of course, England. Disaster struck later in that year when Frittie, who had been playing with his older brother, Ernst Ludwig, tumbled out of a window. Initially, they thought his injuries were not life threatening, but just a few hours later he died from internal hemorrhaging. It was a devastating grief that she could not put aside throughout the rest of her short life.

In March of 1877, Ludwig's beloved father, Prince Karl died, and then three months later, the old Grand Duke died, and Alice and Ludwig inherited the duchy. With this change of circumstances, the family no longer had money worries. Nevertheless, they were overwhelmed with functions, ceremonies and obligations. The little vitality that Alice had left was sapped

The birth of her next child, Alix in 1872, compromised her health further and from then on, her family noticed that she never seemed to fully regain her strength. Nevertheless, she worked hard in the grand duchy often to the by her larger responsibilities and her depressive nature.[15] Nonetheless, she faced them stoically. To be helpful, her family tried to take small breaks from responsibilities, so that Alice might recover

Grand Duchess Alice of Hesse and by Rhine in court dress and wearing the famed Hessian tiara.

Darmstadt, December 1878 – This print, from the Illustrated London News, depicts the coffin of Grand Duchess Alice inside the Hessian family crypt. To the left of her coffin is a smaller one containing the remains of her youngest daughter Princess Marie (insert), who died on November 16.

her strength, but she never seemed to make it up. Indeed, all in the family noticed and it was a constant theme in letters from the eldest, Victoria to her grandmother, the Queen that "Mama" was always tired, headachy, and looked very pale.

On November 5, 1878, Victoria complained of a sore throat. She was quickly put to bed with a hot water bottle by her mother and a physician sent for who diagnosed diphtheria. The family, excepting Alice and sister Ella, quickly came down with the dreaded disease. Alice's delicate condition did not prevent her from once again throwing herself into nursing. All recovered and recuperated slowly, with Alice going from sick room to sick room soothing fevered brows. She never let up while the family physicians struggled to match her twelve-hour schedules.

Tragedy occurred when the youngest child, May, died on November 14, but the worst was yet to come. Alice, worn out by her nursing, and kissing Ernie, who was still ill, to comfort him after breaking the sad news of his little sister's death, caught the disease herself. She succumbed on December 14,

After the loss of Alice, Queen Victoria became a surrogate mother to her Hessian grandchildren. This image was taken in 1879, months after the tragedy that took Grand Duchess Alice and her daughter Marie. Surrounding Queen Victoria, from the left, are: Victoria, Ernst Ludwig, Ludwig IV, Irène, Elisabeth, and Alix.

the same day that her father had died seventeen years before. It was all so sad and mysterious, Queen Victoria wrote. Despite their contentious relationship, the Queen was truly grieved at this first death of a child. Alice, she felt, had her father's disposition, his devotion to duty and his self-sacrificing nature.

After these tragic events, the remaining Hessian children, Victoria, Ella, Irène, Ernst Ludwig and Alix,

From the left: Princess Irène, Princess Victoria, Queen Victoria, Princess Elisabeth, and Princess Alix.

were left motherless, with a father who had very little idea of how to nurture a family. Despite a relationship that was rarely in sync, it was a fact that Ludwig was lost without his wife and he increasingly abdicated his role of parent to his mother and mother-in-law, who was the cynosure of her family. Ludwig was content to let her, and various aunts and uncles take on the raising of his family. They began the slow process of healing with Queen Victoria, taking an active parenting role. The Queen, it must be said was driven by the "*...fear that they would fall under the influence of their 'very cold, very grand' grandmother, Princess Elizabeth* [sic] *of Hesse and By Rhine.*"[16] It is interesting that the Queen felt this way when it had been observed that Princess Karl of Hesse was a shy person, but very broad-minded who was always ready to listen to others.[17]

After Grand Duchess Alice's death, Queen Victoria often invited her Hessian relations to visit her. This image, at Balmoral in 1882, depicts one of these family gatherings. From the left: Grand Duke Ludwig IV, Princess Beatrice, Queen Victoria holding Princess Margaret of Connaught, the Duchess of Connaught, and Princess Alix and Hereditary Grand Duke Ernst Ludwig.

H.R.H. THE PRINCESS VICTORIA OF HESSE.

PRINCE LOUIS OF BATTENBERG.

Prince Louis of Battenberg in British Navy uniform.

A print depicting Prince Louis of Battenberg and Princess Victoria of Hesse and by Rhine. It appeared in a report on their wedding published in the Illustrated London News from April 26, 1884.

Victoria, who was fifteen at the time of her mother's death, also took over the mantle of head of the family. She was a very bossy and intelligent young girl and handled this position beautifully. The Queen also sent beloved aunts[18] and uncles (a great favorite was Prince Leopold, later the Duke of Albany) over to Darmstadt to help mother and father the brood. "Papa," as Victoria often wrote, was out hunting or shooting. Much, though, that she wrote this to her grandmother, the other children felt "Papa's" strong presence during their childhood. They would often gather quietly in their father's study, playing, stitching, reading or some other silent activity, while he worked.

Victoria and her grandmother had a very special bond and the correspondence between them was copious.[19] She reported and discussed her brother and sisters constantly, informing "Grandmama" about their studies, their deportment, their religious studies and as time went on, her views on politics and potential suitors for the younger ones. This correspondence had started when Victoria was about six years old and would end at the death of her grandmother. What began as childish "bread and butter" thank you notes, ended with two women confiding in each other about family matters and long discussions of religion, philosophy and politics. The Queen encouraged Victoria to write about what she thought and felt, and it is easily seen in these letters.

In addition, the entire family spent long periods with Queen Victoria at whatever residence she might be. And, as the years went by, they, indeed, grew up and began to choose their life partners. Princess Victoria married her first cousin once removed, Prince Ludwig (Louis) of Battenberg in 1884; Princess Elisabeth married her cousin Grand Duke Sergei (Serge) Alexandrovich; Princess Irène married her first cousin, Prince Heinrich (Henry) of Prussia in 1888; Prince Ernst Ludwig married his first cousin Princess Victoria Melita of Great Britain and Ireland and Saxe-Coburg and Gotha in 1894 and secondly Prince Eleonore (Onor) of Solms-Hohensolms-Lich in 1905; and, Princess Alix married to her cousin, Tsar Nicholas II in 1894.

Princess Victoria in her wedding dress.

During the wedding festivities for Princess Victoria, Grand Duke Ludwig chose, for reasons best known to himself, to marry Countess Alexandrine de Kolemine, who had been his mistress for some years. Originally a Polish Countess, she had recently divorced the Russian Charge d'affaires in Darmstadt. Far from being unhappy about their father having a mistress, the Hessian children liked her and were glad that their father had found companionship – indeed, the girls even spent time with her. However, they, like the world at large, felt that a mistress should not be made a wife and that she was quite unsuitable to be the second consort of the Grand Duke.

It was literally during the celebrations that the Grand Duke slipped away and forced the Prime Minister to marry him to Madame de Kolemine. His mother-in-law, in whose regard Ludwig basked, was absolutely outraged when she was told. She felt that making a marriage that was so beneath him would make him an outcast from the family.[19] Further, she made it clear that she could never meet his wife. She insisted that the marriage must be annulled at once, saying that the reputation of the lady was such that the unmarried Grand Ducal daughters could not be put in her care. She resolved that both the bride and groom must be told right away and dispatched her son the

Prince of Wales give the news to Ludwig.[20]

Poor Ludwig was in utter shock. He, oddly enough, did not expect such a negative reaction to this second marriage. There seems to have been no comprehension in him about how unsuitable this was or how his benefactress, the Queen, might feel about such a lady (a divorcee, after all) taking the place of her beloved daughter.

However, very quickly, the Grand Duke meekly acquiesced and agreed to the annulment. As this took place during a grand "wedding of the decade," there were many royal families in attendance, especially due to the presence of the Queen at the wedding. These families departed as quickly as possible and decided amongst themselves that Ludwig had brought great disgrace to the fine Hessian Family, then, just as quickly, they forgot all about it.[21] The lady was bought off and decamped to Moscow (she was given the title "Countess of Romrod")[22] where she later remarried and was alive at Ludwig's eventual demise.[23] The lovelorn ex-groom was restored in the Queen's good graces and went for a long visit to Osborne in which they commiserated with each other about their mutual and individual losses.

Despite this sad comedy, Ludwig IV, though alone for the rest of his life, proved to be an excellent ruler for his people. He organized the State's finances and was a reformer who brought *modernisation and prosperity*[24] to Darmstadt. Missing his daughters very much as they married one by one, by the early 1890's there was only Alix and Ernst Ludwig at home.

Ludwig IV was a fairly good constitutional monarch. His lack of meddling in the actions taken by his ministers, allowed his

Grand Duke Ludwig IV with Queen Victoria and Princess Bearice.

Grand Duchess Alice and her sister Crown Princess Victoria of Prussia.

realm to prosper and adopt a democratc government. The style of government Ludwig IV followed was inspired by the British model, whereby he left governmental affairs to senior ministers. This was entirely in his and in the interests of the national liberal majority in the state parliament. The influence Alice played in his political development far overruled the military training Ludwig had received in Potsdam as a young man. Alice believed that it was not the role of a prince to directly rule his people, but to allow democratic institutions to do it in his name. This political view of constitutional monarchy was imbued in her by her father the Prince Consort, who envisioned a European continent ruled by democratic principles and not crowned Prussian-style despots. This was the role that Alice's sister Victoria tried playing in Berlin. Her husband's brief 99-day reign, sadly put an end to the dream of constitutional monarchy in the German Empire before it had a chance to change the course of history. One can but wonder what history would have been like "if" these two sisters had been able to put into practice the teachings of their visionary father.

In his daughter Victoria's opinion, Ludwig IV was

> *"...one of the most valued and fairest men, as liberal as decent, my father understood people, and his people understood him...His sudden death was mourned. He is said to have been Queen Victoria's favorite son-in-law. Soon after the marriage, she gave him the title of Royal Highness, honored him with the Order of the Garter,"* and wanted his company as often as possible.[25]

In the winter of 1891 into 1892, Ludwig, only in his mid-fifties, had to deal with failing health. His condition, which was described as an enlarged heart began to worsen, and all were gravely concerned. During this time, the married daughters and in particular, Victoria, came home to nurse their father.

She had not yet discovered that she was carrying her third child, who would be born in Darmstadt in November. It soon became apparent that the Grand Duke was mortally ill, and he died March 13, 1892 of heart disease and stroke.[26] This time, other English relatives were not on hand to support the Hessian children as the Duke of Clarence, Uncle Bertie's oldest son, had died just the previous January. The Royal Family was still in mourning, and in shock. Ludwig had been lonely up to the end losing his daughters to marriage and perhaps what he considered his one chance of happiness, marriage with Madame de Kolemine.

"This is too terrible! What must your grief be, you who were so devoted to that beloved Father, who was Father and Mother to you, to help & serve whom – your life has been so devoted! It adds to my quite overwhelming grief to think of your distress & poor dear Ernie & Alicky alone – Orphans! It is awful. But I am still there & while I live Alicky, till she is married, will be more than ever my own Child – as you all are," wrote a much-distressed Queen

Grand Duke Ludwig IV and Emperor Friedrich III in the late 1860s.

Victoria to her granddaughter Victoria who was by Ludwig IV's bedside during his last illness.[27] By the end of April, Queen Victoria traveled to Darmstadt to personally express her sympathy to her Hessian grandchildren and pay her respects by Ludwig and Alice's graveside in the Rosenhöhe. Queen Victoria, accompanied by Princess Beatrice and her husband Liko Battenberg, stayed in Darmstadt a week. It was her last visit to the grand ducal capital.

Ludwig's loss was deeply felt by others within the family circle. To her daughter Crown Princess Sophie, in faraway Athens, Vicky, the Empress Friedrich wrote, *"...this new misfortune to our family. Poor Uncle Louis [Ludwig IV], so kind and affectionate, so much beloved by us all. Those poor children! Alicky without Parents and home, Ernie so much too young and inexperienced for that position, poor Victoria who doted on her father and was his pride and support. I am glad indeed that they were all together and could help one another in this sorrow. I hear poor Mama is overwhelmed with grief, she was so particularly fond of Uncle Louis, doubly so for poor Alicky's sake."*[28] Vicky, a widow since 1888, had been immensely keen on Ludwig

Grand Duke Ludwig IV with his two eldest daughters and their husbands. Both Vitoria and Elisabeth married first cousins of their father. From the left: Grand Duke Serge Alexandrovich, Grand Duchess Elisabeth Feodorovna, Prince Louis and Princess Victoria of Battenberg, Grand Duke Ludwig IV, a first cousin of his two sons-in-law.

IV, who had been a close friend of her late husband since his time in Potsdam in the late 1850s.

Princess Victoria, who had recently returned to Darmstadt after living in Malta several years, was a witness to her father's last days. With her family, she settled in apartments her father had given them in the Old Palace. Upon arriving in Darmstadt, she later remembered her father's frailty, *"I did not find Papa well on our return. His heart was giving him much trouble and the doctors had forbidden all strenuous forms of exercise."*[29] His condition took a turn for the worse on March 4, when he suffered a stroke during lunchtime. *"By the time I got up to the house Papa had been put to bed in the library. The stroke had affected his whole right side, and he was very restless. On the next morning he was quieter and drowsy, but his breathing had become very heavy and irregular,"* she remembered.[30]

Meanwhile, news of Ludwig IV's condition reached his other children. Irène and her husband arrived the day after the strike. Prince Louis of Battenberg joined the family the following day. As others traveled toward Darmstadt, the inevitable seemed to approach as Victoria noticed her father's condition *"grew slowly worse, and he could only be roused with difficulty."*[31] Ernie, who received news of his father's condition while he was traveling in the South of France, immediately returned to Darmstadt, where he arrived on March 7. His father recognized Ernie, but the stroke had left him unable to speak. Ella and Serge, who rushed from Russia, arrived two days later. Ludwig IV was able to see them before the end arrived. Although devastated by their loss of such a devoted father, Princess Victoria, the true stalwart of the Hessian family, took his loss with her usual resignation, writing that her father *"was one of the kindest-hearted and most just men I have ever known. He was as liberal as he was fair-minded..."*[32]

Many of the extended family went to Darmstadt for the grand duke's solemn funeral. Among the guests were Vicky and her brother Prince Alfred, Duke of Edinburgh, who represented The Queen. Along with Alfred was his son Alfred Jr. They accompanied their Hessian family in their grief. Princess Victoria later remembered that Alfred Jr. had fallen ill while in Darmstadt, perhaps an early manifestation of the terrible illness that would kill him in 1899. Grand Duchess Marie Alexandrovna, Prince Alfred's wife, came to Darmstadt, accompanied by her daughters, to tend to her son's recovery. Once he was well enough to travel, Victoria (with her daughter Alice), Irène, Ernie, and Alix, went to Coburg to spend Easter with their Edinburgh relations. It is quite likely that the seeds of Ernie's interest in his cousin Victoria Melita of Edinburgh were planted during these emotionally charged and challenging times.

****

Victoria, Ella, Irène, Alix and Ernst Ludwig (1878-1906)

Alice and Ludwig went together to England in March 1863 in order to attend the wedding of Alice's brother "Bertie" to Princes Alexandra of Denmark. The Queen noted that Alice was looking very well in her violet dress and wedding laces, while Ludwig looked handsome in his Garter

Grand Duke Ludwig IV dressed in Garter robes for a fancy-dress ball.

robes. Dresses in those days, with their huge bell-shaped crinolines in Alice's case hid the fact that she was heavily pregnant with her first child. Since there would be no more travel for Alice, the Queen was especially pleased that she would give birth in England.

The following month, on April 5, Victoria Alberta Elisabeth Mathilde Marie of Hesse and by Rhine[33] was born in the Tapestry Room at Windsor Castle. She was christened April 27th in the arms of her grandmother and namesake and was much admired. She was thought to be an attractive baby with blonde fuzz on her head, large heavy-lidded blue eyes, but the best thing was that she was very good during the ceremony and did not cry.

Ludwig IV and Alice with their eldest child, Princess Victoria.

Victoria and her sister Elisabeth, who was born a little over a year later, were raised very much as a pair. Victoria was precocious, tomboyish and bossy and the leader of her siblings from a very early age.

Elisabeth Alexandra Louise Alice or "Ella," as she was called in the family, was born at Bessungen, November 1, 1864.[34] Ella contrasted with her sister in resembling the Hesse side more. She was larger than her elder sister, had darker blue eyes and *"rich brown hair"*[35] and even as a small child was considered by some the most beautiful princess in Europe.

In 1866, when the Austro-Prussian war began,

Alice had prudently sent Victoria and Ella to their Grandmother at Windsor. Since neither was an infant, the Queen appeared to like them more. They were more like regular human beings to her and she wrote very approvingly in her journal that they were *"...such little loves. They have been quite like my own...."*[36] They were also pronounced to be handsome and engaging children.

The pair spent an almost middle-class childhood with a mother who was far more attentive than was customary for most royal families. The elder girls often accompanied their mother when she went to her various charities and hospitals and learned from an early age the meaning of public service. They must have also heard their mother say that she felt that royalty was an anachronism and that people should be useful. These statements, attributed to Alice's socialist leanings, sank in to both sisters and in Elisabeth's case, no doubt contributed to her good works later on in life, if not her fervent religiosity.

Very soon another little one joined the pair. Irène Louise Maria Anna was born on July 11, 1866.[37] She was the third girl and would form a trio that was often called, as they grew, "the three graces". Irène was neither as clever as Victoria nor as beautiful as Ella, and she seemed to have what we might call a "middle child" complex. She was a "pleaser" most of her life, always trying to smooth controversies, while she herself lived as quiet a life as possible. What was not known at the time but would be revealed later was that she, too, carried the gene

Alice with her daughters: Elisabeth, Victoria, and Irène.

The Hessian and Wales cousins gathered in 1875. Standing in the back, from the left: Irène and Ernst Ludwig, with Albert Victor, Victoria, George, and Louise of Wales. Seated at front, same order: Princess Alix, and Princess Maud of Wales.

that passed on hemophilia to her sons. As in everything else, Irène's heroism in dealing with this was never as well-known as her younger sister Alix's. The Empress's guilt and frantic searches for cures from doctors, to mystics and "mad" monks warped her later life. In sum, Irène did not lead a spectacularly public life, and though she certainly had her share of heartache, she did not suffer as beautifully as the Empress Alexandra, or as stoically as the Grand Duchess Elisabeth. She was simply Irène, the Greek word for peace – and the peacemaker.

The Hessian children mixed with the children of Darmstadt, many of who were soon forbidden to play with them. The Grand Ducal daughters were considered far too noisy and un-ladylike for the well-mannered children of the gentry of Darmstadt. In addition, Alice did not necessarily get along well with the elite of Darmstadt. She had difficulty handling their staid ideas and customs and they in turn considered her still a foreigner. Sadly, though she worked hard for the average people of Darmstadt, she was not very popular with those who would have been considered her peers.

Soon after Irène began to take her first steps and speak, Alice was once again pregnant. It was no doubt these constant pregnancies that enervated her strength and stamina. However, this next birth was joyous not only for her family but for the grand duchy itself as Alice, at last, fulfilled the expectations of all and was delivered of a most desired male and heir. He was called Ernst Ludwig Albert Karl Wilhelm and he was born November 25, 1868 at the Neues Palais.[38] His eldest sister was disappointed that he was a boy and only wanted to know why more gun salutes were fired for him than for her little sisters. She later said that their son was namd after Landgrave Ernst Ludwig, his seventeenth century ancestor.

Peace however was fleeting and only two years later, Hesse was involved in the Franco-Prussian War. Alice, pregnant again, was hard at war work and as the war wound down to a close, she gave birth to her second son, Friedrich Wilhelm August Viktor Leopold Ludwig, or "Frittie." He was born on October 7 at the Neues Palais.[39] Little Frittie was healthy, strong and according to his mother, *"the prettiest of all my babies."*[40] His father, who was still away with the occupational forces in France, missed his christening in February 1871. Though Frittie initially seemed like a healthy baby it quickly became apparent to Alice that this was not the case. As he grew, he seemed delicate and thin, and Alice soon noticed little bruises all over his body.

Alice was pregnant again during this worrying time and soon gave birth to Victoria Alix Helena Louise Beatrice or "Alix." She was born on June 6, 1872 at the Neues Palais.[41] Frittie had what was probably his first severe bleeding episode in January 1873. It was a tense and horrifying time, but he managed to pull through and was feeling much better by spring. At the end of May 1873, Frittie and his older brother Ernst Ludwig ("Ernie") were playing together in Alice's bedroom. Ernie later recalled that little Frittie ran to the adjoining sitting room in order to look across at Ernie who stayed in the bedroom. While Alice held Ernie back, Frittie, at the other window, tripped, fell out of the window, hitting his head on the ground below. The toddler was unconscious when he was found, but it appeared that the injuries were slight. He never regained

Ernst Ludwig.

consciousness and died just a few hours later. The family was understandably distraught, and Ernie was heard to remark at the time that he was afraid to die alone and could they not all join hands and go to heaven together?

Alice's last pregnancy and birth took place about a year after this distressing circumstance. Marie Victoria Feodore Leopoldine was born May 24, 1874 at the Neues Palais.[42] This last little girl was christened at Heiligenberg in July of that year. She was, by all accounts, a sweet, cheerful and pretty child. The few photographs of her show a little girl of beauty and as others at the time said of her, of charm. There is little else to say about a child who would tragically die at a young age, but she was the last baby of the family and another cause of great despondency for a mother who was already emotionally fragile.[43]

Raised in strict surroundings, both Ludwig and Alice believed that their children would profit from austere surroundings, but with ample demonstrations of parental concern and love. Alice once wrote to Ernst Ludwig's tutor asking that he be raised like, *"A nobleman in the fullest sense of the word, without pride, but humble, unegotistic, helpful, with those qualities that especially the English educational method strives to develp: compulsory consciousness, ambition, love of truth and and respect for God and the law that alone make you free."*[44]

Friedrich.

For the rest of the family, life would go on as normal for the next few years. Ernie and his sisters would have their lessons, the family would travel to England frequently, and visit other relatives and all was quiet until the fateful November when diphtheria ravaged the Hessians. Unlike the rest of her family, Ella was immune to the disease and was sent to her paternal grandmother, Princess Karl, to keep her safe. She was only allowed home after the disease had spent it course, killing her mother and her little sister Marie.

Afterward, the elder pair, Victoria and Ella felt the need to take their mother's role and care for the family. As mentioned, they were both helped immensely by the voluminous correspondence from the Queen containing lots of wisdom and good counsel. The older woman was involved in their lives as far as it was possible to be from a distance. She supervised their schooling, their social gatherings, their friends and acquaintances, and tried her best to keep her granddaughters as far away from the sons of the Romanov family as was possible. She was tragically unsuccessful in this. Because of their youth, Irène and Alix were the hardest hit by their mother's death. Alix in particular was said to be a happy and carefree child until her mother died when she was only six. From then on, far from living up to her nick-name of "Sunny", she was, from all accounts, slightly melancholy, shy, and reticent. As children in a large family often do, alliances of closeness

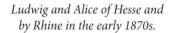

Ludwig and Alice of Hesse and by Rhine in the early 1870s.

had developed: Victoria and Elisabeth as the elder pair, while the younger children, Princess Irène, Prince Ernst Ludwig and Princess Alix made up a triumvirate.

Alice and Ludwig IV's marriage was strained at the start. yet, as the years passed they became good companions to each other. *"I have every reason to hope – please God – that I shall have the joy of seeing Louis come home, and of placing his baby (Frittie) in his arms"* she once wrote.[45] Furthermore, she also feared the length of separation, since he had been fighting in the war against France, would cause her to be emotional upon their reunion, *"My heart is full, as you can fancy, and much as I long to see Louis, I almost dread the moment – the emotion will be so great, and the long pent-up feelings will find vent,"* she wrote.[46]

Alice's contentment was not restricted to her husband. She was deeply caring about their children and wanted to ensure that they would not fall into a life of meaningless self-indulgence.

****

A young and vital family must continue, and the Hessian Grand Ducal Family did so. They visited back and forth with their grandmother at Windsor, Osborne, or one of her other residences and went on with the everyday things necessary

Princesses Victoria, Irène, Alix, and Elisabeth pose in front of a photo of their late mother c. 1879.

Princess Elisabeth of Hesse and by Rhine..

Princess Victoria of Battenberg holding her daughter Princess Alice, with Queen Victoria and Princess Beatrice surrounding them.

for their growth. Much had changed in the household. All still felt a certain amount of dread going into the various rooms of their family home that were most associated with Alice, but they went on.

As Victoria, Ella, and Irène grew, when taken as a threesome, they embodied beauty, intelligence and style and were much admired. They sadly lacked a consistent role model of a grown woman and consequently had to learn much on their own. Princess Victoria mentioned this in her letters to her grandmother and how dinner parties and other entertainments that the Grand Ducal family was obliged to give were more difficult without the guidance of an older woman. It seemed that intermittent visits by aunts and uncles were not the answer.

And as the years went by, they began to think of settling down and having their own families and young suitors started to

Princess Elisabeth (Ella) of Hesse and by Rhine.   *Grand Duke Serge Alexandrovich of Russia.*

present themselves. One in particular was very persistent with Ella. He was one of their least favorite playmates from childhood, Cousin "Willy" (later Kaiser Wilhelm II). He had visited the Hessian court as a youngster, but later on when he was at university, he continued his visits. He insisted on walking and riding with the elder pair and fancied himself very much in love with the already spectacularly lovely Ella. His idea of wooing her was to read aloud to the two girls and give bible lessons. As irresistibly romantic as this was, Ella was not impressed and gently spurned his advances as well as an actual proposal. He never spoke to her again.

At the time she was already well acquainted with her cousin Serge Alexandrovich, a younger son of Alexander II of Russia and his wife, Princess Marie of Hesse and by Rhine. Because of the Tsarina's Hessian association and health concerns, she visited the Grand Duchy quite often and stayed with her brother, Prince Alexander and his wife, Princess Julie of Battenberg at Heiligenberg. The cousins in fact grew up together, Victoria writing that Serge would see his younger cousins in their baths.[47]

The Grand Duke was not Ella's only suitor. Because of her great beauty there were other young men who were quite taken with her. Since her grandmother, the Queen, had such a deep distaste for Russians, she pushed other men into Ella's sphere including Friedrich of Baden, whom she thought such a good and worthy fellow and other lesser admirers. Ultimately, her choice fell on the Grand Duke and her grandmother was resigned.

A little before Ella made her announcement to the family, Victoria too had made a choice. She was courted by another Heiligenberg playmate, Prince Louis of Battenberg. The young prince was in the Royal Navy and a great favorite of Victoria's Uncle Bertie. In her late teens, Victoria was very much involved with raising of her two younger sisters, Irène and Alix, as well as her little brother Ernie, but she became very much aware of Louis as she grew older. Surely, she had heard about his "adventures" at Marlborough House with her uncle, but she and Ella were more interested in his sea adventures and his exotic travels. He had accompanied the Prince of Wales to India and was made the official illustrator of the trip. Many of his drawings were printed in newspapers back home and Victoria and Ella loved them.

In spring 1883, Louis came back to Heiligenberg on leave, proposed and was accepted by Victoria. The Queen was delighted with the match congratulating her granddaughter on finding someone who was, she said, as English as she was. Victoria, who had inherited a lot of her mother's socialist leanings was thrilled with a match with a prince who was not her equal in family or title, in fact, Louis was only a Serene Highness while Victoria was a Grand Ducal Highness. Victoria and Louis were married the following April at Darmstadt and honeymooned at Heiligenberg. It was at this time that Grand Duke Ludwig made his ill-fated second marriage.

In June 1884, the entire Hessian family went to Russia for Ella's marriage to Grand Duke Serge and it was at this point that her younger sister, Alix became better acquainted with Tsesarevich Nicholas Alexandrovich and his sister, Xenia. From then onward, she appears to have had Nicholas on her mind, while Nicholas, who was four years older, was no doubt sowing his wild oats.

Grand Duke Serge Alexandrovich of Russia and his fiancée Princess Elisabeth of Hesse and by Rhine.

After her spectacular wedding, Ella promised her family that she would visit them in Hesse as often as possible. However, she was not always able to make good on this promise and in the interim years, visited but rarely. She continued to be celebrated for her beauty in Russia and throughout Europe as well as her style and spectacular jewelry.

Meanwhile, Victoria gave birth the following year to her first child on February 24, 1885.[48] It was a little girl called Victoria Alice Elisabeth Julie Marie, after her grandmothers and great-grandmothers, and hence forward called Alice. Like her mother, Alice was born in the Tapestry Room at Windsor castle.

That summer, Queen Victoria's youngest daughter, Beatrice married Prince Henry of Battenberg at St Mildred's Whippingham, near Osborne House on

Guests at Princess Beatrice's wedding, Osborne House, July 23, 1885. From left to right: Prince Edward of Saxe-Weimar-Eisenach; Princess Marie of Erbach-Schönberg; Princess Julie of Battenberg; Princess Helena Victoria of Schleswig-Holstein; the Duke of Cambridge; Ludwig IV; Princess Marie of Leiningen; Princess Louis of Battenberg; the Prince of Wales; Princesses Victoria and Louise of Wales; Princess Victoria Melita of Edinburgh; Princess Marie Louise of Schleswig-Holstein (back row); the Princess of Wales; Princess Christian (partly obscured) and Prince Christian of Schleswig-Holstein (behind); Prince Alfred of Edinburgh (in sailor suit) behind his sisters Princess Marie and Princess Alexandra (blurred); Prince George of Wales (center) in front of Prince Philipp of Saxe-Coburg and Gotha; the Duchess of Connaught with her children Princess Margaret and Prince Arthur (Arthur very blurred, the boy in miniature Grenadier uniform); the Duke of Edinburgh; Princess Louise, Marchioness of Lorne; the Duchess of Edinburgh; Prince Alexander of Hesse and by Rhine; Prince Alexander of Bulgaria; Princess Maud of Wales; the Duke of Connaught (superimposed); Prince Albert Victor of Wales; John, Marquess of Lorne; Prince Franz Josef of Battenberg (partly obscured); Princess Alix and Hereditary Grand Duke Ernst Ludwig; Prince Louis of Battenberg; unknown.

the Isle of Wight. The unmarried Hessian Princesses Irène and Alix, were bridesmaids and it was an opportunity for the sisters to be together for a happy occasion. It was also another chance for Grand Duke Ludwig and the Queen to commiserate with one another on their loneliness.

Meanwhile, in the beginning of 1887, the third "grace" was about to make waves for the first and possibly the last time in her life. Irène had made her choice for a husband, Prince Heinrich of Prussia, whom the family called Henry or Harry. The Queen was not pleased with this choice for several reasons. First, she did not think much of Henry whom she believed to be too much under the thumb of his brother, Wilhelm. Secondly, she was worried about how her shy granddaughter would fare in the Prussian Court, which seemed to in many ways have defeated her far more outgoing and intelligent daughter, Vicky. Lastly, she was extremely annoyed with her granddaughter, having found out about the engagement while reading the newspapers. She was infuriated that she was she said, the last to know.

Princess Irène of Hesse and by Rhine.   *Prince Heinrich (Henry) of Prussia.*

Henry was a first cousin and was apparently a match that neither family wanted, but the couple was adamant. The Hessian family closed ranks and came to the rescue, embracing Henry as they had embraced Louis and Serge before him. While acquiescing to their wishes, Queen Victoria did not see the necessity of attending their wedding, though, in the end, a more inoffensive marriage could not be found. On May 24, 1888, Irène and Henry were married in the Royal Chapel at Charlottenburg near Berlin.[49] Significantly, there was a great sadness attached to the wedding, as it was the last event Henry's father, Emperor Friedrich III attended before his untimely death.

In October of that year, Serge and Ella traveled to the area in the Ottoman Empire called Palestine. They went for the dedication of the Russian Orthodox Church on the Mount of Olive called the Church of St Mary Magdalen. The church was dedicated to Serge's mother, the Empress Marie Alexandrovna and stood on the earth where the Orthodox believed that the Garden of Gethsemane was located.[50]

Alix traveled to Russia in January 1889 for her coming out ball. She and her father, the Grand Duke stayed with Ella and Serge and it was here the Nicholas was truly smitten with his little cousin. Alix was at the height of her beauty and it is not surprising that Nicholas fell hard. Not having gotten her way with the marriages of Ella and Irène, Queen Victoria was determined that this youngest of the girls should not go to Russia. She was emphatic on the subject and proposed most notably, Prince Albert Victor (Duke of Clarence), known as "Eddy," the eldest son of the Prince of Wales. Though Alix did not want to marry him, she did say that she would if it was really what the Queen wanted. However, she was singularly

Schloß Charlottenburg, Berlin, May 24, 1888. Even though mortally ill with cancer, Kaiser Friedrich III attended the wedding of his second son Henry to Princess Irène of Hesse and by Rhine. Three weeks later, the 99-day reign of Friedrich III came to an end, thus bringing much-too-early son Wilhelm II to the throne. Henry and Irène shunned court life and preferred to live at Hemmelmark, their estate in Holstein.

unenthusiastic about this particular suitor. The Queen in her turn, could not understand how Alix could refuse the greatest position, in her mind, there was.

Happier news came in March 1889, when Irène, who became pregnant very soon after her wedding, gave birth to her first child. Irène presented her husband with a little boy whose names were: Waldemar Ludwig Wilhelm Friedrich Victor, though he was always called "Toddy." On a sadder note, the boy very soon began to exhibit signs of hemophilia. In that same year in July, Victoria gave birth to her second child, Louise Alexandra Marie Irène. Louise would be a stalwart for her mother through thick and thin and was her close companion especially since Louis was away on voyages for much of their married life.

Ella decided after seven years of marriage, that she would convert to Russian Orthodoxy and did so in March 1891. Besides her fervent and sincere desire to embrace the religion of her husband, she wanted her little sister, Alix, who continued to be interested in the Tsesarevich Nicholas, to see that Orthodoxy was not so very different than Lutheranism. Ella's sisters were not so sanguine about the change in the religion and Irène remarked that her father was very unhappy about the conversion.

Queen Victoria tried to dance other suitors into the life of her young granddaughter. Prince Max of Baden, who caught the eye of many royal princesses because of his good looks, his wealth and his intelligence, was suggested for Alix. However, Alix was not interested, though she was still struggling with the religious question, she would consider no one else but Nicholas unless she was actually forced to do so. As to that, it should be noted that it had always been Alice's and Ludwig's wish that all of their children marry for love if at all possible.

Princess Alix of Hesse and by Rhine.

Tsesarevich Nicholas Alexandrovich of Russia.

Alix's marriage, however, would ultimately not be an issue for the Grand Duke as he had died in March 1892. A much happier event took place much later in the year. Victoria, already pregnant by the time her father died gave birth to her first boy, George Louis Victor Henry Serge. He was born in Darmstadt, November 6, 1892[51], and was named for his cousin George of Wales, his father, the Queen, and his Prussian and Russian uncles.

In 1894, following a rather lukewarm courtship, Ernie, now Grand Duke Ernst Ludwig of Hesse and by Rhine, married Princess Victoria Melita of Edinburgh and Saxe-Coburg and Gotha, and the large family connection gathered in Coburg for the wedding. Many famous photographs were taken here in Coburg of the extended royal family that the Queen called the "Royal Mob." Anyone who has even a passing interest in Queen Victoria has seen the images taken on the steps of the Edinburgh Palais.

Most exciting during another "wedding of the decade," however, was that Alix's drama would finally come to a conclusion when she became engaged to Tsesarevich Nicholas. No doubt to the chagrin of the other couple, the newly affianced couple became the focus of all the attention. Alix had apparently, with the persuasion of Ella and Kaiser Wilhelm II, given up her objections to converting to Russian Orthodoxy, though it came after a long and painful process. Naturally, though the Queen had nothing personal against Nicholas, she was extremely unhappy that this particular granddaughter was going to Russia. It was well known what Victoria thought of Russia, the dissipation of the Imperial family and its corrupt and autocratic government. She had a sincere horror of her delicate Hessian granddaughters going there. In addition, that while liking Nicholas, she thought him lacking in decisiveness and stability. Alix, the erstwhile bride, was delighted with her plight, expressing her joy in a letter to her brother, *"Oh darling, if I could only tell you my happiness – it is too great, but how I miss you, & Papa and Mama is not to be described..."*[52]

Nevertheless, following in Ella's footsteps, go to Russia Alix did and sooner than most people thought. As fall was approaching, the news from Russia was ominous. It appeared that Alexander III, only in his late forties, was seriously ill. He was suffering from kidney disease – nephritis, a malady that could lead to kidney failure at any time. By October, Nicholas summoned Alix to be with him at his father's deathbed. This necessitated a "mad dash" for Alix and Victoria, to Warsaw, where Victoria handed Alix off to Ella who then escorted the young princess the rest of the way to Livadia Palace, in the Crimea.

About ten days after Alix arrived, on November 1, the Tsar died. She was accepted into the Orthodox

While attending her brother's wedding in Coburg in April 1894, Princess Alix became engaged to Tsesarevich Nicholas Alexandrovich of Russia. This image was taken at Schloß Rosenau, a country retreat of their aunt Grand Duchess Marie Alexandrovna.

faith, and was, for a week, Grand Duchess Alexandra Feodorovna. Several weeks later, on November 26, Nicky and Alix were married. The event took place in the Chapel of the Winter Palace and although mourning was discarded for this one day, the atmosphere was grave. Though some of the family were able to attend, due to its hurried nature, not all could – certainly not the Queen, not that she might have if plans even had been made years in advance. Little Alix was now Her Imperial Majesty, the Tsarina Alexandra Feodorovna, a position she was uniquely and tragically unqualified to hold.

However, though they were doomed historically, Alix and Nicholas were an extraordinarily happily

Grand Duke Ludwig IV with some of his children, from the left: The Grand Duke, Alix, Irène, Serge Alexandrovich, Ella, and Ernst Ludwig.

married couple. They were extremely devoted to one another and their personal family life was happy and contented. And, they soon began to produce what would be a large family of four girls and a boy. Beginning with Olga Nikolaevna, the eldest, who was born November 15, 1895, at the Alexander Palace.[53]

Nicholas and Alexandra's Coronation took place on May 14, 1896. Victoria was able to come and used this occasion to have a nice long visit with Ella. However, Irène, who was pregnant, stayed home at Schloß Hemmelmark, which was now her new permanent home. That the estate was far away from Berlin and Potsdam, and the pernicious Prussian Court, only made Hemmelmark even more attractive.

In the fall of that year, Nicholas and Alix traveled with their little daughter Olga to visit the Queen at Balmoral. It was at this time that the first royal newsreel was taken. This would be their only visit while the Queen was alive.

In November 1896, Irène had her second child – a boy. Born at Kiel, he was called Sigismund, according to Irène, *"after Harry's little brother that died."*[54] Thereafter, this little boy was known in the family as "Bobby" and he would be the only completely healthy child that Irène bore.

Alix's second daughter, Tatiana Nikolaevna, was born June 10, 1897 at Peterhof.[55] This was about ten days before the last great jubilee celebration – the Diamond – of Queen Victoria and one of the reasons that Alix did not attend. This was a slightly lower key celebration than the previous jubilee in 1887 as the old Queen was quite infirm at this point. She had difficulty standing and sitting for long periods and was nearly blind. However, many crowned heads and even American President William McKinley attended the celebrations, and this included the Hessians, Victoria, her brother Ernie, Serge and Ella.

Several years later, Alix and Nicholas had another

Ludwig IV with Irène and her first child, Waldemar.

baby girl. She was called Marie Nikolaevna and was born June 26, 1899 at Peterhof.[56] This was a major disappointment to the couple who were naturally under pressure to have a male heir. The stress was immense and certainly made life even more difficult for the naturally depressive and reticent Alix.

At the beginning of the new century, January 9, 1900, Irène's last child, a son, Heinrich was born at Kiel.[57] Unfortunately, this child, too, began to show signs of hemophilia. As time went on, it appeared that Irène and Alix were passing down the gene, but, serendipitously, Victoria had not passed it on to her sons. As for Ella, it cannot be known if she was a carrier since she did not bear children.

Victoria's last child, a boy, Louis Francis Albert Victor Nicholas, was born June 25, 1900, at Frogmore House, Windsor.[58] This was to be the

Princess Louise, Prince George, and Princess Alice of Battenberg.

last great-grandchild of the Queen's born during her lifetime and there is a charming photograph of the two, the elderly Queen and a little baby who had evidently knocked off her spectacles. Even then, however, the Queen was quite weak and a maid out of the view of the camera helped her to hold the child.

The Henrys of Prussia and their sons: Waldemar, Heinrich, Sigismund.

The following year in January 1901, Queen Victoria died. Her death for so many in her family and in the empire itself, was a shattering and seminal event; so completely shattering that afterwards so many said their lives were changed beyond recognition. Many had never known or could conceive a world without the Queen. The Hessian Princess's aunt and eldest daughter of the Queen, Vicky of Prussia, was on her own death bed by this time and expressed her thoughts eloquently, *"the best of mothers and the greatest of Queens, our centre and help and support – all seems a blank, a terrible awful dream. Realise it one cannot."*[59] … and only some months later, in the summer of that year, the lovely and talented but ultimately tragic Vicky died.

Queen Victoria died on January 22, 1901 at Osborne House on the Isle of Wight. She was buried in The Mausoleum, Frogmore, Windsor, on February 4, following a State Funeral in St George's Chapel two days earlier. This image shows her funeral procession from Osborne House to the port, from where her coffin was transported across the Sound to Portsmouth and hence to Windsor. Immediately behind it were King Edward VII, the Duke of Connaught and Kaiser Wilhelm II. They were followed by a bevy of family members and attending royals.

Pregnant with her next child, Alix could not attend her beloved grandmother's funeral. Anastasia Nikolaevna was born June 18, 1901 at Peterhof.[60] Victoria and Irène attended the funeral, but Ella, too, was absent. For the Hessian sisters, for the family and the world, nothing would ever be the same again.

****

…and then there was the only surviving brother: Ernst Ludwig Karl Albrecht Wilhelm, or Ernie as he was called in the family. He was born at the Neues Palais on November 25, 1868.[61] At that point, he was the great-nephew of the reigning Grand Duke and the probable future Grand Duke. Ernie's childhood was filled with devastating deaths that most certainly had an effect on his entire life. His little brother had a tragic accident and died the same day when he was but four years old. When he was ten, he lost his mother and his very closest little sister. From thence forward, he had an immense fear of disease, desertion, death and dying alone. What was apparent, as he grew older and especially later when he was an adult, was that his four remaining sisters tried their best to shield their sensitive brother from great tragedy. One can only imagine the difficulty of this considering what tragedies they suffered.

Left motherless as a young boy, Ernie was mothered by his older sisters and grandmothers and was governed under the tutelage of Herr Müther. His eldest sister, Victoria, took this responsibility very seriously and even when she traveled, she would make sure to write improving letters to Ernie. In one letter she admonished him and advised him to inform his tutor to write progress reports to Queen Victoria on a regular basis.[62] Indeed, the Queen monitored the hereditary Grand Duke's progress as closely as was possible from Britain. At the death of Princess Alice, she told her grandchildren to think of her as their mama an obligation she performed tirelessly through visits and correspondence.

As Ernie grew older, his sisters were more concerned with his habit of dreaming over his lessons and neglecting his focus and concentration. He seemed to lack pride in his schoolwork and did not appear to be ashamed when he did poorly. Victoria, again, wrote to her grandmother that Ernie was more respectful of his Uncle Leopold, than he was his own father.[63] This seems a classic bid for attention to a father who was, perhaps, out shooting a little too much and not paying enough attention to his only son.

As his sisters began marrying and having their own lives, Ernie was taking the route of the typical prince of the time. He had some military training and then went on to study law at the University of Leipzig. As he had done in the past, Ernie was lazy and only applied himself to the subjects he liked, such as art, literature, and history. In due course he returned to Hesse to study politics at the University of Gießen. This was a necessary grounding for a future that came sooner than anyone expected. Certainly, in Ernie's case it was not a future for which he was yet prepared. His father had become the Grand Duke in 1877; in March of 1892 Ernie succeeded him.

Ernie was an attractive young man of twenty-three and completely overwhelmed by work for which he

Three heirs – From the left: Hereditary Prince Alfred of Saxe-Coburg and Gotha, Hereditary Grand Duke Ernst Ludwig of Hesse and by Rhine, and the Duke of York, future King George V.

Siblings gather in Darmstadt. Standing in back, from the left: Nicholas II, Alix, Victoria, Ernst Ludwig. Seated, in the same order: Irène, Elisabeth Feodorovna, Victoria Melita, and Serge Alexandrovich.

1892 – A family in mourning. Clockwise from top: Ernst Ludwig, Victoria, Elisabeth, Alix, and Irène.

initially felt unable to do. Since by then, his three elder sisters were married, he was virtually alone in Darmstadt with only his young sister, Alix for his hostess. Alix, who, herself was shy and broken-hearted at the loss of her father, found it difficult to cope. She had lost her mother at a very young age and had little constant guidance from an older and more experienced woman. Therefore, she had little idea how to make herself appealing or popular and had no instruction about being "first lady" of a Grand Duchy.

The Queen came promptly to visit the youngsters, who at least had their elder sisters there to comfort them for a time immediately after their father's death. She tried to give Ernie an abbreviated course in ruling and worried a great deal about the young man. She need not have. It took time and later on with the right consort he turned out to be an excellent ruler for his people and an ideal patron of the arts for Hesse. He continued to be a man of great sensitivity, with a well-developed artistic temperament. He initiated an extremely forward-thinking program

of arts and sciences and under his reign, Darmstadt became a Mecca for artists and architects. Many lived in what was called the Mathildenhöhe, Darmstadt Artist's Colony, which he supported monetarily. In addition, he attracted various companies to the Duchy including the carmaker, Opel, and continued to encourage one of the oldest pharmaceutical companies in the world, Merck, who have their headquarters in Darmstadt to this day.

After the death of his father, Queen Victoria began what she would later call her last matchmaking schemes for Ernie. She had seen how well he had gotten along with his cousin Victoria Melita of Edinburgh, known as "Ducky" in the family, and somehow decided that these two young people were ideally suited to one another. Her thinking was based on the fact she observed that they had the same sense of humor, musical tastes and, as if to clinch the matter, the same birthdays. Ducky's mother and wife of the Duke of Edinburgh and Saxe-Coburg and Gotha, the Grand Duchess Marie Alexandrovna, did not believe

Ernst Ludwig and Victoria Melita with Nicholas II and Alexandra Feodorovna while on a visit to Russia.

in keeping Princesses on the shelf much past their seventeenth birthday. She was extremely pleased with the idea of her daughter marrying in Germany as she had an acute aversion to Britain and British Princes. The young lady, at seventeen, was no doubt excited about a good-looking Prince as her very much-approved intended, or at least not adverse. However, to the frustration of her mother and her grandmother, the courtship went along at a snail's pace.

The young people were as different as it was possible to be. Ernie was quiet and sensitive, while Ducky was passionate, strong, fearless and quite volatile. It must have been difficult to conduct a courtship while in the depths of mourning his father, but the Queen urged Ernie on…and on. She did it by enlisting other members of the family to "encourage" Ernie since she complained that he was taking the matter much too slowly. His elder sister, Victoria, however, while certainly talking about the subject with him was also sensitive to his state of mind at that time. In addition, she encouraged him to discuss the matter of first cousins marrying quite seriously with his physician, Dr. Eigenbrot.

Ernst Ludwig and his cousin-bride Victoria Melita on their wedding.

By January 1894, Ernie was beaten down in the matter. He proposed and was accepted by Ducky. It should have been an omen for the future that he was so long in coming to the point, but there were high hopes that the marriage between the cousins, who were good friends, might ultimately be successful. It was at their wedding celebrations in Coburg, that Alix and Nicky were engaged, a far more exciting event for the world at large.

The Queen was much pleased with her successful matchmaking, but very soon regretted the entire thing. She complained about the fact that the two were not taking their responsibilities of the Grand Duchy seriously and even expressed her anger that they did not write "thank you" notes in various situations. She felt strongly that Ducky did not become the *Landesmütter* that Alice had been and seemed to have little interest in the charities and social causes that had so much been a part of Alice's life. Ducky however did fulfill one obligation when she gave birth to a daughter in March 1895, Elisabeth.[64] The little girl was a particular favorite in Darmstadt and was greatly loved.

A family group at the Edinburgh Palais, Coburg, April 1894. Standing in back, from the left: Prince Louis of Battenberg, Grand Duke Paul Alexandrovich, Prince Henry of Battenberg, Prince Philipp and Princess Louise of Saxe-Coburg and Gotha, Count Mensdroff-Pouilly, Grand Duke Serge Alexandrovich, Crown Princess Marie and Crown Prince Ferdinand of Romania, Grand Duchess Elisabeth Feodorovna, Grand Duke Vladimir Alexandrovich, the Duke of Connaught, and the Duke of Edinburgh and Saxe-Coburg and Gotha. Middle row, same order: Hereditary Prince Alfred of Saxe-Coburg and Gotha, the Prince of Wales, Tsesarevich Nicholas Alexandrovich, Princess Beatrice of Battenberg, Princess Alix of Hesse and by Rhine, Princess Alexandra of Edinburgh, Princess Victoria of Battenberg, Hereditary Princess Charlotte of Saxe-Meiningen, Princess Irène of Prussia, the Duchess of Connaught, Grand Duchess Marie Pavlovna, and Grand Duchess Marie Alexandrovna. At front: Kaiser Wilhelm II, Queen Victoria, Princess Beatrice of Edinburgh, the Empress Friedrich, and Princess Feodora of Saxe-Meiningen.

However, even by then, the marriage of these two opposites began to fray. Ducky was deeply unhappy, and Ernie was the sort of person who had no idea what to do about it.[65] The two tried to muddle along as best they could and as the century drew to a close, Ducky was once again pregnant. Perhaps this can be seen as a "last ditch" attempt to repair their deteriorating marriage. Tragically, however, the child, a boy, was stillborn. The rumors of their marital issues were so widely known that they were the subject of several audiences with the Queen and her Chargé d'Affaires in Darmstadt, Sir George Buchanan. The old lady took the blame for her part in the disastrous coupling of her grandchildren and vowed never again to a matchmaker.

The Queen was able to keep this vow as the century closed and a new one began. She had been failing for a while and died in January 1901, as previously mentioned. By this time, the marriage was irretrievably lost. In fact, Ducky only waited for the death of her grandmother to leave Darmstadt and live with her mother in Coburg. It was an incredibly distressing time for both families, and painful for their only child, Elisabeth. The Hessian sisters were mostly angry with Ducky, and the youngest, Alix very much so taking sides with her brother against this cousin for whom she had never had more than a lukewarm fondness. Victoria Battenberg, however, played "go-between" and her assessment of the situation as in most things was sage and succinct,

[Ducky] *had often spoken freely to me on the subject of her married life. She had confidence that I hope was not misplaced, in my fairness of judgment, and in spite of my being devoted to my brother. I can only say that I thought then, and still think, that it was best for both that they should part from each other.*[66]

Ernie was devastated by this turn of events, and of course wanted his daughter to stay with him. She more or less

From the top: Grand Duchess Victoria Melita, Empress Alexandra Feodorovna, and Grand Duchess Elisabeth Feodorovna.

did, though she did visit her mother. The terms, it seemed were negotiated by Ernie's sister Victoria Battenberg, who was considered a fair party by both parents. It was a tremendous scandal at the time and the two were divorced. Ducky was free to hope that the man with whom she had fallen deeply in love, Grand Duke Kirill Vladimirovich of Russia, would marry her.[67] Elisabeth, meanwhile, was stuck in the typical situation of divorced parents…living with one for six months and then the other. By the time one visitation was over, the tears in moving to the other parent were all too real. However, what is true is that Elisabeth dearly loved her father and loved her Aunt Alix and her little cousins. Elisabeth and Ernie often visited their Russian family during this time, but it was not to be for long.

Tragedy seemed to dog Ernie during these first years of the century and his daughter was not spared. In November 1903, little Elisabeth died, at the age of eight.[68] She had been visiting her Imperial cousins at the Emperor's shooting lodge

Victoria Melita and her daughter Elisabeth.

Another family gathering, this time in Coburg to attend the wedding of Princess Alexandra of Edinburgh and Hereditary Prince Ernst of Hohenlohe-Langenburg. Standing in back, from the left: Feodora of Saxe-Meiningen, Victoria Melita, Marie of Romania, Beatrice of Edinburgh, Feodora of Saxe-Meiningen, the Duchess of York. Seated, in the same order: Alfred Jr. of Edinburgh and Saxe-Coburg and Gotha, the Duke of York, Max of Baden, Ernst Ludwig, and Ferdinand of Romania.

at Skierniewice. There, she sickened with a rare form of ambulatory typhoid and very quickly died. Both parents mourned the loss deeply and especially Ernie since his daughter had been his mainstay during the divorce ordeal and the aftermath. His family worried about him acutely after this death. In a letter Ernie wrote to Nicholas II, several weeks after the tragedy, he expressed his desolate mood,

"Just a few words to to tell you <u>how</u> I think of you & bless you for all your love to me. Your dear letter was such a comfort to me & never will it go out of my heart what you have been to me during my misery. When I shut my eyes I always see you at your writing table answering telegrams for me; & then I often long to be with you to hear you laugh & see those eyes so good & full of comfort to me...I am getting on all right & will son settle down to my work again, for that is after all the one great thing that helps one over all in every day life."[69]

It was a fearfully lonesome time for the relatively young man of thirty-five who had not really "toughened up". He was still very sensitive and continued to harbor his fears of abandonment and dying alone, as he would for the rest of his life.

Happily, there would soon come some balm for the loss of his daughter when he, in due course, found another princess to marry. The prayers of his family were answered when Eleonore of Solms-Hohensolms-Lich consented to be his wife. "Onor," as she was called in the family, was born in Lich on September 17, 1871 and was the daughter of Fürst Hermann Adolf of Solms-Hohensolms-Lich and Countess Agnes of Stolberg-Wernigerode.[70] She loved riding and was particularly close to her siblings, keeping up a lifelong correspondence with them. She was a sweet, simple girl, and therefore, nothing like the far more flamboyant and complex Victoria Melita. Eleonore's family had been friends of the Hesse family, and she, in fact, had spent time in Darmstadt the previous winter of 1904, staying at the Neues Palais, when her mother, Fürstin Agnes, was ill, and was receiving medical treatment. They became friends, and there was little doubt that she was far more suited to Ernie, who had little idea how to cope with complicated and deeply passionate women.

The couple was married in February 1905 at the Court Chapel of the Old Schloß. The gift of the Duchy was the spectacular "Wedding Tower" at the

Ernst Ludwig and Victoria Melita with their only daughter Elisabeth.

Mathildenhöhe, which was designed by J.M Olbrich and built in 1908. Ernie at last got what he wanted, a family – two boys, Georg Donatus born in 1906 and Ludwig born in 1908, or "Don" and "Lu" as they were called in the family.

Victoria Battenberg wrote:

> *Ernie's second marriage was a great success. She understood him perfectly, thanks to her unselfish but very intelligent nature and they were deeply devoted to each other. There are few people whom I have learned so to respect, love and admire, as my sister-in-law Onor* [as Eleonore was called in the family].[71]

Princess Elisabeth of Hesse and by Rhine.

Chapter V
The Battenbergs

Prince Alexander and His Lady

Prince Alexander of Hesse and by Rhine and Countess Julia von Hauke – the founders of the somewhat short-lived Battenberg dynasty were dramatic and highly romantic lovers. When the couple first met, she was a mere lady-in-waiting in the service of Tsarina Marie Alexandrovna of Russia. He, on the other hand, was the handsome playboy prince, the brother of the Tsarina, the Imperial court's darling who set many hearts a-flutter while he searched for a wife.

Prince Alexander was born in Darmstadt on July 15, 1823.[1] He was the son of Grand Duke Ludwig II and his wife, Wilhelmine of Baden. As has been previously mentioned, he most probably was not the son of the Grand Duke but rather of Wilhelmine's chamberlain, the tall and handsome Swiss-born August von Senarclens de Grancy. After giving birth to an heir and spare, Ludwig and Karl, Wilhelmine set up separate arrangements, eventually leading to a move to Heiligenberg. She managed some years later and without the Grand Duke to give birth to

Prince Alexander of Hesse and by Rhine.

Prince Alexander and Princess Marie, as well as several children who did not survive. Clearly, these last two children were fathered by Senarclens de Grancy.

Alexander not only came into the world on a scandal, but also would afford another one as a young man. He was very close to his very young sister, Marie and accompanied her when she went to Russia to marry the future Tsar Alexander II. While there, he served as Captain in the Chevalier Guards and then Colonel-in-Chief of the Borissoglebosky 17th Lancers, also known as the "Prince Alexander of Hesse's Lancers."[2] In addition to his busy martial life, the young and ardent Prince conducted all sorts of amorous adventures at court.

Marie was highly social as a young woman and gave constant parties, and entertainments. Naturally, the young and handsome Alexander attended these functions and was extremely popular. Judging by his behavior and the observations of others, he was certainly a lady's man and in the parlance of the day an accomplished flirt.

Despite his wandering eye, he evinced a great interest in getting married and sought a wife among the daughters of the Tsar Nicholas I of Russia: either Alexandra, but most especially Olga. Their father, however, had other ideas and was keen to marry his daughters dynastically and importantly. Olga was eventually married to Karl, King of Württemberg, and Alexandra to Prince Friedrich Wilhelm of Hesse-Kassel. Alexander was disappointed but undaunted. Nicholas in turn liked the idea of Alexander marrying his niece, Grand Duchess Catherine Mikhailovna, however Alexander was able to summon no enthusiasm for this idea. She eventually married Duke Georg August of Mecklenburg-Strelitz.

Through accusations of being fickle, Alexander, nevertheless, pressed on in his attempts to find a matrimonial prize. In the interim, and until some other worthy candidate presented herself, the Prince amused himself with the married and aristocratic women of the court. Soon, Alexander found himself in love with Countess Sophie Shuvaloff. Sophie had a close friend and confidant, a young woman who was initially acting as a "go-between" and letter carrier in this affair, Countess Julia von Hauke. The young countess, too, found herself in love and began to vigorously pursue him. Although her feelings for him were one-sided in the beginning, by the summer of 1849, things had changed and the callow prince "...*had grown more and more interested in his sister's clever and good-*

Princess Julia (Julie) of Battenberg.

looking lady-in-waiting....whom he saw daily...."[3]

She was the daughter of a Polish nobleman, Count Maurice von Hauke, Minister of War, and his wife Sophie Lafontaine, a Frenchwoman. He had served with Napoleon during the Peninsular Wars but soon found it expedient to switch sides and fought instead for Russia. He was murdered in the streets of Warsaw in the defense of Russia, and her mother died soon after, so the daughter was brought to the Russian court and educated at the Tsar's expense. Later on, in the course of her duties for Tsarevna Marie Alexandrovna, Julia developed what we might call a "crush" on Prince Alexander the moment she saw him. She managed with cleverness and tenacity to be, at last, the winner of this capricious young man, however not without compromising her virtue and causing a scandal in the eyes of the Imperial Court. Consequently, and searching for happiness and freedom, the couple left Russia, and on October 28, 1851, Prince Alexander married Countess Julia in Breslau.[4]

Prince Alexander and Julia had to flee the disapproval of the Russian Court, and Alexander was stricken from the roll of the Russian Imperial Guard. Alexander's brother, Ludwig III, now the Grand Duke, was more tolerant and allowed the couple to live in Hesse and gave Julia the title of Her Illustrious Highness the Countess of Battenberg,

Darmstadt's Alexander Palais.   and some years later, Her Serene Highness the Princess of Battenberg.[5]

Since Alexander entered the Austrian military, he was stationed at various garrison towns around Italy, where most of the children were born. These, in fact, came quickly: Marie (1852-1923), Louis (1854-1921), Alexander (1857-1893), Henry (1858-1896) and Franz Joseph (1861-1924).[6]

The Battenberg's Darmstadt home was the Alexander Palais. This was a compact building that projected from the old post office on the northwest corner of the Luisenplatz, opposite the building housing the State Chancellery. The palace, built in 1804, initially housed military dependencies. Its design can be assigned to the style of historicism, with Baroque and Classicist principles visible all around. The reddish, probably sandstone from the Odenwald, three-story palace, was set at right angles. It had a prominent, rounded, slightly protruding corner in the direction of Luisenplatz, set like a risalit, known also as an "avant-corps," which refers to a part of the building, such as a porch or pavilion, that juts out from the corps de logis, usually over the full height of the building. It is very common in façades in the Baroque period. On the ground floor as a balcony with four supporting pairs of columns laid out, each of the three corner windows of each additional floor carried a triangular portal. Toward the west, the building had an eight-axis wing, northward the wing was divided: seven-axis to a single-axis entrance portal, this with flanking pillars, the larger windows on the second floor again provided with a portal, the wing now followed by one only two-storey six-axis course with tall windows on the second floor and these crowned by a sandstone frieze. Here in the northern part was probably a large hall. The palace had a wrap-around roof balcony facing the Luisenplatz. The corner risalit above had a three-part frieze, which was crowned in the center with the coat of arms of Hesse, flanked by lions.

Later, the palace was given to Prince Alexander as his private residence in Darmstadt. Hence, the site acquiring the popularly used name "Alexander Palais." From his retirement from Austrian service until his death in 1888, Alexander lived there. After his death, his widow continued living at their home. After her death, in 1895, possession of the Alexander Palais returned to the grand duchy. In June 1944, the palace was almost completely destroyed during the fire-bombing of Darmstadt. Reconstruction deemed too costly, the ghostly shell was demolished and replaced by a modern building.

In the earlier years of their married life, there was no command for Prince Alexander in the Hessian army, so Emperor Franz Joseph of Austria gave him one. Despite his previous amorous adventures, he was apparently a man of great tact and served as a diplomatic mediator between the Emperor and Tsar Alexander II with Napoleon III and King Wilhelm I of Prussia. According to Charlotte Zeepvat: "[Prince Alexander] *was too useful and too skillful to remain in the shadows. As he rose, so too did his family. Not everyone in Europe liked the Battenbergs, but everyone knew who they were."*[7] He was made a general in that army and served the Kaiser for ten years before taking his family back to Hesse in 1862, where he continued his diplomatic duties.

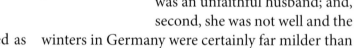

Prince Alexander of Hesse and by Rhine.

In the winter, the family lived in the Alexander Palais, and springs were spent at Heiligenberg, which Alexander had inherited from his mother at the age of thirteen. This pleasant place became the Battenberg's favorite residence. Because Heiligenberg became Alexander's home at such an early age, his sister, Marie, now the Tsarina had an opportunity to become familiar with the house before she left for Russia and loved it nearly as much as her brother did. Consequently, the Russian Imperial Family spent many happy summers with their cousins. It was there that the families, consisting of the Battenbergs, the Hesses and the Romanovs came together for holidays in the spring and summer. These respites were a welcome break from all the duties and responsibilities – at Heiligenberg everyone could relax and be themselves. For the Tsarina, there were further reasons that she came: first, she was not always happy in her marriage to the Tsar, he was an unfaithful husband; and, second, she was not well and the winters in Germany were certainly far milder than the ones in Russia.

The first years that the Battenbergs returned to Hesse can be marked as the beginning of the annual invasions of the Russian Imperial Family. This onslaught continued in one form or another until the First World War. The cousins formed close friendships and in several cases, engagements were made. It may have also been where certain enmities and jealousies were formed, most especially in the case of Marie's eldest son Alexander and his Battenberg cousins. However, for most, these

The Battenbergs attend a performance at the Darmstadt Hoftheater in 1887. From the left: Prince Henry, Prince Louis, Prince Franz Joseph, Count Gustav and Countess Marie of Erbach-Schönberg, Prince Alexander of Bulgaria, Princess Julia of Battenberg, and Prince Alexander of Hesse and by Rhine.

meetings brought with them the fondest of memories. They were counted as halcyon days.

The couple lived on in Hesse seeing their children grow up and, in several cases, making splendid marriages. Prince Alexander died in 1888 and Julia died in 1895.

****

Prince Louis of Battenberg

The four handsome Battenbergs had a story arc that fulfilled all the dramatic urges and had all the important story elements anyone could ask for: great tragedy, lost promise, redemption, and lastly an apotheosis for one, and that strangest of all fates, a peaceful existence, for the other.

They were, in royal terms, an impecunious bunch. They made their way in the world with an extinct title and with only the encouragement and tenacity of their strong mother and supportive father. They had to find their own careers and benefactors and in the marriage market, they had to take the role of supplicants. But what is readily apparent that what they lacked in worldly goods they made up for in manly good looks. Lest this should be thought of as a shallow observation, it helped them tremendously with Queen Victoria, who had a weakness for good-looking men and even their enemy, Otto von Bismarck, who said, no doubt grudgingly, that they were the handsomest princes in Europe. That may not be saying much judging by the competition, but, nevertheless, they were.

Louis was the eldest child, born in Graz, Austria, in 1854. This was the time in which Prince Alexander was serving in the Austro-Hungarian army and was stationed with them in Northern Italy. From an early age, Louis was encouraged to join the Royal Navy by his cousins, Princess Alice of Hesse and later her elder brother Bertie, Prince Albert Edward, the Prince of Wales. At age fourteen, Louis became a naturalized citizen of Great Britain and began a sterling career in the British Navy. He rose through the ranks and would eventually make it to the top, becoming the First Sea Lord in 1912.

When Louis was a young commander, he was very popular with members of his family and particularly enjoyed staying with the Prince and Princess of Wales. Obviously, the young man had inherited the charm and good looks of his father as well as his enjoyment of society and women. While Louis was at Marlborough House between assignments, he met and fell in love with the reigning beauty of the day, Lilly Langtry. She had just finished her affair with the Prince of Wales and seems to have turned to the Prince's young and handsome cousin for solace.[8]

Prince Louis had romantically thought he might marry Lilly to protect her reputation, but he reckoned without his parents and without his own innate sense of duty. Both his father and particularly his mother, Julia of the iron-will, encouraged him to do the right thing and provide for his off-spring, but also to go on a long cruise away from the temptations of Marlborough House. He was

Prince Louis of Battenberg in naval uniform during his early career.

not in London for the birth of his first child, though later on, when he resigned from the Royal Navy she was one of the first persons he told. He was very young and as Jane Austen said, young men must have something to live on as well as young women.

In 1883, Louis began a courtship of his cousin, Princess Victoria of Hesse and by Rhine. It appears, as much any of these things can, to have been a love match and the couple was married in April 1884 at Darmstadt with the bride's beloved grandmother, Queen Victoria, attending. She had certainly strongly approved of the handsome young man, writing to her granddaughter "*...you have done well to choose only a Husband who is quite of your way of thinking & who in many respects is as English as you are...*"[9] While the Queen was enthusiastic, many others of the so-called Royal Mob were not. In particular Victoria's first cousin, Wilhelm was well known for his intense dislike of the Battenberg Princes. It seems they inspired enmity not only because of their good looks but also their morganatic origins; as Wilhelm scoffed, they were not quite "of the blood." This only made the Queen more approving.

Louis and Victoria had four children: Alice (1885-1969), Louise (1889-1965), George (1892-1938), and lastly Louis (1900-1979).[10]

With the patronage of the Queen, Prince Louis continued to rise in the ranks and the young family lived many different places in England and at Malta, the headquarters of the Royal Navy in the Mediterranean. Louis became a captain in 1891 and a Rear Admiral in 1901. He invented the Battenberg Course Indicator that *"was designed for the rapid solution of a series of ordinary speed and distance triangles frequently met in fleet work,"*[11] in other words to calculate relative positions and speeds of other ships when sailing in a fleet. It was adapted by many of the major navies of the world. In addition, Louis also wrote a book on ship's names.

****

Louis and Victoria's first child was Alice. She was born at Windsor in 1885, in the Tapestry Room, the same room her mother was born twenty-two years previous. Alice was married to Prince Andreas of Greece, a son of King George I of the Hellenes and the former Olga Konstantinova, in 1903, and proceeded to have four daughters, Margarita, Theodora, Cecilii and Sophie as well as one son, Philip, in 1921. Alice had many emotional and physical problems during the twenties and thirties and had what amounted to a religious crisis, so the family had to provide the support. In the late 1920s, she had become profoundly religious, so much so that people around her saw it as a mania. She spoke of Jesus in sexual terms

Prince Louis and Princess Victoria of Battenberg with Grand Duke Ludwig IV holding their first child, Princess Alice. Osborne House, 1885.

and later on described marriage and intimacy with him as well as the Buddha. She was checked into a sanatorium at Tegel in 1930 and diagnosed as a paranoid-schizophrenic. She checked herself out of Tegel but continued to be unwell. So much so that her mother, Princess Victoria of Hesse, now the Marchioness of Milford Haven, had her committed to another sanatorium in Switzerland called Bellevue. She was literally taken away and sedated by *"men in white coats"*, a scene that must have been highly distressing.

After her aunt, her cousins and her daughter and grandsons were tragically killed in the air accident in Belgium in 1937, she rather miraculously regained her bearings. She pulled herself together and became a very strong member of the family. No one could quite explain the sudden transformation, though some felt the shock of the tragedy is what did it. Nevertheless, she was always thought of as a little bit odd and certainly different.

She went back to Greece and remained there throughout the war with her sister-in-law Princess Nicholas.[12] She worked hard, nursing and distributing food and without regard for her own personal safety. She also hid a Jewish family, the Cohens, for which she was made Righteous Among Nations in 1993: the highest honor the

Jewish people can give to a non-Jew. As Alice got much older she made her home with her son and daughter-in-law in Buckingham Palace. She died in 1969 and was buried at the Church of St Mary Magdalene in Jerusalem, Israel.

The next child in order of birth was Louise Alexandra Marie Irène (named for her great Aunt Louise, Duchess of Argyll, her father's sister Marie and her mother's sisters, Alix and Irène). She was born at Heiligenberg in 1889. Princess Victoria had had a difficult pregnancy and Louise was a small and somewhat sickly baby. Her father even nicknamed her "Shrimp" and letters to her from Prince Louis generally started with "Dear Shrimp."

Princess Louise and Princess Alice of Battenberg.

in fact the only female member of the royal family to work at the front. She worked in hospitals in Nevers and at Palaves and was secretly engaged several times during the hostilities. However, one young man was sadly killed and the other proved unsuitable because as her father had to explain to her, he was a homosexual. She worked hard during that time though still as frail as she had been as a child and spared herself nothing. Louise's mother, Princess Victoria came to visit her in France and spent her time as her daughter did, bandaging, helping men to the latrines and whatever jobs were given to her.

Louise, in her late twenties, emerged from the Great War heart-whole, or only slightly cracked. She was, as she explained *"figuratively and almost literally in no man's land."*[13] Despite her humor, she was, no doubt, resigned to being her mother's companion and a spinster when something completely unexpected happened. Crown Prince Gustaf Adolf of Sweden (later, King Gustaf VI Adolf) the widower of her cousin Princess Margaret of Connaught, began to court her. She was a reluctant bride, thinking that she was too old and thin to wear white or participate in a full-fledged wedding, but the Crown Prince, with the help of her nieces, Princess Theodora and Princess Margarita of Greece, persuaded her that that was exactly what she should do. She did not wear white – she wore silver, but her marriage

Louise spent her childhood and formative years with governesses, a finishing school, but mostly with her mother, traveling in various locations visiting relatives in Britain, Russia and of course, numerous places in Germany. As a young lady she had several suitors including a supposed secret engagement to Prince Christopher of Greece and King Manoel of Portugal, however Louise married neither of them.

During the Great War, Louise initially worked in the Soldiers and Sailors Families Association, but then later joined the Red Cross in the Voluntary Aid Detachment and served as a nurse in France –

Prince George of Battenberg.

In 1915, during the Great War, Prince George of Battenberg visited Russia. Here he is with his cousins Olga and Maria Nikolaevna.

to the Prince in 1923, proved to be happy and enduring. The couple had many interests in common and was extremely compatible. Their only disappointment was that they were unable to have children – Louise gave birth to one stillborn daughter.

It is noteworthy, that during the Second World War, Louise became the conduit whereby her relations on both sides of the conflict could communicate with one another. Still the Crown Princess, she was in a unique position to clear and forward correspondence from family members to one another. But it was not as easy as it sounds: she had to open, copy and address the correspondence as if coming from herself. On her seventieth birthday she received a gold case *"on which were engraved all the names of the relatives she helped."* She would become Queen of Sweden in 1950 and died in March 1965.

Prince George was born November 6, 1892, at the Old Schloß in Darmstadt.[14] As mentioned previously, his mother had moved to Darmstadt earlier in the year to nurse her father during his last illness. She also, ever the helping hand, was with her brother Ernie to provide guidance and advice as he began his reign. George of Battenberg was Queen Victoria's 14th great-grandchild. Princess Victoria wrote to her grandmother: *"The baby seems a strong, healthy child & is a source of the greatest pleasure & interest to his sisters."*[15] Once recovered from the birthing, and when George was ready to travel, Victoria and her growing family returned to England, much to the delight of her grandmother.

"Georgie" as he was called in the family, attended Cheam and then on to Royal Naval College in Osborne in 1905 in order to serve in the Royal Navy as his father had done. He had a great deal of mechanical ability and creativity. He read calculus books for fun and could do complex calculations in his head. The Prince, according to his master at the college, was a highly intelligent and lazy student who nonetheless

Prince George and Prince Louis Jr. of Battenberg.

graduated fourth in his class and took prizes in German and Science.

In 1911, he attended the Coronation Durbar at Delhi, at the end of the Coronation year of King George V and Queen Mary, as their guest. He was promoted to Lieutenant in February 1914 and present at some of the important naval battles of the Great War including the Battle of Jutland. In 1915, he served the *HMS New Zealand*, and using all those abilities that have been mentioned by his masters as well as his relatives, he was able to air condition his cabin and give himself hot and cold running water before these things were commonplace aboard ships. He also was able to rig a device that would begin his morning tea when his alarm clock went off in the morning. He was most certainly a man of great ingenuity. In the last years of the war, he served in the staff of Admiral Pakenham on the *HMS Lion*. The Queen has stated how much she enjoyed talking to him as he was so interesting and treated her like an equal.

In 1917, as his family and several other branches of the British Royal Family did, he gave up his German titles and took the title Earl of Medina. This is the courtesy title used by the heir of the Marquisate of Milford Haven, the new English title his father received from King George V. Interestingly, four men have held the title of Earl of Medina, starting with George. His son David used it from 1921-1938, his grandson George from 1961-1970, and George's son Henry (Harry), who has been Earl of Medina since his birth in 1991. He is, at the age of 29, the only male Mountbatten of his generation.

The last of Prince and Princess Louis' children is Prince Louis. (For more, see Chapter VII and VIII.)

✶✶✶✶✶✶✶✶

The Other Battenberg Children:
Marie, Alexander, Henry, and Franz Joseph

Then there is the eldest sibling, often neglected, the sister – Marie, Princess of Battenberg, the first-born of the clan. She was born in Geneva in 1852, nearly nine months after her parents' wedding. Several sources erroneously list her place of birth to have been Strasbourg. This is a product of an unsubstantiated

Fürstin Marie of Erbach-Schönberg.

rumor alleging that her parents eloped due to Julia's pre-marital pregnancy. However, we care more for the truth and proof, rather than innuendo. The fact of the matter is that Alexander and Julia married in October 1851, and their daughter arrived nearly nine months later. She was raised closely with the next sibling to be born – her brother Louis – and remained especially devoted to him for the rest of his life.

Marie spent most of her childhood, and it was a very happy one, in various Italian garrison towns where her father was stationed, and where her brothers were born. In the early 1860s, around the time when Marie was ten-years-old, the family settled in Darmstadt and at Heiligenberg. As mentioned, the Russian Imperial family visited a great deal, and, sometimes, but not always, the Tsarina came with her husband. More frequently, however, her younger sons, Serge and Paul and her daughter Marie accompanied her. In fact, despite the Tsarina's second son Alexander III's (known as "Sasha" in the family) hatred for the morganatic Battenbergs, the other children of the family were close playmates. Marie Battenberg and Marie Alexandrovna were actually childhood "best" friends and were close through at least much of the early part of their lives.

According to her cousin Ernst Ludwig, Marie grew up to be a *"beautiful"*[16] woman and in 1871, when she was nineteen, she married Count Gustav Ernst of Erbach-Schönberg, twelve years her senior. She was quite young, but he had fallen in love with her when they met several years previously, and an older man appealed to Marie's lack of frivolity. Once married, Marie pursued good works and charities in her little County. Later, because of his wife's closeness to the British Royal Family, Gustav was made Fürst of Erbach-Schönberg.

The couple had four children: Alexander, Maximilian, Victor, and Marie Elisabeth. Marie, like her mother, was dedicated to her brothers and loved them dearly. She wrote an extremely interesting memoir called *Reminiscences*, where she described how deeply affected she was by the early and untimely deaths of her brothers, Alexander and Henry, and how angry and unhappy she was about the treatment of her brother Louis by the British Press and the Royal Navy – Franz Joseph just seemed like the "little brother." In addition, she beautifully described a visit that she made to Bulgaria when her brother Alexander was the prince. She had an excellent evocative voice and made the entire trip come alive for the reader.

Sadly for her, one of her sons, Maximilian, was mentally and physically challenged, possibly from oxygen deprivation at birth, and though he never stood or talked or seemed to recognize his family, he lived to the age of fourteen. Marie wrote about that as well. She also translated several books from English to German, but that is not mentioned in her memoirs. She, however, lived a very private life, making her primary function in life as a support for her brothers and later her husband and children. She raised her family and dealt with the heartbreak of Maximilian as well as many stillbirths. Still, she also had the blessing of grandchildren and great-grandchildren as she aged.

Marie's son Alexander married Princess Elisabeth of Waldeck-Pyrmont at Arolsen. They had four children: Imma, Georg Ludwig, Wilhelm Ernst, and Helene. Gustav died in 1908 at Darmstadt at the age of 68 and it was after his death that the other two children, Marie Elisabeth ("Edda") and Victor became engaged: Edda to Prince Wilhelm of Stolberg-Wernigerode, and Victor to Countess Elisabeth Széchényi. Edda had two children: Ludwig Christian

Marie of Erbach-Schönberg with her parents, Julia and Alexander.

and Anne Marie while Victor's marriage remained childless. Marie lived on and died in Schönberg in 1923.

****

Alexander, or "Sandro" as he was known in the family, was born in 1857 in Verona. This was during Prince Alexander's time with the Austro-Hungarian army in Northern Italy. No doubt his nickname was from the Italian version of his name, Alessandro. Like his brothers and sister, Sandro spent his early life between his father's postings and the family homes in Darmstadt and Heiligenberg. His cousin Ernie of Hesse described him as "tall" and "beautiful" and said that Sandro was one of his greatest friends.[17] He had a military education and followed his father, volunteering in the Russian Army and fighting bravely in the Russo-Turkish wars in 1877. His family often visited the Russian Court of their Aunt Marie and Uncle Alexander: Sandro, Louis, and their father were actually present in February 1880 when an attempt was made on the life of the Tsar at the Winter Palace. Because of a delay in the dinner, apparently caused by Sandro, the Tsar, his brother-in-law, and nephews were not in the dining room when the bomb went off. Sadly, eleven others were not so fortunate. Speaking of tragic coincidences, much later on, when Crown Prince Rudolf of Austria committed suicide with his mistress, Marie Vetsera, that was a weekend that Alexander was supposed to go to the hunting lodge at Mayerling, but for some unexplained reason was unable to make it.

When he was a young man, his uncle, Tsar Alexander II, was successful in eliminating the de facto Ottoman influence from Bulgaria and was able to declare, with the aid of the Treaty of Berlin the previous year (1878), an independent Bulgarian State. Just as a matter of interest, this Treaty also gave independence to Romania, Serbia and Montenegro. At the time, Sandro was a member of the Prussian Life-Guards at Potsdam, and was recommended, by his Uncle Alexander, to be the sovereign Prince of Bulgaria.

Initially, the crown of Bulgaria had been offered to Prince Alexander of Hesse and then his eldest son, Louis, but both men declined, and Sandro, at the age of twenty-two, having no other tangible prospects except a life in the military, took the position and went to Bulgaria. This was with the backing of his Russian uncle, his other uncle, Ludwig III of Hesse and by Rhine, and Chancellor Otto von Bismarck. This support, however, began to waver after the assassination of Alexander II in 1881, and the disaffection of Sandro by his jealous Russian cousin, now Tsar Alexander III.

In addition, in 1883, Sandro and Princess Viktoria of Prussia, the second daughter of Crown Prince Friedrich and Crown Princess Victoria of Prussia, met and fell in love. Most observers say that the attraction was mutual, though there is also much written about Viktoria, or "Moretta" as she was

Prince Alexander of Bulgaria.

called in the family, being in love with love and that any attractive man would have done for her. At the time, she was, no doubt, what we would call a "boy-crazy" seventeen-year-old, and historians have been a little harsh with her. Queen Victoria and her daughter Vicky supported the engagement, and this may have also had some responsibility for Moretta's enthusiasm, but as time went on and Sandro alienated his sponsors, both in Berlin and St Petersburg, it was thought that a marriage between the two young people would offend either or both of these erstwhile patrons.

Moretta clung to her dream prince as long as she could (certainly longer than he did), even swearing, rather embarrassingly, to cut her hair and come join the Bulgarian army and fight alongside Sandro. By 1885, however, this tenuous engagement or romance or whatever it actually was, was officially terminated by a letter from Prince Alexander to the Kaiser. Poor Moretta had to deal with the harsh reality of being married to Prince Adolf of Schaumburg-Lippe, a son of Adolf I, Prince of Schaumburg-Lippe. From all appearances, he was rather short, stout and certainly hirsute – not the dashing fighting prince of her dreams.[18]

Sandro was not quite as fortunate. After a violent kidnapping at gunpoint and his eventual return to Bulgaria in 1886, he made the mistake of sending a telegram to his cousin Sasha saying that if the

Tsar did not wish him to maintain the throne he would leave. Apparently, Sasha's hatred of Sandro bordered on the pathological and so this telegram gave the Tsar the opening he needed to get rid of this undesirable morganaut for good. Moreover, the Tsar wanted someone far more amenable to Russian influence and malleable, not someone as independent-minded as Sandro, so the young man agreed to leave Bulgaria and did so.[20]

For the next couple of years, he went to Prussia, still keeping alive the idea of marrying Moretta (despite his letter of renunciation), his thinking being that since he was no longer politically controversial then he might be more acceptable to the Prussian Royal family. However, this was absolutely not the case. If Alexander III pathologically hated Sandro because of his dashing good looks and long lean body, then it appears that Willy (later Kaiser Wilhelm II) hated him because he was of tainted and non-royal blood. Wilhelm was in a position to guarantee that such a marriage would never take place.

Eventually, Sandro took the title of Count von Hartenau and spent the last years of his short life married to the lovely Johanna Loisinger (1865-1951), an actress and opera singer.[19] The couple married in 1889 and had two children, Assen Ludwig Alexander (1890-1965) who suffered from cerebral palsy, and Marie Therese Vera Zvetana

The Count and Countess von Hartenau with their son Assen.

(1893-1935). Sandro died in 1893 at the very young age of thirty-six. Most biographers seem to imply that he died of disappointment, possibly of having no spine and being unable to persevere in Bulgaria. It may be a little harsh as he was, after all, extremely young when he took the throne, and though he had strong support from his parents and his brothers, ultimately the two major empires of Russia and Germany were against him. The physical cause of death according to his sister's memoir was appendicitis that for some reason was inoperable, and so he expired, probably because it burst and from the subsequent blood poisoning.

As a side-note, his widow Johanna lived in Vienna after her husband's death and received a pension from Bulgaria, who had moved on to "Foxy Ferdinand."[21] It was with his permission that Sandro's body was moved to Sofia where it is buried. Sandro was always a beloved sovereign in the Bulgarian minds, perhaps in part because he was a virile and daring prince (certainly very unlike his successor), but also no doubt because he exhibited some degree of autonomy from his imperial cousins. The Battenberg Mausoleum was built in Sofia in 1897 and it still exists today.

****

Next in age is Prince Henry (Heinrich) of

Osborne House, The wedding of Prince Henry of Battenberg and Princess Beatrice of the United Kingdom.
Back row: from the left: Prince Louis of Battenberg; Princess Louise of Wales; Princess Irène of Hesse and by Rhine; Princess Victoria of Wales; Prince Franz Joseph of Battenberg. Middle row, same order: Princess Maud of Wales; Princess Alix of Hesse and by Rhine; and Princesses Marie Louise and Helena Victoria of Schleswig-Holstein.
Front row: Princesses Victoria Melita, Marie and Alexandra of Edinburgh; the Bride and Groom.

The Battenberg brothers at Osborne House, 1885. From the left: Alexander, Louis, Henry, and Franz Joseph.

Battenberg. He was born in Milan in 1858. Again, it appears that an Italian governess is responsible for his family nickname of "Liko." This comes from Enrico, which is, of course, the Italian for Henry. Apparently Liko was what the little boy could pronounce and Liko it was for the rest of his life. Henry, like his brothers would have to make his own way in the world. He was educated mostly in the military and served in Prussia. During his brother's tenure as Prince of Bulgaria, Liko was made an Honorary Colonel of the 1st Infantry Regiment of Bulgaria. He was also an avid traveler and in 1879 accompanied his Aunt Marie, the Russian empress, to Egypt, the Sinai, Ottoman Palestine, and Syria.

Henry actually made the most spectacular marriage of his family. During his brother Louis's wedding in 1884 to Princess Victoria, he made the close acquaintance of Queen Victoria's youngest daughter Beatrice. It was not difficult for Beatrice, who had been kept well away from suitors (including Louis when he was at Victoria's court), to fall in love with another handsome Battenberg prince. Henry was slim, with an impressive and highly waxed mustache, and looked incredibly dashing in an uniform. To say that Beatrice was impressed was to say the least of it. However, the Queen was not happy with this arrangement and forbade the engagement. It was not because she was a snob and thought that Henry was not good enough: it was simply because she wanted to keep her daughter unmarried and at her beck and call and to be her unpaid companion. The Queen could not visualize her life without Beatrice.

Standing, from the left: Princess Alix of Hesse and by Rhine; Prince Henry of Battenberg; Princess Victoria of Battenberg. Front row, same order: Princess Beatrice of Battenberg with her son Prince Alexander; Queen Victoria with Prince Leopold of Battenberg; Grand Duke Ludwig IV of Hesse and by Rhine; and Princess Victoria Eugenie of Battenberg.

Beatrice, however, was determined, and after six excruciating months of not speaking to one another and passing notes at the breakfast table, the Queen finally relented. However, she stipulated that the young couple would have to live with her and dance attendance on her during their married life. The Queen oddly noted in her diary that she hoped that there would be no "results" from the union.[22] Beatrice agreed to her mother's stipulations and so, reluctantly, did the much more adventurous and worldly Henry as well. It is interesting to note that his mother was surprised that these two got together, not because she thought that frumpy Beatrice, a shy homebody, did not match Henry in looks, but that Henry was not intellectually enough for *her*.

Standing, from the left: Princess Helena of Schleswig-Holstein, Prince Leopold and Princess Beatrice of Battenberg. Seated, same order: Prince Alexander and Prince Maurice of Battenberg, Queen Victoria, and Princess Victoria Eugenie of Battenberg.

The couple was married in 1885 in a ceremony on the Isle

of Wight with many European royals attending, notably, though, not the Prussians. First, as stated, they did not approve of marriages between themselves and the Battenbergs, and second, they were worried about the proximity of Sandro, who was attending his brother's wedding, to the hapless and unfortunate Princess Moretta, who still lived in hope. The Prussians also created a great fuss about the marriage in the Continental Press, making disparaging remarks about Henry and his parentage. It was highly distressing to everyone; most especially for Beatrice, who apparently lost a great deal of weight and so was quite thin and pale (and far less frumpy) at her wedding. To the Queen's everlasting credit, she was absolutely furious about this condescension, and it was during this time that she talked about giving Wilhelm and his brother Henry a good "skelping".[23]

Prince Franz Joseph of Battenberg.

After a short honeymoon, the couple was ensconced with the Queen for the duration. As time went on, Henry became what the Queen called "the sunshine" of their household. Really, this could have been predicted because the Queen loved a handsome face and she wanted and, indeed, loved having a man around the house. Henry was made Governor of Carisbrooke Castle as well as Captain-General and Governor of the Isle of Wight, given ranks in the British army, and made a member of the Privy Council.

And, despite the Queen's wishes, there were "results": Alexander (1886-1960), Victoria Eugénie (1887-1969), Leopold (1889-1922), and Maurice (1891-1914).[24] There were also some petty jealousies from the Queen's other daughters, most particularly from Louise, who taunted Beatrice, especially after Henry's untimely death. Specifically, Louise said that she was more Henry's confidant than Beatrice, his own wife. Louise told Sir James Reid of *"Prince Henry's attempted relations with her, which she had declined."*[25] If that was truly the case, she certainly ought to have kept it to herself; that Louise was not particularly happy in her marriage was probably more to the point.

Sadly, the untimely death came a little over ten years later, when longing for some manly activities that did not include dancing attendance on his mother-in-law, Prince Henry persuaded the Queen to allow him to go to West Africa to participate in the Ashanti Expedition. Henry had no chance to fight but did come down with malaria and died while being transported back to England. Once again, Queen Victoria embraced the grief as her own as she had done with her husband Prince Albert. Beatrice, however, played out her grief far less dramatically in public and soon went on with her life. It is possible that the marriage was just a footnote in her long single life. At least one of her younger sons inherited the dreaded hemophilia gene, and her elder son, though not really the "marrying kind," did manage to marry and produce one daughter, Lady Iris Mountbatten, who herself had, what was called in those days, quite a "career." Beatrice's daughter made a spectacular marriage to King Alfonso XIII, but this would not prove a lasting and happy marriage. After the King was exiled, the couple chose to live apart.

****

The youngest of the Battenberg Princes was Prince Franz Joseph. Like his older two brothers, "Franzjos," as he was called, was born in what would become Italy, in his case Padua, and thereafter he had a military education. He was a great favorite in the family, being the youngest and especially teased by them. Franzjos accompanied his brother Sandro to Bulgaria and became a Colonel of the Calvary. He was even considered for the throne after Sandro abdicated. He was certainly interested in Bulgaria, and, being more of an academic than a fighter, he went to the University in Leipzig and received his doctorate in 1891 with a dissertation entitled "The Economic Development of Bulgaria from 1879- the present."

Any hopes of Bulgaria were dashed when a Coburg came to the throne, and Prince Franzjos, like his brothers, had to make his mark in the world some

Princess Anna of Battenberg.

A family gathering in Cetinje, Montenegro – King Nicholas and his family. Standing in back, from the left: Grand Duke Peter Nikolaevich of Russia; Prince Franz Joseph of Battenberg; Princesses Vera and Xenia, Crown Prince Danilo, Prince Mirko and Prince Peter of Montenegro. Seated: Crown Princess Militza; Grand Duchess Militza Nikolaevna of Russia; Queen Elena of Italy; Queen Milena and King Nicholas of Montenegro; Princess Anna of Battenberg; King Vittorio Emanuele III of Italy; Princess Natalia of Montenegro. On the ground: Princess Elena Petrovna of Russia; Princess Marina Petrovna of Russia; and Crown Prince Alexander of Serbia, Elena Petrovna's youngest brother.

Clockwise, from top: the Duchess of York, Queen Victoria, Princess Victoria Eugenie of Battenberg, and Princess Anna of Battenberg.

other way. He evidently had little taste for military life, and his option was to find himself an advantageous marriage. In London, he met Consuelo Vanderbilt, and they became further acquainted in Paris. Consuelo was being shown around by her mother in order to attract an English Duke, but the idea of a German Prince temporarily derailed those notions. Franzjos proposed to her, however, Consuelo refused the offer.[26] After this rejection, Franzjos went on a world tour visiting Malta, Suez, Calcutta, Sydney, New Zealand, and then America, traveling from San Francisco to New York.

Several years later, in 1896, Franzjos met Princess Anna of Montenegro[27], a daughter of Nicholas I and Milena of Montenegro, at Balmoral.[28] However, according to the *New York Times*, and other sources, the couple met in Cimiez, near Nice, when Franzjos was visiting Queen Victoria. Anna, who was visiting her sister Militza, was interested in Franzjos and wanted very much to attract him, and he responded to her. *The Times* called her *"...a dark, tall, and unusually beautiful girl."*[29]According to her future sister-in-law, Anna was *".... a woman of rare qualities of heart and character...."*[30] The couple were married in 1897, and Franzjos' father-in-law made him a Colonel in the Montenegrin Army, such as it was. Franzjos, however was not the military man that his brothers were, and so, instead, he and Anna traveled a great deal. At the beginning of World War I, the couple moved to Switzerland and lived there until Franzjos's death in 1924. The couple had never been quite wealthy, but after Franzjos's death, Princess Anna became more impecunious. Rescue came in the form of a particularly generous niece-in-law, Edwina Mountbatten, who contributed financial support. Anna was a great favorite in the family, and there are many photographs of her with various members of the Battenberg "mob." She died in 1971 at the age of 96, and, with her, the House of Battenberg died too, as she was its last surviving member.

An image of Princess Anna of Battenberg from a postcard she mailed to Prince Henry of Prussia, a fellow motor enthusiast.

Chapter VI
The Greek-Battenberg Alliance

Alice and Andreas

As the new century started, there were a few more great occasions, however, that would garner the attention of the world. One was the coronation of King Edward VII in 1902, and the next, closer to the Hesses and Battenbergs was in October 1903, when the entire family came together at Darmstadt for Princess Alice of Battenberg's wedding to Prince Andreas of Greece. It would be the last time there would be a strong Romanov presence at a family event and one of the last events that didn't have the sting of bitterness and anger to it.

Princess Alice had met Prince Andreas when she and her family traveled to London to be present at the Coronation of King Edward VII in June 1902. Alice was a young girl of seventeen, an acknowledged beauty and, unfortunately, almost entirely deaf. She was able to read lips in several languages and was astutely taught by her mother to do everything possible to disguise her disability. She must have been extremely successful as it was rarely remarked upon.

Prince Andreas and Princess Alice of Greece.

Though Alice was much attracted to Andreas, a dashing officer in the Greek military, her parents thought her entirely too young to get married and so discouraged the match at that point. The coronation didn't take place because the King had to go through an emergency appendectomy, and all returned to their respective homes. Prince Andreas however made his presence known in Darmstadt when he became a member of the Hessian 23rd Dragoon Guards.[1] The young couple continued to see one another, and the attraction grew to love. After attending the postponed coronation ceremonies, the couple was unofficially engaged. Their engagement became official in June of 1903. In an effort to stress the bride's Hessian roots, Alice's wedding was scheduled to take place in Darmstadt. Hence, in October, a great royal mob boarded trains and automobiles and headed to the grand duchy's capital.

Prince Andreas was born at the Royal Palace in Athens in 1882, as the fourth son of King George I and Queen Olga.[2] Andreas' father was chosen as King of the Hellenes in 1863. He was born in

Prince Andreas of Greece and Denmark.

Denmark as the second son of future King Christian IX and of his wife, the former Princess Louise of Hesse-Kassel. Andreas began military training at an early age and served in the Greek army. His sister-in-law, Princess Marie Bonaparte considered Andreas, *"a purebred horse,"*[3] and the young prince was described as, *"tall, slim, and intelligent."*[4] He was a thorough soldier and his appointments were substantive rather than honorary. As a child, Andreas was taught English by his nannies, but with his parents he refused to speak anything but Greek. A polyglot as were all members of his family, Andreas also spoke German, French, Danish, and Russian.

In 1867, King George traveled to Russia, where he met and quickly became engaged to Grand Duchess Olga Konstantinovna, the 16-year-old daughter of Grand Duke Konstantin Nikolaevich and his German-born wife Alexandra Josifovna (née Saxe-Altenburg). Once in Athens, where Olga was to remain very popular with her husband's subjects, they soon welcomed the arrival of their first child, Constantine (1868-1923). In 1889, he married Princess Sophie of Prussia, who was a younger sister of Kaiser Wilhelm II, as well as the daughter of the Empress Friedrich, Grand Duchess Alice's older sister. A second son arrived in 1869 and he married the extremely wealthy Princess Marie Bonaparte. In 1870, Olga gave birth to a daughter, Alexandra, who married Grand Duke Paul Alexandrovich, who was one of Ella's brothers-in-law. Two years later a third son was born, Nicholas. He married another Romanov, Grand Duchess Helen Vladimirovna. Four years after Nicholas's birth, Queen Olga gave birth to a second daughter, Marie. She also married a Romanov, Grand Duke George Mikhailovich, but unlike her siblings who married Russians, Marie's marriage was unhappy. In 1880, a third daughter was born, Olga, her mother's namesake, but died that same year. Andreas was next, followed in 1888 by a fifth son, Christopher, basically an afterthought. Christopher married twice, his first wife being an immensely wealthy American named Nancy Leeds, who not only made him a widower, but also left him a considerable legacy.

Princess Alice of Battenberg.

The Royal Mob gathered in Darmstadt's Neues Palais, October 1903. Back row, from the left: Prince Henry and Princess Irène of Prussia, Princess Victoria of Battenberg, Princess Beatrice of Battenberg, Grand Duke Paul Alexandrovich, Queen Alexandra, Grand Duchess Marie Pavlovna the Younger, King George I of the Hellenes, Grand Duke Dimitri Pavlovich, Grand Duke Paul Alexandrovich of Russia, Grand Duke George Mikhailovich and Grand Duches Marie Georgievna, Princess Victoria (Queen Alexandra's daughter), Crown Prince Constantine and Crown Princess Sophie of Greece, Fürstin Marie of Erbach-Schönberg. At front, same order: Grand Duke Ernst Ludwig, Prince Nicholas and Princess Helen of Greece, Queen Olga of Greece, Grand Duchess Vera Konstantinovna, Prince George of Battenberg, Prince Christopher of Greece, Grand Duchess Tatiana Nikolaevna, Princess Elisabeth of Hesse and by Rhine, Princess Louise of Battenberg (looking down), Grand Duchess Olga Nikolaevna, Empress Alexandra Feodorovna holding her daughters Grand Duchesses Anastasia and Maria Nikolaevna, Tsar Nicholas II, Grand Duchess Elisabeth Feodorovna, and Prince George of Greece.

Interestingly, his family oftentimes states that Mrs. Leeds left nothing to her husband. Don't believe it. In 1929, Christopher married Princess Françoise, one of the daughters of the Duke and Duchess de Guise. Christopher's father-in-law, Jean, had become Head of the Royal House of France in 1926, when he succeeded his brother-in-law the Duke d'Orléans.

At the time of his engagement to Alice, Andreas was an impecunious younger son who basically survived on his military salary and a stipend from his parents. While dynastically Alice marrying Andreas was a gigantic leap upward for the Battenbergs, financially it was to be always challenging. Even within his family members, particularly the very imperious Grand Duchess Helen Vladimirovna, Alice was considered a *lesser royal*. Helen's cold treatment of Alice would remain nearly unthawed throughout their long life as members of the Greek Royal House.

It has been suggested that having the wedding in Darmstadt was a show of solidarity with Grand Duke Ernst Ludwig in the wake of his divorce. Considering the trauma and scandal that it engendered

Princess Alice of Battenberg in her wedding dress.

throughout Europe, it's a suggestion that makes sense. Ernie confirmed this in his memoirs saying *"they came together here from all over, and I think that they did this also to show me that they stood by me..."*[5] In attendance, as mentioned were the Romanovs: Ella and her husband Grand Duke Serge; Alix and Nicholas II, as well as Irène and her husband, Prince Henry. In addition, Andreas's parents, Crown Prince Constantine and his wife Sophie, Prince and Princess Nicholas of Greece and many. The Prince of Wales, and his wife Mary, Queen Alexandra were all there along with Princess Henry Battenberg, her daughter Princess Victoria Eugenie (Ena), Princess Victoria of Wales and Princess Christian of Schleswig-Holstein and her children completing the British presence.

Marie of Battenberg left a detailed description of the day. In her memoirs

The Greek Royal Family c. 1904. Standing, from the left: Prince George, Crown Princess Sophie, Prince Andreas, Princess Alice, Grand Duke George Mikhailovich, Prince Nicholas. Seated, same order: Crown Prince Constantine holding Prince Paul, Queen Olga, Princess Helen, King George I, Grand Duchess Marie Georgievna with her daughters Nina and Xenia, Princess Helen holding her daughter Olga. On the floor are: Prince Alexander, Prince Christopher, and Prince George (future George II).

In Athens, Prince Andreas and Princess Alice with Prince Nicholas and his wife Grand Duchess Helen Vladimirovna.

she wrote, *"The arrival at the Russian chapel was wonderful. A fragment of Hellas in the north; deep blue sky, brilliant sunshine, flashing golden cupolas, a scarlet carpet on the steps...The bridal couple, who, of course, came last, stood on a carpet of rose-coloured silk – a symbol of the path of life."*[6]

During the Orthodox wedding ceremony, Princess Alice became confused, even though she had practiced the moment in advance. David Duff recalled the episode writing, *"becoming confused by the complicated procedure, she said "No" when asked if she was marrying of her own free will, and "Yes" when asked if she had plighted her troth elsewhere."*[7]

The shenanigans of the wedding are the stuff of which legends were made. Many witnesses from inside and out saw the dignified royals really "let their hair down" as the bride and groom went off on their honeymoon. The Tsar in particular, to the dismay of his secret service, ran after the car with children and other guests throwing rice into the faces of the bridal couple. Alice famously yelled at him calling him a *"[S]tupid old ass!"*[8]

Alice and Andreas settled in Greece after their wedding. She received some fabulous wedding presents, most prominently a luxury automobile from her uncle Tsar Nicholas II. Two years after their wedding, Andreas and Alice became parents of a baby girl. Her name was Margarita and she went on to marry another descendant of Queen Victoria. The following year, Alice gave birth to a second daughter, Theodora, who would marry into the Grand Ducal House of Baden. A five-year break ensued and in 1911 Alice gave birth to a third daughter, Cecilie, followed three years later by a fourth daughter, Sophie. Seven years, and what seemed a lifetime, separated the birth of Alice's fourth daughter and the arrival of the family's long-awaited son, Philip. These five children are to become important pieces of the life-quilt of the descendants of Ludwig IV and Alice.

Princesses Theodora, Cecilie, Margarita and Sophie of Greece.

Chapter VII

Tragedy, World War, Turmoil, and Survival

From the end of Queen Victoria's reign, through the Great War, the Hesses and the Battenbergs personified the great changes that were rippling through the Royal Families of Europe. If the Victorian Age was the zenith of royal power, it certainly didn't last long. That first sunny decade of the twentieth century heralded, if they but knew, the unraveling of the intricate fabric of familial and monarchical relationships over which the Queen had presided. The families would assemble for a few more great occasions, but the great gatherings of the ruling families of the 19th century were all but gone.

Throughout the first decade of the twentieth century, the Hesse and Battenberg families met constantly. In spite of busy lives, distance, personal obligations, and losses, they sought each other's company either in Hesse under the loving auspices of Ernie and Onor, or in Hemmelmark, Great Britain or Russia. Family reunions were precious, as later and tragic events would inevitably catch up with all the family members.

In 1899, Ernie and Ducky welcomed family at Wolfsgarten for what turned out to be a visit not only filled with hijinks, but also dangerous liaisons. From the top: Grand Duke Boris Vladimirovich, Prince Nicholas of Greece, Tsar Nicholas II, Grand Duke Andrei Vladimirovich, Grand Duke Kirill Vladimirovich, Ernie, Ducky, and Alexandra Feodorovna.

It was in this first decade that the marriage of Ernie and Ducky irretrievably broke down. About nine months after the death of Queen Victoria, Ducky left Darmstadt to live with her mother in Coburg. Divorced proceedings began in earnest and by year's end the marriage was no longer.[1] It was just two years later that the sad and sudden death of little Elisabeth of Hesse, a well-beloved child in the Grand Duchy, occurred. This child of eight was buried in a small white coffin and her fellow Darmstadters lined the streets mourning their lovely little princess.

Neither was Irène spared as the New Year of 1904 rang in. In February, Irène's youngest child had an accident. Ernie wrote to sister Victoria to apprise her of the situation:

I got a telegram from Henry today, saying that their baby had fallen from a chair two days ago & suffers from headaches & sickness, they hear it may be a hemorrhage to the brain & return to Kiel today. Perhaps it is not quite so bad as they think poor things.[2]

The condition of little Heinrich, who was suffering

The Hessian siblings gathered in Darmstadt in 1903. From the left: Grand Duke Ernst Ludwig, Empress Alexandra Feodorovna and Tsar Nicholas II, Princess Irène and Prince Henry of Prussia, Grand Duchess Elisabeth Feodorovna and Grand Duke Serge Alexandrovich, and Princess Victoria and Prince Louis of Battenberg. It was Serge Alexandrovich's last visit.

from fevers and headaches, was grave. There was no hope for the child, Ernie subsequently wrote to Victoria, but Irène was brave and only broke down occasionally. A few weeks later, at the end of February, the little boy died – he was barely four years old. That left her with just two boys: her eldest, Toddy, who also had the dreaded disease, but seemed to manage and even grow up; and, little Bobby – Sigismund, who was completely free from the disease.

In Russia, unbeknownst to the family, a bigger tragedy brewed. In a horrifically miscalculated decision, Nicholas II had taken the empire to war with Japan. At stake was Russian ambition in Manchuria and Japanese dominance over Korea. Russia refused Japan's expansionist policies, instead demanding an area of influence over large portions of the Korean peninsula. After the breakdown of negotiations, the Japanese launched a surprise attacked on the Russian Eastern Fleet, anchored off Port Arthur, China. A disastrous

Henry and Irène of Prussia and their son Sigismund.

Tsar Nicholas II seated between his cousin Prince Nicholas of Greece and his brother Grand Duke Michael Alexandrovich.

war ensued. Russia suffered multiple defeats at the hands of the Japanese, which sent politics tremors throughout the crumbling Romanov dominions. In the end, defeated and humiliated by the Japanese, whom he believed to be beneath him, Nicholas II had to seek peace to prevent a complete collapse of the imperial structure. As revolution and political instability spread, spurred by unimaginable violence on both the side of the imperial forces and revolutionaries, the tsar was forced to grant his people a Duma, a Russian-style parliament. The Russian government reluctantly gave in to demands and accepted the inevitable: autocracy was at an end. The arrival of constitutional government meant the end of the tsar's unquestioned rule over Russia. Nicholas II, a fatalist who saw divine messages where there were none, felt that he had failed in his "god-given" right to protect autocracy and secure its existence into the future. The remaining years of his tragic reign were fraught with efforts to turn back the clock. It was a total failure in governance.

In the midst of these troubles, Nicholas II and Alexandra Feodorovna's longed-for heir finally made his arrival. The birth took place at Peterhof on August 12, 1904. Needless to say, the parents were elated at finally having produced an heir for the Romanov Empire. Joy spread among supporters of the dynasty, as, *"guns roared a full fusillade to mark the birth."*[3] Among the heir's godparents were The Prince of Wales and Kaiser Wilhelm II. And it was hoped that *"splendours of the celebration helped relieve the anxieties over the war."*[4] In the end, the relief was fleeting as it soon became apparent that the Tsesarevich Alexei Nikolaevich was afflicted with a dreaded disease: hemophilia. Realization of the baby's illness changed his parents lives immediately; it affected the course of Russia's history forever.

Empress Alexandra Feodorovna with her son Tsesarevich Alexei Nikolaevich.

Faced with their only son's illness, Nicholas and Alexandra fell victim to healers and quacks who took advantage of their pain to the detriment of their personal

Alexandra and Alexei during one of his hemophiliac attacks.

reputation. The empire did not know that Alexei Nikolaevich was a hemophiliac. Outside the walls of the Alexander Palace, where the secret was kept at all costs, Russia only saw a ruler and his consort who surrounded themselves with an increasingly worrisome coterie of strange and questionable men like Grigorii Rasputin, a dirty, louch charlatan who claimed to possess healing powers. The rumor-mill that emanated from this fact, only further eroded the tsar's reputation.

As for Alexandra Feodorovna, her son's precarious health estranged her from the outside world. Deeply shy, a personality molded by the early losses she experienced, Alexandra Feodorovna retreated inside the confines of her most intimate circles. The outside world rarely got to see the sweet smiles that she gave to those inhabiting her private realm. It was a pity, for had Russians seen this aspect of her personality, she could have won their hearts, Instead, already possessing a tendency toward hypochondria, her self-inflicted isolation only deepened her worse traits. In doing so, she sought solace from the cruelties she blamed the world for inflicting upon her. However, by following this path she showed complete dereliction of the role that she was expected to fulfill. Nicholas and Alexandra were not bad people – they simply lacked the mettle necessary to navigate the troubled waters of Russian politics. One can only wonder how Russia would have reacted to the truth surrounding the Tsesarevich Alexei's illness. It is quite possible that had he and his wife chosen to share their son's health challenges with the empire, Nicholas II's people would have rallied to provide their tsar with much comfort and support.

There was more tragedy in store when Grand Duke Serge Alexandrovich, Ella's husband, was assassinated in early 1905. As in his father's case, there was more than one attempt made on Serge's life. On February 13, the last attempt was successful. At three o'clock in the afternoon, when his carriage was inside the Kremlin walls, a bomb was thrown, and Serge was blown to bits. Ella had heard the explosion from her rooms and rushed out to see what had happened. She numbly began to gather together the parts of

Tsar Nicholas II and his children. Alexei and Anastasia on both his sides, while Maria, Tatiana, and Olga stand behind.

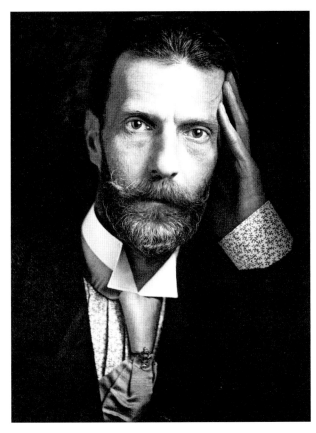

Grand Duke Serge Alexandrovich.

the body strewed everywhere saying *"Hurry, hurry, Serge hates blood and mess."*[5] Though little remained, the pieces of her husband were placed on a stretcher, covered by a cloak, and taken to the Nicholas Palace. Ella wrote telegrams informing the family, though Alexandra and Nicholas were advised not to attend the funeral and did not. Though Irène could not travel to Russia for the funeral, she and Henry as well as Ernie and his wife, were able to travel through Germany several days with sister Victoria, who had rushed from London to be at Ella's side. Wilhelm also made the effort and met them, according to Victoria, *"at the Berlin station and gave me supper. He was very kind and thoughtful and much worried about Ella, for whom since his student days he had felt a strong devotion."*[6]

As the years rolled on, the Hessian sisters spent summers together in Russia and Ella and Victoria discussed her plans to eventually found a nursing order. Since Serge's violent death, Ella took charge of his wards, the children of his brother Grand Duke Paul Alexandrovich – Marie and Dmitri. In addition, Ella busied herself nursing wounded soldiers from the Russo-Japanese War and put as much devotion into this as was possible.

As for the children, Ella favored Dmitri over Marie. The young grand duchess had a difficult character and Ella found her challenging. In due course, she came to accept that the best solution to her quandary would be to find a suitable husband for her niece. The choice landed on Prince Wilhelm of Sweden, second son of King Gustaf V and Queen Victoria of Sweden. Hence, in 1908, Marie was married off and relocated to Stockholm. There she had one child and led a thoroughly unhappy existence. Eventually, Marie left Stockholm and returned to St Petersburg. Her

Grand Duke Serge and Grand Duchess Elisabeth at Illinskoe, his country estate.

marriage ended in divorce, but by then she was no longer Ella's headache. Since Dmitri, the principal heir to Serge's large fortune, came of age in 1909, he was from that day on independent and also no longer under Ella's responsibility and guidance. Dmitri served in the military and led a happy-go-lucky existence in the capital. Close to Nicholas and Alexandra, he was one of the few Romanovs who had access to the imperial family's inner world. The Empress was very fond of him. She was quite shocked when in 1916 he was found to have been involved in Grigorii Rasputin's assassination. Unwilling to deal

The marriage that freed the aunt and trapped the bride. From the left: Grand Duchess Elisabeth, Princess Victoria of Battenberg, Grand Duchess Marie Pavlovna Jr., Prince Wilhelm of Sweden, and Grand Duke Dmitri Pavlovich.

with him harshly, Nicholas II sent his cousin into internal exile. This ultimately saved Dmitri Pavlovich's life as he was thus able to escape the revolutionary turmoil and reach the safety of India, from where he eventually journeyed to Europe.

Grand Duchess Elisabeth after becoming a nun.

With these distractions, Ella was slowly getting past the horrible and violent death of her husband. She began the long process of divesting herself of her worldly goods in order to found something unique in the Russian Orthodox monastic system – a nursing order that would be involved in the actual nursing of patients and the building of hospitals. It took her a long time to get the Metropolitans to agree to what she wanted. For them, the idea that nuns could visit their families and even take holidays wreaked of Protestantism, but Ella persevered. Eventually she was granted permission to found the Convent of SS Martha and Mary. From then onward, she lived at the Convent in three plainly furnished rooms, sleeping *"on a wooden bed without a mattress, and with only one hard pillow."*[7] From all appearances she was able easily to transition from an opulent life to a simple one. She rarely appeared in public again and looked, Meriel Buchanan wrote, like a *"white lily in a garden of exotic flowers."*[8]

Ernie and Onor constantly asked Ella to come to visit Darmstadt, but she was adamant about staying near Alix. Both she and Victoria were horribly aware of the shadow of revolution that was constantly getting larger. Onor however, had better news. She was pregnant and in November of 1906 gave birth to her first child, a boy called Georg Donatus, or "Don" as he was known in the family. He was a handsome child who looked a great deal like his father and grandfather. He was joined two years later in November 1908 by his younger brother, Ludwig known as "Lu." It was the happy little family that Ernie had craved and there are charming photographs of this group enjoying themselves in Wolfsgarten, entertaining their British or Russian cousins and generally living the kind of quiet life that suited them.

It was also the time when Ernie could concentrate on his Darmstadt Artists' Colony, which he had founded in 1899. Artists and architects had homes built in the Mathlidenhöhe and had irregular exhibitions of their works. Ernie was particularly fascinated with the *Jugendstil* or Art Nouveau movement

Grand Duchess Eleonore.

as well as Surrealism. Ernie commissioned a spectacular Wedding Tower to be erected to commemorate his marriage to Onor. It was designed by Joseph Olbrich and was completed in 1908. The colony still exists today with new artists, writers, and architects moving in all the time. Ernie also adored music, which stemmed from piano and violin lessons in his youth and later, after seeing a performance of *Parsifal* at Bayreuth, he began a life-long devotion to Wagner. He actively encouraged music and many leading conductors were invited to Darmstadt to perform. Dance, too, was a love of the Grand Duke's and he invited Isadora and Elizabeth Duncan to found a dance school at the Marienhöhe that became a part of the artists' colony.

Spring 1906 would come with another Battenberg wedding as Prince and Princess Henry's daughter, Ena, married Alfonso XIII of Spain. The couple's engagement was not particularly

Ernie and Onor with their sons Don and Lu.

popular due to the fact that Ena was the daughter of a morganatic father and a Protestant. However, these obstacles were overcome with her conversion to the Catholic church and the ceremony took place in Madrid in May. This type of event attracted many members of the various royal families and there were threats of violence. The happy day was marred by an assassin who threw a bouquet of flowers at the couple. It concealed a bomb. P a n d e m o n i u m ensued as the bomb exploded and the horse guards scrambled around the crowd looking for the murderer. The blast killed twenty-four people and injured dozens. Shaken, the newlyweds changed carriages and proceeded to the palace – a highly inauspicious beginning to a marriage that was later torn by infidelity and disease.

Queen Ena of Spain and her brothers: Maurice, Leopold, Alexander.

The Hesses and Battenbergs, as well as the rest of the family, truly mourned this man who had played such an important part in their lives.

The King's funeral was a grand affair, attended by many royal families. There was the so-called "March of Kings," in which nine kings took part in the funeral procession. The monarchs followed the coffin, as it wound slowly through London. Among those included in the procession were: Kaiser Wilhelm II, Alfonso XIII of Spain, Frederik VIII of Denmark, George I of the Hellenes, Haakon VII of Norway, Manoel II of Portugal, Albert I of the Belgians, Ferdinand of Bulgaria, and Mr. Theodore Roosevelt, now the former US President. On May 17, the actual funeral service took place at Windsor.

The next few years, the last before the war, unfolded gently with little disturbance. The sisters visited back and forth, their children played together, the controversies between Alexandra and her extended family, and, indeed, her country, continued, and the others sought in some way, anyway, to mitigate these controversies. It was a losing battle, but it was fought earnestly. The end of that pre-war world, however, was coming. Many marked it in different events, but certainly one of the most significant was the death of King Edward VII on May 6, 1910 after a short reign of nine years.

That Christmas, Henry and Irène visited Sandringham as guests of the new king, George V and Queen Mary. Victoria, Louis and their family, excepting Alice, were also there. Sandringham was a large edifice, constantly expanded and rebuilt to accommodate the family. In its latest incarnation, it was more gingerbread Victorian house than anything else and very homey. It had originally been bought for the Prince and Princess of Wales when they first married and served as their private country residence. It was far cozier than Balmoral, and certainly much warmer.

Edward VII and Nicholas II onboard the Standart.

The family had their usual festivities before Christmas. There was tree trimming and carol singing, and all joined in with the Christmas charades and games. Inevitably, there was a lot of talk about hostilities between the allies and the so-called Triple Alliance of Germany, Austria-Hungary, and Italy. While he was there, Henry took the opportunity to talk to George about the state of affairs between their two countries. This discussion and one later on just before war was declared became one of the few great storms of Irène and Henry's usually serene life.

The fall of 1910 also marked one of the last meetings of the family of sisters and brother, with all their available children and spouses in Hesse. Alix continued to be sickly and suffering from sciatica and possible heart problems, ailments that she had persistently suffered from since before her marriage. The symptoms were exacerbated now by anxiety over her hemophiliac son and the worsening political situation in Russia. Because of this, she wished to take the waters at Bad Nauheim. Naturally, with so many members of the family coming at once, it was necessary to make detailed arrangements. Letters flew between the siblings, trying to set up accommodations and amusements for the Imperial visitors. However, Ernie was not only concerned with domestic matters but, more urgently with security matters since the Imperial Family could never be without their massive protection apparatus. The towns that they might visit were swept not only by the Okhrana agents, but the local constabularies were on full alert.

The Imperial Family arrived in August and stayed until nearly the end of October at the Schloß in Friedberg while Alix went to the spa in Bad Nauheim. During the visit, Henry and Irène arrived with their children as well as Victoria, Louis along with Louise, George and Dickie, Alice and Andreas and their children. All the cousins played together, with a firm eye kept on all of them by their respective nannies. There were luncheons and dinners, some informal and some, alas, formal, when Wilhelm showed up for several days and required everyone to dress in their uniforms. However, besides this inconvenience, it was a private and relaxing visit.

When Alix had had enough of the waters, they returned

Prince Henry of Prussia at Balmoral.

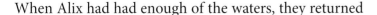

The last meeting of the Hessian siblings before war and revolution changed their lives forever. From the left: Princess Irène, Grand Duke Ernst Ludwig, Grand Duchess Elisabeth Feodorovna, Princess Victoria, and Empress Alexandra Feodorovna.

to Wolfsgarten and spent some quiet days there. There are some last group pictures of the Hessian sisters at their beloved childhood home and Ella now in her nun's habit. She looked, it was remarked, like "Elisabeth" in the opera *Tannhäuser*. Ella became the Abbess of her convent in April 1910. Oddly enough, as fanatically religious as Alix had become, embracing Russian Orthodoxy with a tremendous fervor, she had a hard time understanding why her elder sister would embrace a religious life and doubted her sincerity. However, Victoria defended Ella and the truth was, the Grand Duchess had expressed the desire to be a nun when she was quite a young girl.

Meanwhile, in 1912, Onor took over the running of the *Alice Frauen Verein* in Darmstadt. Victoria Battenberg had been looking after her mother's pride and joy the best that she could considering her peripatetic existence, but it couldn't have been easy. Ducky had never been interested so at last, the people of Darmstadt had a new *Landesmütter*.

In those last years before the Great War, the visits continued across Europe. Princess Victoria, notably, made a visit to Russia in 1912 as well as Irène, who was present at Spala when the Tsesarevich suffered his most dreadful and painful attack of hemophilia. One can imagine the support that the two sisters, who knew this agony so well, were able to give one another. As always, filled with guilt over her son's medical condition, Alix was particularly introspective and

A postcard celebrating the presidency of the Alice Frauen Verein.

Princess Victoria with her sister Ella.

seemed in a state of spiritual melancholy. Moreover, because of Rasputin's seemingly God-given power to alleviate the Tsesarevich's suffering, her dependence on him was all consuming. Alix's sisters all noticed this guilt and fanatical devotion to Rasputin, and like other members of the Romanov family, were worried about her mental health.

The year 1913 was notable for several major royal events. The Romanov dynasty commemorated their Tercentenary with celebrations beginning in February 1913. It was three hundredth anniversary of Michael I, the first Russian Tsar of the House of Romanov. It was also the year of the last gathering of all the glittering royalties of Europe. The occasion was the wedding of Princess Viktoria-Luise of Prussia, the only daughter of Wilhelm, and Prince Ernst August of Hannover, who was also a Prince of Great Britain and Ireland. It was a large assemblage with over twelve hundred guests including, Nicholas II, King George V and Queen Mary, Queen Marie of Romania, Irène and Henry, and countless others.

As a progressive, Ernie hated the war that came. Because he himself was half English and had three sisters on the other side, he did not actively participate in the fighting, which suited him. Sadly, there was much suspicion about him because of his relatives and the perception of where his sympathies lay. Ernie had never whole-heartedly enjoyed the martial life though he served for a time at Kaiser Wilhelm's headquarters. Meanwhile, Onor organized hospitals and general relief for casualties of the war at home in Darmstadt. After leaving the Kaiser's headquarters, he drove an ambulance, visited hospitals, and generally tried to give comfort to fighting men.

As the war was winding down, there is little doubt that Ernie's childhood traumas came back to the surface as he learned of the tragic deaths of his sisters, brother-in-law and nieces and nephews – as well as a great deal of the extended family. His remaining sisters tried to shield him as best as they could and conspired together with Onor not to tell him the exact details of the barbarous murders of the Imperial Family and Ella. Nevertheless, it was immensely difficult to comprehend the scope of the loss.

After the close of the war, revolution swept through Germany. However, Ernie stood up to the revolutionaries and refused to abdicate, refused to leave, but nevertheless lost his throne. As a correspondent from *The Times* of London dramatically described:

The sound of the mob in the streets of Darmstadt had reached the Palace for some time, but the Grand

Duke and his wife stayed to meet them and waited in their Throne Room. Eventually the mob, who had broken into the palace, burst down the doors of the Throne Room and streamed in shouting "Down with the Grand Duke!" "Kill the Grand Duke!" As they approached the Grand Duke, those in the front felt ashamed and there was something like a silence in the Throne Room, broken by the Grand Duke, who said in a loud voice: "I can see no Hessian uniforms among you, but you will form a deputation and tell me what you want; in the meantime, as no one has ever been to the palace without being entertained, my wife will make you tea.

The Grand Duke was one of the few formerly reigning German Princes who, after the revolution of 1918, never abdicated either personally or for their families.[9]

during that time. Alice and Andreas were separated, and Alice was in and out of asylums or other living arrangements. The Princesses often visited their grandmother, Victoria at her apartment in Kensington Palace and their uncle and aunt at Darmstadt. There was a consensus in the family that the four girls were pleasant and well brought up. Ernie wrote to Victoria:

Alice's girls are a great source of joy to us. I have scarcely found such cheery kind-hearted and clever little companions as them. We are all under their charms. Such humor and so absolutely unspoiled. Alice can be indeed very proud of them and their delightful common sense which is so refreshing.[11]

****

Prince Louis of Battenberg at sea.

Prince Louis of Battenberg and the Admiralty

Indeed, the family stayed on in Darmstadt and *"remained popular[,] … well loved…"* and well respected. Ernie made Wolfsgarten his chief residence and his young sons grew during the decade of the twenties. The boys had been raised together in the close-knit home, but eventually they took separate paths. Don had an internship at Opel and also studied law and economics as well as estate management. Lu was the more artistic of the two young brothers and studied art, history, and archeology.

A great comfort to Ernie and Onor was the visits that the Greek Princesses made to Darmstadt

During the pre-war years, Louis moved up the ladder, being appointed a vice-admiral in 1908. Louis continued his rise and by 1911 was Second Sea Lord. At this time, he may have been quietly preparing the Royal Navy for coming war while unofficially gathering intelligence on his trips to Germany. Though some were horrified that a German Prince held such a dominant spot in the Navy, he was strongly supported by Winston Churchill, the head of the Admiralty. From the Admiralty's vantage point, it was a tremendous asset that Louis and his wife had such strong contacts with various Royal Houses. Most especially useful was Victoria's Prussian connection: her sister

Irène. It was also helpful that Wilhelm, boastful as ever, lost no opportunity to engage Prince Louis in discussion about all aspects of his navy, and his pride and conceit usually overpowering his discretion.

In the winter of 1912, Louis was appointed First Sea Lord and the Head of the Royal Navy. It was not an appointment without questions because of Louis's German origins, and there was much talk about it with certain members of the Admiralty who did not admire Louis or were envious of his connections with the Royal Families.

From the left: Margarita of Greece and Louise of Battenberg; George and Louis of Battenberg with Theodora of Greece; Victoria of Battenberg; Alice of Greece; Louis Jr. of Battenberg.

The year 1914 had started quietly. Irène and Henry went on a private seven-week tour of South America and Victoria was making her plans for a summer trip to Russia. At the end of June, the calamitous assassination of the Archduke Franz Ferdinand and his unfortunate wife, Sophie, the Duchess of Hohenberg, heralded in the first great war of the twentieth century. Victoria and Irène had the foresight to exchange lady's maids, Victoria sent Irène her German one, while Irène sent her English maid back to England.

That summer, Victoria and her daughter Louise had gone to visit Alix and Ella in Russia. They visited many cities and small towns in the hinterlands, including, ironically, Perm, and Yekaterinburg. It was the beginning of August when Victoria received a frantic telegram from Louis begging her to return to England as soon as possible. Troops were already being mobilized and it was difficult to get out of Russia and make their way home. She left her jewelry with Alix for safekeeping and eventually got on a train and eventually sailed to Stockholm. They arrived in London, at last on August 17, while Louis was much absorbed with the navy. He had refused to demobilize the navy after war games and so they were ready for whatever would come next.

A fact for which both Victoria and Irène were not prepared was that they would never see Ella and Alix again.

****

As war loomed, the accusations that Louis was somehow working for the Germans multiplied. Of course, it was nonsense, but the jealousy that had been building up against Louis from some of his fellows was coming to the surface. This can most strongly be illustrated by the fact that though he had been a naturalized British citizen for over forty years when the Great War started, because of his German surname, lingering accent and wide German familial connection, he was immediately under suspicion. Though, the First Sea Lord, his name continued to be dragged through the mud by some of his naval fellows, satire magazines and the more lurid press. Nevertheless, as mentioned, Louis had the entire Navy mobilized and doing war exercises and because of this, they were on alert. Still, deciding that this derision was a distraction that should be eliminated, he handed in his resignation in October 1914 and though the King was reluctant to accept it, he did so.

Prince Louis spent the war on the Isle of Wight and eventually he and Princess Victoria helped with the rehabilitation of wounded soldiers and naval men. In 1917, along with the rest of the royal family, Louis and his family divested themselves of their German names and titles and became the Mountbattens. Prince Louis became the First Marquess of Milford Haven and Princess Victoria the Marchioness.

Henry was a Grand Admiral of the Prussian Navy...and ironically, a Vice-Admiral of the British Navy. Irène and Henry's sons were both involved in the German war effort. Toddy, impeded by his hemophilia, drove an ambulance, while Bobby was in the Imperial Navy.

****

Georgie and Nada's Wedding

In November 1916, like many other families, the Battenbergs had a war wedding. George, the eldest of Louis and Victoria's boys married Countess Nadejda de Torby. Nadejda's (or "Nada" as she was called in the family) mother was, among other things, a descendent of the great Russian poet Alexander Pushkin. Countess Sophie von Merenberg was born in Switzerland in 1868 and was the product of a morganatic marriage. Her parents were Prince Nikolaus

Georgie and Nada's wedding, London, November 15, 1916. From the left: Georgie, his sister Louise, Nada, Countess Zia de Torby (Nada's sister), and Princesses Xenia and Nina Georgievna of Russia, first cousins of the bride.

Wilhelm of Nassau and Natalia Alexandrovna Pushkin. When Sophie married her husband, it, too was considered a morganatic marriage and she was granted the title of Countess de Torby by her Uncle Adolphe, Grand Duke of Luxembourg.[12] The title was extended to her daughters Anastasia (Zia) and Nada and her son Michael, known in the family as "Boy."[13]

Nada's father was Grand Duke Michael Mikhailovich, known in the family as "Miche-Miche," son of Grand Duke Michael Nikolaevich of Russia and his wife Olga Feodorovna (née Princess Cecilie of Baden). When Miche-Miche was in his early twenties, he seemed to have been on a mission to marry. This made him much different from the other Grand Dukes in the 1890s who mostly enjoyed, gambling, parties and womanizing.[14] Ironically, he had once been an admirer of George's mother, Princess Victoria and her sister, Princess Irène.

This professional suitor then turned his attention to Great Britain and made an unsuccessful bid for Mary or "May" of Teck. May's father, Francis, Duke of Teck, thought that the Russians were bad husbands, which, of course, they were and so Miche-Miche's pursuit was discouraged. Lastly, he tried Princess Louise of Wales, but according to David Chavchavadze, was honest enough to tell her he wasn't marrying her for love. Possibly, he didn't want to end up like so many other Grand Dukes who married for love, or married their unsuitable mistresses and were exiled, stripped of their various ranks, their possessions and titles or whatever punishments the Tsar might mete out – otherwise his search seems to border on the comical.

Georgie and Nada's wedding.

When this feckless young man fell in love with Sophie von Merenberg, he fell hard and despite the irony and her more (from his point of view) dubious antecedents, was determined to marry her. He succeeded in doing so to the utter dismay of his family, and as a matter of fact, when his mother was informed, she reportedly had a heart attack and died. It's a good story, and that's really

all it is. Nevertheless, his choice was not accepted in the Imperial Family. Miche-Miche was indeed stripped of his titles, etc., etc., and the young couple was exiled, spending most of their married life in Great Britain.[15] From that moment on, he made it his project to pester Tsar Nicholas II, his cousin, into making his wife an Imperial Highness[36], which the Tsar refused to do. Barring that, he wrote the unfortunate Tsar constant letters asking for money from his own accounts or just money period with no apparent shame. The Imperial Family considered him, to be blunt, unintelligent and a fool.

The 1916 wedding itself may have also been an effort to get into the good graces of the Tsar and the Imperial Family. Since the Grand Duke knew that the Imperial Family was partial to the Battenbergs, he thought such a marriage might make them look upon his family with more favor and thus send more money.

The truth is that George's family was pleased with the match though they thought very little of Miche-Miche. Prince Louis, when writing to his daughter Louise about the engagement, went so far as to call him an "asp", an intentional spelling error but obvious in its meaning. He also called "Nada's" grandmother a "vulgarian" and marveled that her mother was such a *thoroughly nice, good woman, without a trace of snobbishness or vulgarity*.[17] However, though they all spoke and wrote about Nada very fondly, no one in the immediate family was well acquainted with her. There was much communication about her being a nice girl despite being the daughter of the erstwhile Miche-Miche and many of the family had their say including the Empress, who was thrilled and sent a letter to her husband, the Tsar saying, *"[i]s it possible that Georgie is getting engaged? Seems quite improbable."*[18]

Nada was dark haired, petite and a beautiful debutante who was often photographed and mentioned in the society pages such as *Tatler*. It is very possible that in the insecure and war-torn world in which George lived, she seemed like something of the lovely, now dream-like past they had been forced to leave behind. As well, she was an active and independent girl who played lawn tennis, rode, shot and loved to dance. She was something of a flamboyant creature and very sophisticated, which appealed to George. After her marriage she continued to be a "party girl," loving bright lights and fast cars and often attending these without her husband.

Louis and Victoria, Georgie and Nada with Tatiana and David.

However, that is not to say that the couple were not happy together, they evidently were and understood each other well. Prince Louis' opinion of Nada was reinforced when he visited the newlyweds some months later. His judgment that she was a "darling" was reinforced and he felt that the couple had found their place with each other.[19]

To the outside world, they were considered to be an unconventional couple, since Nada was perhaps a lesbian, or at least bisexual. She figured very prominently in the custody trial of "Little" Gloria Vanderbilt – with allegations that she was having an affair with "Little Gloria's" mother, also a Gloria. It is from this trial that the accusations of lesbianism came. Today we would probably think of Nada as very uninhibited and possibly someone for whom affection was freely and warmly given no matter the sex of the receiver. Though she spent much of

Georgie and Nada vactioning with Tatiana and David in the French Riviera.

her early life in England, she apparently had none of the penchant for public displays exhibited by Nada. Nevertheless, when these scandals and trials happened, the family stood by Nada as well as "the palace."[20]

They had two children, David, who became the 3rd Marquess of Milford Haven (1919-1970), one of Prince Philip's closest friends who served as his best man, and Lady Tatiana Mountbatten (1917-1988) who was, unfortunately, severely mentally challenged. Aside from this sadness, they settled down well enough together and appeared to be a happy and devoted couple. They both shared a love for erotic art and literature and amassed large collections.

Nada, like many other exiled royalties had a great fondness for the French Riviera and there exists many family photographs taken there. An amusing note in *The New York Times* has her winning a Charleston contest with Prince George, later the Duke of Kent. It seems the two of them were dancing together at The Sporting Casino and won the contest and then did a demonstration in front of the other guests of the evening. According to *The Times*, the Prince was in Cannes to improve his French.[21]

Nada and her sister-in-law, Edwina Mountbatten, the wife of Lord Louis, were also very good friends and companions, and traveled together to a great

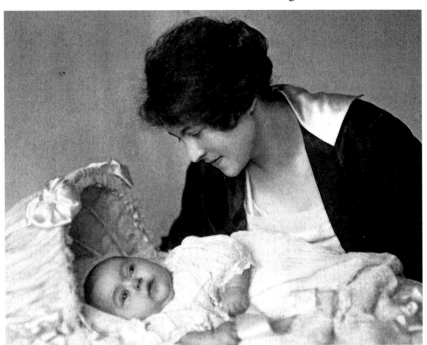

The Countess of Medina, Nada de Torby, and her daughter Tatiana.

many exotic destinations. As Patricia Mountbatten explained, *"Aunt Nada was unconventional and Bohemian in style and she and my mother did some quite adventurous journeys together such as flying across deserts in tiny planes."*[22] They also shared a house together in Malta while their husbands served in the Royal Navy together.

Nada was to survive her husband by nearly twenty-five years. After World War II, she went to live on the French Riviera. She died near Le Cannet at Cannes in January 1963.

****

Alapaievsk and Yekaterinburg

Russia's conduct of the war was nothing short of disastrous. The empire had grossly overestimated its military might and ability to inflict a rapid defeat of Germany and Austria-Hungary. Lackluster military and political leadership, coupled with unimaginable corruption and inadequate supply systems seriously undermined the war effort. Matters worsened when Nicholas II decided to move to the front and set up shop at Moghilev, site of the general headquarters. It was as if the tsar had decided to play soldier, instead of remaining in his capital ensuring that his government was able to support the war effort. In his stead, Alexandra became more involved in the daily governance of Russia. Sycophants and crooks seemed to be the order of the day. Ministers replaced each other with obscene regularity, all while the war became a veritable meat grinder. Millions of soldiers were lost – food shortages worsened the government's hold on the situation. With each defeat, the wedge between the Tsar and people widened.

In early February 1917, workers began striking in Petrograd, the new name given to St Petersburg at the start of the war. On February 22 (Old Style), the workers at the Putilov arms plant announced they were to stage a strike. Further demonstrations took place the following day. Among the workers' demands was bread. By February 25, nearly all industrial enterprises in Petrograd had been shut down

A rare photo of a smiling Alexandra Feodorovna, with Nicholas II and Alexei.

by strikes. Even commercial and service businesses were affected by the work stoppage. Soon enough, students and other workers joined the street protests. When initially informed of the disturbances, Nicholas II and Alexandra discounted them as unpatriotic displays led by leftists. He believed that the troops available in the capital could be relied on to quell the uprising. To his utter astonishment, when he gave the order, troops refused to move on the crowds: officers were shot or disappeared to save their own skin; the military rank and file sided with the protesters. As symbols of tsarism were torn down by the increasingly violent and vociferous crowds, all imperial authority collapsed. Nicholas II did not help the situation by proroguing the Duma that very day in an effort to retake the reigns of the government.

Tsar Nicholas II and Tsesarevich Alexei during the Great War.

By March 1, the capital, the empire, was lost. The imperial train was ordered to return to Petrograd, but Nicholas II did not make it past Pskov, where the military chiefs and some Duma deputies suggested that only his abdication would prevent total chaos. He did so the following day, not just on behalf of himself, but also on behalf of his son Alexei. The imperial mantle landed on the reluctant shoulders of Grand Duke Michael Alexandrovich, who was quick to discover that his succession to the throne lacked the necessary support. On March 3, 1917, Michael declined

The Alexander Palace, Tsarskoe Selo.

the imperial crown, thus bringing the Romanov Dynasty to an ignominious end.

Addressed simply as either "Nicholas Alexandrovich" or "Nicholas Romanov," the former tsar finally reached the Alexander Palace nearly a week after his abdication. He and Alexandra spent time alone. There was much crying and endless tears as the magnitude of their plight became real. A provisional government slowly reestablished control over Petrograd. Then, it placed the Imperial Family under house arrest within the confines of their beloved home in Tsarskoe Selo. While the Romanovs had total privacy inside the palace, outings in the grounds were strictly regulated. Many of the imperial household staff chose to remain in service as they were devoted to the family.

Later that summer, as Russia's military efforts against the Central Powers continued to falter, a Bolshevik uprising took place in Petrograd. Alexander Kerensky, who had assumed control of the government, feared that even though the Bolsheviks were defeated, they could easily reach Tsarskoe Selo and threaten the security of the Imperial Family. He ordered their relocation to the town of Tobolsk in Western Siberia. The town was remote and separated by considerable distance from the nearest railway line. The Romanovs left the Alexander Palace on August 13. They traveled by rail to Tyumen, at the eastern foot of the Ural Mountains. From there, they boarded two ferries, finally reaching Tobolsk on August 19. There, they lived in the Governor's Mansion, a comfortable large house, while their staff and servant were housed nearby. Nicholas not only kept informed of events in Petrograd, but also occupied himself reading books and chopping wood. Alexandra, suffering from many ailments, spent longer periods on a wheelchair while doing needlepoint. The grand duchesses helped their parents, but also tended to a small vegetable garden the family had planted. Alexei found confinement

Nicholas II and Anastasia Nikolaevna chopping wood with staff and guards.

difficult as he longed for physical activity and freedom. In the meantime, life continued in relative peace while events outside the walls of the Governor's Mansion the political situation worsened.

In October 1917, a second Bolshevik coup attempt succeeded in overthrowing the government. Kerensky fled and Vladimir Lenin and his ilk became Russia's new bloodthirsty overlords. Persecution of the Romanovs and aristocrats began in earnest. In faraway Tobolsk,

Nicholas II and Alexei sawing wood in the Governor's Mansion, Tobolsk.

Nicholas II and his family were no exception. By March of the following year, ill-disciplined and disrespectful communist troops replaced the acquiescent guards who kept an eye over the imprisoned Romanovs. Further restrictions were implemented and house arrest basically turned into prison. From Moscow, the Bolsheviks sent Vassily Yakovlev to oversee the Imperial Family. Some within the new Russian government wanted Nicholas II brought to Moscow and put on trial. By late April, Nicholas II was informed that he and his family were to be moved to Yekaterinburg. As Alexei was recovering from a fall, Alexandra left him in the company of Olga, Tatiana, and Anastasia. She, with Maria, journeyed to Yekaterinburg alongside her husband. The remaining Romanovs would travel when Alexei was strong enough to venture out of his confinement.

The tortuous journey to Yekaterinburg began on April 25. En route, the traveling party had to endure long rides in four-wheeled carriages, overnight stops, frozen rivers, and even an abduction attempt by the Yekaterinburg Red Guard. Fearful for his wards' safety if they fell into the hands of the Yekaterinburg Soviet, Yakovlev obtained permission from Moscow to redirect his route to Omsk. His efforts failed after an all-out campaign by the Yekaterinburg soviet to lobby Moscow for custody of the Romanovs. Five days after leaving Tobolsk, exhausted and consumed with worry for the unknown, Nicholas II and his retinue arrived in Yekaterinburg, which was to be their last

The Ipatiev House, Yekaterinburg.

The Church on Spilled Blood, built on the site of the Ipatiev House.

destination. The children left behind in Tobolsk were able to reach Yekaterinburg on May 23. There, the Romanovs were under house arrest in the former home of a rich merchant called the Ipatiev House.

Meanwhile, the situation within Russia continued to worsen. The country was quickly falling into civil war. An anti-Bolshevik revolt led by the Czechoslovak Legion approached Yekaterinburg. The local Bolshevik soviet became alarmed as they feared that the Romanovs could be freed by the revolution's enemies. This was the death sentence for many members of the Imperial Family. The first one to fall was Grand Duke Michael Alexandrovich, who with his loyal secretary Nicholas Johnson, was executed outside Perm, where he had lived in relative peace for some time. Then, on the evening of July 17, 1918, the prisoners of the Ipatiev House were assassinated by the Bolsheviks. Their remains were taken away and buried in a forest, where they remained hidden for decades. The Ipative House was later demolished under orders of Boris Yeltsin, when he served as mayor of Yekaterinburg. Later, a majestic church was built on the spot and dedicated to the memory of the Romanov martyrs.

Ella, though a beloved figure in the poorest sections of Moscow and the Mother Superior of her Convent of SS Martha and Mary, was not spared the atrocities of the Bolsheviks. Arrested in Moscow in early 1918, she was also sent to the Urals. Along with one of her loyal nuns, she was taken to Perm and from there to Yekaterinburg, where she stayed a short while. Other Romanovs joined her, including: Grand Duke Sergei Mikhailovich; Princes Ioan, Konstantin, and Igor Konstantinovich (sons of the late Grand Duke Konstantin Konstantinovich Jr.); and Prince Vladimir Pavlovich Paley (half-brother of Marie Pavlovna Jr. and Dmitri Pavlovich). From Yekaterinburg they were all taken to Alapaievsk on May 20. They were housed in the Napolnaya School, located on the outskirts of town. On July 18, the prisoners were awakened and driven in carts to an abandoned mineshaft near the village of Siniachikha. They were physically abused and thrown down the pit while still alive, with the exception of Sergei Mikhailovich,

The Napolnaya School, Alapaievsk (2006).

who was shot in the head for resisting. Hand grenades were hurled. To finish off their dastardly deed, the executors shoved brushwood into the shaft and set it alight. The Romanov remains were later discovered by soldiers of the White Army. The bodies were kept in a church in Alapaievsk until advancing Red troops forced their keepers to take them eastward, eventually crossing the border into China.

****

In early November, of 1918, Irène and Henry along with Toddy, their eldest, fled from Kiel in their car. They were fleeing the soldiers of the German Revolution and the car was fired upon. According to *The Times* of London Irène

Henry and Irène of Prussia with their sons Waldemar and Sigismund.

was wounded in the arm and a bullet actually went through Henry's coat. After this rather hair-raising escape, the couple eventually returned to their residence in Hemmelmark almost as though nothing had happened and all was seemingly peaceful once again, though deprived of their titles. In fact, wrote the *The Times*, the German Post office refused to deliver letters that were addressed "your royal highness" but only ones, in Irène's case, addressed to "Frau von Preussen".

The remaining members of the Hessian Family, Irène, Ernie, and Victoria, continued to struggle with the rumors and misinformation that began to seep through to Germany and England about the fate of the Imperial Family and Ella. There were endless differing accounts of the events, and people came forward with new and miraculous escapes, or an even grislier version of their sad ends – all incredulous inventions. Later, of course,

between Irène, Victoria, the Dowager Empress, and her daughters, now living in exile in Denmark, they would have to contend with all the imposters parading themselves before the world. They claimed to be the Grand Duchess Anastasia, or Marie, or Olga, or Tatiana, and even, Alexei, who couldn't have possibly survived such an ordeal. Irène and Ernie, in particular, would have to deal with the infamous Anna Anderson case.[23]

Finally, the remaining Hessian siblings had to accept the fact that Alexandra and her family were gone, as was the Grand Duchess Elisabeth. When they discovered that Ella's body was actually in Peking (Beijing), sister Victoria and her husband made arrangements to have the body buried in Jerusalem, as Ella had always wanted. It was Victoria's intention to go to Rome at the end of the year, and, there wait for word that the bodies were on their journey from China to the Levant. However, before she left, certain events occurred.

After all the bad news coming from all sides, one happy note in July of 1919, was the marriage of Bobby, Prince Sigismund, Irène's younger son, and Princess Charlotte Agnes of Saxe-Altenburg, Duchess of Saxony. They had two children, Princess Barbara born at Hemmelmark in 1920, and Prince Alfred born in Guatemala in 1924. Princess Barbara later married Duke Christian Ludwig of Mecklenburg and Irène made her granddaughter her heiress. The following month, Toddy, Prince Waldemar, married Princess Calixta of Lippe. She was a first cousin of Prince Bernhard, who was the father of another Prince Bernhard, who in 1937

Prince Sigismund and Princess Charlotte Agnes of Prussia.

married Princess Juliana of the Netherlands.

Afterward, Victoria and Louis Battenberg attended to the burial of Ella in Jerusalem, she wrote to both Irène and Ernie letters detailing the events. Irène was very moved by the scene at Port Said when Victoria and Louis met the coffins and thought the descriptions of them resting in the little Greek Orthodox Church on a candle lit night, beautiful.[24]

In 1921, Louis was made Admiral of the Fleet on the Retired list. This was thought to be some compensation for the events of October 1914. Louis died at the Naval and Military Club September 1921 at the age of sixty-seven, probably of heart problems.

At war's end, there was a slight bitterness in the relationship between the two sisters, but it healed as well as could be expected, though, since neither traveled as they had before, they saw each other very infrequently. In these circumstances, Irène and Ernie would not be present at family events in England in the 1920s. They missed, for example Victoria's daughter, Louise's marriage to Crown Prince Gustaf Adolf of Sweden. Any anger or bitterness about the war seemed to be kept between the remaining two sisters and was never laid at Ernie's door. Irène, however, didn't hesitate when she wrote to Victoria, to place the blame:

All the sorrow that fell upon our dear ones originated through the net that was systematically begin drawn round us & Austria for years – as we now know! Europe & the World has to thank the so-called Entente for the war & all its consequences. In the End Truth! Will triumph![25]

What Victoria thought of this remark can only be imagined.

****

Meanwhile, Henry and Irène continued their quiet existence. In the 1920s there was barely a ripple in their lives, which had always been calm except for some of Irène's health troubles. However at the beginning of 1929, Henry became ill and died several months later on

Prince Waldemar and Princess Calixta of Prussia.

Prince Henry of Prussia.

April 21. There were newspaper articles asserting that Henry actually had throat cancer like his father, but, according to his son, Toddy, the cause was angina. He had remained, however, a life-long smoker. *The Times* obituary printed an homage to the man they called Germany's *Prince Charming* and praised for what seemed like an assertion of his Englishness during the war and after the German republican revolution. They wrote:

When the dynasty fell he said that he could not, in honour, forswear his house and family; but he promised to give no trouble and kept his word. Republican Germany was well-advised to leave him in peace, and to show that it had no quarrel with a man whose character had been formed from the best qualities of the fallen Hohenzollerns.[26]

Ernie and Onor were there to comfort Irène, but Victoria was not. Victoria had frequently visited Irène at Hemmelmark in the decade of the twenties and would continue to do so – later that summer, as well as continuing to visit Ernie at Wolfsgarten. However, it is possible she felt that she did not want to be seen in such a public fashion, at what became quite a large event in Germany. Maybe the lessons of 1914 were crowding in on her at this volatile time. Indeed, there was virtually no British presence at this grandchild of Queen Victoria's funeral.

****

Dickie and Edwina

The last Battenberg born, Prince Louis Francis Albert Victor Nicholas, arrived on June 25, 1900. "Dickie" as he was called was the last child of Prince and Princess Louis Battenberg. He was the product of a happy childhood with loving parents. Of course, his father, Prince Louis was absent a great deal in the Royal Navy due to his service, but Princess Victoria spent a great deal of time with this child. In fact, she was his first teacher.[27]

He and his sister, Princess Louise, were Princess Victoria's companions, as they traveled, visiting his Aunt Alix, his Aunt Irène or his Uncle Ernie.

Prince Henry and Princess Irène of Prussia.

Prince Louis of Battenberg.

As mentioned, his mother taught him his lessons as a child and he was well known in the family for loving little animals and being attached to his teddy bear, *Sonnenbein*. He was raised with his cousins, the Grand Duchesses of Russia and the Tsesarevich as well as his Hessian and Prussian cousins. He spoke about a "crush" on the Grand Duchess Marie Nikolaevna and told his mother he planned to marry her when he grew up. He told the story that throughout his life and that he traveled with a photograph of the ill-fated Marie.

In 1910, the youngster attended Locker's Park Preparatory school and from there went on to the Royal Naval College at Osborne. After passing out of Osborne he continued at the Royal Naval College at Dartmouth. One of the most traumatic incidents of Dickie's young life was when his father resigned from the Royal Navy in 1914. The story goes that he stood at attention to the British flag with tears running down his face. True or not, it affected him deeply and could be seen as an impetus for his constant striving, his achievements and his research and private publication of his family tree, to which he included as many royal ties as was humanly possible, all the way back to Charlemagne.

Midshipman Battenberg, as he was called, left Dartmouth in 1916 and saw no real action during World War I. However, during this time, there was an event that made an enormous impression on the young man. In 1917, George V announced that he was giving up his German names and titles and requested that other family members do the same. The Battenbergs, considering themselves a British family, pondered long and hard on what Anglicized name they should take. They eventually settled on a sort of translation of their name – Mountbatten. Dickie's father became the First Marquess of Milford Haven, his older brother, George became the Earl of Medina and Dickie became plain Lord Louis Mountbatten. The Battenberg title, after the death of Princess Anna of Battenberg became extinct, and *"fell back into its old obscurity."*[27] These events doubtless seemed to chip away at Mountbatten's sense of his own nobility.

At the conclusion of the war, the young man went to Oxford to study English literature and traveled with

Princess Victoria and her son Dickie.

his good friend, the Prince of Wales (the future Edward VIII, later the Duke of Windsor). Dickie was one of the *"bright young things"* of the early 1920s, tall, handsome, and full of energy and great charm. He, like so many young men, fell in and out of love with great regularity, however, he also had the problem that his father and uncles had – he would need to earn his living. Therefore, it appeared that his choice of bride would have to be someone of financial substance.

She came in the person of Edwina Ashley, the daughter of Wilfred

sincerely worried about the fact that Edwina was so wealthy, and Dickie was relatively poor. However, Dickie soon proposed and was accepted by Edwina. In Dickie's mother, whom Edwina called Aunt Victoria, Edwina had at last found the mother she had lost. The two women had an excellent relationship throughout their lives and Edwina truly loved her.

They were married with all due pomp and royal attendance at St Margaret's Westminster on July 18, 1922. They went on a fabled honeymoon, the first part to stay with

The wedding of Lord Louis Mountbatten and Miss Edwina Ashley, July 18, 1922. From the left: Miss Mary Ashley, Princess Margarita of Greece, Miss Joan Pakenham, Princess Sophie of Greece, the Groom and Bride, The Prince of Wales, Lady Mary Ashley-Cooper, and Princesses Theodora and Cecilie of Greece.

Ashley, First Baron Mount Temple and Maud, Sir Ernest Cassel's daughter. Edwina, as the heiress to a huge fortune was incredibly wealthy, she also had the added charm of being lovely, elegant, intelligent, and relatively unspoiled. She spent most of her childhood at her father's home, Broadlands, which later became the Mountbatten family home. Her mother died when she was ten years old and several years after that Wilfred remarried. With the proverbial stepmother in the wings, Edwina requested and was allowed to live with her grandfather at Brook House in Park Lane.

Dickie was strongly attracted and soon was introducing Edwina to his family. Prince Louis approved wholeheartedly, though he thought Dickie too young to marry. Dickie's parents were

royal cousins in Europe and the second leg was a thorough motoring tour of the United States. It was there, welcomed by such Hollywood Royalty as Douglas Fairbanks, Mary Pickford and Charlie Chaplin (all of whom became lifelong friends) where Dickie learned the technical side of movie making. It was also at this time that he began a lifelong love affair with the United States. While in Hollywood, the newlyweds starred in a fun little film called *Nice and Friendly*[28] with their new friend Charlie Chaplin and a supporting cast. Afterward, Charlie made it clear that as an actor, Dickie made a better sailor! The couple were feted and celebrated wherever they went and were very popular in America.

Chapter VIII

The Next Generation Settles Down and Tragedy Strikes Again

The Greek Princesses

Due to the failure of their parents' marriage, the remaining Hessian sisters, Victoria and Irène, as well as Ernie, focused on the young Greek Princesses and the little prince, Philip. As the girls were entering the age when settling them was of tantamount importance, this became a matter of great interest for all involved. They were pretty, intelligent, well-traveled, polyglots, and exquisitely raised with a sense of *noblesse*

In 1922, Prince Andreas with his family in Greece. From the left: Princess Alice, Princess Theodora, Princess Cecilie, Prince Andreas holding Philip, Princess Sophie, and Princess Margarita.

oblige that was admirable guiven the instability the famkily experienced. They had lived all over Europe and were always willing to make the most of whatever situation they found themselves, whether living in Athens, or exiled in Paris. The absence of their mother was deeply felt by them, but also the need their father had for company. All were very close to their grandmother Victoria and their English relations.

Interestingly, all four of Andreas and Alice's daughters were to marry German princes – all close relations. The first of the weddings of these four lovely girls took place in December 1930: Sophie or "Tiny" as she was known, and the youngest of the four girls married Prince Christoph of Hesse-Kassel. He was one of the six sons of Landgrave Friedrich Karl of Hesse-Lassel and his wife, the former Princess Margarethe of Prussia, youngest child of Kaiser Friedrich III and his wife Victoria. Christoph was not only Sophie's second cousin once-removed, but both were descendants of Queen Victoria and Prince Albert. They had five children: Christina (1933-2011), married firstly to Prince Andrej of Yugoslavia and secondly to Robert Floris van Eyck; Dorothea (b. 1934), married to Prince Friedrich Karl of Windisch-Graetz;

The wedding of Prince Christoph of Hesse-Kassel and Princess Cecilie of Greece – Kronberg-im-Taunus, December 15, 1930.

Karl (b. 1937), married to Countess Yvonne Szapáry von Muraszombath; Rainer (b. 1939), unmarried; and Clarissa (b. 1944), who was married for a few years to Claude-Jean Derrien, before divorcing.[1] Christoph died in an air crash in the Apennines in October 1943. Sophie was pregnant with their fifth child at the time of his death. After becoming a war-widow, Sophie married Prince Georg Wilhelm of Hannover. Sophie's third cousin through Queen Victoria, Georg Wilhelm was the son of Duke Ernst August of Brunswick and his Prussian wife Viktoria Luise, herself a first cousin of Sophie's late husband. The bridal couple were also second cousins through King Christian IX of Denmark. Georg Wilhelm was a brother of Queen Frederica, consort of King Paul of the Hellenes, hence her children were grew up in close contact with the Greek Royal Family. Sophie and her second husband had a further three children: Welf (1947-1981), who married Wibke van Gusteren and died while living in an ashram in India; Georg (b. 1949), married to Victoria Bee; and Friederike (b. 1954), married to Jerry Cyr.[2]

Closer to home, though, was that another of the Greek girls, Cecilie, became very interested in her cousin, Don

Princess Sophie and most of her children. From the left: Georg of Hannover, Rainer of Hesse, Christina of Yugoslavia with her daughter Tatiana, Dorothea and Clarissa of Hesse, Sophie with daughter Friederike, and Welf of Hannover, c. 1957.

The wedding of Hereditary Grand Duke Donatus (Don) of Hesse and by Rhine and Princess Cecilie of Greece – Darmstadt, February 2, 1931.

of Hesse. She had visited with her grandmother, Victoria on several occasions and there were letters back and forth between Ernie and Victoria in which Victoria seemed to be "feeling Ernie out" about Don's feelings for Cecilie. Since Ernie and Onor had such a positive view of all the Greek girls, they put no objections in the way of their engagement. They married in February 1931 with Victoria, Irène, Prince Andreas and young Prince Philip, among many more in attendance. *The Times* remarked upon the great interest by the inhabitants of Darmstadt and personal popularity the family continued to enjoy.[3] Cecilie became very active in the Grand Duchy taking over the presidency of the *Alice Frauen Verein* and other charities. The couple had three children: Ludwig; Alexander; and, Johanna.

Two months after Cecilie and Don's wedding, her older sister Margarita married their cousin Hereditary Prince Gottfried of Hohenlohe-Langenburg. He was the eldest, and only surviving son, of Fürst Ernst II and of his wife Alexandra (née Edinburgh), one of Ducky's sisters. Furthermore, Gottfried's mother was a first cousin of Victoria, both being granddaughters of Queen Victoria. The ceremony and wedding reception, attended by a large contingent of the Royal

The wedding of Hereditary Prince Gottfried of Hohenlohe-Langenburg and Princess Margarita of Greece – Langenburg, April 20, 1931.

Mob, were celebrated at the groom's ancestral home, Schloß Langenburg. It was a truly grand affair attended by family and royalty from near and far.

Gottfried and Margarita firstly settled at Schloß Weikersheim, another Hohenlohe-Langenburg property, located some thirty minutes' drive from Langenburg. While there, Margarita tried her best to become involved in local charities, quickly gaining admiration and appreciation from the population of this ancestral Hohenlohe area. These feelings were shared in an interesting letter, written by her pleased mother-in-law to her daughter Marie Melita of Schleswig-Holstein. They had six children: a stillborn daughter in 1933; Kraft (1935-2004), who succeeded his father as Fürst of Hohenlohe-Langenburg in 1960 and married twice (Princess Charlotte of Croÿ and Irma Pospesch); Beatrix (1936-1998), unmarried; Andreas (b. 1938), married to Princess Louise of Schönburg-Waldenburg; and twins Rupprecht and Albrecht, born in 1944. Rupprecht died by suicide in 1978 and was childless. Albrecht married Maria-Hildegard Fischer in 1976 and had a son, Ludwig, that same year. Albrecht also died by suicide in 1992.[4]

The children of Gottfried and Margarita in the early 1950s. From the left: Albrecht, Rupprecht, Kraft, Ludwig, and Beatrix.

Wedding of Hereditary Prince Gottfried of Hohenlohe-Langenburg and Princess Margarita of Greece, Schloß Langenburg, April 20, 1931 – Front row, from the left: Cecilie of Hesse and by Rhine, Sophie of Hesse-Kassel, Louise of Sweden, Victoria Milford Haven, Andreas of Greece, the Bride and Groom, Alexandra of Hohenlohe-Langenburg, Marie of Romania, Victoria Feodorovna of Russia, Helen of Greece, Archimandrite Legaiki, Marie Melita of Schleswig-Holstein. Second row, same order: Captain v. Zwidineck, Ludwig of Hesse and by Rhine, Elisabeth of Greece, Count v. Oppersdorf, Irma of Hohenlohe-Langenburg, Berthold of Baden, Alexandra of Hohenlohe-Langenburg, Theodora of Baden, Ernst II of Hohenlohe-Langenburg, Christoph of Hesse-Kassel, George of Greece, Feodore and Emich of Leiningen, Viktoria of Solms-Rödelheim, Frau von Raven, Rosa of Hohenlohe-Schillingsfürst, Mr. and Mrs. von Haldenwang. Going up the stairs: Don of Hesse and by Rhine, Karl of Leiningen, Moritz of Hohenlohe-Schillingsfürst, Maria Kirillovna of Russia (married to Karl of Leiningen), Margarita of Bourbon-Parma, Heinrich XLV Reuß, Franz Joseph of Hohenlohe-Schillingsfürst, Kira Kirillovna of Russia, Karl of Hohenlohe-Bartenstein, Johannes of Hohenlohe-Jagstberg, and René of Bourbon Parma.

The Hohenlohe-Langenburg family retains very strong connections with the House of Windsor. They are often among the guests at major royal events, while also being invited privately to visit The Queen and Prince Philip. For example, Fürst Kraft, his sister Beatrix and daughter Cècile, along with Princess Margaret of Hesse, attended the wedding of The Prince of Wales to Lady Diana Spencer in 1981. In 2004, Prince Philip was among the mourners who attended the memorial service in Langenburg for his nephew Fürst Kraft, a gathering attended by hundreds of royals. Furthermore, several years ago, Langenburg was one of the stops on a private farewell visit Prince Philip, accompanied by Lord and Lady Romsey (Countess Mountbatten's son and his wife), made to his German relations. In April 2011, Fürst Philipp and Fürstin Saskia were among the German relations invited to the wedding of the Duke and Duchess of Cambridge. The Prince of Wales has also visited Langenburg as both he and his cousin Fürst Philipp are very prominent figures in the movement toward sustainability. Fürst Philipp, who speaks English fluently and visits Great Britain often, is the current head of this prominent and well-connected mediatized dynasty. He is the late Fürst Kraft's only son, and is married to the former Saskia Binder by whom he has three children: Max Leopold, Gustav, and Marita.

The wedding of Margrave Berthold of Baden and Princess Theodora of Greece – Schloß Salem, August 17, 1931.

The last marriage to happen in quick succession was that of Theodora, the most "regal" of the sisters. She was the second daughter of Andreas and Alice. She married Margrave Berthold of Baden (1906-1963), only son of Margrave Max of Baden, last German Imperial Chancellor, and Marie Louise of Hannover, an aunt of Princess Sophie of Greece's second husband. The couple were also closely related as her father and his mother were first cousins as grandchildren of King Christian IX and Queen Louise of Denmark. Theodora and Berthold had three children: Margarita (1932-2013), whose marriage to Prince Tomislav of Yugoslavia ended in divorce after more than two decades; Maximilian (b. 1933), who married Archduchess Valerie of Austria-Tuscany, a great-granddaughter of Emperor Franz Joseph; and Ludwig (b. 1937), who married Princess Marianne of Auersperg-Breunner.[5] All three Baden siblings, who are frequently seen visiting their English royal cousins, have descendants. They are also regularly seen at major royal events around Europe, often in the company of Queen Sofía of Spain, their cousin.

****

Mountbatten's Girls – Patricia and Pamela

Edwina and Dickie's first child was Patricia Edwina Victoria, born on Valentine's Day, 1924 at Brook House in London.[6] Pamela Carmen Louise was born April 19, 1929[7] in Barcelona Spain. The girl's childhood was filled with the

The children of Berthold and Theodora in the early 1940s. From the left: Max, Ludwig, and Margarita.

166

Prince Andreas of Greece and his children, Schloß Salem, August 17, 1931. From the left: Prince Christoph and Princess Sophie of Hesse-Kassel, Hereditary Prince Gottfried and Hereditary Princess Margarita of Hohenlohe-Langenburg, Prince Andreas, Margravine Theodora and Margrave Berthold of Baden, Hereditary Grand Duchess Princess Cecilie and Hereditary Grand Duke Donatus of Hesse and by Rhine, and Prince Philip of Greece.

The Prince of Wales and Lord Louis Mountbatten.

royal, aristocratic and even Hollywood elites of the day with whom their parents socialized. Patricia and her sister had a similar peripatetic childhood as their father did with Victoria Milford Haven. They traveled a great deal with their mother and father, and various friends and partners of their parents. There was even an instance, recounted in Pamela's book *Daughter of Empire*, where Edwina didn't actually know where the little girls were, but eventually found them in Switzerland with their nanny. It was a bit eccentric, but amazingly it worked well for the entire family.

In July 1940, both girls were sent to the United States because Mountbatten was concerned that their Jewish great-grandfather might put them in greater peril should the Nazi's invade. More likely a greater peril was being a member of a well-known aristocratic and royally connected Naval family. Nonetheless, the two girls stayed with Mrs. Cornelius Vanderbilt at her New York City mansion and also at her summer home in Newport, Rhode Island. They attended classes at Miss Hewitt's in the city and Patricia remained in the States until she had finished school. Pamela returned earlier.

When Patricia returned in 1943, she joined the Women's Royal Naval Service. By the close of the war, Patricia was stationed on her father's staff in Southeast Asia. It was here that she met the man she would marry, John Ulick Knatchbull.

Knatchbull, who would later become 7th Baron Brabourne, was born in India on November 9, 1924.[8] He was the second son of Michael Knatchbull, 5th Baron Brabourne and his wife, Lady Doreen Knatchbull and the grandson of the 6th Marquess of Sligo. He was educated at Eton and Oxford and inherited the title when the SS shot his elder brother, Norton, the 6th Baron, in 1943 after attempting to escape from a prisoner-of-war train. Young Brabourne was an officer in the Coldstream Guards in France and Mountbatten's Aide-de-Camp in Southeast Asia. He met his future wife, Lady Patricia, as she always liked to be called, in 1946 when they were both on Dickie's staff. They had much in common including the fact that Brabourne's father had been Governor

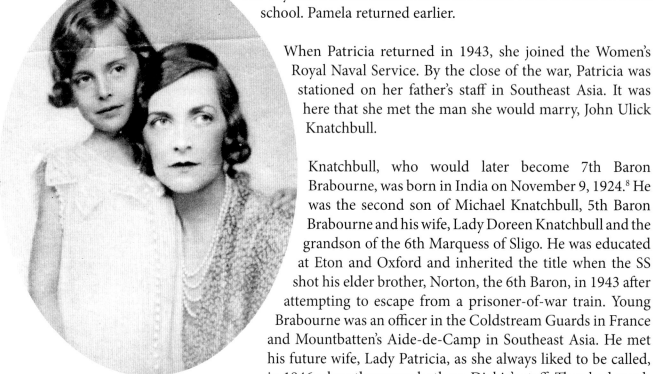

Edwina with her daughter Patricia.

of Bombay and then Governor of Bengal.

Patricia and John were married in October 1946 at Romsey Abbey with King George VI and Queen Elizabeth in attendance. Patricia's bridesmaids were The Princess Elizabeth, Princess Margaret, Princess Alexandra of Kent and her sister Pamela. Among the multitude of guests were Victoria Milford Haven, her daughter, Princess Andreas of Greece, and Lady Patricia Ramsay (the former Princess Patricia of Connaught). As an interesting side note, their wedding was the first occasion that the adult Princess Elizabeth and Prince Philip were photographed together.

Lady Patricia shared an extraordinarily close and special relationship with her father. Their long and enduring connection stemmed, Mountbatten wrote, from the moment he laid eyes on her as an infant. Philip Zeigler's biography of Lord Mountbatten is peppered with the confidences and correspondence they shared. They

Pamela and Patricia Mountbatten.

were in touch constantly when out of the country and telephoned daily when home. Mountbatten had an excellent relationship with Knatchbull, as well: he had, he often said, gained a son and not lost an extremely beloved daughter. Brabourne had a distinguished career in the film business producing such films as: *A Passage to India, Romeo and Juliet, Murder on the Orient Express* and *Death on the Nile.*

The Knatchbulls had a long and happy marriage that lasted until John's death in 2005 at the age of eighty. It was marred by the stillborn death of their son, Anthony in April 1952 and the assassinations of Lord Mountbatten, Lady Brabourne, and their son Nicholas in August 1979.

While in the hospital, recovering from the extensive wounds she suffered during the bombing, Patricia realized that her son Nicholas was absent. *"I think Nicky dead,"* she scribbled on a piece of paper, which she handed to her sister. Pamela confirmed that he had died. *"I was so overwhelmed by grief for Nicky, who was just on the threshold of his life, that I began to feel guilty that I was not able to grieve for my father, whom*

Lord and Lady Brabourne, Norton and Patricia.

The wedding of Lord Brabourne and Lady Patricia Mountbatten. Standing in back, from the left: The Duchess of Kent, Lord Mountbatten, the Groom, King George VI, Lady Mountbatten, and Squadron Leader Charles Duqdale Harris-St John. Middle row, same order: Doreen Lady Brabourne, the Dowager Marchioness of Milford Haven, the Bride, Queen Elizabeth, and the Marchioness of Sligo. The bridesmaids were: Lady Pamela Mountbatten, Princess Alexandra of Kent, Princess Margaret, and Princess Elizabeth.

I really adored, in the same way," she later said.[9]

Patricia became The Countess Mountbatten of Burma in her own right by special remainder after her father's death and she and her husband were one of the rare couples who were both peers in their own right. Lady Patricia harbored no bitterness or anger against the IRA, who had committed the heinous act. She did interviews in recent years talking about the event and had enough of a sense of humor to say that it was her *"IRA face lift."*[10]

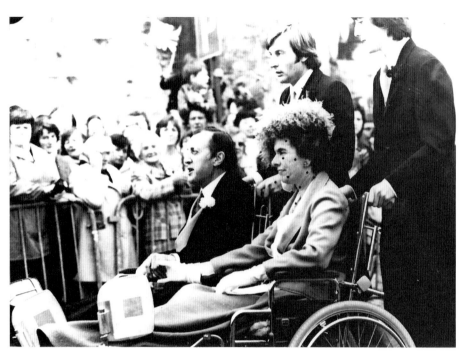

Aided by their sons Michael-John and Philip, the Brabournes heroically attended their eldest son's wedding barely two months after the IRA bombing that ripped the family apart,

Lady Patricia quietly served her country in many different roles during her adult life. Besides being Deputy Lieutenant of the County of Kent, she became Colonel-in-Chief of the Princess Patricia's Canadian Light Infantry in 1974. She replaced her cousin and godmother, Princess Patricia of Connaught who was her grandmother's first cousin. She served in this capacity until 2007 when she herself was replaced by Canadian politician and journalist Adrienne Clarkson.

Besides raising an extensive family and the many different responsibilities in her life, Patricia had a long and abiding interest in her family's history and complex continental relationships. It was well known among historians that she was extraordinarily helpful to anyone of repute who was interested in the family. She was always friendly, accessible and patient. Lady Patricia passed away on June 13, 2017 at the age of ninety-three.[11]

Patricia and John had eight children: Norton (born 1947) who married Penelope Eastwood and had three children; Michael-

The Countess Mountbatten of Burma with her godson The Prince of Wales.

The baptism of Norton Knatchbull (1947). From the left: Lord Mountbatten, Lord Brabourne, Dorren Lady Brabrourne, Patricia holding her son, the Marquess of Milford Haven, Prince Philip, and Crown Princess Louise of Sweden.

John (born 1950) who married Melissa Clare Owen, divorced 1997, married Penelope Coates (1999) had two children; Anthony (b./d. 1952); Joanna (born 1955) married Baron Hubert Pernot du Breuil, divorced 1995, married Azriel Zuckerman and has two children; Amanda (born 1957) married Charles Vincent Ellingworth and has three children; Philip (born 1961) married Atalanta Cowan divorced and married Wendy Amanda Leach and has four children; Nicholas (1964-1979); and Timothy (born 1964) married to Isabella Julia Norman and has five children.[12]

The current Earl Mountbatten of Burma is Norton Knatchbull, who also became the 8th Baron Brabourne at the death of his father. He was born in London on October 8, 1947.[13] One of his godparents was Prince Philip. He was educated at Gordonstoun School and later at the University of Kent. Two months after the IRA tragedy, he married Penelope Meredith Eastwood, the daughter of Reginald Wray Frank Eastwood, founder of the Angus Steakhouse chain in the United Kingdom and Marian Elizabeth Eastwood. Norton and Penny, as she

The Brabournes: Norton, Michael-John, Joanna, Amanda, Philip, Nicholas, and Timothy.

is commonly known, had three children: Nicholas (b. 1981), the current Lord Romsey; Alexandra (b. 1982), who is involved in the management the family estate at Broadlands; and Leonora (1986-1991).[14] Lady Alexandra Knatchbull, who married in 2016 Thomas Hooper, has one son, Inigo Norton Sebastian Mountbatten Hooper (b. 2017).[15]

Some years ago, Earl Mountbatten left his wife and family to live in the Bahamas. However, he has since returned and is thought to be unwell. Countess Mountbatten does most of the duties of the Earldom, which include running the family seat, Broadlands and the role of High Steward of Romsey. Norton and Penny's two surviving children are diametrically opposed in many areas. Nicholas, Lord Romsey, a contemporary of the Duke of Cambridge, as well as a godson of The Prince of Wales, has spent most of his adolescence and young adulthood struggling with addiction issues. After several hard starts, Nicholas seems to be on the mend. He is a musician and and artist. In 2019, there were rumors that he was engaged to be married, but no

Lord Romsey.

wedding date was released. Lady Alexandra, is a forensic accountant working with a major firm of U.S. business consultants. It is more likely that though Nicholas will succeed to the title, Alexandra may be entrusted to run Broadlands, the family home.

Their third child, Leonora Louise Marie Elizabeth died at the age of five of kidney cancer. She was buried on the grounds and the family set up a fund in her name called the Leonora Children's Cancer Fund, later changed to The Edwina Mountbatten and Leonora Children's Foundation.[16]

After Pamela's sojourn in the United States, she returned to England and after the war's conclusion accompanied her parents to the Viceroy's House in Delhi, India when Lord Mountbatten was the last Viceroy. It was during this time that she also served as a bridesmaid for her cousin Princess Elizabeth at her wedding in 1947. She returned permanently to England in 1948. Pamela accompanied the Royal couple on their various trips as a lady-in-waiting and was with them in Kenya, during the 1952 Commonwealth Tour, when King

Lord and Lady Romsey with their children: Nicholas, Alexandra, and Leonora.

Left: The Earl and Countess Mountbatten of Burma.

Above: Patricia, 2nd Countess Mountbatten of Burma, from a postcard she sent to one of the authors.

Below, back row, from left: Secretary of the Duke of Edinburgh; Prince Andreas of Hohenlohe-Langenburg; Count Cyrile de Commarque; Princess Xenia of Hohenlohe-Langenburg; the Countess of Wessex; Princess Cécile of Hohenlohe-Langenburg. Front row, same order: Dowager Fürstin Irma of Hohenlohe-Langenburg; Princess Louise of Hohenlohe-Langenburg; Fürstin Saskia of Hohenlohe-Langenburg; Prince Philip, the Duke of Edinburgh; Prince Edward, the Earl of Wessex; Lady and Lord Romsey, Penelope and Norton.

The wedding of Lady Pamela Mountbatten and David Hicks. Standing, from the left: Earl Mountbatten of Burma; Mrs. Iris Hicks; the Groom and the Bride; Prince Philip, Duke of Edinburgh; Countess Mountbatten of Burma; Lord Brabourne. Seated, same order: Princess Margaret Queen Elizabeth The Queen Mother; Queen Louise of Sweden; the Duchess of Kent; Princess Alexandra of Kent. On the floor: Amanda Knatchbull; Victoria Marten; Princess Clarissa of Hesse; Princess Friederike of Hannover; Joanna Knatchbull; Princess Anne; and Prince Charles.

George VI died. She *"instinctively gave* [the new Queen] *a hug but quickly remembered that her cousin was now the Queen and dropped into a deep curtsey."*[17]

Pamela continued her duties as a lady-in-waiting on various other trips throughout the empire. In 1959, she met David Nightingale Hicks, who was already a famous interior designer. Hicks was born in 1929 in Essex the son of a stockbroker, Herbert Hicks who died when the boy was twelve years old. David attended the Central School of Arts and Crafts and was already something of a media star with clients such as the Duchess of Windsor and Douglas Fairbanks Jr. when he met Pamela. The couple married January 13, 1960. The bridesmaids were Princess Anne, Joanna and Amanda Knatchbull (Pamela's nieces), Princess Clarissa of Hesse (daughter of Princess Sophie of Greece, and Victoria Marten, who was Pamela's goddaughter.

David Hicks went on to become the *"acme of jet-set chic of the 1960s."*[18] He was best known for his bold colors and exciting, modern, designs and patterns. Indeed, he made a style for the age. Some of his eclectic clientele were Vidal Sassoon, Helena Rubinstein, Mrs Condé Nast, and the Prince of Wales's first apartment at Buckingham Palace. In addition, he designed the sets for Richard Lester's ode to the swinging sixties, *Petulia*. Later, Hicks was able to take his brand worldwide with shops virtually everywhere, as well as writing books on design. He was known to be *"talented, charming and mercurial."*[19] David Hicks died of a stroke after being diagnosed with lung cancer on March 29, 1998.

The couple had three children: Edwina (b. 1961) who married the actor Jeremy Brudenell and has three children; Ashley, an architect (b. 1963) who married Allegra Tondato, divorced in 2009 and married secondly Katalina Sharkey de Solis and has two children; and India (b. 1967), who may be best remembered for being the little bridesmaid for Lady Diana Spencer when she married Prince Charles, and as an author, designer and UK television personality, and who with partner David Flint Wood has five children.

The baptism of Edwina Hicks (b. 1961), Church of St Mary Ewelme, South Oxfordshire. From the left: Lady Brabourne; Earl Mountbatten of Burma; Queen Louise of Sweden; Mr. Herbert Hicks; The Queen holding baby Edwina; David Hicks, and Lady Pamela Hicks.

Pamela has served as a director on several boards. She is also the author of two fascinating memoirs: *India Remembered: A Personal Account of the Mountbattens During the Transfer of Power* (2007); and, *Daughter of Empire: My Life As a Mountbatten* (2012).

****

The 1930s

The world continued to change as the decade of the thirties began. Irène and Victoria were now widowed and the constant visits that had been so much a part of their lives were sharply tapered off. After visiting the colossal Imperial palaces and the vast expanse of Russia and her natural wonders, each had now to content themselves with the relative simplicity of Irène or Ernie's various homes in Germany or to those of Louise in Sweden. Expense, which had not seriously impeded any of them in the past, was now an issue always to be considered.

In the summer 1932, Irène briefly made a splash in *The Times*. She was involved in a car accident on the return journey to her home in Hemmelmark from a visit to her brother-in-law, the former Kaiser at Doorn, The Netherlands. She was not hurt, but her car overturned. Although Irène did not visit Wilhelm II frequently, she did make the effort to attend major celebrations. Among these family gatherings, most prominently was his 80th birthday, which she attended and brought her grandson Prince Alfred of Prussia along so he could meet other family members. Even in his old age, Prince Alfred remembered the visit to Doorn clearly. *"Onkel Willy asked if it was true that in Costa Rica I had an alligator for a pet, as some of my younger cousins had told him. I explained to him that there was a confusion, or the cousins had tried to fool him. I had a lagartija, a lizzard, not a lagarto, an alligator. We all laughed about it and I think Onkel Willy was a bit disappointed as he hoped there would be something interesting and exotic about our life in that mysterious country."*[20]

In the summer of 1933, Irène made a visit to Costa Rica. Bobby's attempts to start a coffee plantation in Guatemala had failed. Looking for a better opportunity for success, he moved on to Costa Rica, where he lived the rest of his life. Once settled, Bobby made a lasting friendship with Rafael Beéche, who was governor of Puntarenas Province at the time and had received orders from the President of Costa Rica to help *"el príncipe."* Costa Rica was a peaceful and prosperous country, as well as a haven for many Prussian families that had emigrated there hoping to become successful in the coffee business. Many did, and remain very successful; unfortunately success evaded the Prussians. From his arrival and until his death, Bobby was treated with great deference and courtesy by the small group of Costa Ricans he befriended. As for the Beéche family, that relationship remained close until the death of Prince Alfred.[21]

Irène's visit to that faraway land was unsuccessful. Her grandson, Prince Alfred remembered Irène as a very stern woman who did not like the fact that Bobby was living abroad. After the death of Prince Heinrich, she wanted Bobby to return to Germany. In fact, the purpose of this trip was to attempt to convince her son to come home. However, Bobby and his family were happy where they were, so Irène was disappointed. Prince Alfred's sister Barbara, in fact, did move back to Germany and Irène made the young woman her heir. Barbara had been attending a girl's school in San José, the capital of Costa Rica. Many of her former classmates remembered her very well, while several of them remained in contact with her through the years. She visited her parents several times

Prince Sigismund of Prussia.

At Hemmelmark in the late 1920s. From the left: Prince Sigismund, Princess Irène, Prince Henry holding Prince Alfred, Princes Charlotte Agnes, Princess Barbara, Princess Calixta, and Prince Waldemar.

before Bobby's death. As for Alfred, he returned to Europe and attended school in Germany. At the outbreak of war, Alfred returned to Hemmelmark and stayed with his grandmother and sister. After the end of hostilities, assisted by Louise in Sweden, he was able to board a steamer and return to Finca San Miguel, where he wholeheartedly worked by his father's side in a fortuitous effort to make the farm self-sufficient. They were not very successful, but they were happy. *"My father wanted nothing to do with the old world...while running the farm was challenging, at least he knew that no one would come and take it from him. In Costa Rica, he felt protected from the pain and abuses communists had inflicted on his family,"* Prince Alfred said.[22]

Irène disliked what she saw in Costa Rica. She could not understand how her son could be happy living in such strained circumstances. She had trouble adjusting to the local food and always remembered it as *"ghastly."* Upon returning to Europe from Central America, Irène went first to Wolfsgarten to see her brother and sister.

Prince Sigismund at his farm in Costa Rica.

In July 1936, Irène celebrated a milestone at Hemmelmark – her seventieth birthday. Not only were Victoria and Ernie there with her, but also her two grandnieces, Cecilie and Sophie. This would have been one of the last peaceful visits that the family

Princess Charlotte Agnes of Prussia at home, Finca San Miguel.

would have together. In August, the infamous Olympic games took place in Berlin, which Victoria's son George Milford Haven attended, and apparently enjoyed.

Tragedy struck in 1938, a very difficult year for Princess Victoria. It was in the beginning of the year that George was diagnosed and succumbed to cancer of the bones. This on top of the very tragic accident at Steene the previous year, might have seemed too much to bear. George had left the navy in 1932 and became Chairman and managing director of the Sperry Gyroscope Company, Limited. In addition, he was a director of Electrolux Limited and Marks and Spencer. In 1937, he was promoted to the rank of captain RN, on the retired list. George's funeral took place at Bray near Lynden Manor, the home of the Milford Haven's. Among the attendees were King George VI and the Duke of Kent; the procession behind the coffins went s l o w l y t h r o u g h the little

The 2nd Marquess of Milford Haven.

town. Before the King left the graveside, he kissed Victoria.[23] Nada found herself with the burden of caring for her special needs daughter, while having to play a direct role in the education of her dashing son David. The loss of Georgie, at a time when his private career showed great promise, was deeply felt by his wife and children. Edwina, never one to shy away from assisting where her funds made the most effect, was there to lend her Nada her support. All seemed aware of the heavy load of catastrophes that Victoria Milford Haven had endured throughout her life. The Duke of Connaught, her remaining uncle wrote: *"I can hardly find words to express adequately to you how deeply I feel for you in this new great grief that has fallen upon you...."*[24] However, Victoria stoically did go on, though the death of her son bowed her tremendously.

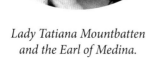

Lady Tatiana Mountbatten and the Earl of Medina.

That summer, Irène and Victoria met at Wolfsgarten, a poignant visit at best, with memories and phantoms at every turn. Irène wrote about the visit:

From the left: Crown Prince Gustaf Adolf of Sweden, Lady Patricia Mountbatten, the Countess Mountbatten of Burma, Victoria Milford Haven, Crown Princess Louise of Sweden, Lady Pamela Mountbatten, and the Earl Mountbatten of Burma.

> It was such a comfort for me & Victoria on arriving here together yesterday for the first time in our dear old home since we lost so many of our loved ones. One has the feeling that dear Ernie & Onor must step in & be there & that they are only just by chance absent – one cannot realize it – & I often feel like in a dream. Peg and Lu are so sweet & kind, doing all they can that one shall not feel the sad change too much – he is quite wonderful, poor boy & Victoria too. We were at the Rosenhohe this morning – their graves are one big one – .... It was very nice being a few days at Langenburg with Sandra, Ernie Hohenlohe & family, where there are so many remembrances of dear Grandmama & her Sister Feodora.[25]

In May 1939, Irène visited Victoria and the two of them visited Queen Mary at Marlborough House. Since the Dowager Queen liked reminiscing about the past, these three ladies most certainly spent a great part of the visit talking about old times, as well as the dear ones from long ago.

On September 1, 1939, the Nazi's marched into Poland and another World War commenced. The remaining two sisters would be separated, and their relationship would be further strained by being once again on opposing sides. Victoria was living in a grace and favor apartment in Kensington Palace and Irène was living at Hemmelmark. Victoria became much closer to Queen Mary and often wrote to her and stayed with her at Badminton during the hostilities. Eventually, she was persuaded to go to her son, Louis's home at Broadlands. During this time, she worked with Baroness Sophie von Buxhoeveden on her unpublished *Recollections*. The rest of the family, Victoria's son, and grandson Philip were very

While Prince Henry was alive, he and Irène frequently visited their relations. After his death, she continued doing so. This image dates from 1925, when Henry and Irène visited his sister Margarete. Standing from the left: Waldemar of Prussia, Christoph of Hesse-Kassel, Henry, Philipp of Hesse-Kassel, Landgrave Friedrich Karl of Hesse-Kassel and his sons Richard and Wolfgang. Seated: Irène, and Mafalda (née Savoy), Landgravine Margarete and Marie Alexandra of Hesse-Kassel (née Baden).

involved in the war effort, as was her daughter-in-law, Edwina. She obviously couldn't see her daughter, Louise, as Crown Princess of Sweden was living in a neutral country, and certainly none of her German relatives.

It was in the spring 1941 that Victoria heard about a death from the very distant past. The Countess Alexandrine de Kolemine, the woman with whom Grand Duke Ludwig IV, her father, had briefly contracted a second marriage had died at Vevey, Switzerland. No doubt that entire scandal all seemed long ago and in a completely different world.

Victoria continued to get news of German relatives through her daughter Louise in neutral Sweden. It was through the Crown Princess that Victoria knew that at least her granddaughters were safe in Germany and that her nephew, Lu and his wife, Peg were safe at Wolfsgarten. Though now in her eighties, Victoria persisted in going back and forth in her own little car to Broadlands and to Badminton to see Queen Mary. By summer 1944, her family did persuade her to go to safety at Windsor. It was at this time that she got to know her little cousins, Elizabeth and Margaret Rose.

It was to the two Princesses that Victoria talked during that time and told them stories of the family history. Princess Elizabeth in particular loved these stories of the family and Victoria's memories of her beloved Grandmama, Queen Victoria. The Princess noted that Victoria's mind seemed as sharp as ever even into her advanced age.

Prince Andreas of Greece and Denmark.

Prince Waldemar of Prussia.

Victoria heard of the death of her son-in-law, Prince Andreas of Greece in December 1944. Alice and Andreas had been separated for many years and had not seen each other during the war. Nevertheless, it, too, was a sad break in the past.

As the war finally wound down, news from the other side was more forthcoming. Irène's son, Toddy died of a hemorrhage at Tutzing, Bavaria since there was no means of blood transfusions, and possibly because the Allies denied it to him. Peg and Lu were sheltering refugees at Wolfsgarten, mostly friends and relatives. More news, the daughters of Alice and their husbands were mostly all right, though the youngest, Sophie, lost her husband, Prince Christoph of Hesse-Kassel, in the war.

Victoria would not travel to Germany again after the war, but Irène was eager to see her last living sister and tried to obtain permission to go to Sweden where Victoria would be visiting, her daughter, Louise. Unfortunately, she was not able to do so.

Like many of her generation, Irène, too, liked to think about those old and golden days before war, loss, and heartache had changed her world.

And then there was much less colorful and different world of the present. Dickie was back in the Royal Navy, having returned from India in the spring of 1948. Irène was still alive but the two wars had the inevitable effect of estranging, at least a little, the sisters, even though they were the last of their immediate family's generation. That did not mean that they did not keep in touch, but it was more sporadic than before.

During the summer of 1950, Victoria suffered from various ailments including bronchitis. Being an inveterate smoker, it is not surprising that she did, and also from circulatory problems that had plagued her throughout her life as well as other issues of advanced age. She would live long enough to see her great-grandchildren, Charles and Anne and died at Kensington Palace on September 24, 1950.[26]

****

Victoria Milford Haven with Fürst Ernst II of Hohenlohe-Langenburg at her granddaughter and his son's wedding in 1931. Both were born in 1863 and died in 1950.

From Germany, Irène wrote to Dickie that the fact *"that I could not see her once more is a great grief to me. ... Mama's courage & loving heart were wonderful & her loving advice I always had from her, in so many ways."*[27] It was unfortunate that the war and its aftermath kept Victoria and Irène from meeting again. However, it may have been just as well, as with so many bitter events to divide them, their relationship would never have been the same.

Irène continued on, living in a smaller house on the Hemmelmark estate. She was Honorary Chairman of the German Red Cross and founded the Heinrich Children's Hospital in Kiel. She kept in touch with relatives in England after Victoria's death, in particular, Queen Mary. She died on November 11, 1953[28] with her granddaughter and heir, Barbara at her side.

Victoria, Dowager Marchioness of Milford Haven.

Princess Irène of Prussia.

Princess Barbara of Prussia.

As for Barbara, she had been interested in marrying Duke Christian Ludwig of Mecklenburg-Schwerin, second son of Grand Duke Friedrich Franz IV and Grand Alexandra, an aunt of Georg Wilhelm of Hannover, Sophie of Greece's second husband. At the end of the war, Christian Ludwig accompanied his parents as they fled west in an effort to outrun the approaching Red Army. They settled at Schloß Glücksburg with their Schleswig-Holstein cousins. Once fighting concluded, Christian Ludwig traveled to Schloß Ludwigslust to retrieve family heirlooms, as it was hoped these would provide the family with some much-needed funding. When the war ended, the area was firstly occupied by the British. However, it was transferred to the Soviet occupation forces and all changed. Unfortunately, he was arrested by communists and was sent to a labor camp in Russia. For years, no one knew if he was alive. Barbara waited. Finally, in 1953 he was released along with other German POWs. He returned to Glücksburg in time for Christmas. His father, sadly, had died in 1945 after Christian Ludwig's arrest.

"My first journey from Glücksburg to Kiel was with my younger sister to Hemmelmark, to visit Barbara," he wrote in his memoirs. *"I had never been to Hemmelmark before and always suspected it was somewhere else. It is located at the north end of the town of Eckernförde, right on the corner of the Bay of Eckernförde. The mansion itself was full of refugees at the time, and Barbara lived in a small room in the so-called Victoria House, a wing of the mansion,"* he recalled.[29] Visits went back and forth and after a few months, Kiki, as Christian Ludwig was known, asked Barbara to marry him while on a trip near Paderborn. Excited, the couple rushed to to Schloß Marienburg, a Hannover property, where his mother was visiting her sister-in-law Viktoria Luise, Duchess of Brünswick, a first cousin of Barbara's father. The wedding was celebrated at Schloß Glücksburg on July 11, 1954. Barbara's parents and brother were unable to attend. Prince Alfred later told one of the authors that, *"Kiki was a truly nice man, and I think he balanced with sister very well."*[30] Right after the wedding, Barbara and Kiki received an invitation from Queen Louise to visit her at

a royal estate near Helsingborg. These visits became a yearly custom until King Gustaf VI Adolf's death in 1973.

Grand Duchess Alexandra of Mecklenburg-Schwerin with her two sons: Hereditary Grand Duke Friedrich Franz and Duke Christian Ludwig.

In Hemmelmark, Kiki quickly took over as manager of the agricultural estate. Meanwhile, Barbara gave birth to their first child, Donata, in March 1956. A second daughter, Edwina, named after Countess Mountbatten of Burma, who had died earlier in the year, was born in September 1960. The Mecklenburg-Schwerin sisters are married and together have six children. They are Prince Henry of Prussia and Princess Irène of Hesse and by Rhine's only descendants.

The wedding of Barbara of Prussia and Christian Ludwig of Mecklenburg-Schwerin – Schloß Glücksburg, July 11, 1954. From the left: Ludwig of Hesse and by Rhine; Adolf Friedrich, Grand Duchess Alexandra, Hereditary Grand Duchess Katrin of Mecklenburg-Schwerin; Friedrich of Schleswig-Holstein; the Bridal Couple; Ernst August of Hannover; Marie Melita, Friedrich Ferdinand, and Anastasia of Schleswig-Holstein; Friedrich Franz of Mecklenburg-Schwerin; and Viktoria Luise of Brunswick.

Barbara died in May 1994, weeks from her fortieth wedding anniversary. Kiki survived his wife by two years years. He passed away on July 18, 1996. In 1998 his very interesting memoirs were published, *Erzählungen aus Meinem Leben*, serving as an excellent testimony to a life dedicated to family and duty.

As for Prince Alfred, once he returned to Costa Rica he lost any interest in settling in Europe. *"The old world held no magnet for me. Everything there was destructioon; hunger was everywhere after the war. My father was right in thinking that Europe was unsafe. My grandmother chose Barbara to inherit Hemmelmark, so there was no incentive for me to return to Germany."*[31] Instead, he worked in several industries in Costa Rica and remained very close to his parents. After Sigismund's death in 1978, the family decided it would be best for Charlotte Agnes to return to Germany, where Barbara awaited her mother at Hemmelmark. She died there in 1989, but her remains were returned to Costa Rica and buried with her husband's in the town of Esparza. They rest not far from Finca San Miguel, their home for so many years, which has now been overtaken by the forest. Alfred was not interested in being a farmer as his spirit and personality sought more exciting and diverse outlets. He worked for a shipping company for many years, later becoming the manager of a private island in the Gulf of Nicoya.

Duchess Donata of Mecklenburg-Schwerin.

Duchess Edwina of Mecklenburg-Schwerin.

Duke Christian Ludwig and Duchess Barbara of Mecklenburg-Schwerin.

"Living on Jesusita Island was a lot of fun. Only left the island whenever absolutely necessary. I learned to live with the bare minimum, often catching my own food from the warm waters surrounding Jesusita. It was as if

I was Robinson Crusoe. Electricity was unreliable, potable water was at a premium. I could swim every day and not be involved in the race that daily life had become," he recalled.[32]

Alfred remained a bachelor until 1984, when he married a wealthy lady by the name of Maritza Farkas. She had been previously married to a friend of Alfred's. With Maritza, Alfred was able to travel to Europe several times, as well as visiting the United States more often. She died in 1996 while undergoing cancer treatment in Rochester, Minnesotta. Unable to deal with the complexity of his late wife's legal and financial affairs, Alfred, sadly, allowed himself to fall prey to Balkan con-artists who eventually took from him all of Maritza's properties in Costa Rica, Spain, and New York City. No amount of warnings by those who really cared for him made Alfred reassess the situation. by then, senile dementia had overtaken his lucidity. He died in June 2013, his mind lost in an impenetrable nebula. He was quietly buried in a cemetery in San José. None of his former close friends knew he had died as in his last years he was kept from them. They want to move his remains to the grave where his parents rest.

Prince Alfred of Prussia in the 1940s.

Prince Alfred with his parents at Finca San Miguel, Costa Rica.

****

Back in Darmstadt ... Young Lu continued his studies during this decade and like most German princes spent time in the military. In 1936, at the invitation of Joachim von Ribbentrop, the Ambassador to England, Lu went to London as a cultural attaché. It was while he was there that he became engaged to Margaret Geddes. A year before, he had met Margaret, a Scottish girl, when they were both studying painting and literature in Southern Germany and the two became better acquainted when Lu was in London.

Margaret or "Peg" as she was known in the family, was born in Dublin in March 18, 1913. She was the daughter of the Rt. Hon. Auckland Campbell Geddes and Isabella Gamble Ross from Staten Island in New York. Sir Auckland was among other things, a prominent member of the military, Principal of McGill University in Montreal and the British Ambassador to the United States. In fact, Peg was raised in New York, London, and many other cities. Their engagement was announced in the summer of 1937. There were objections to Peg, but they were never elucidated in the letters that

Prince Alfred of Prussia in 1999, Heredia, Costa Rica.

went back and forth between the siblings and other relatives. No doubt it was the political climate in the late thirties that gave them pause.

Certainly, it probably cheered none of the English relatives that Don, Cecilie and Lu joined the Nazi Party in May 1937. There is no proof that they were actively involved in the movement, nor is there any proof that they were anti-Semites. At the time, there was considerable pressure for prominent Germans to fall in line and join the movement as there would be political and financial consequences for not doing so. The same argument can be made about Gottfried Hohenlohe-Langenburg, who joined the party as well because it benefitted his position as a large landowner. Not so Christoph and Philipp of Hesse, who were actively involved in Nazi politics and held important positions within the government of the Third Reich. Philipp was introduced to the Nazi Party by their Nazi-obsessed cousin August Wilhelm of Prussia (Auwi), one of Kaiser Wilhelm II's sons, who was a convinced National Socialist, along with cousin Carl Eduard of Saxe-Coburg and Gotha. Christoph joined the party in 1931 and the SS the next year.

Though Ernie knew of his son's engagement, he was already unwell. He had suffered from influenza and colitis in the spring of that year. His sister, Victoria made the trip to Darmstadt and commented that he seemed to be on the mend but was thin and shaky. As the summer progressed, the family began to face the fact that Ernie was not getting better. He went for treatments in Berlin, but they only seemed a temporary respite. Irène was able to visit and Victoria was staying with him, but as September faded into October Ernst Ludwig's condition worsened.

The young boy who had wanted all his loved ones to die together, had grown into a well-respected man whose exit from this world was witnessed by those closest to him. The influenza that had afflicted him since the spring, developed into a bronchial

Prince Ludwig of Hesse and by Rhine and Hon. Margaret Geddes.

187

A family gathering for the 70th birthday of Princess Irène of Prussia, Hemmelmark, July 11, 1936. Standing in back, from the left: Ludwig and Cecilie of Hesse and by Rhine; Crown Princess Louise of Sweden; Georg Donatus of Hesse and by Rhine; Sophie of Hesse-Kassel; Eleonore of Hesse and by Rhine; Eitel Friedrich of Prussia; Marie Melita of Schleswig-Holstein; Eleonore von Oertzen; and Frau von Haxthausen and her daughter Anna-Luise. Seated, at front: Victoria Milford Haven, Irène of Prussia holding Alexander of Hesse and by Rhine; Ernst Ludwig of Hesse and by Rhine holding his grandson Ludwig.

infection that placed undue strain on his heart. On October 9, 1937, surrounded by his loved ones, Ernie passed away in Wolfsgarten at 6:05am.[33]

News of Ernie's death prompted widespread demonstrations of support for his bereaved widow and family. One of the first to arrive in Wolfsgarten to express his condolences to Onor, Don and Lu was Jakob Sprenger, the Reich's Lieutenant and Gauleiter of Hesse. He carried personal condolences from Hitler. Thousands of messages arrived, among them from cousin George

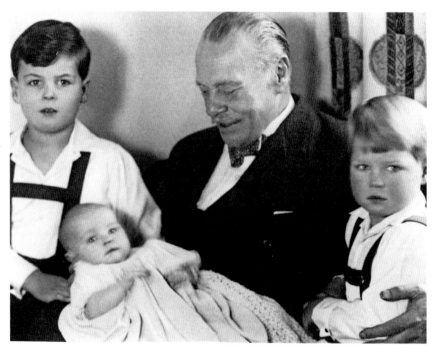

Grand Duke Ernst Ludwig and his grandchildren: Ludwig, Johanna, Alexander.

VI in London, and the Kings of Sweden, Italy, Greece, and Norway. Prince Regent Paul of Yugoslavia, another erudite supporter of the arts, immediately telegrammed the Hessians expressing his support. His wife Olga was a first cousin of Cecilie. Also quick to send condolence telegrams were many of the leading members of the Nazi hierarchy, among them: Adolf Hitler, Rudolf Hess, Hermann Göring, General Field Marshal Werner von Blomberg, and General Baron Werner von Fritsch. From Bayreuth, Wagner's widow Winifred sent her sincere condolences on the loss of a great supporter of her husband's legacy.

Former rulers attending a Hessian wedding in the 1920s. From the right: Prince Max of Baden, Duke Ernst August of Brunswick, Grand Duke Ernst Ludwig of Hesse, Grand Duke Friedrich Franz IV of Mecklenburg-Schwerin, and Grand Duke Friedrich II of Baden.

From Monday, October 11 to the following day, the coffin containing Ernie's remains. Reposed in the entry hall of the Neues Palais. Covering it was his dynastic flag, on which were placed his helmet and dagger. Around it hundreds of wreaths were on display. These included one from Kaiser Wilhelm II, another from pianist Frieda Kwaast-Hodapp; some were elaborately designed, while others were simple garden bunches brought by members of the public.

The funeral service, on October 12, was conducted by Pastor Fiedrich Widmann from Darmstadt, and Pastor Helmut Monnard from Egelsbach. In attendance were close royal relations, among them: the Crown Princely Couple of Sweden (Gustaf Adolf and Louise); Ernie's sisters Victoria Milford Haven and Irène of

The funeral cortège of Grand Duke Ernst Ludwig.

Hereditary Grand Duke Donatus of Hesse and by Rhine.

Hereditary Grand Duchess Cecilie of Hesse and by Rhine.

Prussia; Landgrave Friedrich Karl and Landgravine Margarethe of Hesse-Kassel, Sophie Greece's parents-in-law; Prince Louis Ferdinand of Prussia, representing his grandfather Wilhelm II; Prince Alexander Ferdinand of Prussia, representing his father Prince August Wilhelm, responsible for introducing so many of his relations to National Socialism; Grand Duke Friedrich Franz IV of Mecklenburg-Schwerin; the Margrave and Margravine of Baden, Berthold and Theodora; the 2nd Marquess of Milford Haven, who had less than a year left to live; and Prince Philipp of Hesse-Kassel. State Councilor Reiner represented Gauleiter Jakob Sprenger, while Darmstadt Mayor Otto Wamboldt represented the local government. Among the other funeral guests were royalties from near and far, as well as leaders from the Imperial Army and the Third Reich's revitalized German military.

It was a cold October afternoon as the funeral cortège proceeded along the Wilhelminenstraße, the Upper (Obere) Rheinstraße, past the Old Schloß, and then along the Landgraf Georg Straße until reaching the Rosenhöhe. Thousands lined the streets, most of them with their right hand outstretched in the Nazi salute. By four o'clock in the afternoon, the cortège had reached the New Mausoleum. The atmosphere was somber. Onor and her sons were devastated, as were Victoria and Irène. Yet, in their innocence, Ernie's two grandsons, Ludwig and Alexander, provided a touchingly funny moment when they mimicked the goose-stepping soldiers carrying their grandfather's coffin into the mausoleum. The funeral music and the solemnity surrounding them, were simply too much for the cherubic boys to comprehend. Little did anyone know that just a few weeks later, the scenes of devastating sadness would repeat themselves

Grand Duke Ernst Ludwig of Hesse and by Rhine (1868-1937).

along the black-draped, mourning streets of a shocked Darmstadt.

During the funeral, Hereditary Grand Duke Georg Donatus, now as Head of House, expressed his appreciation for the ample demonstrations of sympathy he witnessed,

"The death of my father has brought from the population of Darmstadt and numerous friends from all Hesse, the most beautiful and deep proofs of sympathy. For that I would like to shake hands with every single one, but that would prevent me to express my appreciation to the thousands who wanted to do accompany us in our sorrow.

So, I have no other choice than to express my cordial thanks, along with our mother and other family members, to all those who wrote in the condolence books at the Neueus Palais, to all who have honored the memory of the Grand Duke by giving flowers, writing their condolences, and by visiting the crypt on the Rosenhöhe.

We will never forget how the population of Darmstadt has behaved during the time of our grave suffering."[34]

Ernie was eulogized in a very positive way by *The Times* of London: *"Thanks to his encouragement, many eminent artists settled in Darmstadt in pre-War days and he was patron of the Great Century Exhibition of German Art[.]"*[35]

Because of Ernie's death, Peg and Lu's wedding was delayed until the following month. The entire Hessian family planned to fly to England for the festivities. On November 16, 1937, Onor, Don, Cecilie, their two boys and various retainers boarded the plane. En-route to Croydon in England, the Hessian family were

Three generations of Hessians: Don, Ludwig, and Ernie.

killed instantly when their plane crashed in bad weather in Steene, Belgium. Besides the tragic deaths, Cecilie's unborn child was also killed. It should be noted that it wasn't just royalty killed at the scene, among the dead were Baron Joachim von Riedesel zu Eisenbach; Fraulein Lina Hahn, the children's nurse; Mr. Martens, a glider pilot; and Antoine Lambotte, the pilot of the plane and his crew, Maurice Courtois and Invan Lansmans.

According to the *New York Times* of that date, the Sabena Junkers J-52 crashed at 2:30 in the afternoon as a consequence of the fog. The pilot made the decision to land in Ostend at the Steene Aerodrome in order to pick up two more passengers -- *"when the plane was sixty feet above the ground in descending ... the left wing hit the chimney of a brick making plant."*[36] *The*

Don and Cecilie with their children Ludwig, Alexander and Johanna.

Prince Ludwig of Hesse and by Rhine, Don's eldest son.

Prince Alexander of Hesse and by Rhine.

A bride in black: Lu and Peg after their quick London wedding.

Times noted that none of the brick factory workers were injured. Apparently although the day had been sunny, the dense fog was sudden and unavoidable. Rockets had been shot off in hopes of helping the plane to land but the pilot could not see them. Rescue workers could not get near the conflagration for an hour because of the extreme heat. Later, fault would be assigned to the official at Steene for not telling the pilot to go on, and the last two of three rockets that misfired.

A witness recalled the accident, *"I saw the aeroplane coming down out of the fog. It hit a chimney of the brickworks at a speed of about 100 miles an hour. One wing and one of the engines broke off, and both crashed through the roof of*

The wreckage of the Sabena Junkers J-52 in Ostend.

the works. The remainder of the aeroplane turned over and crashed to the ground in the brickfield about 50 yards farther on, where it at once burst into flames."[37]

Among the wreckage were the Hessian pearls and the veil of Honiton lace worn by Princess Alice at her wedding. Horribly ironic that Ernie's childhood wish of everyone joining hands and going to heaven together was gruesomely fulfilled. It was a blessing that he had died just a month before.

The family in England was in extreme shock….

Crown Princess Louise of Sweden best expressed everyone's sense of devastation when he wrote, *"My thoughts are hardly here at all & to think of Lu above all is more than one can bear. To lose one's entire nearest & dearest in just over one month is unbelievably awful."*[38] Little did she know that her words were but a preview of what Lu's later life would be – he never truly recovered from the trauma he experienced that cold November of 1937.

Coping with the situation as best as they could, were Sir Auckland and Victoria. All agreed that the wedding ceremony must go on and it did, taking place the following day despite the tragedy that occurred. The bridal couple wore black and according to the *The New York Times*, Lu gave a Nazi salute after the ceremony as he left the chapel. [39] Prince Philip, the brother of Princess Cecilie, did not attend the wedding. Instead of a honeymoon, Peg and Lu went to Ostend, Belgium,

The funeral cortège of the Hessian Grand Ducal family proceeding through the wet and cold streets of Darmstadt. Prince Ludwig walked immediately behind the carriages.

The funeral procession culminated at the Rosenhöhe, where the bodies were buried in the park instead of the grand ducal mausoleum. Ernie's remains also rest with those of his family. In this poignant image, we can see Lu dropping flowers in the family grave, while Peg stands to his side. Behind them are family members, among them: Gottfried and Margarita Hohenlohe-Langenburg, Berthold and Theodora of Baden, Andreas and Alice of Greece, Louis Mountbatten, Philip of Greece, Victoria Milford Haven, and Christian Ludwig of Mecklenburg-Schwerin (tall man with glasses between Philip and Victoria).

near the scene of the accident to take the coffins home to Darmstadt and preside over the burials of their immediate family which took place on November 22. The train ride was mournful, the deadly cargo arriving to Darmstadt on November 18 at 4:10pm. Awaiting inside the Princely Hall at the central train station in Darmstasdt were Onor's sister Fürstin Marie zu Dohna-Schlobitten, Princess Alice with her three surviving daughters (Margarita, Theodora, Sophie), two cousins of Lu's (Countess Johanna Solms-Laubach and Princess Elisabeth Solms-Hohensolms-Lich), as well as members of the Riedesel, Hahn, and Martens families. Peg said later: "*I arrived in the mourning town of Darmstadt as a bride in black.*"[40] Edwina Mountbatten remarked poignantly as the coffins passed by, "[t]*oo ghastly. One by one and quite endless....*"[41] There is a photograph of the mourners, some wearing Nazi armbands, the newlyweds, with Peg, of course, veiled in black, and young Prince Philip marching with the rest slowly through the streets of Darmstadt. It cannot escape one how ominous and tragic the image is for a multitude of reasons.

The family had been so beloved in Darmstadt that the streets were filled with crowds wanting to pay their respects. In addition, people waited hours to file pass the coffins and write in the tribute books. Among the mourners were detachments of the armed forces, representatives of the Nazi Party, and state and local authorities. Family members present included: Prince Andreas and Princess Alice[42] with their young son Prince Philip, the Margrave Berthold and Margravine Theodora of Baden, the Hereditary Prince Gottfried and Princess Margarita of Hohenlohe-Langenburg, Prince and Princess Christoph of Hesse-Kassel with several other members of the Landgrave of Hesse-Kassel's family, Victoria Milford Haven and Irène of Prussia, Prince August Wilhelm of Prussia. Lord Louis Mountbatten attended wearing his British naval uniform.

The plaza in front of the station was closed off for the big parade. Members of the Nazi Party, delegations of the Wehrmacht and the traditional regiments, and the military groups marched with fluttering flags. The Red Cross, which had always been supported by the grand ducal family, was present in large contingents. The funeral procession was led by the Infantry Regiment 115, followed by wreath bearers, religious and parish leaders, all preceding the five carriages transporting the coffins. Each carriage was led by four horses led by two mounted soldiers and two foot-soldiers. Six members of the Hitler Youth escorted each of the carriages. Immediately after the last carriage walked Prince Ludwig, followed by Margrave Berthold of Baden, Prince Philip of Greece, Hereditary Prince Gottfried of Hohenlohe-Langenburg, Prince Philipp of Hesse-Kassel and his brother Christoph. The third row included Lord Louis Mountbatten. They were all stunned, still in shock. As five weeks before, during the funeral parade for Grand Duke Ernst Ludwig, the people of Darmstadt lined the streets again, showing sympathy and solidarity. At the Rosenhöhe, Count von Hardenberg and Baron von Massenbach, who had worked for the Hessians for many years, awaited the arrival of the procession with relatives who had not marched. These included Victoria Milford Haven and Irène of Prussia, accompanied by her nephew Prince August Wilhelm of Prussia.[43] The procession ended with a short ceremony officiated by Provost Dr. Friedrich Müller. It was a gray November day and this time around there were no cute Hessian boys bringing smiles to mourners with their antics. The five victims of Steene were buried in an open area near the mausoleum built by Ernie. A few days later, in agreement with the authorities, Ludwig decided to move his father's coffin and bury it next to Onor's. Today, more than eight decades later, they all rest together for posterity. Ernie's wish to not be alone in death was fulfilled.

Just a few weeks earlier, Don had thanked the people

Lu and Peg with their niece Johanna.

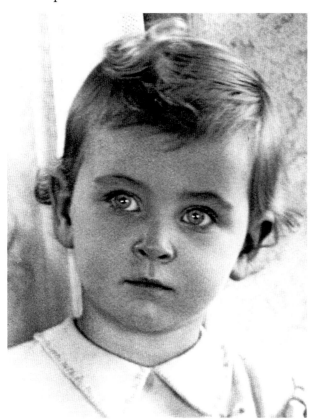

The survivor: Princess Johanna of Hesse and by Rhine.

of Hesse for their great sympathy for the death of his father. Now it was Lu's turn to do it for the unthinkable death of his relatives. On December 1, 1937, he published a note thanking Hessians for their sympathy:

"To the friends in the lands of Hesse!

The incomprehensible stroke of fate, which robbed me so unexpectedly and cruelly of the dearest and nearest people, has caused tremendous demonstrations of support from the whole world, but especially from all parts of Hesse, from which I receive daily proofs. My wife and I feel this sympathy especially deeply and benevolently and thank all those whom we could not thank by letter or with an embrace. Especially noteworthy is the sympathy expressed for the fate of my niece, Princess Johanna. I can only answer to all the many requests of compassionate mothers and ensure that the

Victoria Milford Haven and her family. Standing behind are: Crown Princess Louise and Crown Prince Gustaf Adolf of Sweden, Lady Edwina and Lord Louis Mountbatten, the Marchioness and Marquess of Milford Haven, Princess Alice and Prince Andreas of Greece.

best will be provided for her with all my love. First, she will move with her nurse to the home of Margravine Theodora of Baden, Salem near Lake Constance. There, she has playmates in her children, who were also the friends of her little brothers, who spent a long time in Salem last summer."[44]

Prince Andreas felt the loss of Cecilie deeply, as it was rumored that she had been the one he felt closest to. To his mother-in-law Victoria, he wrote about his sense of loss, *"a very, very hard blow…and the weight of it becomes heavier as time passes."*[45] The tragedy, while consuming Andreas, seems to have provided his estranged wife with the jolt she needed to start the difficult process out of her depression. Her psychiatrist, Dr. Binswanger, later described the tragedy as her, *"first curative shock…contrary to what was expected it apparently tore her out of everything."*[46] Kurt Hahn, the director of Gordonstoun, where

Prince Philip was enrolled, broke the news to his pupil. Hahn later said, *"his sorrow was that of a man."*[47] Gina Wernher, a friend of Philip's and niece of Nada Milford Haven, further revealed his sadness, *"He was very quiet. He didn't talk much about it, but* [later] *showed me a a little bit of wood from the aeroplane. It was just a small piece, but it meant a lot to him."*[48]

In 1939, more tragedy was in store for the remaining family. Johanna, Don and Cecilie's niece and adopted daughter, who had not been on the plane and so did not die with her parents, died in June of meningitis. It was not only obviously very sad that the last of Don's immediate family had perished, but Lu and Peg, her Aunt and Uncle, were not able to have children and so the Hesse and by Rhine line would die with Lu later on.

****

As a young married woman during the 1920s and 1930s, Edwina had a rather checkered career, however, as her daughter recounted, during the Second World War, Edwina really came into her own. She worked hard and diligently with the St Johns

Lord Louis and Lady Edwina Mountbatten dressed for the 1937 Coronation.

Ambulance Brigade, risking her life to stay in London during the blitz. In addition, Edwina quietly financed her sister-in-law Alice's care during her hospitalizations, and also helped her husband's Aunt Anna, the widow of Prince Franz Joseph of Battenberg.

In 1939, Dickie was promoted to Captain and put in command of *HMS Kelly*. He was, in fact, among the party who accompanied King George VI and Queen Elizabeth when they visited Dartmouth Naval College. It was during this particular visit that a young cadet and Dickie's nephew, Prince Philip of Greece and Denmark was put in charge of the entertainment of the two young princesses who had accompanied their parents. The young man made an excellent impression on the eldest, Elizabeth, making sure that they had refreshments and vaulting over a tennis net, which they also seemed to enjoy. The romance of Elizabeth and Philip would blossom during the war and eventually bring them to the altar, but many feel that this was the crucial meeting.

Edwina Mountbatten posing with her dogs.

After World War II was declared, Dickie and his men saw active duty in the English Channel, the North Atlantic and in the Mediterranean. *HMS Kelly* was sunk on May 23, 1941. With scarcely forty survivors, the men had to hang on for four hours before they were rescued. It was a miracle that even that small amount of men survived subjected as they were to constant strafing by German Aircraft.

Noel Coward would dramatize this spectacular and tragic battle in the film *In Which We Serve* and Dickie was celebrated as an intrepid hero. He had previously been appointed by Winston Churchill as the Chief of Combined Operations; a secret task force assigned with the planning of the invasion of Europe that would take place in 1944. Later, in October 1943, he became Supreme Allied Commander in Southeast Asia, affectionately known as "Supremo." Philip Ziegler, Mountbatten's biographer, compared him to his fellow Supreme Commander in the Pacific, Douglas MacArthur. The two "Supremos" were equally and supremely vain, but Mountbatten lacked MacArthur's cold arrogance and *"was endearingly able to laugh at himself."*

In 1945, Mountbatten accepted the surrender of the Japanese at Singapore and was elevated to the title of Viscount Mountbatten of Burma in 1946.

Dickie returned from South East Asia in 1946 and was much involved with the family about discussions of his nephew Philip's future. He was striving toward the pinnacle in the Royal Navy and was still considered the Supreme Commander he had been during the war. As such, the decisions he made during that period after the surrender of the Japanese were, he said, dictated by history and by his mother's excellent advice:

> *"My mother said, 'Don't worry about what people think now. Don't ever work for popularity. Above all, don't care what the newspapers say. What is important is that your decisions should be clear and stand up to history. So all you've got to think about is whether children and grandchildren will think you've done well.'"*[49]

The Mountbattens in India with Jawaharlal Nehru.

Victoria Milford Haven's advice, like her grandmother's, was sound. Dickie came home a hero and was now on his way to being First Sea Lord, the title his father had tragically had to give up in 1914, and for which he had been working for since that sad time.

The Earl Mountbatten of Burma with The Queen and the Duke of Edinburgh on the Buckingham Palace balcony during Trooping the Colour. With them are Prince Charles and Princess Anne.

He is perhaps most famous to the world for being the last Viceroy of India. In 1947, he and Edwina, along with their younger daughter Pamela, who wrote most movingly about this chapter in the family's life in her book *India Remembered*, presided over the "handing over." It was flattering for Dickie to have the responsibility of what would be an extremely delicate situation, but his mother was not amused. She felt that politicians were slippery and

Earl Mountbatten of Burma and Archduchess Helen of Austria at the wedding reception of Prince and Princess Michael of Kent, hosted in Vienna.

incorrigible and if there were problems Mountbatten would make an easy scapegoat. Patricia Mountbatten said this was the first time she saw her grandmother swear. It was also during this time that Dickie and Edwina came to London for a flying visit to attend the wedding of their nephew Philip to Princess Elizabeth.

Just before the wedding, Mountbatten was created Earl Mountbatten of Burma. He returned to the Royal Navy and served as a Rear Admiral. In perhaps the perfect vindication for him and his family, Winston Churchill appointed him First Sea Lord in 1955. Dickie continued all his old friendships, and especially enjoyed people in the entertainment business. He and Edwina hosted many famous entertainers at Broadlands including Frank Sinatra, Shirley MacLaine and Cary Grant. In addition, he had not forgotten his old friend, Charlie Chaplin who was also a guest at Broadlands.

Edwina, who had been feeling unwell during these years, pushed herself more than was reasonable. She was described as a "workaholic" and continued working for many of the charities that she had taken up during the Second World War. She went on a tour of the Far

The Earl Mountbatten of Burma shortly before his assassination by IRA terrorists off the waters of Cliffoney, County Sligo, Ireland.

East on behalf of the St John Ambulance Brigade in 1960 and succumbed in Borneo of a heart attack. It was shocking for all and Dickie received over six thousand telegrams of condolence. Edwina, who had been a bright young thing of the twenties and embroiled in scandal in the thirties, had come into her own as a worker during World War II, Vicereine of India, and champion of many charitable causes. In the end, she was not only mourned by her family but by the world at large. She was buried at sea as she had requested.

Mountbatten retired from active service in 1965. He was also best known to the generations of the sixties and seventies as the beloved mentor and "honorary Grandfather" of Charles, Prince of Wales, who earlier in 1979 had said, *"I admire him almost more than anybody else I know."*[50] Though widowed, both his daughters Patricia and Pamela had provided him with a clutch of grandchildren with whom he spent a great deal of his leisure time. The family used to spend parts of their summer holidays at Classiebawn Castle, one of Edwina's residences located in Ireland. It was here that Lord Mountbatten spent his last days. When he visited, he eschewed security and enjoyed roaming about without surveillance. Everyone knew his daily routine. He was assassinated there along with three others by the IRA on August 27, 1979. According to witnesses it had been, *"a beautiful clear blue sky..."* and a 50-pound bomb, which had been attached to the boat the previous night, was detonated, destroying the boat and resulting in the three deaths. *"The boat was there one minute and the next minute it was like a lot of matchsticks floating on the water,"* a witness recalled.[51] The casualties, as well as Dickie, included his grandson, fourteen-year-old Nicholas Knatchbull, Paul Maxwell, a fifteen-year-old boy who was crewing the boat, *Shadow V*, and Baroness Brabourne, John Brabourne's mother, who actually died from her injuries the following day. Several hours later eighteen soldiers of the British Army were also killed by bomb explosions. Timothy Knatchbull, one of the three survivors later wrote, *"We all have a car crash in our lives. To date I have had one; it happened to be a bomb. I was a boy at the time, on a small boat in Ireland. Three of my family and a friend died in the explosion. One of the dead was my identical twin brother Nicholas. My parents and I were the only survivors."*[52] The IRA called it an execution, *"noble struggle to drive the British intruders out of our native land,"*[53] but *Time Magazine* wrote:

It will stand as one of history's sad ironies that Mountbatten had never taken part in the dispute over the control of Ulster and that, in fact, the Tories counted him a dangerous left-winger and a partisan of self-determination. But he was an English earl and a cousin of the Queen and he died a sacrifice to the kind of tribal hatred he worked so hard in India to overcome.[54]

Chapter IX

The Mountbatten-Windsor Connection

A Greek Prince

Perhaps the most famous and successful Mountbatten of them all, or at least the most well-known in the world of today is the original "fair haired" boy. The son of Princess Alice Battenberg and her husband, Prince Andreas of Greece and Denmark, Prince Philip is the consort of Queen Elizabeth II and the father, grandfather, and great-grandfather to the heirs to the throne of the United Kingdom.

He was born at Mon Repos on the Island of Corfu in June 1921, the last child and only boy of Princess Alice. His family was in constant exile due to the political vicissitudes of the country they had ruled since 1863. When Philip was just a baby, his father barely escaped a firing squad and was banished for life from Greece. The entire family left, of course, and at first they settled in Paris. They never had what felt like enough money, but as time went on, Prince Andreas's brothers George and Christopher[1], and Dickie's Edwina made sure that school fees were paid. In Paris, they lived in a house lent to them by Prince and Princess George

Princess Alice and her son Prince Philip at his baptism.

of Greece (Princess Marie Bonaparte). However, in royal terms, it was a hand to mouth existence and taught Philip to be independent and frugal.

As the twenties waned, Princess Alice's behavior became a matter of much concern and it was at this point that she went out of Philip's life for nearly ten years and his father, Prince Andreas took refuge in the South of France for the remainder of his life. He was the royal equivalent of a latchkey child. All four of his sisters married German Princes in the early 1930s and were then distracted with their own growing families. So there was only his British Family to direct his upbringing.

His Uncle George Milford Haven acted *"in loco parentis"*[2] for much of the early and mid-thirties and Philip was about seven when he started school at Cheam (as would Prince Charles after him), staying with his grandmother and uncles and then later in 1933, he went back to Germany to the Schule Schloß Salem, a school owned by his brother-in-law, Berthold of Baden. The headmaster of the school, Kurt Hahn, was a Jew. He prudently fled the

Prince Philip in the Black Sea while on a visit to the Romanian royal family.

Nazis and Germany and founded the boarding school Gordonstoun in Scotland. After leaving Germany, the prince spent most of his young life in Britain both staying with his Uncle Georgie and visiting his Uncle Dickie or his grandmother, Victoria Milford Haven at Kensington Palace. For a five-year period, from 1932-1937, Philip did not see his mother. In his usual stiff upper lip fashion, Philip said he just had to get on with it, but it was surely difficult for him as a young boy growing up, despite loving relatives.[3]

After Cheam, Philip attended Gordonstoun until his graduation in 1939. But there was a traumatic event that shaped his young life while he was there – the airplane crash in 1937 took one of his beloved sisters, Cecilie and her entire family. There are extremely poignant photographs of Philip at the funeral in Darmstadt. He, his grandmother and uncles are standing at the edge of open graves

A gathering in Langenburg – In April 1931 Prince Philip's sister Margarita married Gottfried of Hohenlohe-Langenburg. From the left: Prince Peter of Greece, Princess Alexandra of Hohenlohe-Langenburg, Count v. Oppersdorff, Prince Peter of Schleswig-Holstein, Princess Irma of Hohenlohe-Langenburg, Prince Philip, The Bride and Grom, Prince Hans of Schleswig-Holstein, Princess Irene of Greece, Margrave Berthold of Baden, Princess Theodora of Greece, and Prince Ludwig of Hesse and by Rhine.

Saint-Cloud, 1928. The Greek defeat in Asia Minor in August 1922 led to revolution. Prince Andreas was arrested, court-martialed, and found guilty of "disobeying an order" and "acting on his own initiative" during the conflict. Many defendants in the treason trials that followed the coup were shot. British diplomats assumed that Andreas was also in grave danger. Though spared, he was banished for life and his family fled into exile aboard a British cruiser, HMS Calypso. The family eventually settled at Saint-Cloud on the outskirts of Paris, in a house loaned to them by Andreas's wealthy sister-in-law, Princess George of Greece. For their silver wedding anniversary the couple posed with their children. From the left: Princess Margarita, Prince Philip, Princess Cecilie, Princess Alice, Princess Sophie, Prince Andreas, and Princess Theodora.

with multiple caskets. In addition to the personal devastation, from our vantage point of today, looking at the Nazi uniforms adds a particularly sinister edge to the images. Barely sixteen, the desolation and heartache must have been incalculable, but nevertheless, Philip got on with it. This tragedy did have one benefit, however, Philip's mother, Alice, seems to have somehow pulled herself together and thrown off her various mental and physical

Darmstadt, November 19, 1937. At the funeral procession for the Steene victims. Leading the procession was Prince Ludwig of Hesse and by Rhine. Behind him, from the left: Hereditary Prince Gottfried of Hohenlohe-Langenburg, Princes Christoph and Philipp of Hesse-Kassel, Prince Philip, and Margrave Berthold of Baden. Lord Louis Mountbatten marches behind Prince Christoph.

illnesses. It was as if the shock of the death of her daughter jolted her back to reality. Nonetheless, her re-emergence was too late to provide Philip with any familial stability – that was provided by his various school situations. Added to the several calamities that Philip and the Hessians and Mountbattens had to deal with was the sad and tragic death of his Uncle George in 1938.

He had a strange and lonely youthful existence where he had the advice and care of his uncles and grandmother, the love of his sisters and his father's influence – he was welcome many places but had no home of his own. Nevertheless, and despite these emotional disadvantages, he appears to have been a boisterous and confident young boy.

From Gordonstoun, he went on to the Royal Naval College at Dartmouth for a year. Philip had thought about going into the Royal Air Force or even one of the Greek armed forces

Prince Philip in Athens, photo by court photographer Boucas.

Above: Front row, third from left is Princess Elizabeth. In front of Lord Louis Mountbatten and Prince Philip are King George VI, Queen Elizabeth and Princess Margaret. This was during a visit to the Naval Academy, when Prince Philip was tasked with entertaining the young princesses. To the right: Prince Philip (then known as Philip Mountbatten) during WWII.

but was wisely persuaded by his father to join the Royal Navy instead. His father, with whom he kept in close contact despite their living apart, didn't like the idea of Greece or its military for Philip. He thought the Royal Navy a more stable situation.

It was during his time at Dartmouth that Philip met the young girl who would later be his bride.[4] In July 1939, King George VI, Queen Elizabeth, and their daughters Princesses Elizabeth and Margaret Rose visited the Naval Academy. While the King and Queen inspected, the young princesses had to be entertained, and Philip was selected to do this arduous task. Refreshments of lemonade and ginger snaps were given while Philip, who probably hadn't the least idea how to amuse the girls, vaulted back and forth over a tennis net. Apparently, he did a good enough job since 13-year-old Elizabeth was quite smitten and has never wavered from it.

He went into the Royal Navy during the Second World War and served on various ships. He was promoted to lieutenant in 1942, one of the youngest in the Royal Navy and was present at the Japanese surrender in January 1946. After the war, Philip continued his naval career. He and Princess Elizabeth

Philip and Elizabeth attending Patricia Mountbatten's wedding.

had been corresponding throughout the war and in summer 1946, he proposed to her. Though Elizabeth's parents were reluctant for her to marry at so young an age and were eager for her to meet other young men, she was steadfast in her devotion to Philip and the King and Queen finally gave their consent. In March 1947, Philip became a naturalized British citizen and renounced his Danish and Greek titles; it was at this point that he took the name Mountbatten, which was, of course, the translation of his mother's maiden name. The day before the wedding King George VI made him the Duke of Edinburgh, Earl of Merioneth and Baron Greenwich of Greenwich. The excitement in the country was unparalleled; it was just what was needed

Wedding of the Duke of Edinburgh and The Princess Elizabeth – Buckingham Palace, November 20, 1947. Standing in the back, from the left: Prince Georg of Denmark, Princess Marie of Greece, King Peter II of Yugoslavia, Countess and Earl Mountbatten of Burma, the Count of Barcelona, the Duchess of Kent, Princess Juliana and Prince Bernhard of the Netherlands, King Haakon VII of Norway, Queen Frederica of Greece, Prince Peter of Greece, Queen Mary, Prince René of Bourbon-Parma, Queen Victoria Eugenia of Spain, King Frederik IX and Queen Ingrid of Denmark, King Michael of Romania, Crown Princess Louise of Sweden, Prince Michel of Bourbon-Parma, the Duchess of Aosta, Hereditary Grand Duke Jean of Luxembourg, Princess Eugenie of Greece. Front row, same order: the Marchioness of Milford Haven, Princess Alice of Greece, Princess Margaret, Prince William of Gloucester, the Marquess of Milford Haven, the Bride and Groom, Prince Michael and Princess Alexandra of Kent, King George VI, Queen Elizabeth, the Duke and Duchess of Gloucester, Prince Richard of Gloucester, Princess Margrethe of Denmark, Princess Helena Victoria, and her sister Princess Marie Louise.

Top left: Prince Philip with his uncle Grand Duke Ernst Ludwig of Hesse and by Rhine and grandmother Victoria Milford Haven. Behind them are Philip's sisters Theodora and Margarita, and his brother-in-law Gottfried Hohenlohe-Langenburg.
Top right: The Duke of Edinburgh.
Left: At Schloß Salem in 1965: Theodora of Baden, Queen Elizabeth II, Kraft of Hohenlohe-Langenburg, Margaret of Hesse and by Rhine, and Prince Philip.
Above: In Langenburg (1950s), Prince Philip tries a new Mercedes Benz while his nephew Kraft of Hohenlohe-Langenburg and cousins Elisabeth and Helen of Törring-Jettenbach stand watching.

after the long and tragic war. The world has time and time again hailed Great Britain for really knowing how to put on a good show, and this wedding would certainly be no exception.

Philip married Princess Elizabeth in November 1947, and there was no end of royalty invited for the occasion – the Danish and Greek connection were there in force as were many other royalties, among them King Michael of Romania and his mother Queen Mother Helen. However, Philip's immediate family was mostly omitted, as were Peg and Lu. His sisters, as has been explained, had all married German Princes and it was decided that it wasn't a good idea to remind the British public about how German Philip was, and indeed most of the British Royal Family as well. As the expression goes, it was "too soon." His father by that time was dead and his mother was thought of as Greek not German. Having said that, it is interesting that his Great-Aunt Irène of Prussia and her family were invited or perhaps Grandmother Victoria had insisted. At any rate, perhaps the German animus didn't extend to elderly Aunts. In

At the Coronation of HM Queen Elizabeth II, Westminster Abbey, June 2, 1953. Prince Philip's mother and family guests: Princess Alice; Margrave Berthold and Margravine Theodora of Baden followed by their son Max; Fürst Gottfried and Fürstin Margarita of Hohenlohe-Langenburg followed by their daughter Beatrix; Prince Georg Wilhelm and Princess Sophie of Hannover followed by her daughter Christina of Hesse-Kassel; Prince George and Princess Marie of Greece. Following them are the Abel Smith family.

due time, contacts with Prince Philip's myriad German relations were reestablished. He oftentimes made private visits to his sisters, while they and their children were guests of The Queen and Prince Philip at countless family events. These private family visits now include the generation of the grandchildren of Prince Philip's sisters. He also invested in strengthening contacts with the Greek royal family and the extended web of relations these royalties represent.

After the wedding, Philip returned to the navy and in 1950 was promoted to Lieutenant Commander. At that point, he and Princess Elizabeth had two children, Charles (b. 1948) and Anne (b.1950). A decade separate the birth of Princess Anne from that of Andrew, The Queen and Prince Philip's third offspring. A fourth child, Edward, arrived in 1964.

As mentioned earlier, Prince Philip's sisters were unable to lend their support to him during his wedding. The government feared the public's reaction to having his German relations in England so soon after the war. However that was not the case in 1953 during his wife's coronation. For that major royal event, Margarita, Theodora, and Sophie, with their husbands and some of their children, walked into Westminster following Prince Alice. For many of the English public, it was the first time they had seen images of the Duke of Edinburgh's family.

Prince Philip in Langenburg with Gottfried and Margarita of Hohenlohe-Langenburg, Georg Wilhelm of Hannover, and Theodora of Baden.

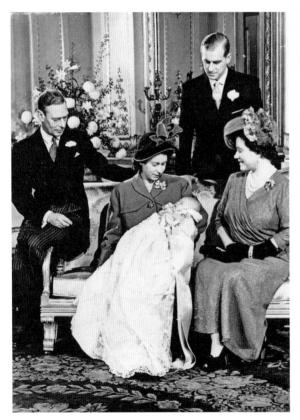

The baptism of Prince Charles. With the baby's parents are his grandparents King George VI and Queen Elizabeth.

For the first years of their marriage, they were able to enjoy the life of a naval family. There are photographs and newsreels of the royal couple and especially Princess Elizabeth enjoying the life of a naval wife – a time that was doubtless over too soon for her. At the death of his father-in-law, Philip had become a full Commander, but had to leave the navy as his wife was now "The Queen." His role would now be the full-time consort of the Queen Regnant and he would be required to subsume his desires for that of his Queen's and the country's.

****

Mountbatten-Windsor

From the wedding onward, despite gossip to the contrary, Philip has remained a steadfast, loyal spouse and support to his wife, the Queen. There have been many family scandals that are so well-known, the issues of Princess Margaret marrying Peter Townsend, her eventual divorce from the Earl of Snowdon, the chaotic chapters of Charles and Diana and Andrew and Sarah, Anne's divorce and remarriage – in all of these the Duke has acted as a major support for the Queen.

Top left: The Prince of Wales, Prince Edward, The Queen, Prince Philip, Prince Andrew, and Princess Anne.
Top right: The Duke of Edinburgh with Earl and Countess Mountbatten of Burma, his Uncle Dickie and Aunt Edwina.
Above: Prince Philip riding a moped.
Middle, right: At the state funeral of Queen Elizabeth the Queen Mother. First row: The Prince of Wales, The Duke of Edinburgh, The Princess Royal. Second row: Prince William and Prince Harry. Third row: The Duke of Kent, The Duke of Gloucester, and Prince Michael of Kent.
Right: a recent photograph of HM The Queen and Prince Philip The Duke of Edinburgh before his retirement from public life.

Notable for this study is that in 1960, the Queen issued Letters of Patent stating that though the Royal House would remain Windsor, if members of the family needed a last name it would be "Mountbatten-Windsor", but that this would only be applicable to her descendants.[5] For Earl Mountbatten of Burma, who was constantly making genealogical charts proving his royal heritage,

A vacation in the Alps – The Prince of Wales and his Aunt Sophie of Hannover.

this must have been a great triumph. More to the point, it was something that Prince Philip wanted.

Many chafe at what are considered his tactless comments and supposed "gaffes", though perhaps he is just amusing himself during what in many cases has to be monumentally boring duties. Whatever the reason, he continues onto this day, with a few health scares and a grumpy yet supremely entertaining disposition upon which many have come to rely. Indeed, his retirement in 2017 is a loss, though no one deserves it more, with the possible exception of his wife, who will never retire.

What is, perhaps, less widely known, is his devotion to his large family circle of cousins and his pleasure in gathering with them on various occasions. Like so many people in their nineties, his

The Prince of Wales and his Aunt Peg, Princess Margaret of Hesse and by Rhine.

circle, despite having the ability to know who his 6th or even 7th cousins, down to the over six hundred descendants of Queen Victoria, is getting smaller and smaller.

The Princess Royal with the Duke of Gloucester, followed by the Duke of York, the Earl of Wessex, and the Duke of Cambridge. (©*Katrina Warne*)

The first of the children to marry was Anne, who in 1973 married Captain Mark Phillips. They had two children, Peter and Zara, before divorcing in 1992. Later that year, Anne, who was granted the title of Princess Royal by her mother in 1987, married secondly Sir Timothy Laurence. Both of her children married and have children.

Prince Charles, The Queen's eldest child and heir, holds the title of Prince of Wales. In 1981, he married Lady Diana Spencer, youngest daughter of the 8th Earl Spencer and his first wife Frances Roche, daughter of the 4th Baron Fermoy and of his wife Ruth (née Gill), who was a confidante and friend of Queen Elizabeth

The Queen Mother. Two children were born to the couple, William and Harry, before their marriage collapsed, leading to a separation in 1992. The marriage ended in divorce in 1996, the year before Diana Princess of Wales died in a horrific automobile accident in Paris. Eight years later, The Prince of Wales married his longtime companion Camilla Parker Bowles (née Shand). They had been involved with each other prior to his marriage to Diana Spencer, who also blamed Camilla for the collapse of her marriage to Prince Charles. Notwithstanding how their marriage came to be, The Prince of Wales and his second wife, who uses the title Duchess of Cornwall, make a thoroughly happy couple who are tireless members of the Royal Family. William and Harry, Camilla's stepchildren, get along very well with her.

On his wedding day to Catherine Middleton,

The Prince of Wales and the Duchess of Cornwall at their wedding.

The wedding of The Duke and Duchess of Cambridge – Buckingham Palace, April 29, 2011.

William was granted the title of Duke of Cambridge. He has three children: George, Charlotte, and Louis. As for Harry, the Duke of Sussex, he married American actress Meghan Markle in 2018. They had a son, Archie Harrison, in 2019. Later that year, the couple caused quite an uproar when they announced their wish to "step back" as senior members of the Royal Family. They argued their wish to be private citizens was behind the controversial decision. As part of the negotiations with Buckingham Palace, the couple agreed not to continue being styled Royal Highness. as for Harry's son, he is known as Master Archie Harrison Mountbatten-Windsor, in

HM The Queen entering St George's Chapel, Windsor. Awaiting her from the left: Sir Timothy Laurence, The Princess Royal, Autumn and Peter Phillips, Princesses Beatrice and Eugenie of York, The Duke and Duchess of Cambridge. (©Katrina Warne)

accordance with his parents' wish that he grow up as a private citizen. Harry and his family have left the United Kingdom and settled in Los Angeles, where Meghan is seeking to restart her acting career.

Prince Andrew entered the Royal Navy and remained in active service until 2001. In 1986, he married Sarah Ferguson, whose father had worked for the Royal Family for years. Through her father, Sarah descends from the 6th Duke of Buccleuch and 8th Duke of Queensberry, and is a distant relation of of the Duke of Gloucester, The Queen's first cousin. The couple had two daughters, Beatrice and Eugenie. Their marriage, rocky from the start, ended in divorce in 1996. Neither has

The 38th birthday of the Duke of Cambridge, with his children: George, Charlotte, and Louis. (©The Duchess of Cambridge)

remarried, but they remain good friends. Sarah has supported her former husband during his many run-ins with the press and myriad public relations missteps.

Lastly, Prince Edward, Earl of Wessex, is married to Sophie Rhys-Jones, a former public relations executive. They have two children, Louise and James. The Wessex's are very active in various charities, as well as conscientious supporters of The Queen. As his father slowed his public obligations, Prince Edward assumed many of the Duke of Edinburgh's duties.

The Earl and Countess of Wessex.

****

The Milford Havens

David Michael Mountbatten, 3rd Marquess of Milford Haven was the son of George, 2nd Marquess of Milford Haven and Nada de Torby. In addition, Prince Philip's close friend, along with their cousin Alex Wernher, only son of Countess Zia de Torby (Nada's older sister) and Sir Harold Wernher. The Wernhers were exceedingly wealthy and Sir Harold was seen by David and Philip as a great influence in their early life. Since both basically lacked a father figure (David because of his father's early death, while Philip due to the breakup of his family), David and Philip were frequent guests at the Wernher homes. Being close in age, David and Philip built a very close

The Milford Havens in 1920: Victoria and Louis Milford Haven; Nada holding David; Georgie with Tatiana.

friendship with Alex. They were all fun-loving, handsome, and protagonists of hijinks. During the Second World War, all three young men served. Alex was stationed with a tank division in Tunisia. In December 1942 his parents' worse nightmare happened. Tragedy, always a constant presence in the lives of David and Philip paid them all an unwanted visit again. Alex was in a tank accident and had his hip and leg were crushed. He died two days later. Some weeks after the tragedy, Prince Philip wrote to Lady Zia a letter of condolence in which he stated his state of mind, *"ever since I got the telegram from Uncle Dickie, I have been*

in a daze."[6] Furthermore, young Prince Philip expressed how important Lady Zia's son had been to him, *"Alex filled a place in my life that was very important to me, he filled the place of a brother and for that alone I am eternally grateful to him. As the older boy he was the guide and the pillow and in a great many ways I tried to model myself on him. As I grew older I was able to find many of my shortcomings by just comparing myself to him and in some cases manage to put them right..."*[7] For the rest of her long life, Zia Wernher could count on both Philip and David's visits and support.

A happy-go-lucky young man, David gave little credence to what people thought of him. Once, shortly after his father's death, he took his cousin Gina Wernher to a nightclub, much agains the wishes of Lady Zia, who was left scandalized at home once she discovered the outing. David minced no words when replying to a stern letter from his aun: *"I wish sometimes you were Gina's age, as you were once...then you would realize how much Gina wants to enjoy herself, as indeed all people of our age do. I know that you can trust Gina, so what is the objection of her going where she wants, whatever the palace is...she knows she is not disgracing anyone, either her or you...Well what does it matter what people think, it is no concern of theirs, and it is only nasty people with dirty, evil minds that start gossiping and inventing stories..."*[8]

David Milford Haven attended Dartmouth Naval College with his cousin and served in the Royal Navy. Like his cousin and uncle, he too was considered a naval hero during the war. He was decorated in 1942 with an OBE as well as a Distinguished Service Cross for taking the British destroyer, the Kandahar through a minefield to rescue another ship. He retired from the Navy in 1947. During the postwar period, he was considered one of the most eligible bachelors on the London social scene. According to the *Los Angeles Times*, he was *"tall, dark and handsome; …a keen theatergoer and nightclub fan."*[9] There were even rumors that he had been engaged to Princess Margaret and was once seen holding hands with her.[10] In 1947, he served as best man at the wedding of his cousin and The Princess Elizabeth.

The hijinks that had caused David's family such concern, did not abate as he entered adulthood. Louise of Sweden, his aunt, was concerned enough to write Lady Zia about it. *"How my heart aches for poor Nada. Really the tragedy to see one's son caught up in a fast, pleasure-loving set…His father died just when he most needed him,"* she wrote.[11] Nada, however, living mostly in faraway Cannes, was not one to judge her son as she had done plenty of wild sowing in her lifetime.

Lady Zia was of the mind that her nephew was *"a fool."*[12] But also commiserated about the undue coverage David received in the papers. *"In my Cannes days any man could go about with a woman without the newspapers hounding him and taking photographs of all their trips abroad!! I am NOT taking his part,"* she wrote, *"but I think it is bad luck in a way."*[13]

In the end, he married Romaine Dahlgren Pierce[14], a wealthy American divorcée, who Nada described as, *"Lots of money! You know I'm mad about good manners, well hers are the best."*[15] However, when soon after their marriage the couple started sporting a large coronet and initials on their paper, Nada lost her initial enthusiasm regarding Romaine and minced now words when expressing

David, 3rd Marquess of Milford Haven.

At the baptism of Norton Katchbull – Patricia Mountbatten holding her son, David Milford Haven, and Prince Philip.

her disapproval, *"Too vulgar for words. Georgie, myself and Aunt V.* [Victoria Milford Haven] *did away with all that."* The marriage, not surprisingly, was a failure and David soon returned to his old ways.[16]

His most notorious love affair was with the actress Eva Bartok. Romaine laid blame on this entanglement for the collapse of their marriage. Lady Zia hoped that their friend Douglas Fairbanks could talk some sense into David. It did not work out.

David, Marquess of Milford Haven with his mother Nada and his fiancée Miss Romaine Dahlgren Pierce. David and Romaine married in 1950, but their union was short-lived.

Lord Milford Haven was part of the London demi-monde of the 1950s. This group of worriless pleasure-seekers brought about a colorful mix of aristocrats and questionable social climbers. Prominent among them was Stephen Ward, later embroiled in the Profumo Affair – a sexual scandal that had broad political implications.

David Milford Haven married Miss Janet Bryce in 1960.

David's second marriage was far more successful. In 1960, he married Janet Bryce, a fashion model was the daughter of Mrs. Francis Bryce of Hamilton, Bermuda and the late Major Bryce. The Bryces had been a successful Scottish shipping family. Janet's mother was a cousin of Lieutenant Colonel Harold Phillips, the husband of Gina Wernher, David's first cousin. Interestingly, Gina and Harold became the parents of two English duchesses, Alexandra, Duchess of Abercorn, and Natalia, Duchess of Westminster.

David and Janet's first son, George, June 6, 1961. He was a premature baby, but from the outset there was no worry.[17] One of George's godparents was Prince Ludwig of Hesse and by Rhine. In 1964, a brother, Ivar, joined him.

On April 15, 1970, David Milford Haven collapsed at Liverpool Street Rail Terminal. He died of a heart attack at the early age of fifty. In an obituary, his close relations with Prince Philip were stressed. They once *"spent one holiday on the Kent coast together and ended up on a Thames barge, where they spent two nights sleeping in the grain cargo.*"[18] This was among the most memorable hijinks that gave such headaches to their elders.

Georgie and Nada's daughter, Lady Tatiana was born December 16, 1917. The story attached to her birth, which took place in Scotland, was that her father, George sent a telegram to his family to the effect that *Tatiana has arrived safely.* When they heard that they initially thought that Grand Duchess Tatiana had miraculously escaped. Tatiana was unfortunately, from birth, mentally challenged and spent a great deal of her life with caregivers and in special facilities. She died in 1988.

The current 4th Marquess of Milford Haven is David's son, George Ivar Louis Mountbatten. He was born June 6, 1961 and became the Marquess at the young age of nine at the death of his father. He was married

George and Clare, Marquesses of Milford Haven. (©Rex Photo)

to Sarah Georgina Walker in 1989. The couple had two children: Tatiana and Henry. They divorced in 1996 and Lord Milford Haven subsequently married Clare Husted Steel, a journalist and social editor for *Tatler*. He is a businessman who in 2000 founded uSwitch, a price comparison website. Several years later, an American conglomerate saw the full potential of the services offered by the company and bought it for a reported £200 million. Lord Milford Haven remains active with the polo set, the Prince of Wales and his sons being friends and fellow polo enthusiasts.

Lord Ivar Mountbatten has a fascinating life story. Born at St Mary's Hospital, Paddington, London, on March 9, 1963, He was only seven-years-old when his father died. With his brother George, Lord Ivar Mountbatten was raised by their mother. In due course, her sons inherited Moyns Park, an estate owned by her cousin Ivar Bryce, a close friend of James Bond-creator Ian Fleming. Lord Ivar studied at Middlebury College in Vermont. His professional career took him to South America, where he lived in Venezuela, and worked in the mining industry. He was co-proprietor of Moyns Park with his older brother. Lord Milford Haven had planned to purchase his brother's share using the sizeable inheritance his first wife was to receive. However, when her father's businesses collapsed, the family lost their financial stability. Marlene Eilers Koenig painted a dire picture of the couple's financial troubles. *"The couple lived the good life – polo, his-and-hers helicopters, tobogganing at St Moritz, lavish parties … until the collapse of George Walker's empire in 1991 … During*

Henry, Earl of Medina. (©Rex Photo)

From the left: Prince Edward, Lord and Lady Ivar Mountbatten, and Princess Margaret.

Penelope Thompson with her former husband Lord Ivar Mountbatten and his husband James Coyle. (©Rex Photo)

the next few months, the Milford Havens were subjected to stories of bounced checks, rumors of separation (which proved true), *and the need to put the family home, Moyns Park in Essex on the market,"* Koenig wrote.[19]

As Lord Ivar returned to Great Britain after spending five years abroad, he looked forward to *"receiving his share of the house."* He stated, *"I spent happy times thinking about the large cash sum which would come to me when I sold my share of the house. I was looking forward to sailing off into the sunset without a care in the world."* It was not to be, for instead, he bought his brother out. *"I don't think I've done this simply out of duty, but I do have an innate sense of history and continuity."*[20]

George and Ivar Mountbatten were friends of The Queen's youngest children, Princes Andrew and Edward. The brothers were childhood playmates and frequent visitors to the palace. As several other members of their extended family, they attended Gordonstoun School. In April 1994, for example, when Lord Ivar married Penelope Thompson (b. 1966), among the guests were Prince Edward (with his wife Sophie) and his Aunt Princess Margaret. The couple had three daughters: Ella (b. 1996), Alexandra (b. 1998), and Louise (b. 2002). In the meantime, plans to turn Moyns Park into a self-supporting conference center did not produce the desired outcome and Lord Ivar decided to sell the property. In 1997, he acquired Bridwell Park, an estate that he converted into a space available for weddings, parties, private and corporate events.

Lord and Lady Ivar separated in 2010 and divorced the following year. They remained on very friendly terms, which allowed an easier time raising their daughters. Penny, as she is known to the family, even lived on the estate. By 2016, Lord Ivar had come to terms with his sexual orientation and announced that he was in a relationship with James Coyle, an airline cabin services director. The couple had met in Verbier, Switzerland, while on a ski holiday. Their wedding ceremony was a private affair celebrated at Bridwell on September 22, 2018.[21] This time without royal presence, however, Lord Ivar was walked down the aisle by none other than Penny. Their three daughters were delighted with their father having found happiness at last.

Chapter X

The End of an Ancient Line

Lu and Peg after Steene

After the funeral of his family, Lu and Peg needed some time to grieve and recoup. With this in mind, they traveled to Italy where they met with his cousins Philipp and Mafalda of Hesse at their beautiful home in Rome, Villa Polissena. They had offered to the grieving Hessians use of their home in the island of Capri, where Lu and Peg headed to seek comfort for their loss. One of their first acts, after the tragedy of Steene, was to legally adopt the youngest child of Don and Cecilie, Johanna. Since the adorable, blonde, and blue-eyed girl was just one year old, she had been left behind in Darmstadt. This kept her from being another victim in the air crash that so violently took her family. Unfortunately, Lu and Peg's experiment with parenthood was to be of short duration. Johanna died on June 14, 1939, of meningitis.[1] This was not an auspicious beginning for a marriage. However, the young people remained devoted to one another for the rest of their lives, though they were not destined to have any children of their own. As the lead-up to inevitable war came, Victoria Milford Haven wrote to Peg's mother

Prince Ludwig of Hesse and by Rhine.

reassuring her of how apolitical and tactful Lu was and that she must not worry about Peg. Louise, Crown Princess of Sweden, was acting as a "go-between" for the royal relatives so that they could communicate with one another during the hostilities.

Lu and Peg made a popular couple among his circle of family and friends. Born Margaret (Peg) Campbell Geddes on March 18, 1913[2], in Dublin, Ireland, she was the only daughter of Sir Auckland Geddes and his American wife, Isabella Gamble Ross. Auckland Campbell-Geddes, later 1st Baron Geddes, was a British academic, soldier, politician, and diplomat. In turn, he was the son of Auckland Campbell-Geddes and his wife, Christina Helena McLeod Anderson and the brother of Sir Eric Campbell-Geddes, First Lord of the Admiralty. Geddes served in the Second Boer War as a Lieutenant (3rd class) in the Highland Light Infantry between 1901 and 1902. He married Isabella Gamble Ross on September 8, 1906, daughter of William Adolphus Ross, a resident of Long Island, New York, and his wife, Annie Eliza Gamble. Growing up, Peg had four siblings, all brothers: Ross Campbell-Geddes,

From the left: Don, Lu, Onor, and Ernie. Little did Lu imagine that he would lose them all within a month of each other, a toll he never truly recovered from.

2nd Baron Geddes, Lieutenant-Colonel the Hon. Alexander Campbell-Geddes, the Hon. John Reay Campbell-Geddes, and the Hon. David Campbell-Geddes.

Auckland Campbell Geddes, a highly respected and learned academic, was an Assistant Professor of Anatomy at Edinburgh University from 1906 to 1909. From 1913 to 1914, he transitioned as Professor of Anatomy at the Royal College of Surgeons in Ireland, in conjunction, with being a Professor of Anatomy at McGill University. In 1919, he was appointed Principal of McGill University, but never undertook his official duties.

At the start of the Great War, Geddes served as a Major in the 17th Northumberland Fusiliers and was on the staff of the General Headquarters in France as a Brevet Lieutenant-Colonel and Honorary Brigadier General. Eventually, he became Director of Recruiting at the War Office from 1916 to 1917. The latter year he was elected Unionist Member of Parliament for Basingstoke, a seat he held until 1920. In recognition of his dedication to duty, he was sworn a member of the Privy Council in 1917.

Geddes served under David Lloyd George as Director of National Service from 1917 to 1918. Then, as President of the Local Government Board from 1918 to 1919, as Minister of Reconstruction in 1919, and as President of the Board of Trade (with a seat in the cabinet) from 1919 to 1920. Geddes was the principal architect of the "Geddes Axe," drastic financial cuts which, led to the painful retrenchment of British public expenditure in an effort to address the enormous debt the country assumed to fight during the First World War.

Upon his appointment in 1920 as British Ambassador to the United States, which he served until 1924, he resigned all of his government positions. As His Majesty's Ambassador, Geddes investigated the

From the left: Don, Cecilie, Lu, and Onor in Bayreuth.

treatment of British immigrants at Ellis Island, for which he wrote a report (1923). Geddes was also heavily involved in the negotiations that led up to the Washington Treaty of 1922, a concerted effort at arms reductions, and which limited the size and number of the world's battleships.

Upon his return to the United Kingdom, he worked (from 1924 to 1947) in the private sector. He was the Chairman of the Rio Tinto Company and Rhokana Corporation, two enormous mining and minerals conglomerates. It was only at the beginning of the Second World War, that he returned to public service as

From the left: Prince Ludwig of Hesse and by Rhine, Hereditary Prince Gottfried of Hohenlohe-Langenburg, and Margrave Berthold of Baden.

Commissioner for Civil Defense for the South-East Region from 1939 to 1944 and for the North-West Region from 1941 to 1942. Later that year, he was raised to the peerage as Baron Geddes, of Rolvenden in the County of Kent, at which time Peg, already a princess on the continent, gained an additional title as the Honorable Margaret Campbell Geddes in her position as a Baron's daughter. Based on her father's accomplishments throughout his life, it is not a surprise how pronounced Peg's sense of duty became, as it was in both her personality and apparently her heredity as well.

Like many of the British between the wars, Peg went on holidays to the Alps. During the Winter Olympics in 1936, she fell in love. The object of her affections and her eventual fiancé, and future husband, was Prince Ludwig of Hesse and by Rhine.

He was once described as *"slim, dark-blond, and blue-eyed."*[3] He liked poetry and was an academic; he had a passion for archaeology and was a decent painter. A product of his environment, Lu could be dilettantish, *"lazy...contemplative...egotistical... roughly said: nice but useless."*[4] As for Peg, she was described as, *"full of energy...smart, erratic, fast-paced, but also brave...always full of fire."*[5] Opposites do definitely attract, which is why many such couples have successful marriages. At the time of their fateful meeting, Lu happened to be stationed as an attaché in the German Embassy in London. They made an instant connection and soon enough looked forward to living a quiet, simple life in a small house in Darmstadt reserved for a dynasty's younger son.

During the 1930s, Lu was sent by his parents to attend many a royal event. As his older brother had found a wife from a former ruling family, Ernie and Onor secretly hoped that their second son would follow suit. Lu, besides being their cousin, was a close friend of Cecilie's sisters, as well as of their cousin Elisabeth of Greece, who had married Count Karl Theodor of Törring-Jettenbach, a first cousin of both King Leopold III of the Belgians and Duke Albrecht of Bavaria. His friendship with the Badens, Hohenlohe-Langenburgs, Hesses, and Hannovers, seemed the perfect environment for Lu to settle his sight on one of many royal bachelorettes. It was not to be. He looked for someone who would adopt his outlook and hoped

Princess Margaret at Woilfsgarten.

to live quietly in a country house dedicated to his esoteric passions. In Peg, he found such a counterpart – a spouse who would take the lead.

Surprisingly, in spite of the differences in rank, it seemed to be of no importance to Lu's family that he settled on Peg. In fact, Grand Duke Ernst Ludwig seemed pleased with his son's choice. Lu's mother didn't raise objections to his choice either, as she was a pretty minor princess herself in the first place. Furthermore, as he had an older brother with two sons, there really wasn't any reason to think his marriage was important dynastically. The only individual who raised any objections to the match was the bride's father, who was disappointed that his daughter was marrying a German. Steene, however, changed Lu and Peg's life forever.

After the tragedy at Steene, Lu ended his career as a German diplomat and took over the family inheritance in Wolfsgarten and Darmstadt. He was drafted into military service in 1939 as a lieutenant in the reserve. He recalled his wartime activities thus: *"from the very beginning I was assigned to meaningless office work where I had to do some chores sitting at desks until the "chief warlord" (Hitler) thought it right to dismiss from service members of aristocratic houses because he saw us as politically unreliable. Hence, from then on (1943) I retreated to Wolfsgarten with my wife, and we lived quietly and privately. We were only startled and disturbed by increasingly heavy bombing raids. During this difficult time, the crowning moment of terror was the attack on Darmstadt, which I witnessed from Wolfsgarten ... one had the feeling that personal tragedy was no longer important – now our city, our people, were touched by grave tragedy..."*[6]

Life at Wolfsgarten, while tranquil, had its perils. When Hitler dismissed the princes from military service, Lu and Peg were under surveillance. Not only was her father involved in the war effort, but Lu's English relations included Louis Mountbatten, by then a prominent officer in the Royal Navy. These close relations to the Windsors, as well as other prominent royal families, were seen as dangerous by the Gestapo. To survive in these troubled waters, the couple had to be extremely careful. Sadly, during this time, the Neues Palais was bombed and completely destroyed by the Allies on the night of September 11, 1944

Schloß Wolfsgarten.

– this happened only months after the Hessian family surrendered the residence to Darmstadt to use in the war effort. The Allies had decided to experiment with what would become a technique called firebombing on Darmstadt and completely destroyed the old city center. On that fateful evening, Darmstadt became one of the lesser Dresdens, one not many people either know or have heard about. The beautiful thousand-year-old city, bound by peaceful and leafy forests, a center of art and culture, once the hub of the Art Nouveau movement, nearly burned to the ground.

A view of the Residenzschloß before September 11, 1944.

Near Darmstadt, some factories (Merck, Rohm, and Hass) produced war material, including some of the drugs the Nazis were using to enhance the performance of German soldiers. In all, however, these factories did not produce even 1% of the German industrial output. Yet, the Royal Air Force (RAF) deemed Darmstadt a major target. Several previous bomb raids, nearly forty, had hit the city and caused some damage. None could compare to the one carried out on that frightful September night. According to records gathered by Darmstadt historians, some 234 bombers dropped thousands of high-explosive and incendiary bombs that caused an unstoppable firestorm. Apparently, Darmstadt was used as a "guinea-pig," a test-run for the pattern that later created the Dresden inferno.

The Louisenplatz before the firebombing.

The consequences of the firebombing of Darmstadt were nothing short of tragically devastating: over 12,000 Darmstadters[7] died as a consequence of the night's bombs, hundreds were severely burned and wounded, while a large number of civilians remained unaccounted for or were missing. Nearly 70,000 civilians were left homeless, while 80% of the population lost all their possessions. A Russian POW camp was also completely destroyed by the firebombing. According to the RAF, the bombing was deemed a complete success as, "*an outstandingly accurate and concentrated raid on an intact city of 120,000 people. A fierce fire area was created in the centre and in the districts immediately south and east of the centre. Property damage in this area was almost complete. Casualties were very heavy.*"[8] The loss to humanity and western culture becomes

A view of the Residenzschloß after September 11, 1944.

more evident when looking at what was destroyed by the fires, for example: the Hessische Landesbibliothek was only one of several ancient cultural institutions devoured by fire that evening, and it lost 760,000 volumes. Also consumed by the unforgiving flames were most of the palaces of the Hessian dynasty: the Residenzschloß, the Alexanderpalais, the Altes Palais (Old Palace), the Neues Palais, and the Rosenhöhe Palais. Left behind, once the flames died out and smoke cleared, were just the shells of these once-beautiful historical buildings.

The firebombing of Darmstadt was but a preamble of further misery headed Lu and Peg's way. As the Third Reich began its slow collapse, the eastern

The Neues Palais before September 11, 1944.

regions of the country became porous and the Red Army breached defense lines. Family and friends from the farthest confines of Germany trekked across the country seeking refuge in the western areas. Princess Tatiana Metternich wrote about this harrowing time in her memoirs, recalling *"the Soviets were advancing rapidly, taking town after town. There was no resistance left to offer, nor had any ever been planned. We heard Carlsbad had become a scene of horror, with women raped and houses plundered...At every moment we had to live with and accept the thought: Now we must be ready to die. Or perhaps even much worse than death, helpless acceptance of horrors inflicted on those dearest to us."*[9] It was during this mayhem, that Lu and Peg opened the gates of Wolfsgarten and welcomed many of their dispossessed

The Neues Palais after September 11, 1944.

family and friends. In a matter of weeks, the estate became the first home-in-exile that many would know, their own properties having been lost forever to the advancing Red Army. No one better remembered the Hesse's hospitality and the meaning of Wolfsgarten as a garden of peace than Prince Heinrich of Hesse, a renowned artist, who later memorialized it in one of his paints as a green and luscious island oasis surrounded by icy waters and a frozen, barren land.

Lu and Peg were ready to share what little they had left with those most in need. People ran away not only from the invading Russians, but also from the occupying Allied armies pouring into Germany. Frankfurt, for example, fell to the Americans, who quickly requisitioned Schloß Friedrichshof, the beautiful home of Landgravine Margarethe of Hesse. Overnight, the landgravine and those living under her roof, found themselves homeless. She and her daughter-in-law, Princess Sophie, Cecilie's youngest sister and Lu's cousin, and her five children and Margarethe's four other grandchildren, had been *"thrown out without previous warning..."*[10] from their home in Kronberg. Both Peg and Lu welcomed all these refugees, never turning anyone away despite being in constant fear and did all they could to house and feed them. Wolfsgarten became Noah's ark for those seeking refuge.

Years later, Landgrave Moritz of Hesse described the time spent in Wolfsgarten as *"a saving island after a terrible shipwreck."*[11] He claimed that the decision to open the gates of Wolfsgarten wide was Peg's, who *"with her persistence and energy...also convinced her husband."* The estate then, Moritz remembered, *"burst like a Noah's ark and everyone was welcomed."* He also described Lu as a, *"somewhat shy man of artistic nature."* In contrast, he saw Peg *"as an energetic, practical, cheerful, no self-doubt woman."*[12] Clearly, Peg was more than the power behind the throne.

The immediate after war period was one of great uncertainty. The Americans came for Lu several times because of his previous rank with the German military. He was soon released as his role had been that of a simple desk-bound officer. Still, this situation caused the family no small amount of worry. In one occasion, a jeep filled with officers arrived at Wolfsgarten to arrest Lu again. *"Peg rushed to get him a change of linen for the night, and was horror-stricken,"* when she opened his drawer only to find an Allied-issued pistol hidden *"into Lu's chest of drawers."* She quickly shut the drawer, *"breathing a sigh of relief when they left without searching the house."*[13] At

The bombed shell of the Neues Palais. It was later demolished.

The bombed Louisenplatz, the Alexander Palais's shell on the lower right corner of the photo. Across the street from it, is the shell of the Old Palace.

The bombed Alexander Palais, compare with the image on page 138.

the time, it was a heinous crime to be caught in the possession of firearms, especially Allied ones. The culprit of this infraction was not Lu, as it turned out. The day before the jeep showed up at Wolfsgarten, Peg's brother, an English officer, had hidden his pistol in Lu's chest of drawers to keep it away from the prying eyes and idle hands of all the children in the house. When he left, he forgot to retrieve the said firearm.

While housing their Hesse cousins, Lu and Peg received two terrible pieces of news: the troops occupying Schloß Friedrichshof had discovered a secret wall into which Margarethe and her family had hidden invaluable family heirlooms. The other

Karl and Rainer of Hesse at Wolfsgarten. Behind them are their mother Sophie, sister Clarissa, and cousin Elisabeth with Lu and Peg.

devastating news affected Moritz and his brother Heinrich: the confirmation of their mother's death. As for Friedrichshof, the damage suffered by the castle was not just restricted to the theft of the Hessian jewels. Other priceless items were destroyed, stolen, or damaged by the Allies. After years of legal efforts, the family received small compensation for the damages suffered. As for Mafalda, Heinrich heard news of his mother's death. Princess Mafalda had been thrown into Buchenwald by the Gestapo after her husband Philipp's fall from Nazi grace. While there, the poor princess was injured and lost an arm. She did not survive the harrowing ordeal. It fell to Sophie and Peg to comfort Heinrich and his siblings.[14]

Despite all that happened during the war, and like his father before him, Lu and Peg continued to be well-beloved in the former Grand Duchy and were very involved in the artistic and cultural life of the

area. In fact, Wolfsgarten became a kind of cultural mecca for musicians and artists. The couple cultivated a cultural salon of sorts at the Schloß and hosted such luminaries from the music world as Yehudi Menuhin, Julian Bream and Mstislav Rostropovitch. In addition, there were readings by poets and writers given frequently. Peg and Lu were, in particular, patrons and close friends of Benjamin Britten, the composer and his partner, Peter Pears and traveled with them on a concert trip to India, Indonesia, and Japan. Pears rendered homage to his friendship with Lu when at his funeral `service on June 6, 1968, he sang the *"Agnus Dei,"* from Britten's *"War Requiem."* Yehudi Menuhin called Peg an ideal friend, while also acknowledging how important she and Lu had been to Britten and Pears.[15]

Over and above all of this, Peg was a tremendous *Landesmütter* in the tradition of Princess Alice and Onor. She was an active patroness of hospitals, orphanages and charities in Darmstadt. She was a cherished and very popular member of the Hesse family and of the British Royal Family and active participant of life throughout the ancient Grand Duchy.

Lu had reveled in his archaeological studies, as well as in his indulgence into art history. He was particularly knowledgeable about ornaments from Darmstadt's long history. In Munich and Lausanne, he had spent time acquiring scientific knowledge, while fulfilling the requirements necessary for him to spend the rest of his life immersed in these erudite endeavors. Steene changed that. Still, in early 1968, months before his death, Lu gave a speech in which he shared his interest in ancient objects. *"I've always considered it my job to convey a little of the things that used to be worth something…I thought it right to collect the old pieces, bring them together and exhibit again, making them accessible to a new person, so that he knows what is good and what our country offers. One should not only think of the bad, but also of the good,"* he said.[16] Interestingly, part of his speech acknowledged modern mass production techniques as a way for the regular person to be able to possess copies of ancient pieces, thus connecting the old with the new.

Lu and Peg with Princess Elisabeth of Greece (Countess of Törring-Jettenbach), and Benjamin Britten and Peter Pears at Wolfsgarten.

Yet, Lu was in all reality, a sad person. The inability to produce an heir weighed heavily on him. Peg felt responsible as well. Their nephew Moritz later wrote that,

"Only a few admitted how much she secretly blamed herself for being the reason for the extinction of the House of Hesse-Darmstadt [and by Rhine]. *She did so because it was while on their way to her London wedding in November 1937, that her husband's family was wiped out in a plane crash. On top of that, what fate, her own marriage would remain childless. This she suffered and it tortured her to the end. So absurd these self-reproaches were, so much betraying a sensitive conscience. Perhaps, however, these made Aunt Peg develop her very special skills. Not only did she become for so many a mother or confidante, but also the center of a large "family" that went far beyond their own family. For this new "family", she was the central uniting figure representing the most diverse people of the most varied circles and professions – she was always accessible for their concerns and worries."*[17]

At Wolfsgarten, Peg with Prince Ernst August of Hannover, Prince Karl of Hesse, and Princess Elisabeth of Greece (Countess of Törring-Jettenbach).

As for Lu, a prominent Darmstadt leader who knew and closely worked with him later recalled that many of his frustrations had to do with feeling as if he had let his family down. *"he was as decent a man as possible,"* yet, Lu *"was more sad than funny, which was the result of frequent drinking and constant smoking."*[18] Manfred Knodt, who worked closely with the family as Director of the Hessian Archive affirmed this reality when he wrote, *"It is no wonder that for such a deeply sensitive, witty and spiritual man this process was lengthy and difficult."*[19] Given what he had to endure in life, it is no wonder that he found living a challenge.

His angst is best exemplified in the pain found in the lines of a poem Lu wrote in 1940:

*"I say father today and hear, son
Your voice sounds to me from inside my chest.
It's a piece of mine, this word from you,
Its tone sounds strong over time and sadness.*

*Those who cut off their roots make it difficult;
The trunk rots, a breath of wind knocks it over.*

*I listen and you say: you are my blood
Loyal, like me, to the people you love,
Do not see what you receive, see that you give
From a strong heart: love, drive and courage.
I hear son and woman: Be as you are,
Only younger, clearer, brighter, tackle fresh
And do your new work, go on and on,
Serve the cause until you lose yourself.
I say: Dear father, see this heart
As it always was, you know it well
With fear and confusion, still his courage is alive,
Love lives, pain is past
And come my day and I have to get away from here
If I lay you, I will stand in front of you
Very light hand on one shoulder to me
And said: That's right, you are my son.*[20]

As military defeats threatened the Reich's eastern borders, Lu became extremely concerned about the fate of Schloß Fischbach and all the masterpieces housed inside the castle. Most prominent among

was Holbein's *Madonna*, perhaps the most exquisite masterpiece still in private hands at the time. Fearful of war raining destruction on Darmstadt and the Rhineland, Lu had the artwork sent to Fischbach in Silesia, where he believed it would escape damage, or even destruction. However, as events turned out, the Russian advance into the Reich presented a clear and present danger to Germany's eastern provinces. Lu took immediate action and arranged for the transportation of the priceless artwork out of Silesia. Prince Heinrich of Hesse recalled the fortuitous escape the *Madonna* made:

Prince Moritz and Prince Heinrich of Hesse, with a friend between them in 1945. Moritz played an important role in recovering Holbein's Madonna from the Veste Coburg.

"Uncle Lu ordered the evacuation of the portrait. It was loaded onto a small car and after eighteen days arrived in Coburg. The journey had taken so long because the streets were full of people fleeing the advancing Russians. It was a journey fraught with danger and near misses. When he reached Dresden, the man transporting the Madonna lodged in a small house outside the city. That night, Dresden was bombed by the RAF and razed to the ground. Then, shortly before Coburg, the transport was nearly missed by a low-flying enemy fighter. The carrier finally arrived in Coburg, where the Madonna was housed in the vast Veste fortress. The man no longer had the energy to continue the journey to Wolfsgarten and did not want to risk his life. This is how the painting became, along with many other works of art, housed in there."[21]

Eventually, the *Madonna* made it to Wolfsgarten, where Lu hid it under Peg's bed. Prince Heinrich later told an interesting story about how he discovered the whereabouts of *"the most precious privately owned painting."* Lu and Peg decided to clue Heinrich into an important secret:

"There was one treasure in Wolfsgarten that outshone all. It was shortly after the war that one evening after dinner Uncle Lu told me in a muffled voice: "Come with me, I have something for you see, but you mustn't talk to anyone else about it ..." Uncle and Aunt took me to her bedroom and pulled one rough, flat mahogany box under the double bed. Are you ready? I couldn't believe my eyes because I saw the Madonna in front of me ... the Madonna of Holbein the Younger, the famous image commissioned by the Mayor of Basel, Jakob Meyer zum Hasen, and one of the greatest masterpieces ever painted."[22]

From the left: Lu and Peg, an American officer known as "Blackie", and Hesse-Kassel cousins: Prince Richard, Landgravine Margarete, and Princess Sophie.

As Coburg fell under the American Zone, Lu thought the *Madonna* was safe inside the Veste. After the war, however, he was horrified to learn that the Veste Coburg was plundered. The worst was to be feared. *"Uncle Lu and Aunt Peg were extremely worried"*, Heinrich wrote. *"But they managed to persuade and American officer, who was in charge of art treasures, to allow my brother Moritz to bring the precious painting back if it still existed."* With this in mind, Moritz traveled to Coburg with the single mission of retrieving the artwork.

"Behind empty, looted boxes and all kinds of junk that the looters left behind they found, leaning against the back wall, the mahogany box, barely recognizable in the semidarkness of the hall. Perhaps it had escaped the plunderers, they hoped. Their prayers were heard and that was the box I was shown at Wolfsgarten,"* Heinrich later recalled.[23]

For decades, the Holbein *Madonna* was displayed inside the Residenzschloß Museum in Darmstadt. Before Darmstadt was rebuilt after the war, there was a period (1953-1958) when Lu loaned the portrait to a museum in Switzerland. In exchange, the museum paid for a group of twenty Darmstadt children to go on vacation every summer. The children who benefitted from this arrangement were commonly known in Darmstadt as *"the Madonna Children."*[24]

Through the power of their personality and the strength of their hearts, Lu and Peg increased the role of the family in Darmstadt's long reconstruction process. They were involved in countless projects to speed the city's revival, whether it was the porcelain museum, or the hunting museum that was located in Schloß Kranichstein. Musicians and artists were encouraged personally by Lu and Peg to visit Darmstadt and participate the city's cultural revival. Also, every time a building restoration was completed, the couple were invariably among the many dignitaries invited. Furthermore, as a bridge between the old and new Darmstadt, Lu participated in the creation of various artistic institutions among them: the Institute for New Technical Form, the German Design Council, the Bauhaus Archive at the artists' colony in the

A gathering at Wolfsgarten on May 10, 1965. From the left: Lu, The Queen, Princess Beatrix of Hohenlohe-Langenburg, Peg, Princess Dorothea of Windischgrätz, and Prince Philip.

Mathildenhöhe (which had been his father's creation). He also played a significant role in the design of the German pavilion at the Brussels World Exhibition in 1958. It is not surprising that because of his work to benefit Darmstadt, the city of Darmstadt recognized him that same year by awarding him the silver plaque, its highest honor. Lu and Peg, throughout their productive lives, were to receive many other honors.

In 1965, during The Queen's official visit to Germany, Prince Philip's family had the opportunity to host the royal couple to private family gatherings. One took place at Schloß Salem, where Margravine Theodora was the hostess. The other reunion was hosted at Wolfsgarten by Lu and Peg. Fürstin Tatiana Metternich, one of the guests, recalled the gathering, writing:

"Lu and Peg hosted a lovely dinner at Wolfsgarten, in the closest family circle, for The Queen and Prince Philip. They were on an official visit to Germany. All protocols stopped at the gate. We gathered, as so often before, in the beautiful large hall for a cocktail, then in the red saloon covered with Spanish leather to dine. The table, exquisitely decorated, was covered by a forest of May bell, that lit up in the light of the candles. Our hosts said that they opted for not using their fine silver and porcelain – no such thing could have impressed The Queen. Lu, therefore, preferred to use simple spring flowers to pay homage to a lovely woman."[25]

Health problems had been affecting Lu for years. Smoking did not help. He looked prematurely aged he was only 59 years old. Already in photographs taken just before the start of the Second World War, he looked much older than someone in his early thirties. He died in Frankfurt on May 30, 1968. He was the last male in the Hesse and by Rhine line, and the properties went to Moritz of Hesse, whom he had adopted in 1963. In fact, after Lu's death, the Hesse-Kassel line became simply the House of Hesse.

After Prince Ludwig's death Heinz Winnfried Sabais, former councilor and Darmstadt cultural officer, eulogized his lifelong dedication to their city:

"His example commits the living ... He was a worthy representative of his house in a deep and far-reaching sense, his legacy will preserve the urban cultural history, he was a worthy successor of his father as patron and friend of the arts." Furthermore, Sabais, wrote, "the daring idea of setting up a new form of intellectually and artistically productive neighborhood next to the old art colony of Grand Duke Ernst Ludwig

at the Mathildenhöhe was engineered by Prince Ludwig as the initiator and long-time supporter of the New Artist Colony on the Rosenhöhe ... For the same reason, Prince Ludwig worked tirelessly for a humanization of the personal environment in modern industrial society. As Chairman of the Bauhaus Archive, as a member of the Design Council, and as a director of the Institute of Technical Design, he repeatedly encouraged and inspired the social aspects of the arts. His involvement in the Standing Committee of Darmstadt Talks also made this social avant-gardism stand out in productive dialogue with science. If the School of Wisdom founded by Grand Duke Ernst Ludwig, with the assistance of Count Hermann von Keyserling was still a place of elitist exchange, the Darmstadt Talks, with the participation of Prince Ludwig, turned to a wider public.

Vacationing in the Alps at Schloß Tarasp, from the left: Prince Charles, Princess Sophie of Hannover, Lu, Prince Georg Wilhelm of Hannover, Peg, and Princess Friederike of Hannover.

In addition to activities that sought to be effective in the widest sense of the word, the prince, as modern as he was traditional, also took care of the preservation of traditional culture in our city. The re-establishment of the castle museum is his very own thought, and in it Holbein's Darmstadt Madonna, one the greatest works of art in our country, has found the most beautiful setting. In the future, this great picture will also bear witness to its after-glory, as the subtle collector has set a memorial for it in the porcelain museum.

The witty conversational partner who was able to generate and formulate good and right in the exchange of ideas and who as a writer in the international pen-club was in favor of freedom of expression in this country, we will never forget."[26]

****

The war was scarcely over when Peg took up a very important mission doing everything in her power to nurse the wounds and smooth the way toward a reconciliation of the warring nations. She was uniquely positioned as *"a native of Britain by birth... not to apportion blame but instead"* extend her hand in reconciliation.[27] Peg found a calling in bridging people, while acting with the interests of *"a shared future"* for the former combatants.[28] If there was going to be lasting peace in Europe, an understanding among former enemies had to be reached. After her death, an old postcard of St Francis of Assisi's prayer for peace was found among her papers, on it, *"she once drew a cross beside the words "Where there is hate, let me bring love"* and added the word Yes and after it, a full-stop. Yes and full-stop." Undoubtedly, this embodies who she truly was, *"a woman of not too many words, but if necessary, the words were closely linked to her deeds."*[29]

Widowhood did not wilt Peg. While she missed her husband deeply, she continued her social work. Serving as patron and sponsor of countless charities provided her with a solid and long-lasting "raîson d'être." In her own way she became the

232

Lady Pamela Mountbatten with Lu and Peg.

'Landesmutter' that Alice would have become had she not died so soon and tragically in 1878.

She continued to preside over her household after the death of her husband. Both were intimate friends of Benjamin Britten and Peter Pears, with whom they frequently went on long holidays. Britten often worked at Wolfsgarten, although he found the German Christmas *"very holy and serious but inclined to be a bit sloppy and 'heilig Nacht'* (holy-nightish)." Peg became President of the Aldeburgh Foundation and in 1959 set up the "Hesse Students" scheme to enable young people to attend the Aldeburgh Festival in return for practical help.

Although not royal by birth, "Peg" (as most people came to know her) certainly immersed herself in her role of princess so that in a way she came to represent what one should be. This is particularly poignant as she accomplished this feat in the second half to the late 20th century, when her kind were fast being considered obsolete. It is due to her credit, undoubtedly, that her single-handed championship of her late husband's family heritage ensured that it has survived intact to this day, and quite likely for posterity.

During his life, and certainly after becoming a widow, Peg shared and supported Lu's love for artistic and literary life of Darmstadt. After his death, she diligently took care of his legacy. *"It seems like a forgiving wave of history today that the woman who once came as a stranger took up a legacy overshadowed by graves; soon she became so welcoming that the spirit of her greatest predecessors – I only think of the Great Landgravine Karoline and the Grand Duchess Alice,"* Landgrave Moritz recalled.[30] In fact, Peg *"followed the tradition of all those caring and active ladies in the Grand Ducal family, which dates back to*

At Wolfsgarten, Peg hosting family members for the confirmation of Mafalda of Hesse.

the great Landgravine Karoline, whose motto Princess Margaret had adopted in her activities, namely: "Charity, regardless of whether Christian or otherwise, should be practised in such a way that it is an end in itself.[31] Today, the legacy of the Hesse and by Rhine dynasty lives on in no small part due to Peg's indefatigable efforts. Peg, and Lu even, saw in a name not privilege, *"but understood as an obligation, to get involved with what was given to her, what was important to her: culture, friends, the needy, the sick and the disabled."*[32]

At Wolfsgarten, Peg surrounded by Beatrix of Hohenlohe-Langenburg (who worked as her secretary) and Heinrich of Hesse.

This opinion of Peg was echoed by the late Fürstin Tatiana von Metternich. *"Throughout her life, many depended on her. Arrived in Darmstadt as a "black bride" behind coffins, she soon selflessly took over the earlier duties of the Grand Ducal Family and won all hearts. I am glad afterwards to have written to her about what her loyal friendship meant to me. Her answer was that we had a lot in common: the same English upbringing; our active husbands who relied so much on us; our consistent social engagement despite our dazzling life; we both had moved to foreign countries; we also shared the memory of the tragic Russian past, me through exile, her through her husband's tragic family,"* she wrote.[33]

Landgrave Moritz of Hesse had a high opinion of his Aunt Peg. *"She brought in a fresh Scottish-Irish wind to the old clan of the continent. She was relaxed and understanding, and she clear up immediately any problems instead of holding them back for a long time. I don't know anyone who could do it like that – to encourage your counterpart with a few direct questions during a talk about the problem that was worrying you and then direct you to look for a solution right away."*[34]

Peg at Schloß Langenburg talking to Fürstin Eilika of Leiningen. Behind them are: Grand Duke Wladimir Kirillovich of Russia, Prince Georg Wilhelm of Hannover, and Archduchess Alexandra of Austria-Tuscany.

In a conversation one of the authors had with Archduchess Helen of Austria (née Törring-Jettenbach), she fondly remembered the Hesses, *"We knew Aunt Peg and Uncle Lu very well because they were intimate friends of our parents. We often spent time at Wolfsgarten and loved being*

Peg with King Gustaf VI Adolf of Sweden, widower of her husband's cousin Louise.

there. And the couple used to come to Winhöring [a Törring-Jettenbach estate in Bavaria] *which was nice for old and young. My mother loved having friends to stay and enjoyed speaking English with Peg."*[35] As for Peg's love of children, the archduchess recalled,

"Peg was extremely amusing and witty and loved children. She used to invent endless games with us and made us perform small shows and theatre performances using the old billiard table as a stage. Peg loved music – classic and entertainment- and whenever there was an opportunity in Wolfsgarten, she used to wind up the old Gramophone and we would dance! A lot of classic music was played in her house and I remember many evenings when Benjamin Britten used to play the piano accompanying Peter Pears singing ancient English folksongs (which we found boring). Peg seemed to have endless energy and a lot of her energy was used on good works. (Red Cross – children's home, etc.). She was always ready to help and when our beloved mother died, she came and stayed with us numerous times in Munich and Winhöring. Etty, my sister-in-law [Princess Henriette zu Hohenlohe-Bartenstein] *stayed and worked at Wolfsgarten and she liked her very much!"*[36]

To accompany her, Peg had Princess Beatrix of Hohenlohe-Langenburg, who became her secretary and inseparable companion, almost like a daughter. Under Peg's stewardship, Wolfsgarten continued welcoming Lu's extended family. Often times the palace would witness large gatherings, including the rambunctious voices of the younger generation, many of them playing in the still-standing playhouse Ernst Ludwig had built for his daughter Elisabeth.

In a remembrance he penned in honor of his Aunt Peg, Heinrich of Hesse wrote,

"Thanks to Aunt Peg's generous commitment and warmth, in the post-

Peg with the Earl Mountbatten of Burma, her husband's first cousin.

war years, it [Wolfsgarten] *appeared like one inviting nursery where you felt protected, in which you found comfort and nourishment, bodily and spiritual. Because of her background, our aunt also enjoyed sympathy from Scottish-origin English and American officers, some of whom were of high rank. Sometimes she influenced them to assist us in finding solutions for one or two of our problems, mainly among them food. One day an influential American general came for dinner, and Aunt Peg intended to talk to him about my father, who was in detention. She instructed us in detail to make the guest's stay as pleasant as possible. Towards the end of the meal,*

London, July 29, 1981 – At the wedding of The Prince of Wales and Lady Diana Spencer: Peg with Kraft, Cécile and Beatrix of Hohenlohe-Langenburg.

when it was favorable for our request to be placed, the general started rocking on his chair. The piece of furniture was antique and fragile, and the general corpulent. Suddenly, he lost his balance, fell down, medals jingling over the back and hit his head violently against the wall. Angry, he scrambled up and ran from the room and the house, taking with him our chance to inquire about father. After some time in Wolfsgarten, I realized an important fact of life there: Aunt Peg kept coming up with something new to keep everyone busy. I had hoped for a little loneliness and quiet as I wanted to spend time in my interests and above all finding

The baptism of Leonora Knatchbull, Romsey, 1986. From the left: Queen Sofía and King Juan Carlos of Spain, Lord Brabourne and Countess Mountbatten of Burma, Michael-John Knatchbull, Queen Anne Marie of Greece, Lady Romsey holding baby Leonora, King Constantine II of the Hellenes (behind him is Landgrave Moritz of Hesse); Lord Romsey with his children Nicholas and Alexandra, and Peg.

Over the years, Prince Philip frequently conducted private visits to Peg in Darmstadt and Wolfsgarten. This image was taken during one such occasion. From the left: Prince Philip, Peg, Moritz of Hesse, and Sophie of Hannover.

myself again and coming to terms with my fate. I was looking for one area that was mine alone, where I could do what I wanted. And what I wanted was to intensely paint, and devote myself to studying art. Then I remembered Schloß Adolfseck, our big baroque palace, that after the war got its old name again, Schloß Fasanerie … Yet it was Wolfsgarten's warmth and peace that allowed us all to start rebuilding our relief after so much loss…."[37]

According to Peg's obituary in the *Independent* dated January 30, 1997, it was actually through her that the British Royal Family was able to start to revive contact with their German relatives after the war. In addition, they were able to recover some of the Hesse Crown Jewels that had been stolen by US Army officers right after the war was concluded.[38]

Princess Margaret of Hesse and by Rhine, Aunt Peg, Peg, arts patron and humanitarian, died on January 26, 1997, weeks short of her 84th birthday. Her funeral took place five days later and was attended by a large gathering of the "Royal Mob," prominently among them Prince Philip, The Prince of Wales, Queen Anne Marie of Greece, Landgrave Moritz of Hesse, Prince Georg Wilhelm and Princess Sophie of Hannover, among a throng of many of Peg's "adopted" family.

Later that year, a memorial book in honor of Peg was published in Darmstadt. Many family, friends and colleagues, sent their contributions. Principally among them was The Duke of Edinburgh, whose dedication follows:

In November 1937 Prince Ludwig of Hessen was to be married to Miss Margaret Geddes in London. His mother, brother and sister-in-law and their two sons were flying to London for the wedding when their aircraft crashed in fog at Ostend. I have the very clearest recollection of the profound shock with which I heard the news of the crash

Schloß Langenburg: Peg with Count Hans Veit of Törring-Jettenbach.

and the death of my sister and her family. Whatever I may have felt was as nothing compared to the shattering effect it must have had on the couple about to be married. It was a cruel way to start married life, but worse was to follow. Within a matter of months, his brother's surviving daughter, Johanna, was to die of meningitis. If that was not enough, war was soon to break out between the home countries of Margaret and Ludwig. She was thus completely cut off from family and friends and her husband was away fighting.

Peg at Schloß Langenburg attending the 60th birthday of her nephew Fürst Kraft of Hohenlohe-Langenburg. Greeting her is Princess Pimpinela of Hohenlohe-Langenburg, Marquesa de Belvis de las Navas, with Kraft behind Peg.

It says a very great deal for their strength of character that they came through all these dreadful ordeals with unimpaired enthusiasm and a burning dedication to help others in trouble. At the end of the war, Princess Margaret had to cope with a husband taken to prison by the Allies, because he had been in the German Army, and a constant stream of refugees from eastern Germany seeking rest and re-settlement. Not only did she manage to care for all these unexpected guests, she made a special effort to accommodate disabled and disadvantaged children. All this at a time of severe food shortages and crippling transport problems.

Six years of war took a dreadful toll of Darmstadt. No-one knows better than the people of Darmstadt how the Prince and Princess devoted themselves to the rehabilitation of the town and its inhabitants. They also threw themselves into the task of repairing and refurbishing their home at Wolfsgarten, the old Schloss in the town and the farm at Kranichstein. All this on top of their active involvement in the re-establishment of the arts and the encouragement of charities and voluntary organizations.

The Prince of Wales and his Aunt Peg at her 80th birthday celebration

Wars have been sweeping through Europe for thousands of years and anyone with an interest in history will know about the campaigns and the battles. What is frequently overlooked is the vital part played by those who set about repairing the damage and breathing new life into shattered

communities. *Prince and Princess Ludwig were heroes of the post-war reconstruction of cult reconstruction of culture in Germany. It was a contribution that is difficult to exaggerate but there is no doubt that it was fully and generously recognised by the people of Darmstadt and Hessen.*"[38]

The pastor who officiated at her funeral on January 31, 1997, said of Peg, "*The charisma of this remarkable woman was also apparent in the effect she had on other people, the effect she had on you who are here today, for example, and in the respectful and sometimes almost affectionate manner in which the people of Darmstadt*

Darmstadt, January 31, 1997 – The funeral of Princess Margaret of Hesse and by Rhine.

spoke of her." Furthermore, he expressed his opinion of Peg's moral character when he said that she was, "*Something very special indeed which, sadly, will never come again. That much we know. And as has become apparent over the past few days, her Royal Highness Princess Margaret of Hesse and by Rhine was indeed something very special, was indeed a very special gift to our city, just as our city of Darmstadt was to her. Born in Dublin, raised in New York, at home in London and numerous other cities of the world, it was Darmstadt that was her city, the city in which she was not only respected and esteemed but also the city in which the people knew her, loved her as well. How else can we describe the relationship between the Princess and the city of Darmstadt if not as a love affair? And that's why today is a sad day not only for you, Prince Moritz and your family, but for Darmstadt as well.*"[39]

The Prince of Wales felt the loss of his Aunt Peg deeply as well. In his tribute to this beloved member of the extended family, he wrote,

> "*She very soon became an important feature of my life, as did her husband, Prince Ludwig, who was also my godfather. I was still quite young when my father first took me to Wolfsgarten and I fell in love with that magical house at once. The love and devotion my aunt felt for the house meant that her spirit pervaded the entire atmosphere of the place.*
>
> *She was, above all, a life-enhancer whose presence immediately injected a positive element into everything. I shall never forget her constant refrain – "Accentuate the positive; eliminate the negative!" She followed her own advice through thick and thin and this was exemplified by her unstoppable sense of humor.*
>
> *I greatly admired her constant support for artists, musicians, poets and writers of every description and it is so wonderful to know that she won the hearts of the people of Darmstadt as a result of all the special*

qualities she possessed – most particularly that of unbounded energy and enthusiasm. I, like so many others, miss he more than words can describe. But her gloriously bright spirit lives on in our hearts as an inspiration for our own lives and for the way in which one heart can touch so many others during the brief course of an earthly existence...."[41]

The talented Yehudi Menuhin recalled at her memorial service in London (June 20, 1997) a vignette that described her character. *"She delighted in recounting the American liberation at Wolfsgarten and the disbelief and amazement on the officer's face when she introduced one after the other of her extensive family of all ages with their full titles. The real and tangible transaction occurred finally with a welcome and generous gift of loo-paper and toothpaste from the local American PX store,"* he shared with the concurrence.[42]

The Duke of Edinburgh accompanied by his sister Princess Sophie of Hannover attending the funeral of Princess Margaret – The Prince of Wales following them.

Another meaningful tribute was paid by Herbert Heckmann, former president of the German Academy of Language and Poetry, of which Peg was patron for many years. He longingly spoke of the *"great good fortune which only late are we becoming aware of,"*[43] which was having her patronage and support. Other such organizations given support by her included: The Multiple Sclerosis Society, the Associations for the Spastics, the Association for the Victims of Muscular Atrophy, and of course, the Red Cross.

Perhaps, no better tribute best described Peg's life than the one contributed by Landgrave Moritz, wrote:

One of her typical habits was to jot notes on a notepad with *"Don't forget ..."* on it – some notes were important, others just as menial as a little message to place chocolates on someone's bedside table. On one of these notes we found the following lines by Lady Ryder of Warsaw, an Englishwoman who worked tirelessly in the Polish capital assisting those displaced by war, as well as caring for imprisoned deportees. The words don't just bring aunt Peg's essence, but also what she wanted to convey to us:

"Don't forget ..."
Think deeply, speak gently,
love much, laugh often,
work hard, give freely,
pay promptly, pray earnestly.[44]

★★★★★★★★

Princess Mafalda of Savoy and Prince Philipp of Hesse-Kassel.

The House of Hesse Today

Despite the numerous traumas of Moritz's early life, he faced the postwar world with determination to preserve and protect his family's heritage.[45]

And one might add for all the traumas of the House of Hesse and by Rhine. The post-war years were somewhat difficult since many of the members of the Hesse family had joined the Nazi party and went through de-Nazification of some form or other, while others who had been persecuted by them were either dead or getting over the horrific suffering.

Landgrave Moritz of Hesse was born in Racconigi Castle, Italy on August 6, 1926[46], the eldest son of Prince Philipp of Hesse (himself the son of Landgrave Friedrich Karl of Hesse and Princess Margarethe, nèe Prussia) and Princess Mafalda of Savoy, the daughter of King Victor Emmanuel III of Italy and his wife, the former Princess Elena of Montenegro. Moritz spent his early childhood in Italy and made occasional visits to Germany to see his paternal grandparents. He was educated with his younger brothers at Villa Polissena in Rome. In the early thirties, with the rise of the Nazis, Prince Philipp, a member in good standing of the Nazi party since 1930, and his family spent more time in Germany. Philipp *"joined the NSDAP in part because of the personal conviction he had with Nazi leaders,"* but also due to *"ideological reasons for becoming a Nazi."*[47]

Being the son-in-law of the Italian monarch decidedly improved Philipp's position within the Third Reich. For several years he served as Governor of the province of Hesse-Nassau. Philipp later claimed that he had been cajoled into accepting by Hermann

Princess Mafalda of Hesse-Kassel with her sons Heinrich, Otto, and Moritz.

Göring, and had finally accepted as it *"could be in the best interest of your homeland,"*[48] his father reportedly advised. However, when Mussolini fell and the Savoys abandoned their German alliance, Philipp's star lost its former luster. Eventually, he was arrested by the Nazis, who also aprehended Mafalda and imprisoned her. Philipp languished in prison until the end of the war, when his hope to be free was quickly dashed after the Allies arrested him for his involvement with the Third Reich. It was not until 1948, that Philipp finally emerged from incarceration. From then onward, he focused all his energy on rebuilding his life.

As a teenager, without much say in the matter, Moritz became a member of the Jungvolk, and other Nazi youth movements as befitted the son of an early party member. Besides, it was an obligatory requirement at the school Moritz and Heinrich were attending.[49] During the war, he witnessed the devastation rained upon Frankfurt by the firebombing carried out by the Allies. On October 22, 1943, for example, *"as 444 British Lancaster bombers*

Moritz and Tatiana of Hesse.

turned the streets into a sea of liquid phosphorus,"[50] Moritz was serving on a flak battery outside the city.

Prince Heinrich of Hesse.

Princess Mafalda ended in Buchenwald Concentration Camp, where she died from loss of blood in August, 1944 after her arm had been amputated due to injury. As horrible as her death was, the family also became refugees at this point, thrown out of their home by the advancing allies. Moritz and his young siblings, Heinrich, Otto and Princess Elisabeth, sought and were given refuge at Wolfsgarten with Peg and Lu. Moritz worked at Gut Kranichstein, his Uncle Lu's farm, while Heinrich later went to Fulda to complete his diploma. Their younger siblings, Otto and Elisabeth remained in Wolfsgarten under Lu and Peg's care. It took the famkily some time to recover fro the trauma suffered during the war. Moritz later said that he never discussed with his father his involvement with the Third Reich or Mafalda's death as, *"it was simply too painful for him."*[51] Moritz, years later, took the admirable initiative to bring much-needed light into his family's historical involvement with the Third Reich. During his last meeting with one of the authors he was quite certain that he had done the right thing, *"it is best to open up to responsible academics, so the family's history can be better understood,"* he said.[52]

Eventually, Moritz became fully engaged in running the

German Heads of House – From the left: Duke Carl of Württemberg, Fürst Friedrich Wilhelm of Hohenzollern, and Landgrave Moritz of Hesse.

Hessian family legacy. His brother Heinrich dedicated himself to his artistic pursuits and lived in the family's Roman home, Villa Polissena. He died in Wolfsgarten in 1999. Heinrich remained a life-long bachelor and although the press constantly coupled him with several princesses, among them Irene of Greece, he was not interested in such matters; not the marrying kind.

Philipp and Mafalda's youngest children, Otto and Elisabeth, eventually returned to live with their father after his release from detention. Otto married morganatically, twice, and left no descendants. He died in January 1998 aged sixty. As for Elisabeth, she married in 1962 Count Friedrich Carl von Oppersdorff (1925-1985), by whom she had two sons children. After becoming a widow, Elisabeth did not remarry. She leads a very private life and is rarely seen, her brother Morit'z funeral being the last such large outing she attended.

According to his obituary, after the war, Prince Moritz was something of a playboy and got himself into scrapes with other members of the social circles he frequented.[53] Prince Moritz studied agriculture and estate management at Darmstadt (working for a time for Lu at Schloß Kranichstein) and then went on to the University of Kiel. He married Princess Tatiana of Sayn-Wittgenstein-Berleburg in 1964. Princess Tatiana is the sister-in-law of Princess Benedikte of Denmark and the daughter of Gustav Albrecht, 5th Prince of Sayn-Wittgenstein-Berleburg and Margareta Fouché d'Otrante, a descendent of Napoleon's Chief of Police. The couple had four children: Mafalda who married Enrico dei Conti Marone Cinzano in 1989, divorced and married Carlo Galdo in 1991, had two children, divorced and married Ferdinando dei Conti Brachetti Peretti in 2000 and had two children, before her third divorce; Donatus (the current Head of House), who married Countess Floria von Faber-Castell in 2003 and has three

Schloß Greinburg, Austria, 2003: Moritz and Duchess Sophie of Württemberg.

children; Elena, unmarried with one child; lastly, Philipp who married Laetitia Bechtolf in 2006 and has three children: Elena (b. 2006), Tito (b. 2008), and Mafalda (b. 2014). Moritz's three grandsons will carry the family name into the late XXI century since all other Hessian princes of his and his sons' generations have not fathered any sons.

Moritz and Tatiana were divorced in 1974 but were often seen at family occasions together, so their split must have been somewhat amicable or their relationship repaired in due time.

In 2003, Landgraf Moritz of Hesse and his former wife Tatiana at their son Don's wedding.

Moritz lived through a botched kidnapping attempt in 1978. His kidnappers had been studying his movements for several months and of course, their motive was monetary. When he was snatched, his housekeeper had the presence of mind to call the police and the whole thing was over in several hours. However, it served to panic Lord Mountbatten since the kidnappers had said they knew that the two men were related. He quickly set up a meeting with the Metropolitan Police Commissioner to review his security. In the end, Mountbatten's heightened sense of security did little to prevent his being assassinated by the IRA.

Landgraf Moritz of Hesse and Prince Georg Wilhelm of Hannover.

Moritz became Head of House in 1980 at the death of his father, Prince Philipp. It was then that he took the title Landgrave along with his title of Prince. He made

Copenhagen, May 2004, Wedding of Crown Prince Frederik of Denmark – Princess Xenia of Hohenlohe-Langenburg, Prince Georg Friedrich of Prussia, and Prince Philipp of Hesse.

his home at Schloß Panker, in Northern Germany, and at Wolfsgarten. He was also in charge of his family's vast art collection and landholdings. He remained active in promoting the fortunes of the family through art, wine, and the beautiful Schloßhotel Friedrichshof at Kronberg, a property the Hesse family turned into a luxury hotel in 1954. It has been suggested that the Hesse family is the possessor of the richest private art collection in Germany and one of the finest in Europe.[54] He was appreciative and a modest custodian of his family's art collection. Once, as he showed a visitor round who said how wonderful it all was, *"We rather think so,"* replied Landgrave Moritz.[55] However, the art collection is under a legal instrument known as the Hesse Foundation, which prevents its contents to be sold. Moritz could come across as stern and distant, but in reality he was a hospitable, amiable,

Don of Hesse, Madrid, May 2004.

and knowledgeable raconteur once he felt at ease. In 2004, the Hesse family announced that they wanted to sell Schloß Tarasp, which Grand Duke Ernst Ludwig had obtained in 1916 from a wealthy Saxon friend. A worrisome taxation issue was forcing serious reestructuring. In 2008, the municipality of Tarasp agreed to investigate purchasing the property and converting it into a cultural and tourist attraction. Two years later, the *Fundaziun Chastè da Tarasp* was created to seek funding and administer the castle after it was purchased. Since the *Fundaziun* struggled to raise funding, in 2015 Swiss artist Not Vital announced that he would purchase the castle. In March 2016, Not Vital acquired the castle for CHF 7.9 million.[56]

Don and Floria of Hesse with Ignaz and Robinia of Törring-Jettenbach in Salzburg.

One year after the sale of Tarasp, Moritz and his son Don decided to dispose of Holbein's *Madonna*, the precious masterpiece that Moritz had recovered from the plundered Veste Coburg. As the German government declared it a national treasure, the House of Hesse was unable to sell it to a foreign collector or institution. Instead, it was sold to a German billionaire who offered a reputed €50 million for it. The painting is now on display in a museum on Schwäbisch Hall.

As the decade proceeded, Moritz's health suffered more deterioration. A smoker for many years, his lungs had suffered grave damage. He died after a long battle with lung disease on May 23, 2013.[57] Moritz's funeral, a major gathering of royalty from across Europe took place on June 3 at the St Johanneskirche in Kronberg-im-Taunus. Among the mourners were: Queen Sofía of Spain, King Constantine II of the Hellenes, King Simeon of Bulgaria (his first cousin), the Prince of Naples (first cousin), as well as members of nearly every German dynasty. All of Moritz's children, as well as his sister Princess Elisabeth and his former wife, along with some of the grandchildren, attended the funeral

Philipp and Letitia of Hesse, Schloß Panker, 2006.

Donatus, the current Head of House Hesse was born October 17, 1966 in Kiel, Germany.[58] He trained in Economics and is currently not just the head of The Hesse House Foundation, but manages his family's many and varied business and cultural interests. He is a passsionate equestrian. As mentioned, Donatus is married to Countess Floria von Faber-Castell. She is from the famous pen and pencil manufacturing family. The couple have three children: twins Paulina and Moritz (b. 2007), and August (b. 2012).

Chapter XI

The Women of Darmstadt

The Darmstadt branch of the Hesse dynasty produced many more females than males. This eventually led to its extinction when the last generation was wiped out by tragedy and childlessness. None of the five grand dukes of Hesse and by Rhine managed to produce a collateral male line that could have stepped in as a "spare" in the event that the main line died out. Examples abound of landgraves and grand dukes producing several sons, who in turn failed to establish collateral lines: for example, Ludwig I's sons: Ludwig II, Georg, Friedrich, Emil, and Gustav. Of these five siblings, only Ludwig II produced sons. Among them, the eldest (Ludwig III) was childless, the middle (Karl) left three sons, and the younger (Alexander) left morganatic descendants who could not inherit the grand ducal throne. Prince Karl fathered three sons, but only one of them (Ludwig IV) left a male heir (Ernst Ludwig). The last grand duke produced two sons (Georg Donatus and Ludwig) who were deeply affected by tragedy and bad luck, and were thus unable to produce a viable next generation: the elder had two sons who died in the same air accident that wiped out his family, while the younger son was childless. What one of the authors of this book calls "genealogical Russian roulette" finally won the hand and in 1968 the Hesse and by Rhine family came to an end after more than four-hundred years of being one of Europe's most prominent dynasties.

While the family was notoriously short of males, generation after generation, landgraves and grand dukes produced a large number of female offspring who survived childhood illnesses and proliferated. These women, landgravines and princesses, were to be mainly responsible for linking their house to many of Europe's leading dynasties. Not only were their own marriages exquisitely dynastic, but their descendants, in most cases, spread the Hessian bloodlines throughout the continent. Today, in fact, there are hardly any ruling and formerly ruling dynasties that do not have a spot in the intricate quilt build by the women of Darmstadt.

Ernst Ludwig, Eleonor and their two sons: Don and Lu.

When looking at family trees, one can clearly see the relationships established through genealogical lines. The overwhelming majority of family trees follow the descendants in the male line; female lines are not usually displayed in family trees. Genealogists attempt to demonstrate degrees of consanguinity by explaining through family trees how closely or distantly related people are. And, only following the male lines of descent fails to display the whole gamut of a person's genealogical connections as female lines oftentimes demonstrate very interesting and previously ignored family relations between royalty.

This last chapter brings to life eighteen fascinating Hessian women. They were chosen for the purpose of illustrating not only their role in expanding the dynasty's intricate genealogical web, but also because of their own achievements.

****

Duchess Anna Eleonora of Brunswick-Lüneburg (1601-1659)

Anna Eleonore was a daughter of Landgrave Ludwig V of Hesse-Darmstadt (1577-1626) from his marriage to Magdalena (1582-1616), daughter of the Elector Johann Georg of Brandenburg. She was born in Darmstadt on July 30, 1601.[1]

Duchess Anna Eleonora of Brunswick-Lüneburg.

Through her marriage, she is of particular importance to the English royal house. She married on December 14, 1617 in Darmstadt the future Duke Georg of Brunswick-Lüneburg (1582-1641).[2] The marriage, in which a large number of princelings were present in Darmstadt, was elaborately celebrated. Through this marital alliance Duke Georg was able to exert considerable influence in the ongoing conflict between the Hessian branches of Darmstadt and Kassel. The Brunswicker also astutely knew how to use for his benefit the good relations of his father-in-law with the Habsburg court in Vienna. Anna Eleonore unknowingly became an important recorder of history, doing so through the voluminous political correspondence she maintained with her father.

Anna Eleonore and Georg were the parents of eight children: Magdalena (b./d. 1618); Duke Christian Ludwig of Brunswick-Lüneburg (1622-1665), who married Dorothea of Schleswig-Holstein-

Sonderburg-Glücksburg (1636-1689), but was childless; Duke Georg Wilhelm of Brunswick-Celle (1624-1705), who entered into a semi-morganatic marriage with Eléonore Desmier d'Olbreuse (1639-1722); Duke Johann Friedrich of Hannover (1625-1679), married to Countess Palatine Benedikta Henriette of Simmern (1652-1730); Sophia Amalie (1628-1685); Elector Ernst August of Hannover (1629-1698), who married Princess Palatine Sophia (1630-1714); Dorothea Magdalena (1629-1630), and Anne (1630-1636).[3]

In his will, Duke Georg appointed his wife Anna Eleonore, together with his brother and brother-in-law, the guardian of his young sons. Anna Eleonore devoted to her father's house immediately procured her brother Johann the command of the Brunswick-Lüneburg troops. Anna Eleonore lived until her death in her widow's residence Schloß Herzberg, where all her children were born. It is therefore considered the cradle of the English royal family as her son Ernst August was to become the father of future King George I, who inherited English succession rights from his mother Sophia of the Palatinate, a daughter of Princess Elizabeth Stuart and her unlucky husband Friedrich, Elector Palatine and Winter King. Anna Eleonore did not live long enough to meet her grandson, as she died in 1659, a year before the birth of the future King George, first of the Hannoverian kings of Great Britain.

Anna Eleonore was buried in the royal crypt in the town church of St Mary in Celle, Brunswick. Her descendants are present today in nearly all families in the Gotha. Indeed, both The Queen and Prince Philip are among their many descendants.

****

Electress Palatine Elisabeth-Amalia of Neuburg
(1635-1709)

Elisabeth Amalia was born in Giessen on March 20, 1635.[4] She was the third daughter of Landgrave Georg II and his wife, the former Sophie Eleonora of Saxony. Elisabeth Amalia was strictly raised by her Lutheran mother, a convinced follower of the strictest interpretation of Luther's reforms. The young landgravine was considered quite a beauty and striking blond hair is said to have remained so until advanced age.

On September 3, 1653, Elisabeth Amalia married Philipp Wilhelm of Neuburg (1615-1690) in Langenschwalbach.[5] Ten days after their wedding, he inherited the County Palatinate of Neuburg from his father. The groom was twenty years' Elisabeth Amalie's elder and by the time of their wedding he was already a widower. Philipp Wilhelm's first wife was Anna Catherine Vasa, daughter of King Sigismund III of Poland and of his wife Archduchess Constance of Austria. They had married in 1642 and had a son who died at birth. Anna Catherine died in 1651 without any surviving issue. Philipp Wilhelm's second marriage came about through the mediation of Landgrave Ernst of Hesse-Rheinfels, after Elisabeth Amalia had initially secretly and without the knowledge and consent of her family converted the Catholicism, her groom's religion.

She publicly and solemnly accepted her new confession on November 1 of the same year. Her official welcome into the Catholic Church took place in Dusseldorf in the presence of the Elector Archbishop of Cologne, Maximilian Heinrich of Bavaria.

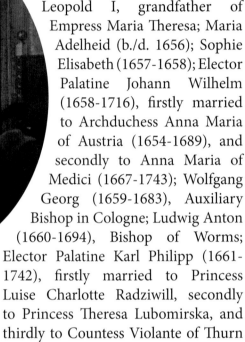

Electress Elisabeth Amalia of Palatinate-Neuburg.

The marriage of Philipp Wilhelm and Elisabeth Amalia not only lasted nearly forty years but was also a very happy one. They settled in Dusseldorf, where they demonstrated their true piety by founding and equipping several churches and monasteries. As a couple, they took procreation with great seriousness and an astounding 17 children were born to them between 1655-1679. They were: Eleonore (1655-1720), wife of Emperor Leopold I, grandfather of Empress Maria Theresa; Maria Adelheid (b./d. 1656); Sophie Elisabeth (1657-1658); Elector Palatine Johann Wilhelm (1658-1716), firstly married to Archduchess Anna Maria of Austria (1654-1689), and secondly to Anna Maria of Medici (1667-1743); Wolfgang Georg (1659-1683), Auxiliary Bishop in Cologne; Ludwig Anton (1660-1694), Bishop of Worms; Elector Palatine Karl Philipp (1661-1742), firstly married to Princess Luise Charlotte Radziwill, secondly to Princess Theresa Lubomirska, and thirdly to Countess Violante of Thurn und Taxis; Alexander Sigismund (1663-1737), Prince Bishop of Augsburg; Franz Ludwig (1664-1732), Archbishop of Trier and Mainz; Friedrich Wilhelm (1665-1689), unmarried; Marie Sophie (1666-1699), consort of King Pedro II of Portugal; Maria Anna (1667-1740), consort of King Carlos II of Spain; Dorothea Sophie (1670-1748), firstly married to Odoardo Farnese, Duke of Parma and Piacenza (by whom she became the mother of Elisabeth Farnese, second wife of King Felipe V of Spain), and secondly to her brother-in-law Francesco Farnese, his brother's successor; Hedwig Elisabeth (1673-1722), married to Jakub Sobieski of Poland; Johann (b./d. 1675); and Leopoldine (1679-1693).[6]

In 1685, Philipp Wilhelm became Elector Palatine with the death of his cousin Elector Palatine Karl

II, a grandson of the Winter King and Queen. This succession also brought a change in religion in the Electoral Palatinate as Philipp Wilhelm was a Catholic, while his predecessor had been a Protestant. However, Philipp Wilhelm was not to enjoy his new throne since his late cousin's sister, Elisabeth Charlotte, Duchess d'Orléans, also laid claim to the Palatinate. In this adventure, she was encouraged by King Louis XIV who had been looking for a pretext to send his armies over the border and into the Palatinate, a wealthy region he had coveted for some time. This claim ignited a war between France and Germany, a conflict that spread misery all along the Rhine.

Due to the Nine Years' War with France, Philipp Wilhelm established his court in Neuburg, instead of Heidelberg, the traditional capital of the Electoral Palatinate. A talented and pious ruler, Philipp Wilhelm was unable to achieve any lasting political accomplishments since during the entire duration of his reign, he was at war with France. Dynastically however, Philipp Wilhelm and Elisabeth Amalia became the ancestors of every Catholic royal house in Europe.

****

Duchess Maria Hedwig of Saxe-Meiningen (1647-1680)

The youngest child of Landgrave Georg II and Landgravine Sophie Eleonora, Maria Hedwig was born in Giessen on November 26, 1647.[7] She lost her father at the age of 14-years-old, while her mother died in 1671, the same year Maria

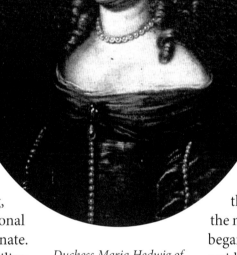

Duchess Maria Hedwig of Saxe-Meiningen.

Hedwig married Prince Bernhard of Saxe-Gotha, whose father Duke Ernst I "the Pious," was the foundational stone for the Ernestine ducal lines of the Wettin dynasty (Saxony). These lines, three of them existing still today, included: Saxe-Gotha-Altenburg, Saxe-Coburg, Saxe-Meiningen, Saxe-Römhild, Saxe-Eisenberg, Saxe-Hildburghausen, and Saxe-Saalfeld. Coincidentally, Maria Hedwig's brother Landgrave Ludwig VI married her husband's sister, Princess Elisabeth Dorothea.

Maria Hedwig married on November 20, 1671, in Gotha's vast Schloß Friedenstein.[8] Her father-in-law Ernst "the Pious" was approaching the end of his long and fruitful reign, while his seven sons planned how to handle the huge inheritance their father would leave behind. In the meantime, Bernhard and his wife began their family. They eventually resided in Ichtershausen. Here he built Schloß Marienburg, which was named in honor of his wife. The year after their wedding, their first son, Ernst Ludwig was born in Gotha. Two more sons arrived in quick succession, Bernhard (1673-1694) and Johann Ernst (1674-1675). In 1676 she gave birth to Maria Elisabeth, who died soon after. Johann Georg was born in 1677, but died the following year. In 1679 a fifth son arrived, Friedrich Wilhelm, who in 1743 succeeded a nephew as the fifth Duke of Saxe-Meiningen, the title his father had received in 1680. That same year, Maria Hedwig gave birth to a sixth son, Georg Ernst. It was a complicated birth that cost his mother's life. Bernhard remarried the following year Elisabeth Eleonore of Brunswick-Wolfenbüttel.

Ernst "the Pious" died in 1675.[9] His sons all ruled the

parental inheritance together for a few years, until the large realm was divided into seven different duchies. Hence, in 1680, Bernhard became the reigning Duke of Saxe-Meiningen. His male-line descendants today are the representatives of this long line of Wettins. The late Archduchess Regina of Austria (née Saxe-Meiningen), wife of Archduke Otto, was also a descendant of Duke Bernhard.

When in 1680 Bernhard divided the family's lands with his brothers he became the first Duke of Saxe-Meiningen. The largest part of his newly formed country was the former county of Henneberg, in whose coat of arms a black hen was depicted. At the time, this symbol was associated with witchcraft and the evil powers of the occult. Maria Hedwig very definitely noticed, shortly before the relocation of their residence from Ichtershausen to Meiningen, that she would never enter the land of the black hen. She was not mistaken as she died shortly after the birth of her last child, a mere nine weeks before their relocation to Meiningen. Her body was transferred there and buried in the crypt of the city church.

Years later, Duke Bernhard built a new palace in Meiningen that would be fitting to his station. The palace, Schloß Elisabethenburg, was completed in 1692 and was named after his second wife. The interestingly shaped structure is an excellent example of Baroque architecture. Inside, the duke built an absolutely gorgeous reception room called the "Hessian Hall,"[10] in memory of his beloved first wife. The room was to be decorated with tribute pictures to honor both dynasties, Saxe-Meiningen and Hesse-Darmstadt.

****

Duchess Magdalena-Sibylla of Württemberg (1652-1712)

Magdalena-Sibylla was the daughter of Landgrave Ludwig VI and his wife, the former Duchess Maria Elisabeth of Holstein-Gottorp. She was born in Darmstadt on April 28, 1652.[11] As a child she lost her mother and came into the care of her aunt, the Queen Dowager Hedwig Eleonore of Sweden. Magdalena-Sybilla moved to Stockholm, where she manifested deep religious beliefs. It was while living there, that in 1671 she met the man who would become her husband. He was Hereditary Prince Wilhelm Ludwig of Württemberg, who was born in Stuttgart in 1647 as the son of Duke Eberhard III (1614-1674) and of his first wife Countess Anna Catharina of Salm-Kyrburg (1614-1655). At the time of his visit to the Swedish court, the young Württemberger was on a multi-year educational tour through Western Europe. Magdalena-Sibylla and Wilhelm Ludwig quickly became engaged and were married in Darmstadt on November 6, 1673.[12]

On July 2, 1674, Wilhelm Ludwig succeeded his father as Duke of Württemberg. The following month Ludwig Wilhelm and Magdalena-Sibylla became parents when a daughter, Eleonore Dorothea, was born in Stuttgart. A second daughter, Eberhardine Louise, also born in Stuttgart, arrived in October 1675. A much-expected heir, Eberhard Ludwig, was born in Stuttgart in September 1676. Magdalena Sibylla was in the midst of her fourth

Duchess Magdalena Sibylla of Württemberg.

pregnancy when her young husband suffered a heart attack. Pregnant and in mourning, the 25-year-old widow had to assume the regency for her son, who reigned as Duke of Württemberg until his death in 1733.

After the birth of her last child, Magdalena Sophie (1677-1742), Dowager Duchess Magdalena-Sibylla concentrated on ruling Württemberg in her son's behalf. Her regency lasted until 1693, when her son took over ruling his duchy. In her free time, she continued religious studies. Like her Aunt Anna Sophia of Hesse-Darmstadt, Abbess of Quedlinburg, she wrote numerous hymns and poems. Many of these hymns found a permanent place in Protestant hymnals. Her music composition was assisted by Johann Pachelbel, who was under her employment in the 1690s.

Duchess Maria Elisabeth of Saxe-Römhild.

Upon her son's accession, Magdalena-Sibylla, with a satisfying sense of accomplishment retired to Kirchheim unter Teck, where she died on August 11, 1712.[13] By then, her son had married Margravine Johanna Elisabeth of Baden-Durlach and made her a grandmother. This grandson was Hereditary Prince Friedrich Ludwig (1698-1731), who predeceased his father and did not have a surviving son. Hence, on Duke Erberhard Ludwig's death, the Duchy of Württemberg passed to his first cousin Karl Alexander, whose modern-day descendants include Duke Carl, Head of the Royal House of Württemberg.

****

Duchess Maria Elisabeth of Saxe-Römhild (1656-1715)

Born in Darmstadt on March 3, 1656, Maria Elisabeth was the child of Landgrave Ludwig VI and Landgravine Maria Elisabeth of Hesse-Darmstadt.[14] On March 1, 1676, a few weeks before her 20th birthday, Maria Elisabeth married in Darmstadt the future Duke Heinrich of Saxe-Römhild, who from the year prior had been co-ruling their father's vast inheritance with his six brothers. He was a younger brother of Duke Bernhard of Saxe-Meiningen, who had married Maria Elisabeth's aunt.

Once in Thüringen, the newlyweds settled in Römhild's Schloß Glücksburg. Heinrich was deeply in love with his wife and always called her "Marielies."[15] In her honor, he had several buildings constructed, including a new grotto which he named "Marie-Elisabethenlust" (Marie-Elisabeth's Pleasure). Around it a beautiful garden grew that provided the Duke of Saxe-Römhild's wife with much joy. In 1680, after the seven brothers decided to partition their paternal inheritance, Heinrich officially became Duke of Saxe-Römhild.

Duke Heinrich entered the military at an early age. He served in Brandenburg and later transferred to Imperial service in the Austrian cavalry. As a ruler, he was less effective. Heinrich had a tendency to spend more than his exchequer would allow. Either building, remodeling, renovating, or adding luxurious pieces to his residences, his expenditures were unsustainable. When he died in 1710, Heinrich left the ducal treasury deeply in debt. Still, the valuable land he left behind was fought over by his relations until they reached a final settlement in 1765.

In spite of their deep love for each other, their marriage lasting nearly three-and-a-half decades, Heinrich and Maria Elisabeth remained childless. After his death, Maria Elisabeth remained undisturbed in Römhild, even as his relatives argued over the spoils around her. She died there on August 16, 1715.[16]

****

Duchess Sophia Maria of Saxe-Eisenberg (1661-1712)

Sophia Maria was born in Darmstadt on May 7, 1661.[17] She was one of the many daughters of Landgrave Ludwig VI and his wife Maria Elisabeth. As was the case with her aunt and sister, Sophia Maria married one of the seven sons of Ernst the Pious. On February 9, 1681, she married in Darmstadt Duke Christian of Saxe-Eisenberg, who at the time was already a widower and father of a daughter.

Duke Christian was interested in history and art. He was educated at the University of Strasbourg, and along with his brothers Bernhard and Heinrich, went on a lengthy educational tour that included visits to the Netherlands, Switzerland, Savoy, France, and Italy. After the division of his father's domains, Christian received Eisenberg, Ronneburg, Roda, and Camburg, using the title of Duke of Saxe-Eisenberg. He relocated to his new duchy and began building a sizeable residence called Schloß Christiansburg, in his name. He

Duchess Sophia Maria of Saxe-Eisenberg.

later expanded the structure and added a castle church in memory of his first wife, Christine of Saxe-Merseburg. Christian's penchant for building quickly plunged his small duchy into debt. During his reign, he was in contact with many of the leading scholars of his time and developed a troubling interest in alchemy and the occult. He promoted the school system and set up a mint. Another of his improvements was installing Eisenberg with a water system using lead pipes that supplied his quaint little capital with spring water. Along with her husband, Sophia Maria busied herself with projects to improve the lives of their subjects. She was a diligent housewife and had a predilection for spinning. Oftentimes, and disguised as a simple woman, she would provide wool and yarn supplies to local spinners. Doing so, allowed a cottage industry to be built around clothmaking.

As was the case with her sister Maria Elisabeth, Sophia Maria's marriage remained childless. She cared for her husband's daughter Princess Christina as her own child and saw her married to Duke Philipp Ernst of Holstein-Glücksburg (1673-1729).[18]

Duke Christian died at Eisenberg in 1707. Behind, he left a depleted treasury and a duchy deeply in debt. As he lacked a direct male heir, his domains were partitioned among his brothers and their descendants, the lion's share going to the Saxe-Gotha-Altenburg line. As for Sophia Maria, she survived her husband five years and died in Gotha's Schloß Friedenstein on August 8, 1712.[19]

****

Landgravine Elisabeth Dorothea of Hesse-Homburg (1676-1721)

The youngest daughter of her mother and namesake, Elisabeth Dorothea was born in Darmstadt on April 24, 1676.[20] She lost her father Landgrave Ludwig VI on her second birthday. Her mother, Elisabeth Dorothea of Saxe-Gotha, was very fond of her daughter and called her affectionately "Lisa Dorthgen."[21] At the end of her mother's regency, Elisabeth Dorothea accompanied her to Butzbach in Upper Hesse, the residence designated as a widow's seat. The young landgravine was considered to be very educated, spoke several languages, and wrote poetry.

Landgravine Elisabeth Dorothea of Hesse-Homburg.

Such an alluring prospective bride as Elisabeth Dorothea soon attracted the attention of important suitors, most prominent among them the King of the Romans, Archduke Joseph of Austria (later Emperor Joseph I). Negotiations between Vienna and Butzbach began in earnest and for a while it seemed as if Elisabeth Dorothea was destined to wear the Imperial mantle. However, the negotiations broke down and Joseph instead married Amalie Wilhelmine of Brunswick-Lüneburg (1673-1742). Elisabeth Dorothea did not wait long to find a groom as her mother had already arranged her betrothal to Landgrave Friedrich III Jakob of Hesse-Homburg (1673-1746). The wedding ceremony took place in Schloß Butzbach's audience chamber on February 24, 1700.[22]

Landgrave Friedrich III Jakob was one the sons of Landgrave Friedrich II from his marriage to Louise Elisabeth of Courland. He was born at court in Berlin and was educated in its culturally and spiritually progressive atmosphere. Elisabeth Dorothea was a true match to her husband as she also received a thorough education and mastered German, French, Latin, Italian, and Greek. She invested great efforts in participating in their children's education as well.

Friedrich III Jakob entered the military while in his teens, attending an academy in Wolfenbüttel in 1687. Then he transferred to a cavalry regiment in Württemberg. In 1690, he went to serve for the Dutch with the rank of Captain. Two years later he was raised to Colonel of the Cavalry Regiment Groningen. Over the following years, he remained in Dutch service and continued being regularly promoted until his retirement after the signing of the Treaty of Utrecht. As a Dutch officer, Friedrich III Jakob saw action in the War of the Spanish Succession, and spent time in Spain, where Elisabeth Dorothea followed him.

In twenty-one years of marriage, the couple had ten children, most rather unhealthy. The first, a stillborn arrived in Homburg in November 1700. Friederike was born in Groningen in 1701 but died in Homburg three years later. The third child, Friedrich Wilhelm, was born in Groningen in 1702 and died there the following year. The fourth pregnancy brought Louise Wilhelmine, born in Homburg in December 1703, who died some eight months later. By the end of 1704 all Elisabeth Dorothea's children had died. In January 1705, she gave birth to a fifth child Ludwig Johann, born at Homburg. He married Princess Anastasia Ivannovna Trubetzkoy, but died childless. Child number six was Johan Karl, born in Homburg in 1706. He died childless in Fellin, Livonia, in 1728. Ernestine Louise was born in Homburg in 1707 but only lived a month. Two more stillbirths followed. Lastly, and tragically, in 1721 Elisabeth Dorothea gave birth yet again. The birthing was complicated, and she died a week after giving birth to Friedrich Ulrich, who survived his mother by two months.

Seven years after becoming a widower, Friedrich III Jakob married secondly. His new wife was Countess Christianne Charlotte of Nassau-Ottweiler (1685-1761), the widow of Count Karl Ludwig of Nassau-Saarbrücken. As his second wife was already in her forties, there were no children.

Since Friedrich III Jakob served many years in the Dutch military and administrative service, he was not preoccupied with the administration of his realm. Worth mentioning, however, is the founding of the Homburg orphanage 1721, which still exists today as a foundation. The Landgrave of Hesse-Homburg being a worldly and educated man, supported religious toleration in his realm. Unfortunately, during his reign Hesse-Homburg fell into serious debt. An imperial debt commission acted to solve the precarious financial situation in Homburg and Friedrich was forced to return to military service in Holland in 1738. He became governor of the Belgian city of Tournai, then governor of Breda in 1741. Promoted to General of the Cavalry in 1742, he died as Governor of s-Hertogenbosch in 1746. He was buried in the family crypt in Schloß Homburg, where his first

Landgravine Friederike Charlotte of Hesse-Kassel.

wife was buried a quarter of a century earlier. Since none of his children survived him, his nephew Friedrich Karl (1724-1751), succeed him as Landgrave of Hesse-Homburg.

****

Landgravine Friederike Charlotte of Hesse-Kassel (1698-1777)

Friederike Charlotte was a daughter of Landgrave Ernst Ludwig of Hesse-Darmstadt from his marriage to Dorothea Charlotte (1661-1705), daughter of Margrave Albrecht of Brandenburg-Ansbach. Her education was initially conducted at home by members of her father's court. In 1711, Landgrave Ernst Ludwig sent Friederike Charlotte to live with his sister Sophia Louise, who lived in Oettingen. This the landgrave hoped, would provide his daughter with a more careful upbringing and training for her future responsibilities. Considerable doubts exist whether this was a wise choice as years later the young landgravine would turn into a careless and somewhat irresponsible woman. On October 6, 1720, she became engaged to Maximilian of Hesse-Kassel (1689-1753), whom she married seven weeks later on November 28, 1720 in Darmstadt.[23] This marriage, it was hoped, would serve as reconciliation between the two main branches of the Hessian dynasty, for it was the first time that a Hesse-Kassel and a Hesse-Darmstadt had married the other since the territorial division of 1567. However, within a few years both families would come to regret the alliance as Maximilian and Friederike Charlotte led a lavish and scandalously frivolous existence.

Maximilian was the ninth son of Landgrave Karl of Hesse-Kassel (1654-1730) from his marriage to Marie Amalia (1653-1711), daughter of Duke Jakob Kettler of Courland. He was born in Marburg on May 28, 1689. His father bought him in 1713 the estate of Betzigerode for the purpose of providing his son with independent means. Eight years later, when the Lords of Linsingen died out, Landgrave Karl acquired large portions of their estate and passed it to his son Maximilian, including the territory of Jesberg, as well as several villages and bailiwicks. Landgrave Maximilian then sold the estate of Betzigerode to raise the necessary funding for the building of a baroque palace in Treisbachgrund in Jesberg and create a garden for his four daughters. Maximilian was not a good administrator and incurred large debts. He was, however, a passionate musician, an indulging husband, a loving father, and the creator of a splendor-filled, fun-loving court.

Landgrave Maximilian of Hesse-Kassel.

Landgrave Maximilian and Landgravine Friederike Charlotte were married over three decades. They were the parents of eight children: Karl (1721-1722); Ulrike Friederike (1722-1787), who married Friedrich August, Duke of Oldenburg; Charlotte (1725-1782), Canoness and Coadjutrix (assistant) of the Abbey of Herford; Marie (1726-1727); Wilhelmine (1726-1808), married to Prince Heinrich of Prussia, a brother of King Friedrich II "the Great" of Prussia; a stillborn in 1729; Elisabeth Sophie (1730-1731); and Caroline (1732-1759), who married Prince Friedrich August of Anhalt-Zerbst, a brother of Empress Catherine "the Great" of Russia.

In Kassel, the princess from Darmstadt, who soon came to be thought of as wasteful and selfish, did not have an easy time. The fact that she had a good relationship with the widower Landgrave Karl's mistress Madame de Langallerie, was not appreciated by her successor in the landgrave's bedchamber, Barbara Christine von Bernhold. This situation was particularly more complicated when in 1730, in spite of Landgrave Karl's death, his son and successor King Frederik of Sweden retained von Bernhold in her position as First Lady of the Court in Kassel. Landgrave Maximilian's long absences were viewed very critically in the family. Criticism and misunderstanding were also caused by Friederike Charlotte's permissive and lavish lifestyle. Hence, as she did not like Kassel nor her husband's estate at Jesberg, and to avoid the hated von Bernhold, in the 1730s, Friederike Charlotte traveled more frequently, for weeks and months, to Darmstadt and to her friend Princess Maria Augusta of Thurn und Taxis in Frankfurt.

After the death of her husband, she rejected her brother-in-law Wilhelm VIII's suggestion to use the former monastery of Heydau as her widow's seat. That offer was something she saw as an effort to deny her the pleasures her husband had always provided for her in Jesberg. Instead, and leaving considerable debts behind, she moved in 1755 to Darmstadt. Life there was not always what she had expected as her tendency to live beyond her means, her penchant for extravagance, brought her little sympathy from the landgraviate's administrators.

Friederike Charlotte died in Darmstadt on 22

March 1777.[24] Of her eight children, only three survived their mother. Her remains were placed in the family crypt inside Darmstadt's City Church (Stadtkirche).

****

Duchess Maria Theodora (Dorothea) of Guastalla (1706-1784)

Landgravine Theodora was born in Vienna on February 6, 1704.[23] She was the only daughter of Landgrave Philipp of Hesse-Darmstadt (a younger son of Landgrave Ludwig VI) and his wife Princess Maria Theresa of Croÿ Havré. She was raised in the Imperial capital due to her father serving in the Habsburg army.

On February 23, 1727, Theodora married in Mantua Antonio Ferrante Gonzaga (1687-1729), Duke of Guastalla and Sabionetta, a small Italian state in the Emilia-Romagna, on the right bank of the Po River. The county of Guastalla was established in 1406 and became a duchy in 1621. In 1539, Ferrante Gonzaga, a son of the Duke of Mantua, purchased Guastalla from Countess Ludovica Torelli, who had inherited the county from her father. Ferrante's descendants ruled over Guastalla until their line became extinct in 1746.

Antonio Ferrante Gonzaga was born in December 1687. He was the son of Vincenzo Gonzaga, Duke of Guastalla, and his wife, and cousin, Maria Vittoria Gonzaga. In 1714, Antonio Ferrante succeeded his father as Duke of Guastalla. For a brief period, he was engaged to Maria Karolina Sobieska, daughter of Jan III Sobieski, King of

Antonio Ferrante Gonzaga, Duke of Guastalla.

Poland. The marriage was derailed by Maria Karolina's refusal to go ahead with it. Instead, Antonio Ferrante married Margherita Cesarini, an Italian aristocrat. It is worth mentioning that Antonio Ferrante's sister Eleonora Luisa Gonzaga had been engaged to Landgrave Philipp of Hesse after the death of Theodora's mother. However, after several years, the engagement was abandoned, and she married Francesco Maria de Medici rather than the much-older Hessian suitor. Unfortunately, Theodora was not Duchess of Guastalla for long. Her husband met an untimely and ghastly death when he was burned alive in an accident in Guastalla on April 16, 1729. Their short-lived marriage was childless.

Guastalla passed to Theodora's brother-in-law Giuseppe (1690-1746), who married Eleonore of Schleswig-Holstein-Sonderburg-Wiessenburg (1715-1760). The marriage of the last Duke of Guastalla being childless, on his death the duchy was annexed by Austria. Later, it was ceded to the Spanish, together with the Duchy of Parma and Piacenza, to which it was merged.

Duchess Theodora of Guastalla's widowhood lasted nearly five decades. She served as Canoness of the Endowment for Highborn Ladies of Thorn bei Roermond. Having survived her brothers, husband, and brother and sister-in-law, Theodora died in Parma on January 23, 1784.[24] She was the last-living Duchess of Guastalla and Sabionetta.

****

Margravine Karoline Luise of Baden-Durlach (1723-1783)

Karoline Luise was the second daughter of Landgrave Ludwig VIII of Hesse-Darmstadt from his marriage to Charlotte, daughter and heiress of Count Johann Reinhard III of Hanau-Lichtenberg. After the early death of her mother, Karoline Luise was carefully educated with her siblings mainly by her father in Buchsweiler. Landgravine Charlotte died in 1726, leaving her widower with five young children; Karoline Luise was three-years-old when she lost her mother, who did not recover after giving birth to a sixth child.

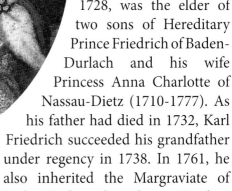

Margravine Karoline Luise of Baden-Durlach.

The education of Ludwig VIII's young daughters became a matter of great concern for him. The Landgrave of Hesse-Darmstadt knew only too well that their marital prospects would increase if Karoline Luise and her sister Louisa Augusta were well-prepared and ready to fulfill their future obligations. In 1733, Karoline Luise was confirmed in the Lutheran faith by a chaplain, Johann Peter Job, sent by her Hanauer grandfather. At her home, her father, who did not remarry, granted her the title of "First Lady of the Darmstadt Court," and as such she became the hostess of her father's very important guests.[25] In 1742, for example, she hosted Elector Karl of Bavaria (Emperor Charles VII), who was in the midst of his rivalry with the Habsburgs. That same year, Louisa Augusta died two months after celebrating her 17th birthday, causing Karoline Luise much sadness as she was her only sister.

Soon enough, marriage proposals began arriving

in Darmstadt as Karoline Luise's fame was well-known across Germany. A marriage project with the Duke of Cumberland failed. Fürst Johann Friedrich of Schwarzburg-Rudolstadt also made approaches but walked away as he felt threatened by the independent-thinking and gifted landgravine. Finally, in 1750, a marriage proposal was accepted. The groom was Margrave Karl Friedrich of Baden-Durlach, a powerful ruler who was seven years Karoline Luise's junior. The wedding ceremony was celebrated in Darmstadt on January 28, 1751.[26]

Karl Friedrich, who was born in Karlsruhe in 1728, was the elder of two sons of Hereditary Prince Friedrich of Baden-Durlach and his wife Princess Anna Charlotte of Nassau-Dietz (1710-1777). As his father had died in 1732, Karl Friedrich succeeded his grandfather under regency in 1738. In 1761, he also inherited the Margraviate of Baden-Baden when that senior line of his family became extinct. From then on, he would be known as Margrave of Baden. In 1803, he was elevated to Elector of Baden, and three years later Baden became a grand duchy.

Due to his father's early death and his mother's mental illness, his grandmother, Margravine Magdalena Wilhelmine (née Württemberg), took over the education of Karl Friedrich and his brother Wilhelm Ludwig. In 1743, Karl Friedrich attended the Académie de Lausanne, where he studied for two years. In 1745, he traveled to Paris, England, and the Netherlands, where he lived with his uncle Wilhelm Carl Heinrich Friso of Nassau-Dietz, later heir to the succession of the United Provinces of the Netherlands.

On October 13, 1746, the imperial declaration of consent took place and Karl Friedrich was officially recognized as the ruler of the margraviate of Baden-Durlach. Karl Friedrich returned to Karlsruhe via the princely courts of Kassel and Darmstadt and formally took over the regency on his 18th birthday on November 22, 1746. However, for the following five years, he paid little attention to the daily task of governing his vast realm.

Soon after assuming the throne of Baden-Durlach, Karl Friedrich's troublesome lifestyle gave much cause for concern. Not only was it rumored that he wanted to adopt Catholicism, but there was disconcerting news about a loose lifestyle involving card games and countless amorous adventures. This caused his Dutch uncle to worry and caution his nephew against his behavior and a proposed visit to Italy, where temptations of all sorts awaited the young margrave.

In 1748, he returned to the Netherlands and visited his family. Then at the beginning of 1749 he asked for the hand of Karoline Luise of Hesse-Darmstadt. Negotiations were slow and complicated, but by October the marriage contract was ready. Meanwhile, Karl Friedrich was in the throes of a relationship with one Elise Barbara Schlutter, who gave him a son. News about this matter did not hinder the marriage plans as the Landgrave of Hesse-Darmstadt was happy with finally finding a befitting husband for his beloved daughter. This began as a political alliance, a marriage of convenience. However, Karl Friedrich and Karoline Luise were extraordinary people who found a way to build a happy union. As for Ms. Schlutter, she was married to a court huntsman and her son Carl Friedrich Hermann was granted the title Baron von Freystedt. He served in Baden military, married and left descendants.

From mid-January to mid-September 1750, Karl Friedrich visited Italy with the excuse of furthering his education. It was nothing but a pleasure journey that brought endless distraction and temptation to the margrave. So troubling was news arriving in Baden, that the head of the council was forced to warn his master of the consequences his behavior and lifestyle could bring. Settling him with an appropriate wife became ever more necessary. The wedding finally took place in Darmstadt on January 28, 1751, but in May Karl Friedrich – without his wife – embarked on a second trip to England, from which he did not return until September. From then on, Karl Friedrich seems to have become seriously concerned with the government of his country.

In 1771, he inherited the Margraviate of Baden-Baden upon the extinction of the senior line of the House of Zähringen, which had ruled Baden for centuries. As Baden-Baden was Catholic and Baden-Durlach Lutheran, the joining of both margraviates created a Protestant Margraviate of Baden, with Karl Friedrich as its ruler. The religious rights of Baden-Baden's Catholics were respected. Karl Friedrich is considered a model of an enlightened absolutist ruler. He promoted schools and universities, jurisdiction, administration, business, culture, urban planning. Above all, he earned merit for the reorganization of the University of Heidelberg, which has since been given the surname "Karl" in his honor. He abolished torture in 1767 and in 1783 serfdom. On his initiative, the foundations were laid of the jewelry and watch industry, and the first drawing school for craftsmen (1767) was opened in Pforzheim. Around 1780, Karl Friedrich brought the Gutedel vines from the Swiss town of Vevey to Baden, which greatly improved the wine industry.

The "Reichsdeputationshauptschluss," the all-encompassing political, territorial, and economic redrawing of Germany, in 1803 gave him the title of Elector and from 1806 onward he was Grand Duke of the new and greatly enlarged Baden. Due to the policies of Chief Minister Baron Sigismund von Reitzenstein, the right bank parts of the Palatinate and parts of the bishoprics of Konstanz, Basel, Strasbourg and Speyer, Breisgau, and Ortenau were added to Baden.

Margravine Karoline Luise was also a force to be reckoned with – she designed the courtly life followed in Karlsruhe. She was deeply involved in the humanities and cultural topics. Karoline Luise mastered five languages and was proficient in numerous fields. Many of her contemporaries called her a "Hessian Minerva."[27] As an ardent admirer of Voltaire, she maintained with him an important correspondence. It was under her patronage that Karlsruhe, the margraviate's capital, developed during this time into one of the spiritual and artistic centers of the empire. Her guests included, in addition to Voltaire, such important contemporaries as Johann Gottfried von Herder, Johann Caspar Lavater, Johann Wolfgang von Goethe, Friedrich Gottlieb Klopstock, Christoph Willibald Gluck, and Christoph Martin Wieland.

Karoline Luise was at times a harpsichordist member of the Baden Margravial Court Chapel, which was greatly expanded and promoted by her and Karl Friedrich. She was also a talented draftsman, and numerous red chalk drawings and pastels with portraits from the hand of the Margravine have been preserved. As such, she was a member of the Copenhagen Academy of Arts.

The Margravine had a special fondness for science and was intensively involved in botany,

Margrave Karl Friedrich of Baden-Durlach.

zoology, physics, medicine, mineralogy, geology, and chemistry. Lavater described her in a letter to Goethe as the *"Wonder of Baden."* In addition to a studio, her living quarters in the Karlsruhe Palace also included a laboratory in which she performed physical and chemical experiments. Karoline Luise planned to publish a comprehensive botanical compilation with illustrations of all plants according to the Linnaeus system, but the venture failed for lack of funds. In addition, the botanist Friedrich Wilhelm von Leysser was for many years the official mineral collector on behalf of the Margravine.

Karoline Luise herself managed her possessions on the right bank of the Rhine. She was extraordinarily successful in this area, supported agriculture, founded a paper mill, and maintained a soap and candle manufactory. After falling down a flight of stairs in 1779 her health was impaired. This accident did not stop her zest for life. Unfortunately, the life of this remarkable woman came to an end while visiting Paris in 1783 with her son Prince Friedrich.

Karoline Luise and her husband had had nine children, but only three survived into adulthood. In 1751 and 1753, she gave birth to babies who died during birthing. In 1755, Karl Ludwig, the Hereditary Prince of Baden, was born. In 1774, he married his first cousin Amalia of Hesse-Darmstadt. A second son was born in 1756, Friedrich, who in 1791 married Princess Christiane Luise of Nassau-Usingen. They were childless. Two more unsuccessful pregnancies followed. Then in

1763 Karoline Luise gave birth to Ludwig, who would rule as Grand Duke of Baden from 1811-1830 but died childless and unmarried.[28]

Still a vibrant and vigorous man when his beloved wife died, Karl Friedrich soon enough found companionship in the arms of a young mistress forty-years his junior. Her name was Luise Karoline Geyer von Geyersberg. While her father was registered the baronial title on his baptismal record, no document exists pointing to who granted his family the title. It is certain that they were ennobled in Austria in 1595 but without a title. Luise Karoline was born in Karlsruhe in 1768, her parents being "Baron" Ludwig Heinrich Geyer von Geyersberg and Countess Maximiliana von Sponeck.[29]

Landgravine Karoline of Hesse-Homburg.

Karl Friedrich was enthralled with his young companion and in November 1787 he led her to the altar. The marriage, inarguably, was not equal, and any children would lack inheritance rights. Genealogical Russian roulette would dictate otherwise. In 1787, she was created Baroness von Hochberg, the title being upgraded to that of Imperial Countess von Hochberg in 1796 by Emperor Franz II.[30]

In due time, children arrived. In 1790 Luise Karoline gave birth to Leopold. Two years later a second son, Wilhelm, arrived. Friedrich Alexander was born in 1793 but lived only a few days. Amalia-Christina born in 1795, went on to marry Fürst Karl Egon II of Fürstenberg, and died in 1869. Finally, Maximilian was born in 1796 and died unmarried and childless in 1832.

The Hochberg children are mentioned because although morganatic at birth, years later they were elevated to full membership in the grand ducal house. That, however, is a story that falls under the section dedicated to their half-brother Hereditary Prince Karl Ludwig and his wife Amalie.

****

Landgravine Karoline of Hesse-Homburg (1746-1821)

Karoline was the eldest daughter of Landgrave Ludwig IX of Hesse-Darmstadt and his wife, Countess Palatine Caroline of Zweibrücken-Birkenfeld. She was born in Buchsweiler on March 2, 1746.[31] Four years later, Karoline was left behind in the hands of caretakers when her parents moved to Prenzlau in Prussia, where her father served in the military. It was not until 1756 that Karoline reconnected with her parents and met the siblings who were born during the multi-year separation. Not surprisingly, Karoline remained strongly independent.

On September 27, 1768, Karoline married Landgrave Friedrich Ludwig of Hesse-Homburg.[32] The marriage was arranged for purely dynastic and diplomatic reasons, without any concern given about Karoline's thoughts on the matter. Karoline's grandfather Landgrave Ludwig VIII had led the regency in Hesse-Homburg with Dowager Landgravine Luise Ulrike for her son Landgrave Friedrich Ludwig, who was five-years-old. Part of the marriage contract mandated that Darmstadt would renounce to the sovereign rights it still held over Homburg. In this treaty, Homburg received a considerable degree of inner sovereignty, while Darmstadt continued to represent Homburg at the imperial level, which included raising imperial taxes. At the time of Karoline's wedding, the ducal family patiently awaited the passing of her grandfather. He passed away three weeks later.

While Karoline and her husband's marriage was prolific, as a couple they remained alien and failed to coalesce. Landgrave Friedrich noted in his memoirs that he had never known love. That, however, did not prevent them from procreating, which after all was the reason why they married. During the first two decades of her marriage, Karoline gave birth 15 times. Friedrich VI was born in 1769 and married in 1818 Princess Elizabeth of Great Britain, a daughter of King George III. He ruled as landgrave from his father's death in 1820 to his own nine years later. Ludwig, born in 1770, married Princess Augusta of Nassau-Usingen, but they divorced the following year.

Landgrave Friedrich VI of Hesse-Homburg.

He ruled as Landgrave of Hesse-Homburg from his brother's death to his own in 1839. Karoline (1771-1854) married Fürst Ludwig Friedrich of Schwarzburg-Rudolstadt. Luise Ulrike (1772-1854) married Prince Karl of Schwarzburg-Rudolstadt. Amalia (1774-1846) married Hereditary Prince Friedrich of Anhalt-Dessau. Paul Emil (1775-1776) was the couple's sixth child and Augusta followed him in 1776. She married Hereditary Grand Duke Friedrich Ludwig of Mecklenburg-Schwerin in 1818 and died in her ninety-fifth year in 1871. Victor, the fourth son, was born in 1778 and died two years later. Philipp (1779-1846) ruled as Landgrave of Hesse-Homburg 1839-1846. He married morganatically Antonia Pototschnigg (1806-1845), whom he created Countess of

Naumburg. Son number six was Gustav (1781-1848), who married Princess Luise of Anhalt-Dessau (1798-1858). He ruled for two years and was succeeded by his brother Ferdinand since his only son predeceased him a few months before his own death. In 1782 Karoline had a stillborn, followed in 1783 by Ferdinand who ruled from 1848-1866 and was the last Landgrave of Hesse-Homburg. Maria Anne (1785-1846) came next and she married Prince Wilhelm of Prussia. Leopold (1787-1813) died in the Battle of Grossgörchen during the Napoleonic Wars. He was unmarried and childless. Karoline last child was a stillborn in 1788.[33] Coincidentally, two of Karoline's granddaughters, Elisabeth and Marie of Prussia made noteworthy marriages as the former married Prince Karl of Hesse and by Rhine, while the latter was the consort of King Maximilian II of Bavaria, as well as the mother of King Ludwig II and his brother "Mad" King Otto.

It is both amazing and tragic, that in spite of having eight sons, six reaching adulthood, they only gave Friedrich V and Karoline one male heir. This was Hereditary Prince Friedrich, born in Homburg in 1830. He was attending university in Bonn when he died three months short of his 18th birthday. Had he survived, he would have succeeded his father and could have possibly replenished the family's empty nursery.

To entertain herself away from her husband, Karoline built a small house on an island in a forest near Homburg. There she found the peace and solitude that endless pregnancies denied her. From Homburg, she also maintained contacts with her mother. Karoline was regarded as one of the most educated ladies of her time and owned a library that was much admired.

The landgrave did not approve of the temporary enthusiasm of his wife for Napoleon, which also distinguished her from her sister-in-law in Darmstadt. Friedrich Ludwig was not a bellicose man. In fact, he was more interested in intellectual discourse, than in soldiers, parades, and anything military. He was a sponsor of German intellectual history and maintained an intriguing and deep correspondence with many of the best-known philosophers and intellectuals of his time. Although he had a speech impediment (he stuttered) that inhibited his public speaking, he devoted himself to philosophy, mathematics, architecture, and other humanities. He was also a passionate chess and piano player. He was an even-handed ruler who tried to rule as honestly as he could. He received a mismanaged legacy and tried throughout his life to cleanse the exchequer and rid Hesse-Homburg of generations of debt.

Scholars, poets, and musicians were always welcome at the small Homburg Court. Even Johann Wolfgang von Goethe was a guest for a short time and fell in love with Homburg. A big concern for the landgrave was the school system and his library. But even then he made no purchases, if he was in arrears with the salary payments at court. Fiction was not his thing – in contrast to his wife Karoline, who was very fond of reading French works. He was more attracted to historical, philosophical, military, and theological literature. As a passionate traveler (about which he wrote detailed descriptions) he devoured travelogues. He *"liked to write, philosophical-religious essays mostly,"* yet was a supporter of the Enlightenment.[34]

The French Revolution and the Napoleonic Wars disrupted the placid life Friedrich V and Karoline enjoyed in Homburg. In 1795, the French Revolutionary Army crossed the Rhine and made its way to Homburg. It was not to be an isolated event. Homburg was surrounded, occupied, and forced to pay ransom several times. In 1798, Marshals Saint-Cyr and Ney even moved their headquarters to the vacant Schloß Homburg. Friedrich Ludwig and his family relocated to private properties they owned, while his sons joined the fight by serving in various German armies.

In 1806, Holy Roman Emperor Franz II not only laid down the German imperial crown, but also dissolved the empire. After Friedrich Ludwig refused to join the Confederation of the Rhine, his landgraviate was sequestered and mediatized under control of Hesse-Darmstadt. The administration was relocated to Giessen and sovereignty was lost. Friedrich Ludwig withdrew to a property he owned at the foot of the Taunus Mountains, went to Schlangenbad, or lived in several rooms he kept in an inn in Frankfurt.

After Napoleon's fall, Hesse-Homburg was re-established as the only one of the mediatized states to have its sovereign rights restored. This political coup was achieved due to several factors: Landgrave Friedrich Ludwig's daughter Maria Anne had married into the Prussian Royal Family and advocated for her father; his six sons had fought alongside Napoleon's enemies with great distinction; and the significance of his family, as the House of Hesse was one of Europe's most respected ruling dynasties. Landgrave Friedrich Ludwig received his lands back in 1815 in the Congress of Vienna. Hesse-Homburg gained some territories previously belonging to France's Sarre Department. Friedrich Ludwig ironically grumbled, *"What should I do with this district in China?"*[35] However, Hesse-Homburg was a sovereign state and that was something worth celebrating.

In September 1818, the landgraves celebrated their golden wedding anniversary, a veritable milestone for a couple that was basically robbed of their choice of spouse. The quirky and conservative but popular Landgrave of Hesse-Homburg died in his capital on January 20, 1820.[36] He was buried in the crypt of the Schloß Bad Homburg. Karoline survived her husband by a little over a year. She died in Homburg on September 19, 1821.[37]

Queen Friederike Luise of Prussia (1751-1805)

Friederike was the second of many daughters of Landgrave Ludwig IX of Hesse-Darmstadt and his wife Karoline, daughter of the Count Palatine and Duke Christian III of Zweibrücken-Birkenfeld and his wife Caroline of Nassau-Saarbrücken. She was born on October 16, 1751 in Prenzlau, where her father was stationed with the Prussian army. The princess, with her inconspicuous appearance, was considered quiet, introspective, and reserved. Friederike was raised mainly by her mother, who as a woman of great intellect was commonly referred to as the "Grand Landgravine." King Friedrich the Great, who was a close friend of Friederike's mother and was chosen as her godfather, had sought to secure the young girl for his nephew and heir. The Prussian monarch, in fact, thought very little of this difficult, indolent, pleasure-seeking nephew who one day would inherit his throne.

Friederike married on July 14, 1769, in the Charlottenburg Schloß Chapel the future King Friedrich Wilhelm II of Prussia.[38] This was the groom's second marriage as he had divorced his first wife Elisabeth of Brunswick because of their outrageous infidelities. "*This animal is incorrigible,*" wrote his disappointed uncle Friedrich the Great.[39] "*The King was disgusted by his dissolute ways and*

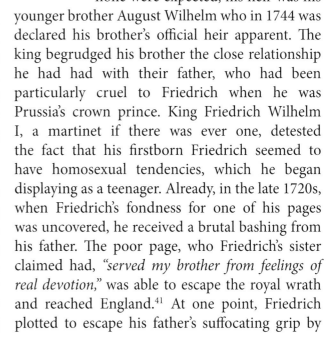

Queen Friederike of Prussia.

by his dabbling into occultism...he was useless for the serious task of government," a biographer of Friedrich II wrote about the disappointing king's nephew and heir.[40] Still, Friedrich Wilhelm managed to impregnate his first wife once and she gave birth to their only child, Friederike, in 1767. She went on to marry Prince Frederick, Duke of York, a son of King George III of Great Britain. Elisabeth, whom King Friedrich the Great held in high esteem, was set with her own small court. She found happiness involved in her own endeavors and lived to the ripe old age of 95. She died in Stettin in 1840.

Friedrich Wilhelm was born on 25 September 1744 in Berlin, as the eldest son of the Prince August Wilhelm of Prussia and Princess Luise Amalie of Brunswick-Wolfenbüttel. As Friedrich the Great did not have children, and given his orientation none were expected, his heir was his younger brother August Wilhelm who in 1744 was declared his brother's official heir apparent. The king begrudged his brother the close relationship he had had with their father, who had been particularly cruel to Friedrich when he was Prussia's crown prince. King Friedrich Wilhelm I, a martinet if there was ever one, detested the fact that his firstborn Friedrich seemed to have homosexual tendencies, which he began displaying as a teenager. Already, in the late 1720s, when Friedrich's fondness for one of his pages was uncovered, he received a brutal bashing from his father. The poor page, who Friedrich's sister claimed had, "*served my brother from feelings of real devotion,*" was able to escape the royal wrath and reached England.[41] At one point, Friedrich plotted to escape his father's suffocating grip by running away to England with his close friend Hans Hermann von Katte, a military officer several years his senior, whom many claimed was his lover. The King had his son and Katte arrested and imprisoned. His father threatened Friedrich with execution, while he considered forcing his wayward son to renounce the succession in favor of his brother August Wilhelm. Instead, Friedrich Wilhelm I forced his son to witness the execution of his friend Katte. The young crown prince fainted just before the fatal blow severed Katte's head.

Friedrich Wilhelm was born into a warlike time, since Prussia was once again in a state of war with Austria. In 1740, upon the death of Habsburg Emperor Karl VI the Imperial succession was in question due to the late ruler lacking a male heir. He had tried to get the European Powers to agree to his Pragmatic Sanction, allowing his eldest daughter Maria Theresa to succeed to the throne.

King Friedrich Wilhelm III of Prussia, Friederike's son.

While some monarchs agreed to the succession plan, others remained aloof and waited for events. Friedrich the Great saw an opportunity to wrest Silesia from Austria and attacked. This was the world Friedrich Wilhelm was born into at Berlin's massive Stadtschloß.

This was the family into which the unfortunate Landgravine Friederike of Hesse-Darmstadt married.

The marriage of the unattractive Friederike of Hesse-Darmstadt and the sensible, but capricious, prince who became king in 1786, was not happy. Friedrich Wilhelm had many love affairs and spent most of his time with his mistress Wilhelmine

von Lichtenau. Friederike often took advice from her clever mother, who tried to influence her increasingly despondent daughter. After the death of Friederike's mother, Friedrich Wilhelm II twice entered bigamous morganatic marriages with the Countess of Ingenheim and Countess von Dönhoff. The queen, who suffered from financial difficulties all her life, knew how to negotiate funds out of granting her husband's wishes to bigamously wed his mistresses.

In spite of Friedrich Wilhelm's disrespect and lack of interest in his wife, Friederike provided her husband with eight children. They were: Friedrich Wilhelm III (1770-1840), whose first wife was Luise of Mecklenburg-Strelitz, a daughter of Friederike's first cousin Charlotte of Hesse-Darmstadt; Friederike (1772-1773); Ludwig (1773-1796), who married Friederike of Mecklenburg-Strelitz, a sister of his sister-in-law Luise; Wilhelmine (1774-1837), who married King Willem I of the Netherlands; a stillborn in 1777; Augusta (1780-1841), married to Elector Friedrich Wilhelm of Hesse-Kassel; Heinrich (1781-1846); Wilhelm (1783-1851), who married his cousin Maria Anne of Hesse-Homburg, and, as previously mentioned were the parents of Princess Karl of Hesse and by Rhine and Queen Marie of Bavaria.[42]

Friederike paid little attention to the upbringing of her children. A neglected wife, she became a neglectful mother. The children were raised by tutors at her home in Schloß Monbijou. Their father, not surprisingly, was too consumed with his own distractions to pay them much attention. As time passed, Friederike became more despondent with her marital situation. She felt like nothing more than a baby-making machine, hence she didn't bother with personal appearance. Year after year she became more whimsical and neglectful. Her tortured mind began drifting into a different reality and she would claim to have been visited by ghosts and spirits. She slept by day and remained awake at night as she feared these visits. Slowly, Friederike retreated from public life and by the time she died, the Dowager Queen of Prussia had basically been forgotten by her son's subjects.

From 1788 onward, Friederike spent summers in the resort town of Freienwalde in Brandenburg. This contributed to the town's economy and created a cultural boom, particularly as its spa became a popular destination. Friederike had a palace built to house her court and entourage. After the death of her wayward husband in 1797, her stays in Freienwalde became longer.

Hereditary Princess Amalie of Baden.

His body weakened by a life dedicated to pleasure and excess, Friedrich Wilhelm II, who had succeeded his uncle in 1786, died in Potsdam's Marmorpalais on November 16, 1797.[43] He was 53-years-old. Behind, he not only left his surviving children by Friederike, but also a tribe of illegitimate children from his various lovers and morganatic bigamist wives. His heir, King Friedrich Wilhelm III, who had been repulsed by his father's lasciviousness and decadent lifestyle, moved quickly to sanitize the Berlin court and rid it of any remnant of this unmemorable past.

As for Dowager Queen Friedrike, she continued living away from court. One Swedish princess who

visited during her widowhood wrote, *"The Queen Dowager had invited us at déjeuner, and we left for Montbijou, a very simple manor slightly outside of Berlin, where she resides all year. It is sweet and well tendered but terribly small. She had it built herself, as well as the park and the garden. She is a small, very fat, middle-aged lady, who walks so crooked that she looks like an old woman. You could mistake her for one of these fairies from an ancient tale. She is very polite and talkative and shines of a goodness which gives the witness of a kind heart and a noble character."*[44] Having grown stout due to her own fall into lethargy, Friederike suffered a stroke and died at Monbijou on February 25, 1805.[45]

****

Hereditary Princess Amalie of Baden (1754-1832)

Amalie was the third daughter of Landgrave Ludwig IX of Hesse-Darmstadt and his wife Karoline. She was born on June 20, 1754[46], in Prenzlau, where her father was stationed in Prussian service and was raised in Buchsweiler by her mother. In 1772, Amalie traveled with her mother and her sisters Wilhelmine and Louise to St Petersburg, so that the future Tsar Paul could choose among the sisters a bride. He chose Wilhelmine.

She married in Darmstadt, on 15 July 1774, her slightly younger first cousin, the Hereditary Prince Karl Ludwig of Baden, born in Karlsruhe on February 14, 1755.[47] At first she felt uncomfortable in her Baden home as she had trouble adapting to her in-laws; particularly challenging was her relationship with her mother-in-law and aunt

Margravine Karoline Luise. She complained about the coldness of Margrave Karl Friedrich and the childish behavior of her husband, who was only 19-years-old at the time of their marriage. Truthfully, she missed the splendor and dignity she had come to know, for example, at the Prussian and Russian courts.

In spite of her personal hesitations and worries, Amalie's main responsibility was to assist in replenishing the Baden nursery. In all, Karl Ludwig and Amalie had nine children: Amalia (1776-1823), doyenne of the Abbey of Quedlinburg; Karoline (1776-1841), second wife of the future King Maximilian I Joseph of Bavaria; Luise (1779-1826), wife of Tsar Alexander I as Empress Elisabeth Alexeievna; Friederike (1781-1826), wife of King Gustaf IV of Sweden (divorced in 1812); Marie (1782-1808), married to Friedrich Wilhelm, Duke of Brunswick-Wolfenbüttel; Karl Friedrich (1784-1785); Karl Ludwig (1786-1818), Grand Duke of Baden; Wilhelmine (1788-1836), consort of her cousin Grand Duke Ludwig II of Hesse and by Rhine; and a stillborn (1791).[48] Through their descendants Karl Ludwig and Amalie are the ancestors of an impressive number of heads and heirs of royal and princely families, among them: the United Kingdom, Austria-Hungary, Prussia, Russia, Spain, Bavaria, Belgium, Italy, Saxony, Romania, Yugoslavia, Luxembourg, Monaco, Liechtenstein, Schleswig-Holstein, Baden, Mecklenburg-Schwerin, Hohenzollern, Thurn und Taxis, Törring-Jettenbach, Hohenlohe-Langenburg, Leiningen, Erbach-Schönberg, and Urach, to name but a few. In fact, Karl Ludwig and Amalie provide the closest link of the Princely House of Monaco to the rest of Gotha.

Hereditary Prince Karl Ludwig of Baden.

After the death of her mother-in-law in 1783, Amalie became the first lady at the Baden court. She was tasked with assisting her father-in-law when needed, while also continuing to accept the approaches of her unattractive husband. Karl Ludwig was described as obese and constantly in poor health. For all his life he was in the shadow of his father. Although since 1773 he participated in the meetings of the Privy Council in Karlsruhe, his opinion counted for naught.

Conditions at court became tense in 1787, when the Margrave married morganatically a young woman four decades his junior, the previously mentioned Luise Geyer von Geyersberg. Neither Karl Ludwig nor Amalie felt comfortable with the situation as both felt it was a blot on the family's standing and respectability. When Luise, eventually created Countess of Hochberg, began providing her husband with healthy children, matters only worsened between both couples. The succession tethered on the infant son Amalie had in 1786, since both her brothers-in-law Friedrich and Ludwig remained childless. Meanwhile, "la Geyersberg," as the stepmother was called, produced several strong and healthy little morganauts.

It was in this atmosphere of domestic tension, that Karl Ludwig and Amalie's daughters began marrying. The first to do so was Luise, who was invited by Catherine the Great to visit St Petersburg for inspection as a possible bride for her grandson Grand Duke Alexander (future Tsar Alexander I). The marriage took place in 1793 after Luise adopted Orthodoxy and changed her name to Elisabeth Alexeievna. Four years later, Karoline married the future Maximilian I of Bavaria in the spring, while Friederike married in the fall Gustav IV of Sweden.

From the start, Amalie was a vocal opponent of the French and Napoleon Bonaparte. During the Napoleonic Wars, Baden was ransacked several times due to its strategic position along the eastern bank of the Rhine. As the mother-in-law of the future Russian emperor, the King of Sweden, and the Elector of Bavaria, she was uniquely positioned to opine on the most important political matters of her time.

In 1801, soon after the assassination of Tsar Paul I, his son Alexander, wishing to assist his wife in recovering from the shock, invited her parents to Russia. The Badens brought along three of their children (Karl, Amalia, and Marie) and stayed several months. Amalia remained in St Petersburg as a companion to her sister for several years. In September, the Badens left Russia and traveled to Sweden, where they also visited their daughter Friederike, the Queen of Sweden. The final leg to Germany started on December 15. After departing Gripsholm Castle, the caravan was approaching Arboga when their carriage slipped off the road and tipped. Karl Ludwig received a serious head injury and suffered a stroke.[49] He died in Arboga on December 16, 1801. His remains were transported to Stockholm and buried in the Riddarholmskyrkan on January 17, 1802.[50] Karl Ludwig's heart was taken to Baden and deposited in an urn in the castle church in Pforzheim.

After the death of her husband Amalie returned to Baden. She retained the position of first lady until 1806, when Stéphanie de Beauharnais

Grand Duke Karl of Baden.

married her son Karl. As an opponent of Napoleon Bonaparte, she had tried to prevent the wedding of her son with Napoleon's niece and later adoptive daughter. Stéphanie was a cousin of Empress Josephine's children and Napoleon was very fond and protective of the young lady. The groom was also most displeased with having to ally himself to a parvenu dynasty. Yet, confronted with what basically was an imperial command to marry Stéphanie, Karl had no choice but to fall back in line with Napoleon's grand plan to ally his family with Europe's most prestigious dynasties. As for Amalie, since she did not get along with her new daughter-in-law or with her father-in-law's second wife Countess Luise von Hochberg, she retired from court and moved to Schloß Bruchsal, which was previously owned by the Prince-Bishops of Speyer. To assist with her expenses, Amalie was granted a yearly appanage of 120,000 gulden. Her summer residence was Schloß Rohrbach near Heidelberg, which her son-in-law King Maximilian I Joseph of Bavaria gifted her. Over the years, Rohrbach received important guests, including Tsar Alexander I, Emperor Franz of Austria, and Johann Wolfgang von Goethe.

After the unexpected death of his son, Margrave Karl Friedrich, supported by Minister Reitzenstein, focused on preparing his only grandson for the legacy that would land on his young shoulders. In 1803, due to the secularization of the abbeys and the redistribution that ensued, Baden became an electorate. Three years later, as the Holy Roman Empire of the German Nation expired, Karl Friedrich became a Grand Duke.

Amalie exerted her influence during the Congress of Vienna through strong lobbying on her son-in-law Tsar Alexander I. She convinced him to allow Baden to remain a grand duchy without the loss of any territory gained from Napoleon's allocations. This was appreciated by her son, as Baden remained a grand duchy and its territorial borders were preserved.

Tragedy, however, always seemed to lay around the corner in Amalie's long life. One of the saddest episodes of her unfortunate story was the fate of her only surviving son, who in 1811 had succeeded his grandfather as the 2nd Grand Duke of Baden. Karl had overcome his reticence and impregnated his wife after five years of marriage. The year her husband ascended the throne, Stéphanie gave birth to their first child, Luise (d. 1854), who married her cousin Prince Gustaf Vasa, former Crown Prince of Sweden. A stillborn followed in 1812, and a second daughter in 1813, Josephine. She married in 1834 Hereditary Prince Karl Anton of Hohenzollern and in due course became the mother of King Carol of Romania and grandmother of King Ferdinand, Carol's successor. In 1816 Stéphanie gave birth to a son, Alexander, but the boy died a week after his first birthday. Lastly, in 1817 Marie was born. She married William Hamilton, Duke of Hamilton and Brandon, and their daughter Lady Mary Victoria Hamilton married Prince Albert I of Monaco.

After the death of his only son, Grand Duke Karl made an important provision concerning his succession. Since he lacked a son and his only surviving uncle was unmarried and childless, a succession formula had to be set up to protect the sovereignty of his realm. He decided to elevate the station of his Hochberg half-uncles. Had

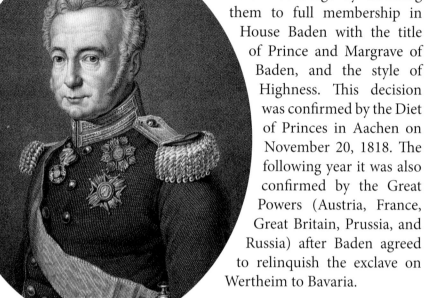

Grand Duke Ludwig I of Baden.

he not done so the closest living relative who could lay claim to Baden was the powerful King of Bavaria, whose wife was Karl's sister. If Baden was inherited by the Wittelsbachs, the grand duke and his council feared the country would lose its independence and simply become a Bavarian province. Therefore, on October 4, 1817, Karl confirmed the succession rights of the Hochbergs by elevating them to full membership in House Baden with the title of Prince and Margrave of Baden, and the style of Highness. This decision was confirmed by the Diet of Princes in Aachen on November 20, 1818. The following year it was also confirmed by the Great Powers (Austria, France, Great Britain, Prussia, and Russia) after Baden agreed to relinquish the exclave on Wertheim to Bavaria.

Grand Duke Karl of Baden died in Rastatt on December 8, 1818, weeks after the Diet of Princes approved the grand duchy's new line of succession. He was succeeded by his uncle as Ludwig I, who earlier in the year had married morganatically Countess Katharina Werner von Langenstein. The 3rd Grand Duke of Baden died in 1830 and was succeeded by his half-brother Leopold I.

One can only speculate what Amalie thought of what destiny had forced her to witness. Not only did she bury her husband at a relatively young age, but in 1809 she provided shelter to her daughter and her children when King Gustaf IV of Sweden was deposed and forced into exile. Amalie also buried her only surviving son Grand Duke Karl when he was 32-years old. Furthermore, between 1823-1826, she lost three of her daughters. She had already lost her daughter Marie in 1808. Further injury to her ego came when the hated Hochbergs were made dynasts. One can only but imagine her ire when in 1819 her granddaughter Princess Sophie of Sweden married her half-grand uncle Leopold of Baden, formerly Count of Hochberg. A man with a huge chip on his shoulder, married to a haughty, selfish woman became the founders of the renewed House of Baden. The proud Badens had been succeeded by the even prouder former Hochbergs. Surely, Amalie's last blow must have been witnessing her late husband's former morganatic half-brother inherit the grand ducal throne.

Amalie, Dowager Hereditary Princess of Baden, died at Schloß Bruchsal on June 21, 1832, one day after her 78th birthday.[51]

There is an interesting addendum to the story of the grand ducal family. In 1828, a young man appeared out of nowhere in the streets of Nuremberg. On him he carried a letter claiming that he was born in 1812 and had been mysteriously handed to a man who raised him in seclusion, as he "*never let him out of my house.*"[52] The letter also said that his father was a cavalryman. Another letter found on him claimed that his name was Kaspar. In history we know him as Kaspar Hauser, a trickster who apparently wrote both letters and eventually claimed to be the "stillborn" child Stéphanie of Baden had given birth to in 1812. Hauser claimed that he was spirited out of the grand ducal palace by people involved in a cabal organized by the Hochbergs and court officials. The stillborn baby, he claimed was a dead child that had been clandestinely brought to the palace and handed over to the exhausted mother, who then believed the child was stillborn. The story of Kaspar Hauser captivated

the imagination of conspiracy theorists and much of it resembles the extraordinary hoax carried out by one Franziska Schankowska, aka the lost Grand Duchess Anastasia Nikolaevna. Today we know that he was an impostor, very much like myriad free-loaders who have claimed to be miraculous survivors of assassinations, children spirited away from their birth chamber, or surreptitiously extricated from prison cells. Kaspar Hauser was fatally stabbed in prison in 1833.

****

Tsarevna Natalia Alexeievna of Russia
(1755-1776)

Landgrave Ludwig IX and Landgravine Karoline were exceedingly successful in finding suitable spouses for their many daughters. That is not to say that each of their sons-in-law was the best groom available for the young Hessian landgravines. This is the case of Tsesarevich Paul Petrovich of Russia, who on paper seemed as the best match possible, but in reality was not so great a partner for any young woman. Such was the sad fate of Landgravine Wilhelmine, the couple's fourth daughter, whose three older sisters were also married off exquisitely, but to wretched men.

Landgravine Wilhelmine was born in Prenzlau, on June 25, 1755.[53] She was the last of her parents' children born in the Prussian garrison outpost where Ludwig was stationed. In due course, Wilhelmine relocated to Hesse, where she was raised along with her sisters at Buchsweiler under the supervision of their erudite mother.

As early as 1762, Landgravine Karoline reached out

Tsarevna Natalia Alexeievna of Russia.

to the Russian court reminding several friends that she had available daughters. Late in 1761 Empress Elisabeth of Russia died. She was succeeded by her nephew Tsar Peter III, who could not conceal his glee at his aunt's death. Peter, who was born a Duke of Holstein-Gottorp, was not only pro-German, but had disdain for the Russians. Instead of focusing on governing his vast realm, which was a difficult task for a man who *"had only contempt for the nation whose leadership he had assumed."*[54] It was just a matter of time before opposition forces at the Russian court struck with deadly force. Peter had been married by his aunt to Princess Sophie Augusta of Anhalt-Zerbst, a vivacious, fun-loving, calculating, and intelligent young woman who quickly realized her husband was a nitwit. As he could not muster the interest to impregnate her, Catherine (the name Sophie Augusta adopted upon converting to Russian-Orthodoxy) sought passion somewhere else. Presto … pregnancy … son … succession secured. This child was Paul Petrovich.

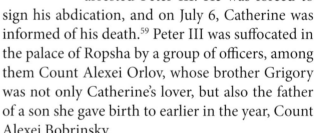

Tsar Peter III of Russia.

The short reign of Peter III lasted 186 days. Years before ascending the throne, Peter had failed to hide the scorn he felt for all things Russian: language, culture, Orthodoxy, military. He even went as far as designing uniforms that were embarrassingly similar to Prussian ones. *"Drowned in wine, unable to stand upright or articulate his words,"* he once went to the Prussian ambassador and said, *"Let us drink to the health of your King, our master."*[55] before a portrait of Friedrich the Great. This behavior infuriated the Russian aristocracy, politicians, and the army, particularly when he insinuated that he would put his whole army at the disposal of the Prussian king, *"if he gives the*

order."[56] Not surprisingly, Catherine, by then a fearless survivor and talented plotter, was actively plotting to overthrow Peter III.

In June 1796, matters between the spouses came to a boil when Peter berated her publicly, calling her a *"fool"*[57] in what many believed was his first move to repudiate her. Four days later, Peter had given the order for Catherine's arrest. His uncle Duke Georg of Holstein intervened and saved Catherine from prison.[58] However, she and her supporters knew that the time had come to strike. On June 28, Catherine left Peterhof for St Petersburg, where she was enthusiastically welcomed by the capital's most renowned regiments and army units. She was proclaimed Empress of Russia at a large gathering outside Kazan Cathedral on the Nevsky Prospekt, and her son Paul confirmed as heir. The following day, the conspirators arrested Peter III. He was forced to sign his abdication, and on July 6, Catherine was informed of his death.[59] Peter III was suffocated in the palace of Ropsha by a group of officers, among them Count Alexei Orlov, whose brother Grigory was not only Catherine's lover, but also the father of a son she gave birth to earlier in the year, Count Alexei Bobrinsky.

By the beginning of the 1770s, Catherine II was solidly in control of Russia. As Paul Petrovich was the only viable heir, his marriage was a matter of state. Being aware of several German candidates for his hand, Catherine II sent an emissary to tour various courts. Baron von Asseburg reported to his master in Russia that of the 15 eligible princesses he had found, six were from Darmstadt. She received glowing reports about the unmarried daughters of Landgrave Ludwig IX. Oil paintings of the young landgravines were shipped to Russia and invitations arrived to travel to St Petersburg.

Landgravine Karoline was invited to St Petersburg with three of her daughters: Wilhelmine, Amalie, and Luise. Along with her daughters and a small retinue, Karoline embarked on a fateful journey to Russia. From the Rhineland they traveled to Lübeck, having made a stop in Berlin, where King Friedrich the Great not only welcomed them, but also contributed a travel allowance. From the Baltic coast, a Russian flotilla sailed the august travelers to Reval and then onward to St Petersburg. It is said that upon meeting the young Hessian candidates, Catherine II chose Wilhelmine as her son's bride. However, that seems not to have been the case.

When informed that three Hessian princesses were headed to Russia for him to choose, Paul Petrovich feigned ignorance. He also said, *"that he had no trust in Asseburg's veracity,"* concerning the descriptions he had sent the empress.[60] The heir assured anyone who would listen that *"he detested the idea"* of the visit and would do his utmost *"to be ill at that time."*[61] Paul Petrovich's sullen demeanor irked his mother so, that she informed him that as his empress, Catherine II had *"the right to expect compliance with her wishes."*[62] Either he behaved appropriately, or he would face serious consequences. As usual when confronted by someone with a strong personality Paul Petrovich acquiesced.

As the Russian court prepared to welcome the Hessians, Paul Petrovich formed a *"sudden*

and vehement"[63] friendship with Count Andrei Razumovsky, who would later play an important role in the Tsesarevich's marriage. He spoke to Paul Petrovich candidly but with certitude. He counseled compliance to avoid insulting his mother. As the weeks passed, Paul Petrovich's prior aloofness cooled and he wrote to his friend, *"I am convinced… that (I) must not continue in such a morbid state…I have followed your advice…I have been reading, walking, meditating, getting rid of worries and anxieties… You may remember how I hated the mere idea of the princesses' arrival…Now I am looking forward to it…I am determined to seek more and more opportunities to draw closer to my mother, to win her confidence, and to protect her from possible intrigues in the future…Our own mistakes give rise to our anxieties…I am trying to control my temper…I am trying not to indulge in gossip…"*[64]

Empress Catherine "the Great" of Russia.

When Landgravine Karoline and her daughters approached Tsarskoe Selo, Paul Petrovich impulsively mounted a horse and rode to meet them. *"At the sight of the carriage, Paul leapt out of the saddle and swept one of his famously perfect bows. At a sign from their mother, the three princesses left the carriage and curtseyed low. They were tall and slim, very blonde and blue-eyed, but Wilhelmina, standing between her sisters, was the only one to smile at his wildly disheveled hair and dusty blue velvet coat. Paul looked at her again. She was still smiling in a way which informed him of her pleasure at his eagerness to meet them. He then looked at her sisters. Their lips stayed grave. Wilhelmina's smile decided him."*[65]

Marriage contract negotiations began in earnest.

271

As they awaited the arrival of Landgrave Ludwig IX's formal consent to the betrothal Catherine II became better acquainted with her future daughter-in-law. Wilhelmine *"was pretty, gay, exuberant. And then Razumovsky liked her so much."*[66] The Empress admitted that Wilhelmine must have been disappointed with Paul as much as she had been with his father. The Landgravine of Hesse-Darmstadt did her utmost to reassure everyone writing, *"the distinction of which the heir to the throne has made her the object does not seem to be disagreeable to her."*[67]

The engagement of Tsesarevich Paul Petrovich and Landgravine Wilhelmine of Hesse-Darmstadt was announced shortly thereafter. She was received in the Russian Orthodox Church and took the name Natalia Alexeievna. The magnificent wedding followed in early October 10, 1773. *"She looks born to wear a crown,"* said some court ladies.[68] As compensation for losing their daughter, the mother received precious, priceless gifts, while Ludwig IX, received a field marshal's rank with a pension of 7000 rubles, an astronomical sum at the time. The Russian marriage project consolidated the ailing financial conditions of the country Hesse-Darmstadt greatly. Landgravine Karoline, however, was to survive the grueling return journey only a few months.

In the end, and in spite of being showered with precious gifts and large stipends (50,000 rubles per year), there was no happy ending for Natalia Alexeievna. Even though she had the temporary support of a chambermaid brought from Darmstadt and her brother Hereditary Prince Ludwig, appointed to a Russian command, she found life in Russia enormously challenging. The fact that Paul Petrovich was an unstable, unreliable, and unattractive partner only worsened matters. Natalia Alexeievna was described as gracious and witty, dominated her husband almost completely, and urged co-government when he succeeded. Even Catherine II did not think much of her son, whom she sought to distance from court and from matters of state. Soon after the honeymoon ended, problems between Paul and his mother once again erupted and everyone's mood soured. Emotionally unfulfilled by her husband and fearful of the feud between husband and mother-in-law, Natalia Alexeievna soon became entangled in a love affair with Paul's friend Razumovsky. The Russian court, as it turned, was a cauldron of poisonous passions and dangerous pitfalls.

Initially, Catherine was enthralled with Natalia Alexeievna, admitting that she *"was charming and affectionate. I am very pleased and my son is quite in love..."*[69] The Empress was truly delighted with the effect Wilhelmine had on Paul's character as he no longer, *"made mordant remarks about his mother's favorites, his scowl had gone, his eyes looked remarkably clear, he was even courteous to Gregory Orlov* (Catherine's lover).*"*[70]

Yet, as months passed Natalia Alexeievna's relationship with Catherine soon became embittered. To her friend Baron Melchior Grimm, Catherine wrote, *"The Grand Duchess is perpetually ill, and who would wonder at it? She always rushes to extremes. If she goes for a walk, she needs to trudge for something like twenty versts. If she dances, it must be quite twenty minutes. To avoid excessive heat in their apartments, she orders that they are not to be heated at all... She has no confidence in anyone...(she) will have her way in everything...In eighteen months she has not learned a single word of Russian. She says she does mean to learn, and she keeps on saying it...Her debts have swollen to twice the amount of her yearly allowance, and yet there is hardly a princess in Europe who receives as much as she does..."*[71]

In the summer of 1775, Natalia Alexeievna realized she was pregnant. During a visit to Moscow, her physical condition had given cause for concern. She felt cramped inside the Kremlin, she suffered from devastating migraines heightened by the incessant ringing of church bells. Her claim of ill-health kept her from participating in hardly any public appearances. Besides these natural reactions caused by pregnancy, her pregnancy proceeded so smoothly that the Empress even ordered a search for wet-nurses for the new baby. Catherine was delighted with the possibility of a grandchild finally arriving.

Labor pains came early in the morning of April 10, 1776, and Paul alerted his mother that the Grand Duchess had had been in torment since midnight. *"The Czarina tied a big apron over her dress and helped the midwife in her work."*[72] As hours passed, the attending physicians realized that both Natalia and the child were in trouble. The problem was that the child was too large to enter the birth canal. Still no obstetric forceps were used nor a caesarean section performed when it would have been

Tsar Paul I of Russia.

safe to do. For five days and five nights, Paul, the Empress, and the ablest physicians and surgeons hardly left the room where she lay. By the end of the third day they knew the unborn child was dead, but Natalia's own agony lingered on for another forty-eight hours. Exhausted by the five-day vigil she kept next to Natalia, Empress Catherine, later complained that she was exhausted and her *"back hurts as much as hers,"* – the difference was that Natalia was dead.[73] The postmortem revealed a most extraordinary malformation of bone structure: *"the Grand Duchess could never have given birth to a living child,"* wrote Paul's biographer.[74]

There has always been speculation that the stillborn baby was Count Razumovsky's, not Paul's. Catherine II, an expert at keeping many pregnancies secret did not care who the father was. Yet, to protect the dynasty's reputation Razumovsky was banished from court. No

one dared speak again of Natalia Alexeievna's friendship with the young and handsome count. Still, and above all, Catherine needed an heir, plain and simple. Honestly, whoever deposited the seed did not matter, as long as her daughter-in-law carried the baby to term. Still, Natalia Alexeievna's death was shocking to all, both in St Petersburg and Darmstadt. Catherine the Great was badly shaken, but a realist foremost, she knew that a grand duchess who could not bear children was of no use to Mother Russia. Unlike his mother, Paul Petrovich was devastated. *"He had enjoyed her caresses and her companionship, and even her grievances had found an echo in him,"* his biographer wrote.[75] Such was his pain after his wife's death, that he could not attend her funeral. To Archbishop Platon, his confessor, Paul Petrovich wrote, *"I have always been conscious of my great debt to you. Now, after all you have done to help her in her dying, I feel more deeply than ever…You know the state of my heart…nothing except my faith in God upheld me through those difficult days…"*[76]

Still, Mother Russia demanded an heir. Paul Petrovich had to produce the next generation as the Romanov nursery had been dangerously empty for more than two decades. His mother lost little time in finding her son a second wife. Her choice fell on Sophia Dorothea of Württemberg, whom she had initially hoped her son would marry. However, since she was only 13-years old at the time, marriage to Paul Petrovich was not advisable. Now, five years later, she seemed the right choice. That she was engaged to Natalia Alexeievna's brother Ludwig mattered not. He was told by Russia and Prussia to move along and was paid off.

Tsesarevich Paul Petrovich married Duchess Sophia Dorothea of Württemberg in October 1776. After being received in the Russian Orthodox Church, she took the name Marie Feodorovna. They were married for nearly a quarter of a century and had ten children. Their eldest son, Tsar Alexander I, married, as previously mentioned, Princess Luise of Baden, a niece of Natalia Alexeievna.

****

Grand Duchess Louise of Saxe-Weimar-Eisenach (1757-1830)

Landgravine Louise was the youngest daughter of Landgrave Ludwig IX and Landgravine Karoline. As her father's service in Prenzlau had recently come to an end, Louise was born in Berlin on January 30, 1757.[77] Her father was a Prussian general fighting in the Seven Years' War (1756-1763) between Austria and Prussia. With her siblings, she was raised at Buchsweiler, the Hanau palace her father had inherited from his maternal grandfather. Louise grew up to be studious and introverted, but also compassionate and sympathetic.

Grand Duchess Louise of Saxe-Weimar-Eisenach.

Her life would be dedicated to culture and music, as well as to turning her husband's capital, Weimar, into one of the leading centers for intellectual activity of their time.

As the youngest daughter among eight siblings, the education of Louise was an important aspect for her chances of landing a good marital arrangement. Since her father, consumed by his militaristic hobbies showed little interest in his offspring, the marriage of the daughters remained in the hands of Landgravine Karoline, who as we know was a deeply respected intellectual who maintained close contacts with many of the leading philosophers and prominent intellectuals of her time. This is

the reason why so many of her acquaintances referred to Karoline as the "grand landgravine," most prominently among them King Friedrich the Great. For the purpose of finding Louise a future, she accompanied her mother and sisters Amalie and Wilhelmine on the fateful journey to the Russian court. There, they were inspected by Catherine II, but Louise was unsuccessful in finding a husband. She was lucky not to be the chosen one since her destiny lay elsewhere.

Nevertheless, this trip was not without influence in Louise's future. On their journey to Lübeck, where they were scheduled to board a Russian flotilla, the Hessians made several stops. One of them was in Erfurt, where Dowager Duchess Anna Amalia of Saxe-Weimar-Eisenach hosted the travelers. She was a niece of Friedrich the Great of Prussia and had served as regent for her son Carl August, a promising young man with an even brighter future. It was during this visit that Louise met her future husband. Upon her return from Russia, Louise's future as Duchess of Saxe-Weimar-Eisenach began taking shape as marriage negotiations between Darmstadt and Weimar started.

Due to the fact that her father lived primarily in Pirmasens and her mother had died soon after returning from Russia, court life in Darmstadt was basically non-existent. After her mother's death, Louise, the last unmarried daughter went to live in Karlsruhe with her sister Amalie. The Baden capital being her new home, Louise and Carl August's marriage was celebrated there on October 3, 1775.[78]

In Weimar, Louise was to find a difficult environment. Her first obstacle was her indomitable mother-in-law, a strong personality who refused to retire from the main stage after relinquishing the regency for her son. Anna Amalia of Brunswick-Wolfenbüttel had married Ernst August II of Saxe-Weimar-Eisenach in 1756. She was 16-years old, while her husband was only two years her senior. He had inherited the ducal throne in 1748 as the eldest son of his father's second marriage. A sickly child, Ernst August was urged to marry quickly to replenish the ducal nursery and thus guarantee not only the succession, but also his duchy's sovereignty and integrity. As the last male of his family, if he were to die without heirs the duchy would be redistributed among the surviving branches of the Ernestine line of the House of Wettin.

Anna Amalia had not reached her 18th birthday by the time she became a mother. Her child was named Carl August. Within months Anna Amalia discovered that she was pregnant again. But then tragedy struck, and her husband's precarious health brought his demise five days before his 21st birthday. Pregnant and months short of her 19th birthday, Anna Amalia had to assume the regency for her infant son. Three months after her husband's death, she gave birth posthumously to a second son, Friedrich Ferdinand, who would die unmarried in 1793.

Louise's reception in Weimar was not enthusiastic. Anna Amalia simply was a larger than life figure who refused to share the stage with her daughter-in-law. As for Louise and Carl August, contemporary witnesses and existing literature agree that their connection was anything but happy. This situation hindered the couple's main purpose and the nursery remained empty for several years. Finally, in 1779, Louise gave birth to a daughter, Louise, who died in 1784. Two years later a stillborn princess made a sad entry into the family's mausoleum. Finally, in 1783 Louise gave birth to a son, Carl Friedrich. Four other children were born to the couple: a son who was born and died the same day in 1785; Caroline (1786-1816), who married Hereditary Grand Duke Friedrich Ludwig of Mecklenburg-Schwerin; a son who was born and died the same day in 1789; and Bernhard (1792-1862), married to Princess Ida of Saxe-Meiningen. Having produced an heir and a spare, Louise's marital obligations were fulfilled after the birth of her youngest son.

While bedding his wife due to obligation, Carl August conducted himself lasciviously with several women. His excesses, many in the company of his close friend Johann Wolfgang von Goethe, became legendary. Carl August's relationship with Karoline Jagemann lasted long enough for them to produce several offspring. Eventually he granted his mistress the noble title of "Lady von Heygendorff," the name inherited by their three children. Perhaps thankful that she had freed her from her wifely bedchamber duties, Louise became a close friend of Karoline. Husband and wife, realizing that there never was love or attraction between them, accepted the personal freedom of the other partner. Louise dedicated herself to their children and her artistic and intellectual pursuits, while Carl August continued bedding as many women as he could and eventually fathered nearly 40 illegitimate children.

During his trip to Karlsruhe where he was to marry Louise, Carl August met Goethe again in Frankfurt and invited him to Weimar. Weeks later on November 7, 1775, Goethe arrived in Weimar, which was to become his adopted home town. From this renewed encounter, a solid friendship arose, uniting the two men for a lifetime of ups and downs, mischief and glory. Their friendship is responsible for the cultural revival that Weimar personified, a time known in history as Weimar's "Classical Period." Inviting other intellectuals, artists, philosophers made Carl August's capital a vibrant city on Europe's cultural map. It also led to Goethe and Schiller developing a classical poetry program in Weimar and Jena that can be largely attributed to their ducal benefactor.[79]

Legendary stories abound concerning Carl August and Goethe, carousing in Weimar. As young men they ran through Weimar's alleys noisily stirring up the sleepy city. They partied until collapsing. Yet, Carl August in spite of his wild lifestyle, was a responsible ruler who took his administerial responsibilities rather seriously. He worked consistently to cleanse the ducal administration of excesses and waste, while also striving to reduce the country's debt, curtail the military, and promoting mercantile programs. This was followed by reforms in the economy, administration, and justice. He was inevitably dependent on his privy council. Goethe was admitted to this body as a secretary with a seat and vote, even though the Duke had come up against strong resistance to do so. To his critics, Carl August announced, *"People of discernment congratulate me on possessing this man. His intellect, his genius is known. It makes no difference if the world is offended because I have made Dr. Goethe a member of my most important collegium without his having passed through the stages of minor official professor and councilor of state."*[80]

Goethe's main role resembled that of a minister of economics. He was also responsible for infrastructure matters like road construction or mining. Later, the duke transferred to his friend overall supervision of the court library and the reconstruction of the ducal castle in Weimar, destroyed by a fire in 1774. This multi-year project was finally completed in 1804. In all, Carl August granted his friend extensive freedom, influence, and security. In return the duke only wanted one condition: almost everlasting loyalty.

Grand Duke Carl Friedrich, Luise's son and father-in-law of Kaiser Wilhelm I.

Carl August's leadership also brought other achievements. The Weimaraner, a breed of dog, is said to have been developed by him and his court for hunting. Carl August was also interested in literature, in art, in science, funding Goethe, and the foundation of the Weimar Princely Free Drawing School. Critics praised his judgment in painting; biologists found in him an expert in anatomy. His aim was to educate his people to work out their own political and social salvation, the object of education being in his view, as he explained later to the dismay of Austrian Chancellor Prince of Metternich, to help men achieve independence of judgment. To this end Johann Gottfried Herder was summoned to Weimar to reform the educational system. During his rule, the University of Jena attained the zenith of its fame under his rule. Undoubtedly, under Carl August's leadership Weimar became the intellectual center of Germany, the epicenter of a cultural reform movement with lasting effects throughout the country.

Meanwhile, Duchess Louise focused on her own pursuits and raising her children in an atmosphere that allowed them to thrive in the cultural epicenter their parents had created. In due course, she also did her part in finding them suitable spouses. The first such project was concluded in 1804 when her son Carl Friedrich was married to Grand Duchess Maria Pavlovna, one of the daughters of Paul I and his second wife. Within a few years, noisy children's voices once again could be heard in the ducal nursery. Louise lived long enough to become a great-grandmother through her granddaughter Marie of Saxe-Weimar-Eisenach who in 1827 married Prince Carl of Prussia, a grandson of Luise's sister Friederike.

In October 1806, Louise had her moment of glory, essentially determining her image for posterity. This episode occupies considerable space in the history pages of Weimar. After the twin battles of Jena and Auerstedt (October 14), which led to a decisive defeat of the Prussian-Saxon armies, the victorious Frenchmen reached Weimar and proceeded to sack it. As other members of the dynasty had fled or, like the Prussian sovereign, was not available in the ensuing turmoil, Louise was left in Weimar to handle matters. It was up to her to fulfill her role as "Landesmütter" and save her capital and its people from the marauding hordes. Two days after the battle, she faced Emperor Napoleon. She made it quite undiplomatically clear that her husband, out of duty could not withdraw from his alliance with Prussia and Austria. His honor was at stake, and a man without his word was a worthless one, particularly a ruling prince. Napoleon seems to have been impressed by Louise and her message. On his orders, the looting stopped, and Weimar came off lightly. Whether Napoleon let himself be softened by Louise, or rather followed powerful political considerations, must remain an open question. What is a fact, is that due to her intervention the Duchy of Saxe-Weimar-Eisenach remained generally unscathed by further military upheavals. The duchy had to join the Confederation of the Rhine and, as much of Germany, became a satellite state of the French Empire. As for Louise, since her intercession with Napoleon, she was considered the savior of the motherland.[81]

After Napoleon's defeat, Saxe-Weimar-Eisenach did fairly well at the Congress of Vienna. Not only

was Carl August granted the higher title of Grand Duke, but his realm received new territories from Prussia and Electoral Hesse. As for Louise, after peace arrived, her daily life was occupied by her expanding family, her intellectual interests and hobbies, and her role as first lady of the grand duchy. As official hostess in Weimar, she was constantly welcoming prominent visitors, including Tsar Alexander I and his brother Grand Duke Nicholas Pavlovich, who came to visit their sister Maria Pavlovna.

Princess Augusta of Saxe-Weimar-Eisenach, who in 1830 married future Kaiser Wilhelm I.

Grand Duke Carl August of Saxe-Weimar-Eisenach died in Graditz on June 14, 1828. He was succeeded by his eldest son Carl Friedrich. By then, Louise had lived away from the public eye for several years. She passed away in Weimar on February 14, 1830. Had she lived a few years longer, she would have witnessed her granddaughter Duchess Helene of Mecklenburg-Schwerin marry Prince Ferdinand, Duke d'Orléans, heir of King Louis Philippe of the French. It is through this marriage that today's Count of Paris, Prince Jean, is a descendant of the House of Hesse and by Rhine. She also would have witnessed another granddaughter, Augusta of Saxe-Weimer-Eisenach, marry her cousin Wilhelm of Prussia. In due time this couple not only became the first German emperor and empress, but also the grandparents of Kaiser Wilhelm II and his brother Heinrich. Both were to play a role in the Hessian dynasty decades after the death of their great-great-grandmother Louise of Hesse-Darmstadt.

****

Hereditary Princess Friederike of Mecklenburg-Strelitz (1752-1782)

&

Hereditary Princess Charlotte of Mecklenburg-Strelitz (1755-1785)

Friederike and Charlotte were daughters of Prince Georg Wilhelm of Hesse-Darmstadt (1722-1782) from his marriage to Luise (1729-1818), daughter of Count Christian Carl Reinhard von Leiningen-Dagsburg and his wife Catharina Polyxena of Solms-Rödelheim. Both were born in Darmstadt, Friederike on August 20, 1752, Charlotte on November 5, 1755.[82]

Hereditary Princess Friederike of Mecklenburg-Strelitz.

Friederike, the most attractive of the two, was the first to marry. Her wedding was celebrated in Darmstadt on September 18, 1768. The groom was Prince Karl, one of the sons of Duke Karl Ludwig of Mecklenburg-Strelitz and his wife Princess Elisabeth Albertine of Saxe-Hildburghausen. Karl was born at Mirow, on October 10, 1741.[83] One of his siblings was Queen Charlotte, consort of King George III of Great Britain. This marriage would play an important role in Karl's life and career.

Hereditary Princess Charlotte of Mecklenburg-Strelitz.

Along with his siblings, Karl lived in Mirow, his father's seat until late 1752. When in December his older brother Adolf Friedrich succeeded their childless uncle Adolf Friedrich III as Duke of Mecklenburg-Strelitz, Karl was taken with the rest of the family from Mirow to the capital Strelitz.

From an early age, Karl appeared set for a military career. He received a commission as a captain when only four-years-old. When his sister Charlotte married King George III, who was also Elector of Hannover, Karl made the first of many visits to Great Britain. He received a commission from his brother-in-law and served in Spain, followed by an appointment at Hannover. It was while there that he began searching for a wife. Initially, he sought to marry a Princess of Denmark and a Princess of Saxe-Gotha. These marriage prospects not having prospered, Karl then set his sights on Darmstadt. On September 18, 1768, he married sixteen-year-old Landgravine Friederike.[84] The groom, an experienced man in many realms, was eleven years older than his bride.

Between 1769-1782, Friederike gave birth ten times: Charlotte (1769-1818), married to Duke Friedrich of Saxe-Altenburg; Karoline (1771-1773); Georg (1772-1773); Therese (1773-1839), married to Fürst Carl Alexander of Thurn und Taxis; Friedrich (b./d. 1774); Luise (1776-1810), married to her cousin King Friedrich Wilhelm III of Prussia; Friederike (1778-1841), who married three times, her last husband being her first cousin King Ernst August of Hannover; Grand Duke Georg of Mecklenburg-Strelitz (1779-1860), married to Landgravine Marie of Hesse-Kassel; Friedrich (1781-1783); and Augusta (b./d. 1782).[85] Through their children, Karl and Friederike became a common ancestor to several dynasties, among them Prussia (Wilhelm I was his grandson), Baden, Greece, Hannover, Hesse-Kassel, Mecklenburg-Strelitz, Mecklenburg-Schwerin, and Denmark, to name but a few.

As Duke Karl served under the Hannoverian banner, he was stationed in Hannover for many years. This is the reason behind all his children being born there. Furthermore, in the autumn of 1776, Karl was appointed General-Governor of Hannover by his brother-in-law King George III. As such, Karl effectively held all the powers of a sovereign ruler. His brother-in-law had no wish to reside in Germany, being thoroughly English. This setup suited the English monarch perfectly as he was not interested in visiting or settling in his German territories.

In May 1782, Duchess Friederike prepared for the arrival of her tenth child. Since marrying her husband thirteen years earlier, she had been repeatedly pregnant, giving birth regularly year after year. Surely, her body must have taken a considerable toll, yet nothing prepared the family for the tragedy that was about to ensue. On May 5, Friederike went into labor. It was a difficult labor and the child, a daughter named Augusta, lived only for one day. Friederike, exhausted, was unable to recover from the birthing and died two days after her daughter.

In shock, Duke Karl was devastated by the loss of a wife for whom he cared so deeply. Yet, he also realized that he had the responsibility of raising and caring for their five surviving children. He felt a second wife was needed, and what better option than asking his unmarried sister-in-law Charlotte to marry him and become stepmother to her nieces and nephews.

Blue-eyed, blonde Charlotte was an attractive woman. She had pinned her hopes to marrying Hereditary Prince Peter Friedrich of Schleswig-Holstein. However, the prince's mental instability prevented the betrothal. Charlotte was left in Darmstadt to dry her tears and wait for another suitor. Years passed without any inquiries and as she entered her late twenties, Charlotte began to resign herself to spinsterhood. Her situation changed with the death of her sister Friederike. Wishing a life of her own away from her parental home, she accepted Karl's proposal. Their marriage took place in Darmstadt on September 28, 1784, and the newlyweds settled in his residence in Hannover. However, the following year Charlotte, like her older sister, died as a result of complications during childbirth. The child, a boy named Karl, served in the Prussian army and died unmarried in 1837.

Shortly after becoming a widower for a second time, Karl requested permission to retire from his military post in Hannover and resign from the governorship. In appreciation for more than two decades of service, King George III not only raised Karl to the rank of field marshal, but also granted him a pension. He spent some time traveling around the continent before settling in Darmstadt, with his six children, at the residence of his mother-in-law. While residing there, he became the President of the Imperial Credit Commission, an important office in charge of guaranteeing that all member states' financial conditions were optimal. It was a difficult, complicated, and thankless job, particularly given spendthrift habits of many of his fellow royals, particularly those bitten by the architectural bug, or wishing to introduce luxury into their courts.

Following the death of his childless older brother Adolf Friedrich IV on June 2, 1794, Karl succeeded as the ruling Duke of Mecklenburg-Strelitz.[86] His family relocated to Neustrelitz, his capital, where he took over the daily ruling of his realm. As a ruler Karl encouraged agricultural innovation, established a new police force, and implemented compulsory education. As the Holy Roman Empire crumbled, Karl had to join to Confederation of the Rhine or face Napoleon's ire. However, his close connections to Prussia and Great Britain guaranteed him favorable treatment during the Congress of Vienna, where he was elevated to the rank of grand duke.

In the summer of 1816, Karl went on as lengthy journey to various places around Germany. Shortly after his return to Neustrelitz, he was taken ill. He suffered respiratory complications and his lungs were seriously compromised. He died on November 6 after suffering an attack of apoplexy. Karl was buried in Mirow, where the Mecklenburg-Strelitz dynasty had its crypt. Both his wives had been buried there three decades earlier.

****

Countess and Duchess Palatine Augusta of Zweibrücken (1765-1796)

Born in Darmstadt on April 14, 1765, Marie Wilhelmine "Augusta" was the youngest child of Landgrave Georg Wilhelm and his wife Luise Albertina.[87] Known by the name Augusta, she was carefully educated by her mother, who hoped to make advantageous matches for her daughters. Through her sister Luise, Augusta was able to establish a friendship with Queen Marie-Antoinette. During a visit to Paris, a meeting between Augusta and a potential suitor was arranged. He had served in the French regiment "Royal Alsace" and had led a rather extravagant bachelorhood. The couple liked each other and plans for a wedding began in earnest.

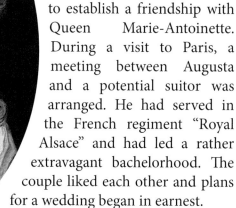

Countess and Duchess Palatine Auguste of Zweibrücken.

Augusta's future husband resided in Strasbourg, where he had lived aor many years. The young man in question was Count and Duke Palatine Maximilian (Max) Joseph of Zweibrücken. Born in Mannheim on May 27, 1756, Max Joseph was the second son of Count Palatine Friedrich Michael of Zweibrücken and his cousin Countess Palatine Maria Franziska of Sulzbach.[88] By then, the once prolific House of Wittelsbach was dangerously approaching extinction. Four branches remained: the Elector Palatine (childless), the Elector of Bavaria (childless), the Counts and Dukes of Zweibrücken, and the distant Counts Palatine of Gelnhausen. As the two electors had failed to produce heirs, the dynasty's succession would fall on the Zweibrücken line. If the Zweibrückens failed to father a new generation, then the entire legacy would land on the Gelnhausens, who were direct descendants Count Palatine Wolfgang of Zweibrücken.

In 1777, Elector Max Joseph of Bavaria died without issue. His vast domains were inherited by his cousin Elector Palatine Karl Theodor, who also had failed to produce offspring. Complicating matters even more, Max Joseph of Zweibrücken's older brother, Karl II, Count and Duke of Zweibrücken, also was childless as his only child had died at the age of eight. Hence when his nephew died in 1784, young Max Joseph was the last remaining Zweibrücken of marriageable age. From Munich, his cousin the Elector urged him to find a suitable wife immediately. That choice was Landgravine Augusta of Hesse-Darmstadt.

On September 30, 1785, Augusta and Max Joseph were married in Darmstadt.[89] It was a rare ecumenical marriage as he was Catholic, while the bride a Lutheran. The children, because their father one day would rule over Bavaria, were raised in the Roman Catholic Church. After their wedding, the couple lived primarily in Strasbourg's "Hôtel des Deux-Ponts" (Zweibrücken Palais), while their summer residence was at Rappoltstein, a small territory Max Joseph had previously inherited.

Count and Duke Palatine Max Joseph of Zweibrüchen.

The Elector of Bavaria did not have to wait long to see a new generation of Wittelsbachs make its entrance. On August 25, 1786, Augusta gave birth in the family's Strasbourg home to a son, Ludwig. Nearly two years later, on June 21, 1788, also in Strasbourg, a second child, Augusta Amalie, arrived. The following year, the placid, carefree existence Max Joseph and Augusta enjoyed in Alsace's beautiful capital city of Strasbourg was uprooted by revolution. On July 14, 1789, the Bastille was stormed by crowds in Paris. Overnight, the sparks of revolution blowing from Paris infected the rest of the kingdom. Strasbourg was not immune to revolutionary fervor. To escape advancing turmoil, Max Joseph, along with his young family, departed and headed to Darmstadt, where they stayed briefly. Then, they moved to Mannheim, where they lived in reduced circumstances.

While in Mannheim, on October 9, 1790, Augusta gave birth to a second daughter, Amalie. This child would die in 1794, in the midst of very difficult times of war. A third daughter, Karoline, was also born in Mannheim on February 8, 1792.

All around Max Joseph and Augusta everything was war, destruction, and desolation. France's revolutionary fervor had spilled over the country's borders and Germany was ransacked, particularly the Rhineland. As Mannheim erupted in riots, Augusta and the children fled to faraway Ansbach. Eventually, they reached Munich, where on July 7, 1795, Augusta gave birth to a second son named Karl. Earlier in the year, Max Joseph's brother Karl II had died without issue, leaving him as his only heir. Yet, because of war and the tenuous political situation in the Rhineland, Max Joseph was unable to assume his ducal legacy.

Stress, exhaustion, war, and revolution, the constant moves searching for safety, all took a heavy toll on Augusta's health. She developed pulmonary tuberculosis and died at Schloß Rohrbach, near Heidelberg, on March 30, 1796.[90] In death, she returned to Darmstadt, setting of her happy childhood. Augusta was buried in the Darmstadt Schloßkirche.

In order to care for his remaining children, Max Joseph married Augusta's 20-year-old niece

Princess Karoline of Baden in 1797. Two years later he inherited the Electorate of Bavaria and all of the remaining Palatinate territories belonging to the House of Wittelsbach, with the exception to those lands owned by the Counts Palatine of Gelnhausen. Overnight, Max Joseph became one of Germany's most prominent and important rulers. Together with his second wife, they had a further eight children, including the mothers of Emperor Franz Joseph and Empress Elisabeth of Austria.

It is worth noting that Max Joseph was perspicacious enough to see Napoleon's mastery of Europe take shape before the continent fell to him. Early on, he allied himself with France, and Napoleon granted him the title of King of Bavaria, an elevation later accepted by the Congress of Vienna. His descendants, including those by his first wife include not only Duke Franz of Bavaria, Head of House, but also the Hereditary Princess of Liechtenstein, and Gisela, the Margravine of Meißen.

Empress Marie Alexandrovna of Russia.

****

Empress Marie Alexandrovna of Russia (1824-1880)

Princess Maximiliane Wilhelmine Auguste Sophie Marie of Hesse and by Rhine was born in Darmstadt on August 8, 1824.[91] She was the youngest of Grand Duchess Wilhelmine's second set of children. As a child, she was called Wilhelmine, like her mother. Later, she was known as Marie. Rumors abounded regarding the real identity of her father: was it Baron Senarclens de Grancy or was it her

mother's official husband? Regardless, Grand Duke Ludwig II recognized her as his child, just as he had done with all of his wife's children. It is not an exaggeration to state that Marie's parents were incompatible: Ludwig was bashful and introverted, Wilhelmine, eleven years his junior, was sweet, enchanting, vivacious. She was fifteen-years old when she married her first cousin Ludwig. A mother at seventeen, by her 21st birthday Wilhelmine had given birth three times.

Another complication in Ludwig and Wilhelmine's relationship was caused by his many absences. As his father's heir, Ludwig was required to participate in myriad diplomatic missions, as well as in the endless warring that took place during the turbulent years of the Napoleonic Wars. Consequently, the couple grew apart and began leading separate lives. The entry of Baron August Senarclens de Grancy into Wilhelmine's employment guaranteed a more pronounced estrangement. In due course, Ludwig and Wilhelmine reached an entente that allowed each to live as they wished, while keeping up appearances. At times they would have long periods of not seeing each other, while at other times Ludwig II would join his wife at Heiligenberg. It may have been an unorthodox setup, but it worked for them and a reconciliation ensued, while also ensuring each party their privacy.

Marie spent long periods of her childhood in Heiligenberg. Wilhelmine assumed direct responsibility for her daughter's education. She included topics on French culture and literature, areas in which Wilhelmine was deeply interested. She also placed emphasis on teaching Marie literature and history, as well as languages. Marie's mother placed Marianne von Senarclens de Grancy, August's sister, in charge of her daughter's education. This idyllic existence came to an abrupt end in 1836 when Wilhelmine died of tuberculosis. Marie and her brother Alexander moved permanently to their father's court in Darmstadt, although many of their mother's closest servants remained in charge of continuing the education of the siblings along the path set in motion by their mother. While Marie's older brothers, Ludwig III and Karl, were close to their younger siblings, that was not the case with their legal father who remained distant and aloof toward Wilhelmine's youngest children.

In 1839, Tsesarevich Alexander Nikolaevich, eldest son and heir of Tsar Nicholas I of Russia, embarked on a lengthy journey to western Europe. After visiting several faraway regions of the Russian Empire, including Yekaterinburg, where his dynasty would meet its ignominious end nearly eight decades later, Alexander crossed over the border into Germany. The voyage had a dual purpose: to introduce the Russian heir to several European courts, thus increasing his knowledge, and to assist him in finding a wife. Initially, his parents had chosen Princess Alexandrine of Baden, eldest daughter of Grand Duke Leopold (he of Hochberg origin). However, the meeting did not go too well, and Alexander was unmoved by the rather plain-looking princess. He continued his search – Alexandrine ended marrying one of the most rakish of royals, Duke Ernst II of Saxe-Coburg and Gotha, Queen Victoria's brother-in-law. Alexander's tour through Germany brought

Tsesarevich Alexander Nikolaevich of Russia.

him to Prussia and Württemberg, where he had relatives aplenty. Fate played its furtive hand when the Russian entourage made an unexpected visit to Darmstadt. The stop, lasting only one day, changed Alexander and Marie's lives forever. Due to her youth, she had not been on the list of eligible princesses for Alexander to consider. Marie was not yet fourteen-years old, while Alexander was weeks away from his 21st birthday. Marie was a sight to behold: slender and tall for her age, girlish, fragile with a small waist, golden-haired and blue-eyed. Alexander was *"stopped in his tracks"* and the *"aim of all our travels travels is at last achieved,"* wrote his tutor.[92] She is said to have been eating cherries, and had to spit the seeds in her hands, when she was unexpectedly introduced to the Russian heir. She made an immediate impression and Alexander's heart was lost after that unscheduled meeting that evening at the opera. This Romanov was to find his own bride, not just accept one issued to him.

The following day, just before he departed Darmstadt Marie gave Alexander a locket with strands of her hair. Infatuated, Alexander wrote to his father, informing the tsar of what happened in Darmstadt: *"I like her terribly at first sight. If you permit it father, I will come back to Darmstadt after England."*[93] Delighted with the news, Nicholas gave his approval. Alexandra Feodorovna, Nicholas' consort, was hesitant because of Marie's disputed parentage and her mother's death by consumption. To his mother, Alexander wrote, *"My dear Maman, I absolutely do not care about the secrets of Maria. I love her, and I would sooner rather abdicate the throne, than give her up. I will marry only her, that is my decision!"*[94] Nicholas held no such worries for if Marie's father had accepted her as his own, that settled matters. The Romanovs had enough sizable skeletons in their own closet. On the other hand, this would not be the first marriage between the houses of Romanov and Hesse. Two generations earlier, a princess of Hesse-Darmstadt was the first wife of Tsesarevich Paul Petrovich, Alexander's grandfather; two generations afterward two Romanovs would marry Hessian princesses.

After a successful visit to Queen Victoria, Alexander traveled to The Hague to stay with his Aunt Maria Pavlovna, consort of King Willem II. In early June, the Russians arrived in Darmstadt to allow Alexander more time with Marie. The engagement was sealed during this visit, although a public announcement was delayed given the bride's young age. Later in the year, Alexander returned to Darmstadt. Among his companions was a Russian Orthodox priest who would begin Marie's instruction in Orthodoxy. Their engagement was officially announced in April 1840.

Alexander Nikolaevich was born in Moscow on April 29, 1818[95] (April 17, Old Style), the eldest son of the Grand Duke Nicholas Pavlovich and his wife Alexandra Feodorovna, née Charlotte of Prussia, whose grandmothers were Hessians, Friederike, Duchess of Mecklenburg-Strelitz, and Friederike, Queen of Prussia. As his older uncles Tsar Alexander I (his namesake) and Konstantin Pavlovich were childless, Alexander's birth assured the Romanov dynasty's survival. In due course, his parents produced three more sons (Konstantin, Nicholas, and Mikhail), who would fill the Imperial nursery with a further 12 grand dukes. Alexander Nikolaevich was *"unusually handsome, a true prince. His father thought him too feminine, with a too-tender heart. He adored solitude and daydreaming. Nicholas wanted his son to be manly,"* wrote one of his biographers.[96] The Marquis de Custine, a contemporary wrote, *"if he ever comes to the throne, he will obtain obedience through the constraint of a gracious character rather than by terror."*[97]

Furthermore, Alexander was also described as, *"not an original character and he was not perverse. He was used to having someone at his elbow to tell him what was good or wise and he readily assimilated good advice. He had tact or was merely disinclined to quarrel. While he failed to share his father's military enthusiasm, he meekly fulfilled arduous duties on the parade ground and in the field. He had sympathy for the victims of his father's tyranny, but seldom interceded for anyone. He seemed colourless and did not promise to be a great tsar. What won him most favour was the mildness and graciousness of his disposition."*[98]

In August 1840, Marie set out on her historic journey to Russia. Along with her came her brother Prince Alexander and Mademoiselle Senarclens de Grancy – both would remain in Russia for years to come. She liked St Petersburg and found the Imperial capital more beautiful than she thought it would be. The sprawling views of the city and the Neva River from her apartments in the Winter Palace she found spellbinding. Romanov pomp and circumstance were on full display to welcome Marie to St Petersburg, the Russian capital being Europe's most luxurious court. Banquets, balls, concerts, and plays occupied the young Hessian princess, who also received priceless gifts and was showered with awe-striking jewels. And yet, Marie's bourgeois upbringing in Heiligenberg and Darmstadt did not prepare her for life in the splendor of the Imperial Russian court. She found court life in Russia to be suffocating and tiresome. Her lady-in-waiting, Anna Tiutcheva, later wrote about Marie's feelings: *"Having been raised in seclusion and even, one might say, in austerity, in the little castle of Jugenheim (sic. Heiligenberg), where she saw her father only rarely, she was more frightened than bedazzled, when she was suddenly brought to Court, to the most opulent, most splendid, most brilliant Court of all European nations. She told me that many times, after constant battles of overcoming her timidity and awkwardness, later on, under cover of darkness and in the stillness of her own room, she would give freedom to her tears and muffled cries."*[99]

Marie was raised a Protestant, but as the future wife of the Russian heir she had to be received into the Russian Orthodox Church. After months of preparation and direction from priests tending to the spiritual needs of the Imperial Family, she became an Orthodox on December 17, 1840. Her Russian name onward was Marie Alexandrovna. The next day, in the presence of the Imperial Family, the whole court, the Russian nobility, notable foreign guests, and the diplomatic corps, the official betrothal was held.

Alexander and Marie's wedding took place in the Cathedral Church of the Winter Palace in St Petersburg on April 18, 1841. She wore a white dress sewn with silver and diamonds. A crimson velvet robe with white satin and red ermine hung from her shoulders. Diamonds adorned a tiara she wore, as did her earrings, necklace, and bracelets. Orange blossoms, a tradition for brides, were intertwined with the diamonds in her tiara.

After the wedding celebrations were concluded, Alexander and Marie occupied a suite of rooms in the south-west block of the Winter Palace. Summers were spent in apartments in the Zubov wing of the Catherine Palace in Tsarskoe-Selo. Yet all this splendor failed to astonish Marie Alexandrovna, who instead struggled to assimilate. She slowly retreated into her private realm and had trouble fulfilling many of her duties as Tsarevna of Russia. *"La petite bourgeois Allemande,"* her Russian critics called her when pointing to her *"excessive"* fondness for domesticity. Her shyness would win the day –

Tsar Alexander II and Empress Marie Alexandrovna.

she enjoyed more the private life of the countryside more than the dazzling world of the Russian court. While she and Alexander built a loyal coterie of close friends, both led a very bourgeois and domestic existence. These first years of marriage were blissful, yet they would not last. Marie was comforted, until 1851, by the company of her brother Alexander. His decision to marry one of her ladies-in-waiting forced not only the end of his military career, but also his departure from Russia.

Marie Alexandrovna's main purpose in Russia was to provide the Romanov nursery with occupants. In this respect, she would not disappoint. In 1842, she gave birth to their first child, Alexandra. Unfortunately, the little girl died in 1849 after a life cut short by tubercular meningitis. Both parents were devastated by this unexpected loss. Years later Alexander remembered his daughter as, *"so devoted to him she used to entreat to be allowed to sit in his room even when He was busy, and would remain there hours, quite silent, if only she might see her Papa."*[100] Even in the 1870s, Alexandra's loss was still present in her mother's heart as shared by her niece Princess Alice in a letter to her mother Queen Victoria, *"Aunt Marie was so sympathizing, motherly, and loving; it touched me much…At such moments she is peculiarly soft and womanly, and she loves her own children so tenderly. She cried much, and told me of the sad death of her eldest girl…"*[101]

Seven other children were born to Alexander and Marie: Nicholas (1843-1865); Tsar Alexander III

(1845-1894); Vladimir (1847-1909), married to his distant cousin Marie of Mecklenburg-Schwerin; Alexei (1850-1908), unmarried; Marie (1853-1920), married to Prince Alfred, Duke of Edinburgh and Saxe-Coburg and Gotha; Sergei (1857-1905), married to his cousin Elisabeth of Hesse and by Rhine; and Paul (1860-1919), firstly married to his cousin Alexandra of Greece, and secondly to Olga Karnovich, created Princess Paley.[102]

At the Russian Court, Marie befriended Grand Duchess Elena Pavlovna, Alexander's aunt. Born a Württemberger, Elena Pavlovna had married Grand Duke Mikhail Pavlovich, Tsar Nicholas I's youngest brother. The arranged marriage was a disaster and after the birth of several children, the couple separated. A respected intellectual, Elena Pavlovna led an important, progressive

Tsar Alexander II.

salon inside the Mikhailovsky Palace, her vast residence in St Petersburg. The grand duchess was also a confidante of her nephew Alexander Nikolaevich, whom she hoped would implement long-needed reforms to all of Russia's institutions, serfdom most importantly above all. Alexander and Marie attended these gatherings frequently mingling with intellectuals, men of letters, artists, and progressives. Hence, in their aunt, they found a kindred spirit who inspired their intellectual pursuits and political goals, as well as Alexander's *"resolve to change matters and allow greater freedom from a climate of admittedly ineffectual censorship once he ascended the imperial throne."*

Marie Alexandrovna cherished reading. Together with her husband, they would read some of the most progressive books of their time. Writers critical of tsardom and autocracy made their thoughts known to the heir and his wife through their books. Mikhail Lermontov, Nikolai Gogol, Fyodor Dostoevsky, Ivan Turgenev, contributed to shaping Alexander's sympathies for the plight of serfs, while also inspiring his ardent abolitionist stand. Vassili Zhukovsky, Alexander's tutor and confidante, had stressed on his pupil the heavy legacy his shoulders would one day carry. *"Zhukovsky brought up the heir to be a true Christian, with feelings of compassion,"* wrote Edvard Radzinsky.[103] The devoted tutor advised Alexander that, *"if a ruler would be loved by his people he must show first that he loved them."*[104] Marie not only enjoyed Alexander's confidence, but she supported his ideals of introducing political reforms.

These were heady days filled with discussions and preparation to ready for the time when Alexander would sit on the throne, Marie by his side. It was at this time when Anna Tiutcheva first came into Marie's employment as a maid-of-honor. *"The first time I set eyes on the Grand Duchess,"* wrote Tiutcheva, *"she was already twenty-eight years old, but still looked very young. She retained that youthful appearance all her life; when she was forty, she could have been taken for a woman of thirty. Although she was tall and slender, she was in fact so thin and fragile, that at first glance she gave no impression of a 'belle dame'; however, she was unusually elegant, with that special kind of grace, which can only be found in old German paintings, or Madonnas by Albert Dürer. Her facial features were regular. Her beauty lay in the wonderful, delicate color of her skin, and her large, slightly bulging, blue eyes, which looked at you with timidity and perception...she seemed almost out of place and uneasy in her role as mother, wife, and empress. She was tenderly attached to her husband and children, and conscientiously fulfilled the duties which her family and exalted rank demanded of her. The Empress's mind was like her soul: subtle, refined, penetrating, extremely ironic, but lacking in ardor, breadth and initiative."*[105]

The couple's peaceful existence was deeply affected when in 1853 Tsar Nicholas I plunged Russia into an unnecessary war. Both Alexander and Marie opposed the very idea of war, yet they could not deter it as doing so would have been perceived as treasonous. The conflict erupted when Russian troops invaded the Danubian principalities of Wallachia and Moldavia, which were part of the Turkish Empire. The Sultan of Turkey demanded withdrawal, Russia ignored his request and declared war instead. London and Paris insisted on Russia's evacuation, while Vienna offered diplomatic intervention. War ignited in March 1854.

From the start, Russia's conduct of the war was dismal. Soldiers were unprepared, infrastructure insufficient, organization lacking, medical supplies inadequate, corruption rampant. Six decades later, the same ills were still hampering the battle-readiness and efficiency of the Russian army, which had become a thoroughly corrupted institution. The war also painfully demonstrated the rot devouring autocracy from within. The Russians suffered

Empress Marie Alexandrovna.

grave casualties; one defeat followed another. Nicholas I, in shock and disheartened, ceded some governmental responsibilities to his son. Alexander, tired of military ineptitude, dismissed Prince Menshikov, commander-in-chief; the more able Prince Mikhail Gorchakov replaced him. Yet, with full realization of his dismal error, Nicholas I collapsed physically. To his heir, the dying tsar said, *"I am passing command to you that is not in desirable order. I am leaving you many disappointments and cares."*[106] His demise was brought on by a deadly combination of stress, bitterness, frustration, and a weakened constitution. Pneumonia set in; his respiratory system collapsed. Tsar Nicholas I died on March 2, 1855.[107]

When he ascended the mighty Russian throne, all that Alexander could see was disaster, corruption, and deceit. The war had quickly tarnished the image of a powerful Russia upon autocracy based its raîson d'être. Alexander II knew that for his reign to be successful, the war had to conclude. *"Everything is crashing, but we will have to be quiet now,"* Alexander said.[108] Once this was achieved, Alexander set about, with his wife's support, on reforming Imperial Russia.

During the Crimean War, Marie Alexandrovna assisted the medical efforts to bring relief to the extremely high casualty numbers. At the same time, she supported her husband in the first decisive moves of his reign, particularly when suing for peace to prevent the outright invasion of Russia. This would have been a devastating blow to all their reformist goals. However, the double stress caused by worry and continued pregnancies took a toll on her physical condition. After the birth of a fifth son in 1857, she collapsed as depression set in. She was sent to Bad Kissingen in Bavaria to recuperate. Her last pregnancy in 1860 did little to better her condition and she spent months on bedrest in an effort to regain her strength.

That same year, after the death of her mother-in-law, Marie Alexandrovna assumed many of her responsibilities. She played a pivotal role in charitable activities, among them supporting the establishment of the Red Cross in Russia and becoming its chief patron. She also patronized hospitals, alms-houses, shelters, high schools, primary schools, and countless other charitable institutions. She was particularly interested in furthering women's education and supported the establishment of many women's educational institutions throughout Russia. She also played an important role in advising and supporting her husband's decision to bringing an end to the pernicious institution of serfdom. To achieve his life-long goal to free the peasants, on March 3 (February 19, OS), 1861, Alexander II proclaimed the Emancipation Proclamation.[109] Nicholas I's prediction that during his son's reign nothing great would be done proved false.

Initially, Alexander was happy with his marriage. The early years were described as, *"years of untroubled family happiness...There were almost daily gatherings at the young court...there would be reading aloud, music, cards...the host and the hostess charmed everyone by their manner."*[110] As to their

Nixa and Dagmar.

children, Alexander and Marie paid great attention to their upbringing and education. They carefully chose their tutors and had the children learn several languages. Both parents were particularly involved in the education of their eldest son, Nicholas Alexandrovich, known to the family as "Nixa." He represented their hope for further reform in Russia. In him, Alexander and Marie saw someone who would complete the work that the father would leave unfinished. However, Nixa suffered from weak health, accentuated by a fall from a horse in the early 1860s. Not surprisingly, his early death of spinal meningitis in 1865 was a devastating blow to everyone in the family. Nixa had been convalescing in Nice, where his doctors hoped the climate would improve his health. Marie Alexandrovna never left her ailing son's bedside. Numb with shock, the Romanovs proceeded to Heiligenberg before continuing to Russia to bury their son. In her diary, Princess Marie of Battenberg wrote, *"we have prayed for him and his poor parents. Yesterday he died, it is very distressing after the happiness of last year – Anna's marriage and Nixa's betrothal – and now both are dead."*[111] By his deathbed had also stood his fiancée, Princess Dagmar of Denmark, second daughter of King Christian IX and Queen Louise. Aged seventeen-years old, Dagmar was now without her beloved Nixa. Eventually, the parents agreed that she would do as wife of Nixa's next brother, who in 1881 succeeded as Tsar Alexander III. Upon entering the Russian Imperial Family, she became baptized as Marie Feodorovna. Their son, Nicholas II, was to marry in 1894 Princess Alix of Hesse and by

Rhine, Marie Alexandrovna's great-niece.

Marie's coping with Nixa's death was to withdraw further from public life. Her health, already compromised, suffered a major setback after her son's death. She had already embarked on long sojourns to various spas in Europe. In 1864, while on a visit to Bad Kissingen, she met King Ludwig II of Bavaria, who became infatuated with her. Many of these visits to western Europe also included stays with her brother Alexander at their beloved Heiligenberg, still full of memories of long-gone happy days. She also, from 1861 onward, began visiting the Crimea, where the mild climate was beneficial for her health. She was delighted by the flora, the warm climate, the abundant colors. Alexander bought Livadia for her, an estate with a two-story villa that had belonged to Count Lev Potocki. The original villa was later replaced by a large palace, a small palace, and a church built under the direction of renowned architect Ippolito Monighetti. Her choice for this beautiful region turned the Black Sea coast into a playground not just for the Romanovs, but eventually for the Russian nobility and officialdom as well.

Marie Feodorovna with George Alexandrovich, Nicholas Alexandrovich, and Tsesarevich Alexander Alexandrovich.

While Alexander had always loved his wife, fidelity was not one of his virtues. He had had several sexual adventures since their marriage, but none had been threatening to his wife's position. Extramarital affairs only increased as Marie Alexandrovna's health declined and her absences from St Petersburg became more frequent. None

had been more than dalliances that were not worth her worry. However, all that changed when a young woman by the name of Ekaterina was noticed by Alexander II's roving eye.

In 1866, Alexander and Marie celebrated their silver wedding anniversary. To the outside world, all seemed to be fine with the Imperial couple. In private, however, the reality was quite different. Alexander's gaze was captured by a young woman who was enrolled in the Smolny Institute, a school that provided an education for young ladies of the nobility. The object of Alexander's infatuation was Princess Ekaterina Mikahilovna Dolgoruky, whose father had been an acquaintance of Alexander's and had died leaving his children his debts. As was tradition when cases like the Dolgoruky happened, the children became Imperial wards.

Alexander II had first met Ekaterina in 1857, when he visited her father's estate near Poltava. He later saw her during a visit to the Smolny. She captivated him. His visits to the school increased in frequency. His relentless hunt of Ekaterina began, but she resisted his approaches as she would not succumb to him unless marriage was part of their future. *"Ekaterina was not born to be a mistress: her lineage was longer and prouder than Alexander's own, and it was not in her nature to love lightly,"* wrote Charlotte Zeepvat.[112] For a year, Alexander tried his wiles on Ekaterina, who was but a teenager. Finally, and to his lascivious delight, his campaign bore fruit when she finally submitted to him in July

Top left: *Tsar Alexander II and Empress Marie Alexandrovna.*
Top right: *Grand Duchess Elisabeth Feodorovna.*
Left: *Grand Duchess Elisabeth Feodorovna, Grand Duke Paul Alexandrovich, and Grand Duke Serge Alexandrovich.*
Above: *Empress Marie Alexandrovna with her daughter the Duchess of Edinburgh and her son Grand Duke Paul Alexandrovich.*

1866. Alexander promised Ekaterina that if ever he could, he would marry her. Hence, with this pledge in her hand, Ekaterina embarked on the love affair of her life. Alexander called Katya his *"wife before God."*[113] When their secret dalliance became known to her family, she was taken to Italy. After five months apart, Alexander requested Ekaterina to meet him in Paris. By 1869, he set her up with a home in the exclusive Millionnaya, a street not far from the Winter Palace.

Not surprisingly, children began to arrive. Alexander II, throwing discretion overboard, eventually moved Ekaterina to apartments in the Winter Palace whenever she was approaching childbirth. Ekaterina gave birth to a son in 1872. He was named George and granted the title Prince Yourievsky. By late 1873, a second child, Olga, arrived. Three years later Boris was born, but died soon after birth. In 1878 Ekaterina gave birth to a second daughter who was named after her.[114]

Against convention, the tsar did not even bother finding his mistress a pliable husband who would recognize her children as his own. Alexander, to the consternation of his older children, quite openly lived with Ekaterina. She became very domestic and focused her attention on the children and her lover. Every day, *"at three, when the Tsar was in St Petersburg, he would visit Ekaterina and the children would be taken to join him: in their*

company Alexander rediscovered the untroubled happiness he had known with Maria when their own children were small."[115]

Marie Alexandrovna knew about her husband's relationship with Ekaterina. With time, everyone in the family knew about it. The affair with Ekaterina brought about discord within the ranks of the Imperial Family. Tsesarevich Alexander Alexandrovich could not comprehend why his father acted in this despicable manner. He and his wife Marie Feodorovna led the anti-Dolgorouky party, and all through her years as Tsarevna, the Romanov family was divided and the animosity to Ekaterina flowed like an undercurrent beneath the surface. Alexander II's brothers, embroiled in marital scandals of their own, as well as his son Alexei Alexandrovich, whose moral code left much to be desired, sided with the tsar. Alexander II's other sons opposed Ekaterina, while his daughter Marie tried her best to remain neutral.[116] The children sided with their mother, who in turn took a passive stand when informed of her husband's affair. In her memoirs, Princess Marie of Battenberg expressed everyone's dismay with the situation:

"One day, it was at Heiligenberg, one of the gentlemen of the Darmstadt Court said to me as I wished him good-morning, 'Oh, I have seen you already this morning, when you were walking down

From the left: Grand Duke Paul Alexandrovich, Grand Duke Serge Alexandrovich, Tsar Alexander II, Grand Duchess Marie Alexandrovna, Grand Duke Alexei Alexandrovich, Tsesarevich Alexander Alexandrovich, Tsesarevna Marie Feodorovna with Grand Duke Nicholas Nikolaevich, and Grand Duke Vladimir Alexandrovich.

in the valley with the Tsar, and your little son.' I denied having met him, but I was rather surprised, as I had been at home all the morning, and my little four-year-old son was at Schönberg. Only after the Tsar's departure did my mother tell me who the young lady, who was so like me, and the little boy were. Then something died in me."[117]

The last decade of Marie Alexandrovna's life witnessed her increased withdrawal from public view. In 1870, Alexander renamed the Imperial Palace in Kiev after his wife. The Mariinsky Palace had undergone extensive reconstruction to be used as a rest-stop along the long route between St Petersburg and the Crimea. Marie, who was a horticulturist, had a large park built to one side of the palace. The Mariinsky Palace was used by the Imperial Family until the dynasty's last days. Previously, the Mariinsky Theater in St Petersburg was named in her honor. As her visits to Darmstadt increased, Alexander also contributed to Prince Alexander's plans to expand Heiligenberg so all the Russian visitors could be comfortably housed. Having come to terms with her many tragedies, life took a peaceful route for the ailing tsarina. Queen Victoria thought her, *"very lady like.. and very kind and amiable…she has a sad expression and looks so delicate. I think we should get on very well together, poor thing I pity her much."*[118]

As 1879 came to an end, so did Marie Alexandrovna's waning light begin flickering to its expected early end. Princess Marie of Battenberg later wrote about realizing her aunt's life was coming to an end: *"In the late Summer of this*

From the left: Serge Alexandrovich, Elisabeth Feodorovna, Paul Alexandrovich, Marie of Greece and Marie Pavlovna.

year, 1879, my beloved aunt, the Tsarina Marie, already in very bad health, stayed some weeks with us at Heiligenberg. A year later her melancholy dark blue eyes closed forever in her Russian home. For my father, and all of us, her death was a heavy sorrow."[119] In spite of his betrayal, Alexander and Marie remained on good terms until her last day. In February 1880 after a bomb ripped through the Winter Palace, his first reaction was to rush to his wife's apartments to make sure she was unharmed. Since she was asleep through the ordeal, Alexander remained outside her door so he could be the one to let her know what happened and reassure her. To the end, this couple that had started life together with such hope and love, remained terribly fond of each other. This can be best demonstrated by a story later told by Vera Borovikova, the nanny of the Yourievsky children, after Alexander brought George and Olga to meet his first wife. Alexander, *"took them himself to the Tsarina's room,"* she wrote, *"and introduced Maria to them as 'Aunty', as Maria kissed and blessed her husband's children by his mistress, the couple were both in tears."*[120]

Death finally released Marie Alexandrovna of her earthly turmoil on June 3, 1880. She passed away alone in her rooms at the Winter Palace and her remains were laid to rest inside the Imperial Crypt at the Peter and Paul Cathedral in St Petersburg. Living above her room were Ekaterina and her children, who had moved into the Winter Palace for their, and the Tsar's, protection. An apocryphal story claims that she was tortured by hearing the little feet of the Yourievsky children, which

Top left: Empress Marie Alexandrovna at a time when her health had started deteriorating.

Top right: The Vladimirovichi grandchildren: Andrei, Kirill, Helen, and Boris.

Left: Grand Duchess Marie Alexandrovna with her son Prince Alfred Jr. Upon marrying Queen Victoria's second son, she became Duchess of Edinburgh, later also gaining the title of Duchess of Saxe-Coburg and Gotha when her husband succeeded to that ducal throne. Alfred Jr. died childless in his twenties, victim of excess and dissipation.

Above: Tsar Nicholas II and his wife Empress Alexandra Feodorovna.

many historians have used as further proof of the torture Alexander inflicted on her. And yet, we know through Borovikova's account how Marie Alexandrovna reacted to meeting her husband's other family.

Undeniable is the near indecent haste with which Alexander married Ekaterina. Only forty-six days after his wife's death, the Tsar married Princess Yourievsky. The secret wedding took place in Tsarskoe Selo on July 18. Three days later, Alexander II shocked his family when he informed them of his second marriage. To Alexander Alexandrovich and Marie Feodorovna, he explained his concern to do his duty by Ekaterina and their children. He also informed the Tsesarevich and his wife of the marriage, alleging that he had done so to, *"do his duty by Catherine and their children, to regularise their position and to ease her conscience."*[121] When news reached her in Berlin, Crown Princess Victoria expressed her disgust by writing to her mother Queen Victoria, "(he) *presented his wife to them and asked them to be kind to them…What one must feel bitterly is the want of respect for the poor Empress's memory."*[122] Further shock came when rumors reached the Imperial Family that Alexander intended to have Ekaterina crowned. This would mean that his daughters-in-law would have to bow to her. Marie Feodorovna, threatened to leave Russia – the Tsar retaliated by announcing the Imperial yacht was unavailable. In case of his death, Alexander II asked his son Alexander to take care of his second family. Marie Feodorovna, however, was relentless in her spite toward Ekaterina. *"Come my dear, say how*

Tsar Alexander II with his second wife, Ekaterina Princess Yourievsky, and their eldest children, George and Olga.

do you do to the princess," he said. His unforgiving daughter-in-law curtseyed to him, *"and swept off, her proud head held high, without even a glance at Catherine."*[123]

Tsar Alexander II's marital bliss was of short duration, however. The target of several assassination attempts, nihilists finally got him on March 13, 1881. He had signed a manifesto earlier that morning for the reform of the Council of State, *"paving the way for full franchise in the future."*[124] With the document still in his coat pocket, Alexander II called on his cousin Grand Duchess Ekaterina Mikhailovna. Along the Catherine Canal on his way back to the Winter Palace a bomb was thrown at his carriage. Shaken but unharmed, Alexander alighted from his carriage to surmise the damage. A second bomb was hurled and landed at Alexander's feet. His contorted body lay on the blood-soaked snow. *"Take me home quickly,"*[125] Alexander muttered to his brother Michael Nikolaevich. Forty-five minutes after arriving in the Winter Palace, Tsar Alexander II of Russia expired as Ekaterina's *"soul-tearing shrieks"* curdled everyone's blood.[126]

The death of Alexander II not only inaugurated the repressive reign of his successor Alexander III, but also brought all plans for reform to a screeching halt. While the new tsar's reign of terror managed to curtail revolutionary activity, it wrote the script that would bring the Romanovs to an ignominious end in 1917.

Epilogue

In the beautiful woods and forests of Hesse, the hunting lodges, palaces, and castles positively ring of myths, legends and tales of romance, calamities and sadness. There is a hoary old legend that a monk put a curse on the family in the 13th century, the fabled Curse of the Hessians or perhaps, because of the intermarriages, the Curse of the Coburgs in the 19th century might also apply. Sadly, like the curses of many famous families it seemed played out in the numerous tragedies that have occurred. The disintegration of empires, the horrible executions, the deaths due to inherited disease or horrific accidents can all be explained by something far simpler than the maledictions of a vicious monk. It was, frankly, the way things are with a large family that is closely recorded in history for century upon century.

The life and death of one branch of the family, horrible and sad as it was, coincided with the real and difficult birth of another arm of the family. Named for a small village with an extinct title, they had a patriarch who succumbed to love and a mother who was quietly ambitious for her four handsome sons. They presented a united front that held steadfast, one for the other. The family extended its reach to Great Britain achieving great success as well as experiencing great tragedy. To say that tragedy followed the Hesse and by Rhines, Battenbergs and Mountbattens, though, is, as was said, an oversimplification and a disservice to the accomplishments of family members. It implies helplessness, which was certainly not the case. Ultimately, through prejudice and slights, they evolved into a modern aristocratic family: successful, hardworking and non-complacent.

Our book is their story. While much attention was given to the historical presence and contributions of the House of Hesse-Darmstadt (later Hesse and by Rhine), we also sought a more human approach to its study. As historians, we know full well how policies and theories shape the destiny of humankind. Yet, we also realize that the human aspect of history is of great importance and meaning. What would have history been without a Grand Landgravine Karoline shaping culture; what would the course of Russia had been without Marie Alexandrovna and her influence of her husband the tsar. It is simply inconceivable to comprehend the calamitous collapse of Imperial Russia without the shared responsibility held for that tragedy by both Nicholas II and his Hessian wife, Alexandra Feodorovna. Just imagine, if you can, what the fate of the Romanovs would have been had she not brought hemophilia into the Imperial family.

It is our sincere hope, as we end our visit with the passionate and tragic, uplifting and sad, fulfilling and exemplary, history of the Grand Dukes of Hesse, that we managed to convey to you their joys and foibles from a human perspective. As Lord Mountbatten once said, *"No biography has any value unless it is written with warts and all!"* This, we have attempted to portray in a fair and balanced manner.

Personally, we feel inspired by the exemplary life led by the late Princess Margaret of Hesse and by Rhine, Peg, beloved and respected, admired and persuasive. Her life serves as a road map for creating your own devoted family of choice, when life granted you none. Hence, *"Don't forget … Think deeply, speak gently, love much, laugh often, work hard, give freely, pay promptly, pray earnestly..."* for life is only lived once and we must make it matter …

The Landgraves of Hesse

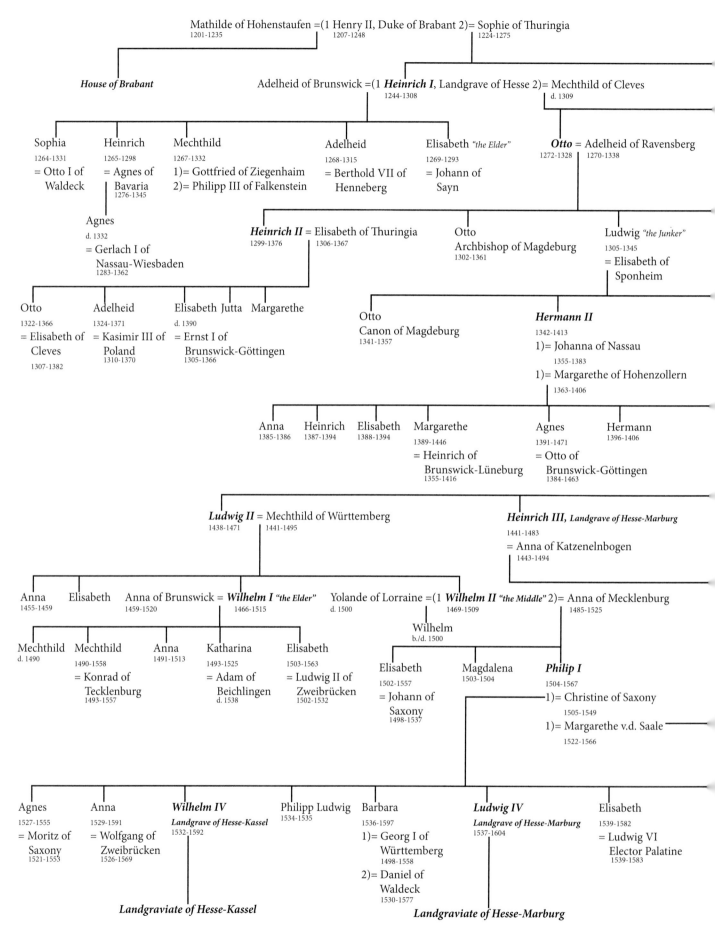

Mathilde of Hohenstaufen =(1 Henry II, Duke of Brabant 2)= Sophie of Thuringia
1201-1235   1207-1248   1224-1275

House of Brabant

Adelheid of Brunswick =(1 **Heinrich I**, Landgrave of Hesse 2)= Mechthild of Cleves
1244-1308   d. 1309

Sophia
1264-1331
= Otto I of
Waldeck

Heinrich
1265-1298
= Agnes of
Bavaria
1276-1345

Mechthild
1267-1332
1)= Gottfried of Ziegenhaim
2)= Philipp III of Falkenstein

Adelheid
1268-1315
= Berthold VII of
Henneberg

Elisabeth *"the Elder"*
1269-1293
= Johann of
Sayn

Otto = Adelheid of Ravensberg
1272-1328   1270-1338

Agnes
d. 1332
= Gerlach I of
Nassau-Wiesbaden
1283-1362

Heinrich II = Elisabeth of Thuringia
1299-1376   1306-1367

Otto
Archbishop of Magdeburg
1302-1361

Ludwig *"the Junker"*
1305-1345
= Elisabeth of
Sponheim

Otto
1322-1366
= Elisabeth of
Cleves
1307-1382

Adelheid
1324-1371
= Kasimir III of
Poland
1310-1370

Elisabeth Jutta
d. 1390
= Ernst I of
Brunswick-Göttingen
1305-1366

Margarethe

Otto
Canon of Magdeburg
1341-1357

Hermann II
1342-1413
1)= Johanna of Nassau
1355-1383
1)= Margarethe of Hohenzollern
1363-1406

Anna
1385-1386

Heinrich
1387-1394

Elisabeth
1388-1394

Margarethe
1389-1446
= Heinrich of
Brunswick-Lüneburg
1355-1416

Agnes
1391-1471
= Otto of
Brunswick-Göttingen
1384-1463

Hermann
1396-1406

Ludwig II = Mechthild of Württemberg
1438-1471   1441-1495

Heinrich III, *Landgrave of Hesse-Marburg*
1441-1483
= Anna of Katzenelnbogen
1443-1494

Anna
1455-1459

Elisabeth

Anna of Brunswick = **Wilhelm I** *"the Elder"*
1459-1520   1466-1515

Yolande of Lorraine =(1 **Wilhelm II** *"the Middle"* 2)= Anna of Mecklenburg
d. 1500   1469-1509   1485-1525

Wilhelm
b./d. 1500

Mechthild
d. 1490

Mechthild
1490-1558
= Konrad of
Tecklenburg
1493-1557

Anna
1491-1513

Katharina
1493-1525
= Adam of
Beichlingen
d. 1538

Elisabeth
1503-1563
= Ludwig II of
Zweibrücken
1502-1532

Elisabeth
1502-1557
= Johann of
Saxony
1498-1537

Magdalena
1503-1504

Philip I
1504-1567
1)= Christine of Saxony
1505-1549
1)= Margarethe v.d. Saale
1522-1566

Agnes
1527-1555
= Moritz of
Saxony
1521-1553

Anna
1529-1591
= Wolfgang of
Zweibrücken
1526-1569

Wilhelm IV
Landgrave of Hesse-Kassel
1532-1592

Philipp Ludwig
1534-1535

Barbara
1536-1597
1)= Georg I of
Württemberg
1498-1558
2)= Daniel of
Waldeck
1530-1577

Ludwig IV
Landgrave of Hesse-Marburg
1537-1604

Elisabeth
1539-1582
= Ludwig VI
Elector Palatine
1539-1583

Landgraviate of Hesse-Kassel

Landgraviate of Hesse-Marburg

296

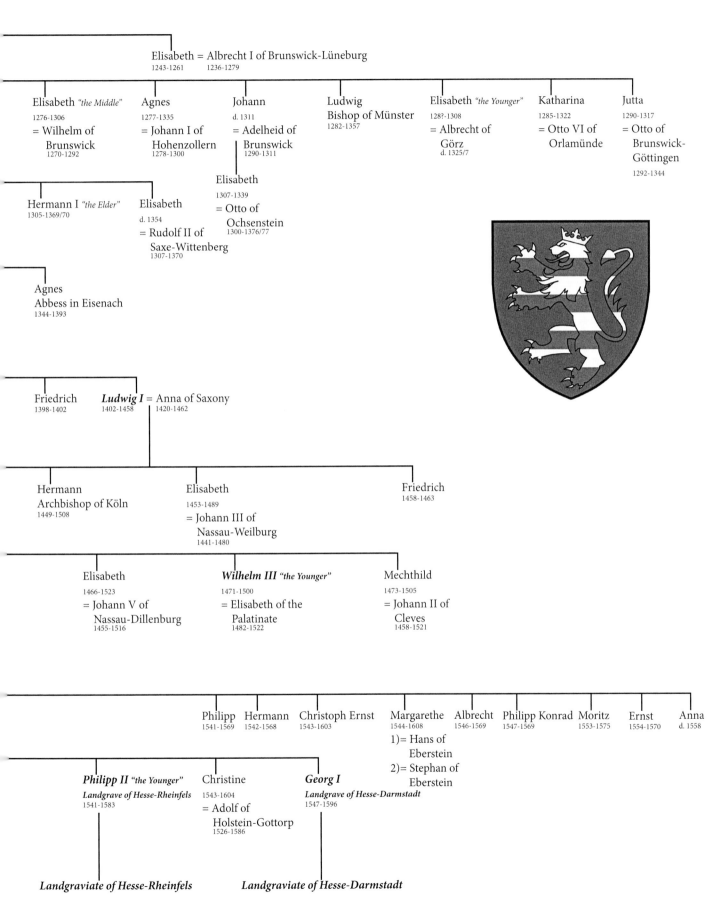

Elisabeth = Albrecht I of Brunswick-Lüneburg
1243-1261   1236-1279

Elisabeth *"the Middle"*
1276-1306
= Wilhelm of
Brunswick
1270-1292

Agnes
1277-1335
= Johann I of
Hohenzollern
1278-1300

Johann
d. 1311
= Adelheid of
Brunswick
1290-1311

Ludwig
Bishop of Münster
1282-1357

Elisabeth *"the Younger"*
128?-1308
= Albrecht of
Görz
d. 1325/7

Katharina
1285-1322
= Otto VI of
Orlamünde

Jutta
1290-1317
= Otto of
Brunswick-
Göttingen
1292-1344

Elisabeth
1307-1339
= Otto of
Ochsenstein
1300-1376/77

Hermann I *"the Elder"*
1305-1369/70

Elisabeth
d. 1354
= Rudolf II of
Saxe-Wittenberg
1307-1370

Agnes
Abbess in Eisenach
1344-1393

Friedrich
1398-1402

Ludwig I = Anna of Saxony
1402-1458   1420-1462

Hermann
Archbishop of Köln
1449-1508

Elisabeth
1453-1489
= Johann III of
Nassau-Weilburg
1441-1480

Friedrich
1458-1463

Elisabeth
1466-1523
= Johann V of
Nassau-Dillenburg
1455-1516

Wilhelm III *"the Younger"*
1471-1500
= Elisabeth of the
Palatinate
1482-1522

Mechthild
1473-1505
= Johann II of
Cleves
1458-1521

Philipp
1541-1569

Hermann
1542-1568

Christoph Ernst
1543-1603

Margarethe
1544-1608
1)= Hans of
Eberstein
2)= Stephan of
Eberstein

Albrecht
1546-1569

Philipp Konrad
1547-1569

Moritz
1553-1575

Ernst
1554-1570

Anna
d. 1558

Philipp II "the Younger"
Landgrave of Hesse-Rheinfels
1541-1583

Christine
1543-1604
= Adolf of
Holstein-Gottorp
1526-1586

Georg I
Landgrave of Hesse-Darmstadt
1547-1596

Landgraviate of Hesse-Rheinfels

Landgraviate of Hesse-Darmstadt

The Landgraves of Hesse-Darmstadt

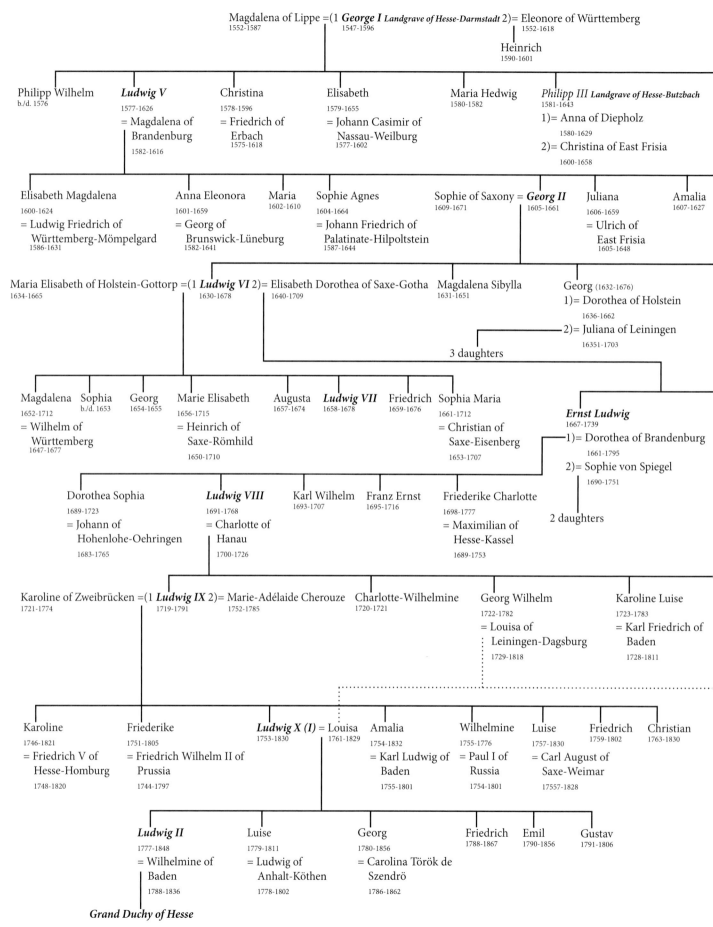

Magdalena of Lippe =(1 **George I** *Landgrave of Hesse-Darmstadt* 2)= Eleonore of Württemberg
1552-1587   1547-1596   1552-1618

Heinrich
1590-1601

Philipp Wilhelm   **Ludwig V**   Christina   Elisabeth   Maria Hedwig   *Philipp III* *Landgrave of Hesse-Butzbach*
b./d. 1576   1577-1626   1578-1596   1579-1655   1580-1582   1581-1643
   = Magdalena of   = Friedrich of   = Johann Casimir of   1)= Anna of Diepholz
   Brandenburg   Erbach   Nassau-Weilburg   1580-1629
   1582-1616   1575-1618   1577-1602   2)= Christina of East Frisia
   1600-1658

Elisabeth Magdalena   Anna Eleonora   Maria   Sophie Agnes   Sophie of Saxony = **Georg II**   Juliana   Amalia
1600-1624   1601-1659   1602-1610   1604-1664   1609-1671   1605-1661   1606-1659   1607-1627
= Ludwig Friedrich of   = Georg of   = Johann Friedrich of   = Ulrich of
Württemberg-Mömpelgard   Brunswick-Lüneburg   Palatinate-Hilpoltstein   East Frisia
1586-1631   1582-1641   1587-1644   1605-1648

Maria Elisabeth of Holstein-Gottorp =(1 **Ludwig VI** 2)= Elisabeth Dorothea of Saxe-Gotha   Magdalena Sibylla   Georg (1632-1676)
1634-1665   1630-1678   1640-1709   1631-1651   1)= Dorothea of Holstein
   1636-1662
   2)= Juliana of Leiningen
   1635?-1703

3 daughters

Magdalena   Sophia   Georg   Marie Elisabeth   Augusta   **Ludwig VII**   Friedrich   Sophia Maria   ***Ernst Ludwig***
1652-1712   b./d. 1653   1654-1655   1656-1715   1657-1674   1658-1678   1659-1676   1661-1712   1667-1739
= Wilhelm of   = Heinrich of   = Christian of   1)= Dorothea of Brandenburg
Württemberg   Saxe-Römhild   Saxe-Eisenberg   1661-1795
1647-1677   1650-1710   1653-1707   2)= Sophie von Spiegel
   1690-1751

2 daughters

Dorothea Sophia   **Ludwig VIII**   Karl Wilhelm   Franz Ernst   Friederike Charlotte
1689-1723   1691-1768   1693-1707   1695-1716   1698-1777
= Johann of   = Charlotte of   = Maximilian of
Hohenlohe-Oehringen   Hanau   Hesse-Kassel
1683-1765   1700-1726   1689-1753

Karoline of Zweibrücken =(1 **Ludwig IX** 2)= Marie-Adélaïde Cherouze   Charlotte-Wilhelmine   Georg Wilhelm   Karoline Luise
1721-1774   1719-1791   1752-1785   1720-1721   1722-1782   1723-1783
   = Louisa of   = Karl Friedrich of
   Leiningen-Dagsburg   Baden
   1729-1818   1728-1811

Karoline   Friederike   **Ludwig X (I)** = Louisa   Amalia   Wilhelmine   Luise   Friedrich   Christian
1746-1821   1751-1805   1753-1830   1761-1829   1754-1832   1755-1776   1757-1830   1759-1802   1763-1830
= Friedrich V of   = Friedrich Wilhelm II of   = Karl Ludwig of   = Paul I of   = Carl August of
Hesse-Homburg   Prussia   Baden   Russia   Saxe-Weimar
1748-1820   1744-1797   1755-1801   1754-1801   1755?-1828

Ludwig II   Luise   Georg   Friedrich   Emil   Gustav
1777-1848   1779-1811   1780-1856   1788-1867   1790-1856   1791-1806
= Wilhelmine of   = Ludwig of   = Carolina Török de
Baden   Anhalt-Köthen   Szendrö
1788-1836   1778-1802   1786-1862

Grand Duchy of Hesse

298

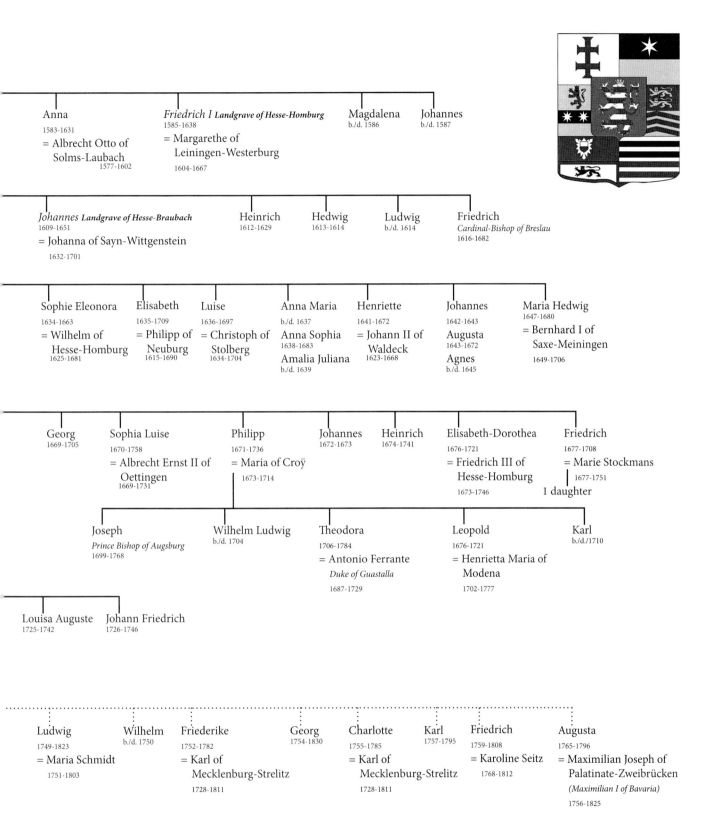

Anna
1583-1631
= Albrecht Otto of
Solms-Laubach
1577-1602

Friedrich I **Landgrave of Hesse-Homburg**
1585-1638
= Margarethe of
Leiningen-Westerburg
1604-1667

Magdalena
b./d. 1586

Johannes
b./d. 1587

Johannes **Landgrave of Hesse-Braubach**
1609-1651
= Johanna of Sayn-Wittgenstein
1632-1701

Heinrich
1612-1629

Hedwig
1613-1614

Ludwig
b./d. 1614

Friedrich
Cardinal-Bishop of Breslau
1616-1682

Sophie Eleonora
1634-1663
= Wilhelm of
Hesse-Homburg
1625-1681

Elisabeth
1635-1709
= Philipp of
Neuburg
1615-1690

Luise
1636-1697
= Christoph of
Stolberg
1634-1704

Anna Maria
b./d. 1637
Anna Sophia
1638-1683
Amalia Juliana
b./d. 1639

Henriette
1641-1672
= Johann II of
Waldeck
1623-1668

Johannes
1642-1643
Augusta
1643-1672
Agnes
b./d. 1645

Maria Hedwig
1647-1680
= Bernhard I of
Saxe-Meiningen
1649-1706

Georg
1669-1705

Sophia Luise
1670-1758
= Albrecht Ernst II of
Oettingen
1669-1731

Philipp
1671-1736
= Maria of Croÿ
1673-1714

Johannes
1672-1673

Heinrich
1674-1741

Elisabeth-Dorothea
1676-1721
= Friedrich III of
Hesse-Homburg
1673-1746

Friedrich
1677-1708
= Marie Stockmans
1677-1751
1 daughter

Joseph
Prince Bishop of Augsburg
1699-1768

Wilhelm Ludwig
b./d. 1704

Theodora
1706-1784
= Antonio Ferrante
Duke of Guastalla
1687-1729

Leopold
1676-1721
= Henrietta Maria of
Modena
1702-1777

Karl
b./d./1710

Louisa Auguste
1725-1742

Johann Friedrich
1726-1746

Ludwig
1749-1823
= Maria Schmidt
1751-1803

Wilhelm
b./d. 1750

Friederike
1752-1782
= Karl of
Mecklenburg-Strelitz
1728-1811

Georg
1754-1830

Charlotte
1755-1785
= Karl of
Mecklenburg-Strelitz
1728-1811

Karl
1757-1795

Friedrich
1759-1808
= Karoline Seitz
1768-1812

Augusta
1765-1796
= Maximilian Joseph of
Palatinate-Zweibrücken
(Maximilian I of Bavaria)
1756-1825

The Grand Dukes of Hesse (Hesse and by Rhine)

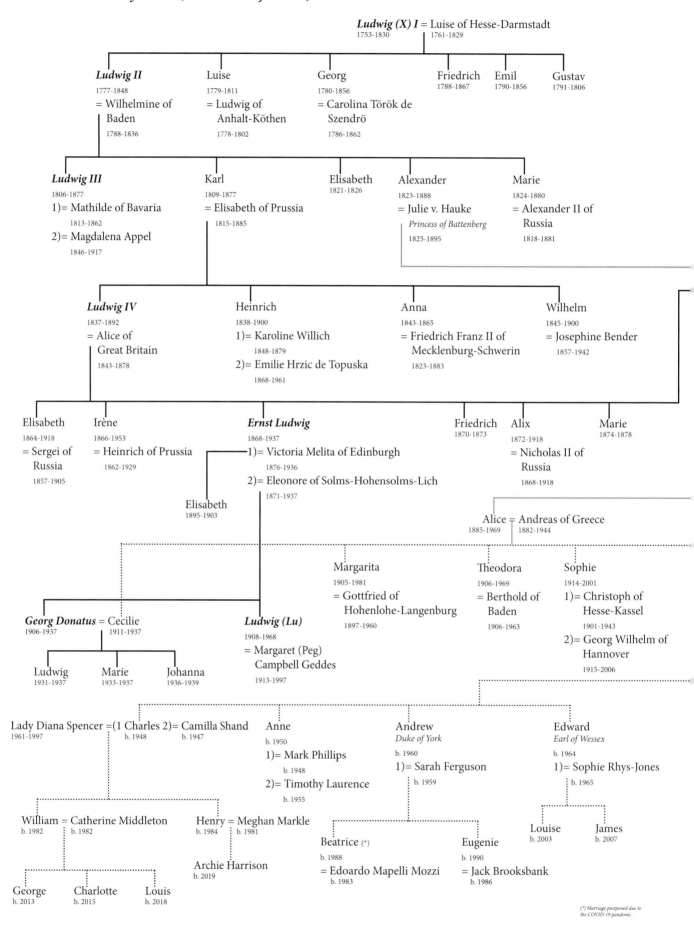

Ludwig (X) I = Luise of Hesse-Darmstadt
1753-1830   1761-1829

Ludwig II 1777-1848 = Wilhelmine of Baden 1788-1836

Luise 1779-1811 = Ludwig of Anhalt-Köthen 1778-1802

Georg 1780-1856 = Carolina Török de Szendrö 1786-1862

Friedrich 1788-1867

Emil 1790-1856

Gustav 1791-1806

Ludwig III 1806-1877 1)= Mathilde of Bavaria 1813-1862 2)= Magdalena Appel 1846-1917

Karl 1809-1877 = Elisabeth of Prussia 1815-1885

Elisabeth 1821-1826

Alexander 1823-1888 = Julie v. Hauke *Princess of Battenberg* 1825-1895

Marie 1824-1880 = Alexander II of Russia 1818-1881

Ludwig IV 1837-1892 = Alice of Great Britain 1843-1878

Heinrich 1838-1900 1)= Karoline Willich 1848-1879 2)= Emilie Hrzic de Topuska 1868-1961

Anna 1843-1865 = Friedrich Franz II of Mecklenburg-Schwerin 1823-1883

Wilhelm 1845-1900 = Josephine Bender 1857-1942

Elisabeth 1864-1918 = Sergei of Russia 1857-1905

Irène 1866-1953 = Heinrich of Prussia 1862-1929

Ernst Ludwig 1868-1937 1)= Victoria Melita of Edinburgh 1876-1936 2)= Eleonore of Solms-Hohensolms-Lich 1871-1937

Friedrich 1870-1873

Alix 1872-1918 = Nicholas II of Russia 1868-1918

Marie 1874-1878

Elisabeth 1895-1903

Alice 1885-1969 = Andreas of Greece 1882-1944

Georg Donatus = Cecilie 1906-1937   1911-1937

Ludwig (Lu) 1908-1968 = Margaret (Peg) Campbell Geddes 1913-1997

Margarita 1905-1981 = Gottfried of Hohenlohe-Langenburg 1897-1960

Theodora 1906-1969 = Berthold of Baden 1906-1963

Sophie 1914-2001 1)= Christoph of Hesse-Kassel 1901-1943 2)= Georg Wilhelm of Hannover 1915-2006

Ludwig 1931-1937

Marie 1933-1937

Johanna 1936-1939

Lady Diana Spencer =(1 Charles 2)= Camilla Shand 1961-1997   b. 1948   b. 1947

Anne b. 1950 1)= Mark Phillips b. 1948 2)= Timothy Laurence b. 1955

Andrew *Duke of York* b. 1960 1)= Sarah Ferguson b. 1959

Edward *Earl of Wessex* b. 1964 1)= Sophie Rhys-Jones b. 1965

William = Catherine Middleton b. 1982   b. 1982

Henry = Meghan Markle b. 1984   b. 1981

Beatrice (*) b. 1988 = Edoardo Mapelli Mozzi b. 1983

Eugenie b. 1990 = Jack Brooksbank b. 1986

Louise b. 2003

James b. 2007

Archie Harrison b. 2019

George b. 2013

Charlotte b. 2015

Louis b. 2018

(*) Marriage postponed due to the COVID-19 pandemic.

300

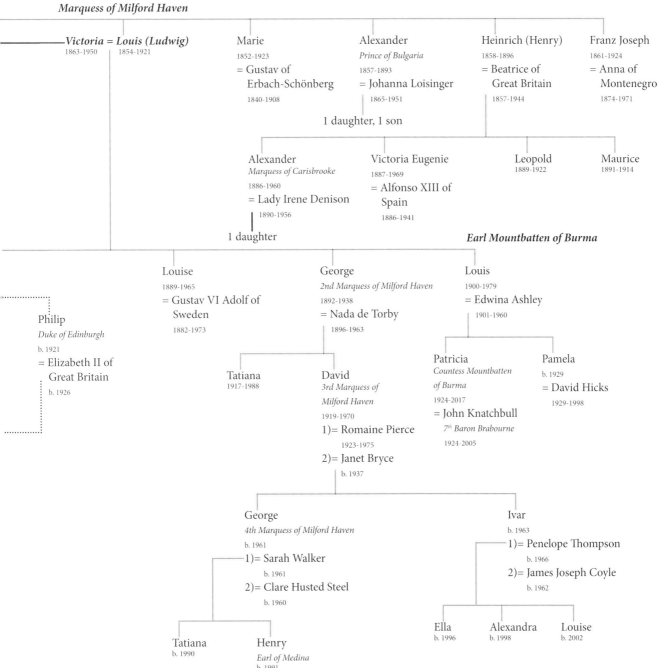

Marquess of Milford Haven

Victoria = Louis (Ludwig)
1863-1950   1854-1921

Marie
1852-1923
= Gustav of
Erbach-Schönberg
1840-1908

Alexander
Prince of Bulgaria
1857-1893
= Johanna Loisinger
1865-1951

Heinrich (Henry)
1858-1896
= Beatrice of
Great Britain
1857-1944

Franz Joseph
1861-1924
= Anna of
Montenegro
1874-1971

1 daughter, 1 son

Alexander
Marquess of Carisbrooke
1886-1960
= Lady Irene Denison
1890-1956

Victoria Eugenie
1887-1969
= Alfonso XIII of
Spain
1886-1941

Leopold
1889-1922

Maurice
1891-1914

1 daughter

Earl Mountbatten of Burma

Philip
Duke of Edinburgh
b. 1921
= Elizabeth II of
Great Britain
b. 1926

Louise
1889-1965
= Gustav VI Adolf of
Sweden
1882-1973

George
2nd Marquess of Milford Haven
1892-1938
= Nada de Torby
1896-1963

Louis
1900-1979
= Edwina Ashley
1901-1960

Tatiana
1917-1988

David
*3rd Marquess of
Milford Haven*
1919-1970
1)= Romaine Pierce
1923-1975
2)= Janet Bryce
b. 1937

Patricia
*Countess Mountbatten
of Burma*
1924-2017
= John Knatchbull
7th Baron Brabourne
1924-2005

Pamela
b. 1929
= David Hicks
1929-1998

George
4th Marquess of Milford Haven
b. 1961
1)= Sarah Walker
b. 1961
2)= Clare Husted Steel
b. 1960

Ivar
b. 1963
1)= Penelope Thompson
b. 1966
2)= James Joseph Coyle
b. 1962

Tatiana
b. 1990

Henry
Earl of Medina
b. 1991

Ella
b. 1996

Alexandra
b. 1998

Louise
b. 2002

Endnotes

Chapter I

1. *Haus Hessen Biografisches Lexikon* (edited by Eckhart G. Franz), p. 267.
2. Earl Mountbatten of Burma, *The Mountbatten Lineage*, p. 147.
3. Ibid.
4. Ibid.
5. Ibid.
6. *Haus Hessen*, p. 267.
7. Manfred Knodt, *Die Regenten von Hessen-Darmstadt*, p. 13.
8. *Haus Hessen*, p. 267.
9. Mountbatten, p. 149.
10. Haus Hessen, p. 271.
11. Mountbatten, p. 151.
12. Ibid.
13. Ibid.
14. Ibid., p. 152
15. Mountbatten, p. 152.
16. *Alice, Grand Duchess of Hesse*, p. 71.
17. Ibid., p. 72.
18. Ibid., p. 289.
19. *Haus Hessen*, p. 268.
20. Mountbatten, pp. 147-148.
21. *Haus Hessen*, p. 267.
22. Ibid.
23. Mountbatten, p. 152.
24. Knodt, p. 17
25. *Haus Hessen*, p. 269
26. Mountbatten, pp. 159-162.
27. *Haus Hessen*, p. 279.
28. Mountbatten, 164.
29. Ibid.
30. *Haus Hessen*, p. 281.
31. Ibid., p. 280.
32. Mountbatten, p. 164.
33. Knodt, pp. 19-20.
34. Ibid., p. 17.
35. *Haus Hessen*, p. 269.
36. Ibid., p. 276.
37. Ibid.
38. Michel Huberty, et al, *L'Allemagne Dynastique* (LAD1), Tome I, pp. 94-95.
39. Mountbatten, p. 169.
40. Ibid.
41. LAD1, p. 73.
42. *Haus Hessen*, p. 227.
43. Knodt, pp. 22-23.
44. *Haus Hessen*, p. 277.
45. Mountbatten, p. 175.
46. Ibid.
47. LAD1, p. 94.
48. Ibid.
49. Ibid., p. 111.
50. *Haus Hessen*, p. 282.
51. Knodt, pp. 26-27.
52. Ibid., p. 28.
53. Ibid.
54. Ibid., p. 29.
55. LAD1, p. 94.
56. *Haus Hessen*, p. 297.
57. Ibid., pp. 297-298.
58. LAD1, p. 112.
59. Ibid., p. 132.
60. *Haus Hessen*, p. 299.
61. LAD1, p. 112.
62. *Haus Hessen*, p. 300.
63. LAD1, p. 113.
64. *Haus Hessen*, p. 302.
65. Ibid.
66. LAD1, p. 111.
67. Ibid.
68. Ibid., p. 438.
69. Ibid., p. 457.
70. Knodt, p. 33.
71. Ibid.
72. Mountbatten, p. 198.
73. Knodt, p. 36.
74. Ibid., p. 37.
75. LAD1, p. 295.
76. Ibid., p. 131.
77. Ibid., p. 112.
78. Ibid., p. 132.
79. Ibid. p. 112.
80. *Haus Hessen*, p. 303.
81. Ibid., p. 304.
82. LAD1, pp. 148-149.
83. *Haus Hessen*, p. 303.
84. Knodt, p. 38.
85. Ibid., p. 41.
86. Arturo Beéche and Coryne Hall, *The Royal House of Bavaria* (RHB), p. 10.
87. Knodt, p. 41.
88. LAD1, p. 131.
89. Ibid., p. 148.
90. Knodt, p. 42.
91. RHB, p. 22.
92. LAD1, p. 148.
93. Ibid. pp. 164-168.
94. Mountbatten, p. 93.
95. Knodt, p. 60.
96. Ibid.
97. Mountbatten, p. 236.
98. Ibid., p. 234.
99. *Haus Hessen*, p. 311.
100. LAD1, p. 148.
101. Ibid., p. 316.
102. Ibid., pp. 168-169.
103. *Haus Hessen*, p. 316.
104. Ibid.
105. LAD1, p. 148.
106. Ibid.

Chapter II

1. LAD1, p. 164.
2. Knodt, p. 72.
3. E.M. Almedingen, *So Dark a Stream: A Study of the Emperor Paul I of Russia*, pp. 44-45.
4. Mountbatten, p. 239.
5. Ibid.
6. *Haus Hessen*, p. 373.
7. LAD1, p. 167.
8. Ibid., p. 192.
9. Knodt, p. 74.
10. Mountbatten, p. 239.
11. *Haus Hessen*, p. 323.
12. Mountbatten, p. 241.
13. https://en.wikipedia.org/wiki/Treaty_of_Lunéville
14. Interview conducted by Arturo E. Beéche with Hereditary Count Ignaz of Törring-Jettenbach, April 20, 2020.
15. Ibid.
16. LAD1, pp. 164-167.
17. Knodt, p. 80.
18. LAD1, pp. 164-167.
19. Knodt, pp. 89-90.
20. Ilana D. Miller, *The Four Graces*, p. 84.
21. David Duff, *Hessian Tapestry*, p. 274.
22. Alan Palmer, *Alexander I*, p. 273.
23. *Haus Hessen*, p. 323; Knodt, p. 81.
24. LAD1, pp. 164-1676.
25. Knodt, p. 84; Mountbatten, p. 246.
26. Knodt, p. 83.
27. Ibid.
28. Ibid., p. 85.
29. Ibid.
30. Ibid.
31. LAD1, p. 167.
32. Ibid.
33. Ibid., 192.
34. *Haus Hessen*, p. 338.
35. Ibid., p. 339.
36. Ibid.
37. Ibid.
38. LAD1, p. 204.
39. Ibid., p. 205.
40. *Haus Hessen*, p. 341.
41. Ibid.
42. Miller, p. 5.
43. Princess Marie of Battenberg, *Reminiscences*, p. 33.
44. Ibid.
45. LAD1, p. 205.
46. *Haus Hessen*, p. 341.
47. LAD1, p. 205.
48. Ibid.
49. Ibid., p. 206.
50. *Haus Hessen*, 341.
51. Shelton, Darren (1998) "Royal Quarterings: The ahnenreihe of the grandchildren of the last Grand Duke of Hesse and by Rhine", *European Royal History Journal*, I (VI:August), p. 19-22.
52. *Haus Hessen*, p. 339.
53. Knodt, pp. 97-98.
54. https://de.wikisource.org/wiki/ADB:Ludwig_II._(Großherzog_von_Hessen_und_bei_Rhein)
55. Knodt, p. 93
56. Ibid.
57. LAD1, p. 192.

Chapter III

1. LAD1, p. 205.
2. Victoria, Marchioness of Milford Haven (VMH), *Recollections*, p. 6.
3. Ibid.
4. Ibid., p. 7.
5. Ibid.
6. Ibid., p. 8.
7. *Haus Hessen*, p. 347.
8. Ibid.
9. Ibid.
10. https://de.wikisource.org/wiki/ADB:Ludwig_III._(Großherzog_von_Hessen-Darmstadt)
11. *Haus Hessen*, p. 347.
12. LAD1, p. 205.
13. RHB, p. 50.
14. *Haus Hessen*, p. 349.
15. Ibid.

16. Knodt, p. 112.
17. LAD1, p. 205.
18. *Haus Hessen*, p.350.
19. Ibid.
20. Ibid.
21. Knodt, p. 108.
22. Mountbatten, p. 260.
23. Knodt, p. 110.
24. Ibid, p. 111.
25. LAD1, p. 150.
26. Ibid., p. 133.
27. Ibid., pp. 149-150.
28. Ibid., p. 169.
29. *Haus Hessen*, p. 348.
30. https://de.wikisource.
org/wiki/ADB:Ludwig_III._
(Großherzog_von_Hessen-
Darmstadt)
31. LAD1, p. 205.
32. Ibid.
33. VMH, p. 8.
34. https://de.wikisource.
org/wiki/ADB:Ludwig_III._
(Großherzog_von_Hessen-
Darmstadt)
35. LAD1, p. 205.
36. Ibid.
37. *Haus Hessen*, p. 350.
38. VMH, p. 8.
39. Ibid.
40. Ibid.
41. *Haus Hessen*, p. 350.
42. Ibid.
43. Ibid.
44. Ibid., p. 351.
45. Ibid.
46. Ibid., p. 352.
47. RHB, p. 82.
48. LAD1, p. 205.
49. Ibid., p. 217.
50. Ibid.
51. Ibid., pp. 217-218.
52. Ibid., p. 218.
53. Roger Fulford, *Dearest Mama*, p. 81.
54. *Haus Hessen*, p. 352.
55. Roger Fulford, *Dearest Child*, pp. 218-219.
56. Ibid., p. 219.
57. *Haus Hessen*, p. 359.
58. *Dearest Child*, 211.
59. *Haus Hessen*, p. 360.
60. LAD1, p. 217.
61. Ibid.
62. Gerard Noel, *Princess Alice*, p. 122.
63. Ibid.
64. Ibid.
65. Michel Huberty et al, *L'Allemagne Dynastique, Tome VI* (LAD6), p. 240.
66. LAD1, p. 217.
67. Ibid.

68. Ibid., p. 230.
69. Ibid., p. 217.
70. Ibid.
71. VMH, p. 6.
72. LAD1, p. 231.
73. *Haus Hessen*, 360.
74. LAD1, p. 218.
75. Ibid., p. 231.
76. Ibid., p. 242.
77. Ibid., p. 231.

Chapter IV

1. LAD1, p. 217.
2. Noel, p. 83.
3. *Alice*, p. 10.
4. *Dearest Mama*, p. 271.
5. We see them coming out in a very healthy fashion in Victoria and Elisabeth.
6. LAD1, p. 217.
7. LAD1, pp. 229-230.
8. Unfortunately, completely destroyed during World War II.
9. Which among other things called for strict hygiene in the sick room and plenty of fresh air.
10. Duff, p. 80.
11. Queen Victoria to Victoria Milford Haven (hence forward referred to as VMHLetters: August 22, 1883, RA VIC/Z 88/12.
12. Bismarck offered Hesse and by Rhine territorial compensations should she ally herself with Prussia. Hesse however decided to side with Austria as, of course, Ludwig III wanted to keep his throne. https://en.wikipedia.org/wiki/Austro-Prussian_War
13. A florin or gulden is worth approximately $10.00 in today's currency.
14. It had suffered a terrific setback in 1865, when Alice and the Queen became estranged over the matter of the marriage of Alice's younger sister, Helena. Alice disapproved of the match since Prince Christian of Schleswig-Holstein-Sonderburg-Augustenburg was fifteen years older than Helena. Eventually Alice was persuaded that Helena was happy with her fiancé.
15. Treading on dangerous ground here, but one feels that in disregarding her physical

wellbeing time after time and year after year, there was perhaps something of a "death wish".
16. Greg King, "The Hessian Royal Family", *Atlantis Magazine: In the Courts of Memory, vol.2, no.2*, p.15.
17. …Especially the talkative and highly opinionated Princess Victoria.
18. Princess Helena, Princess Louise and Princess Beatrice who was a mere six years older than Princess Victoria.
19. *Advice to My Granddaughter* by Richard Hough is a selection of this correspondence and an invaluable resource.
20. It's good to be the Queen.
21. All except Chancellor Bismarck who would never forget such a thing and urged an immediate departure by the Prussian Imperial Family who were not to be thus polluted by such marriages.
22. One of the Hessian properties.
23. She was paid 500,000 marks and also appears to have had a child, which would be interesting to investigate.
24. Charlotte Zeepvat "Riding to Russia: The First Grand Dukes of Hesse-Darmstadt," *Royalty Digest, vol.VII*, No. 2, August 1997, p.38.
25. Huff, p. 225.
26. Ibid.
27. Richard Hough, *Advice to my Grand-daughter*, p. 116.
28. Arthur Gould Lee, *The Empress Frederick Writes to Sophie*, p. 110.
29. VMH, p. 73.
30. Ibid., 74.
31. Ibid.
32. Ibid.
33. *Haus Hessen*, p. 368.
34. LAD1, 229.
35. Christopher Warwick, *Ella: Princess, Saint & Martyr*, p.21.
36. VMHLetters, RA VIC/QVJ: 23rd August 1866.
37. LAD1, p. 230.
38. Ibid.
39. Ibid.
40. *Alice*, p.256, quoted by Kevin Brady "His Grand Ducal Highness Prince Friedrich Wilhelm of Hesse and by Rhine." *The European Royal*

History Journal, Issue XIV, November-December 1999, p.3.
41. LAD1, p. 230.
42. Ibid.
43. Elizabeth Jane Timms, "Princess Marie of Hesse, 1874-1878." *Royalty Digest Quarterly, no. 1*, 2014, pp.60-62.
44. Knodt, p. 132.
45. *Alice*, p. 235.
46. Ibid.
47. This was not at all disturbing for the time.
48. LAD1, p. 231.
49. *Haus Hessen*, p. 371.
50. Lord Kitchener thought it was located in another spot in East Jerusalem, which today is right next to the Arab Central Bus Station.
51. LAD1, p. 231.
52. Petra H. Kleinpenning, *The Correspondence of the Empress Alexandra of Russia with Ernst Ludwig and Eleonore Grand Duke and Duchess of Hesse*, p. 146.
53. Nicolas Enache, *La Descendance de Pierre le Grand, Tsar de Russie*, p. 160.
54. Ilana Miller, *The Four Graces*, p. 103.
55. Enache, p. 160.
56. Ibid.
57. Montgomery-Massingberd, Hugh, *Burke's Royal Families of the World, Volume I: Europe and Latin America*, p. 142.
58. LAD1, p. 232.
59. Miller, p. 110.
60. Enache, p. 160.
61. LAD1, p. 230.
62. Victoria was good at managing and did so, it appears, without much resentment from whichever relative she was directing. Later on she would also manage her sons and grandsons when she thought it necessary.
63. The Duke of Albany, the fourth, and hemophiliac, son of Queen Victoria.
64. LAD1, p. 241.
65. There were and are, of course, the rumors that Ernie was a homosexual and was neglectful of his wife while he pursued men and boys, however, this was not common knowledge though his biographer Manfred Knodt confirmed to Marlene Eilers

Koenig that he had "uncovered numerous homosexual relationships between the Grand Duke and members of the Hessian Court" (King, Atlantis, p.19) which were not included in the biography.
66. VMH, p. 212.
67. …in fact had been in love with the Grand Duke since attending the coronation of her sister-in-law, Alix in 1896.
68. LAD1, p. 241.
69. Kleinpenning, p. 251.
70. LAD1, p. 230.
71. VMH, p. 23.

Chapter V

1. LAD1, p. 205.
2. Greg King, "The Battenberg Family" *Atlantis Magazine, vol.2* no.2, p.28.
3. Count Egon von Corti, *The Downfall of Three Dynasties*, pp. 63-64.
4. LAD1, pp. 205-206.
5. A small town near near Hesse-Nassau and an extinct title.
6. LAD1, pp. 218-219.
7. Charlotte Zeepvat, "Dear Marie Erbach" *Royalty Digest: A Journal of Record* no.165, March 2005, p.259.
8. The result of the affair was the only child Miss Langtry would have, Jeanne-Marie. Jeanne-Marie later married Sir Ian Malcolm and Lord Mountbatten was in touch with the Malcolms. As an aside, Jeanne-Marie always thought that Miss Langtry was her aunt, not her mother. She found out the truth when a malicious gossip disclosed it in her presence at a dinner party.
9. Miller, p. 41.
10. LAD1, pp. 231-232.
11. *Remarks on Handling Ships*, Great War Primary Document Archive, 1934.
12. Formerly, Grand Duchess Helen Vladimirovna of Russia.
13. Theo Aronson, *Grandmama of Europe*, p. 268.
14. LAD1, p. 231.
15. VMHLetters, November 24, 1892 Royal Archives VIC / Z 90 / 33.
16. *Ernst Ludwig, Grand Duke of Hesse and by Rhine*, ed, by Eckhart G. Franz, p. 38.
17. Grand Duke Ernst Ludwig of Hesse, *Erinnertes*, p. 39.
18. However, her self-delusion continued for the remainder of her life and she trumpeted to the world that she had at last found the man for whom she had been waiting. This time, she went against her brother and married him. His name was Alexander Zoubkoff, and he was thirty-five years her junior. She was defiant about him in her boilerplate memoirs, professing to be in love and she didn't care what anyone else thought. That she alienated her family didn't bother her at that point and frankly, who can blame her. What was sad, though, was that he spent all her money and then deserted her. It was a wretched and pointless melodrama for the princess that had been described as "a kind of wild, Scandinavian woman, with much of her mother's impetuosity and a streak of her brother Willy's eccentricity." Hannah Pakula, *An Uncommon Woman*, p. 412.
19. According to Ernst Ludwig's memoirs, Prince Alexander was extremely bitter about his son's treatment at the hands of Alexander II and Bismark. When Sandro married, he did so in order to rid himself of the "eternal persecution" of the Bulgarian adventure; *Erinnertes*, p. 36.
20. Apparently, they were happier with the far more malleable Ferdinand ("Foxy Ferdinand") of Saxe-Coburg and Gotha.
21. Prince Ferdinand of Saxe-Coburg and Gotha who eventually became Prince then King of Bulgaria.
22. Elizabeth Longford, *Born to Succeed*, p. 478.
23. Which pretty much is what it sounds like…
24. LAD1, pp. 232-233.
25. Matthew Dennison, *The Last Princess*, p. 199.
26. She thought him oily and continental with all the prejudices of a German Princeling. She went on to marry the Duke of Marlborough and was extremely unhappy. Later divorced him and married a Frenchman with whom she was much happier.
27. Anna was born August 18, 1874 in Cetinje, Montenegro, the daughter of Nicholas I and Milena Vukotić.
28. Their first meeting occurred here according to Dr. Franz in his biographical lexicon of the Hesses, Battenbergs and Mountbattens.
29. "Royal Wedding At Cettinje: Francis Joseph of Battenberg United to Princess Anna of Montenegro" *The New York Times*, May 19, 1897.
30. Battenberg, p. 54.

Chapter VI

1. Miller, p. 114.
2. Arturo Beéche and Coryne Hall, *APAPA*, p. 167.
3. Celia Bertin, *Marie Bonaparte: A Life*, p. 92.
4. Beéche and Hall, p. 167.
5. *Erinnertes*, p. 94.
6. Battenberg, p. 294.
7. Duff, p. 274.
8. Miller, p. 119.

Chapter VII

1. LAD1, p. 230.
2. Duff, p. 349.
3. Ibid., p . 256.
4. Ibid.
5. LAD1, p. 229.
6. Ernst Ludwig to VMH, Darmstadt, December 2, 1928, HS Abt. D 24 Nr. 35 /
7. *The Times of London*, February 4, 1931.
8. Montgomery-Massingberd, p. 309.
9. *The Times of London*, October 22, 1937.
10. Duff, p. 349.
11. Ernst Ludwig to VMH, Darmstadt, December 2, 1928, HS Abt. D 24 Nr. 35 /
12. LAD1, p. 231.
13. Count Michael Mikhailovich de Torby or "Boy" was born in 1898 in Weisbaden. He was an artist of some talent and had a special love for Chinoiserie. Some of his paintings can be viewed here: http://www. invaluable.com/artist/torby-count-michael-rrzlse3wg5. He never married and died in London May 8, 1959.
14. …and marrying unequally.
15. Which, no doubt, saved their lives.
16. Reminding the reader of the Duke of Windsor's attempts to make an even less worthy candidate a Royal Highness.
17. Prince Louis of Battenberg to Princess Louise May 27,1916 SA MB1 / T90.
18. Joseph T. Fuhrmann, ed., *The Complete Wartime Correspondence of Tsar Nicholas II and the Empress Alexandra: April 1914 – March 1917*, p.445, Alexandra to Nicholas, Tsarskoe Selo, April 8 /20 1916.
19. During this visit in June 1917 the name change for the Battenberg family to Mountbatten went in force. Prince Louis famously wrote in a visitors' book: *"Arrived Prince Hyde…. Departed Lord Jekyll."* Mark Kerr, Prince Louis of Battenberg, p. 289.
20. Janet Morgan, *Edwina Mountbatten: A Life of Her Own*, pp. 237-238.
21. *New York Times*, March 28, 1927.
22. Email Lady Mountbatten to author, January 31, 2006.
23. Irène did visit Anna Anderson and was persuaded that she was not her niece. According to Charlotte Zeepvat, this created a division in the family since her son Sigismund was a supporter of the claimant as was his brother-in-law, Prince Friedrich of Saxe-Altenburg. ("The Name Irène…" *Royalty Digest: A Journal of Record. No. 147*, September 2003, p.71.). Also, along with Sigismund came to meet Anna Anderson his son Alfred. He initially believed she was Anastasia, but later, when DNA studies were done on her organs, came to believe that she had conned him and Sigismund.
24. Ella's assistant, Sister Barbara was murdered with her and her coffin, too, was found with Ella's.
25. Princess Henry to Victoria Milford Haven, June 14, 1922, Hemmelmark Archives.

304

26. *The Times of London*, April 22, 1929.
27. Princess Victoria had expressed from a young age that she wanted to be a teacher.
28. Richard Hough, *Mountbatten*, p. 61.

Chapter VIII

1. LAD1, pp. 240-241.
2. Montgomery-Massingberd, p. 170.
3. *The Times of London*, February 4, 1931.
4. Arturo E. Beéche and David McIntosh, *German Princely Houses: Hohenlohe-Langenburg*.
5. Marlene Eilers Koenig, *Queen Victoria's Descendants*, pp. 141-142.
6. LAD1, p. 242.
7. Ibid.
8. Montgomery-Massingberd, p. 214.
9. https://www.nytimes.com/2017/06/14/world/europe/patricia-knatchbull-countess-mountbatten-dead.html?searchResultPosition=1
10. Email from Lady Mountbatten to Arturo E. Beéche, February 25, 2012.
11. https://www.nytimes.com/2017/06/14/world/europe/patricia-knatchbull-countess-mountbatten-dead.html?searchResultPosition=1
12. http://heinbruins.nl/Battenberg.html
13. Email from Lady Mountbatten to Arturo E. Beéche, August 11, 2007.
14. http://heinbruins.nl/Battenberg.html
15. Ibid.
16. This fund specially provides specially trained nurses to look after children with cancer.
17. India Hicks, "What Lady Pamela Hicks, Queen Elizabeth's Lady-in-Waiting, Thinks of The Crown". http://www.townandcountrymag.com/society/tradition/news/a8741/the-crown-india-hicks/
18. *The New York Times*, April 2, 1998
19. Ibid.
20. Interview with Prince Alfred of Prussia by Arturo E. Beéche, San José, Costa Rica, July 9,

1999 – Eurohistory Archive, Prussia File II.
21. In October 2000, Prince Alfred attended the 3rd Eurohistory Conference hosted by Arturo Beéche in San Francisco, CA. Prince Alfred remained at the Beéche home for an extended five-week-long stay. During his visit, Arturo Beéche arranged for the prince to meet his distant relations King Michael and Queen Anne of Romania, and their daughter Princess Margarita, who gave a speech at the Eurohistory Conference.
22. Interview with Prince Alfred of Prussia by Arturo E. Beéche, Punta Leona, Costa Rica, September 30, 2004 – Eurohistory Archive, Prussia File II.
23. *The Times of London*, April 14, 1938.
24. Duke of Connaught to VMH, April 8, 1938, BA S 368.
25. Irène to Princess Louise, July 12, 1938, RA VIC / Add A / 17 / 1679
26. LAD1, p. 229.
27. Irène to Mountbatten, September 24, 1950, BA S 354.
28. LAD1, p. 230.
29. Duke Christian Ludwig of Mecklenburg-Schwerin, *Erzählungen aus Meinem Leben*, p. 261.
30. Interview with Prince Alfred of Prussia by Arturo E. Beéche, Punta Leona, Costa Rica, September 30, 2004 – Eurohistory Archive, Prussia File II.
31. Ibid.
32. Interview with Prince Alfred of Prussia by Arturo E. Beéche, Punta Leona, Costa Rica, February 28, 2007 – Eurohistory Archive, Prussia File II.
33. *Haus Hessen*, p.
34. Manfred Knodt, *Ernst Ludwig Grossherzog von Hessen und bei Rhein*, p. 404.
35. *The Times of London*, October 11, 1937.
36. *The New York Times*, November 16, 1937.
37. Hugo Vickers, *Alice: Princess Andrew of Greece*, p. 273.
38. Ibid.
39. *The New York Times*, November 17, 1937.

40. Eckhart G. Franz, Schlapp, Karl-Eugen (eds.) *Margaret Prinzessin von Hessen und bei Rhein: Ein Gedenkbuch*, p.167.
41. Morgan, p. 259.
42. It was evident to Princess Alice's mother that this terrible tragedy and the loss of her daughter, Cecilie, "snapped" Alice back into sanity.
43. *The Times of London*, November 24, 1937.
44. Vickers, p. 274.
45. Ibid.
46. Philip Eade, *Prince Philip*, p. 114.
47. Ibid.
48. Ibid.
49. Words many of our politicians today could live by…. Hough, p. 213.
50. https://www.nytimes.com/1979/08/28/archives/lord-mountbatten-is-killed-as-his-fishing-boat-explodes-ira-faction.html?searchResultPosition=2
51. Ibid.
52. Timothy Knatchbull, *From a Clear Blue Sky*, p. xi.
52. https://www.nytimes.com/1979/08/28/archives/lord-mountbatten-is-killed-as-his-fishing-boat-explodes-ira-faction.html?searchResultPosition=2
53. http://www.time.com/time/magazine/article/0,9171,968220-1,00.html

Chapter IX

1. Thanks to his wealthy American wife, Nancy Leeds.
2. Eade, p. 62.
3. Ibid., pp. 67-68.
4. Much has been made about Uncle Dickie's orchestrating the Royal Family's visit to Dartmouth in the summer of 1939, and certainly this is nothing that anyone would put passed the ambitious Mountbatten, but no amount of persuasion would have been possible if the parties had not eventually been willing.
5. Marlene Eilers-Koenig "Windsor or Mountbatten-Windsor" Royal Musings, March 24, 2009. http://royalmusingsblogspotcom.

blogspot
6. Raleigh Trevelyan, *Grand Dukes and Diamonds*, p. 375.
7. Ibid.
8. Ibid., p. 347.
9. "U.S. Envoy's Daughter Now Dating Two of Princess Margaret's Beaux", *Los Angeles Times*, October 5, 1948.
10. Ibid.
11. Trevelyan, p. 405.
12. Ibid.
13. Ibid.
14. http://heinbruins.nl/Battenberg.html
15. Trevelyan, p. 405.
16. Ibid.
17. *Eurohistory Archive*, Mountbatten file (newspaper clipping).
18. Ibid.
19. Eilers, p. 51.
20. Ibid., p. 52.
21. https://www.townandcountrymag.com/society/tradition/a23398501/royal-family-same-sex-wedding-lord-ivar-mountbatten/

Chapter X

1. LAD1, p. 248.
2. Ibid., p. 241.
3. Franz, p. 39.
4. Ibid., p. 40.
5. Ibid.
6. Ibid., p. 47; Richard Thornton, *Royal Digest June 2002*, p.370. In a small article the author recounts having some moments to spend, and did so doing some genealogical research. He found out that von Stauffenberg's wife, Nina von Lerchenfeld was the daughter of Anna von Stackelberg, who herself was the daughter of Alexander von Stackelberg, who himself was the son of Baron Karl von Stackelberg and Emilie von Hauke, the sister of Julie von Hauke.
7. These attacks killed 12,300 inhabitants – Jörg Friedrich, Jörg, *The Fire: The Bombing of Germany, 1940–1945*, p. 313.
8. https://www.raf.mod.uk/what-we-do/centre-for-air-and-space-power-studies/documents1/ahb-narrative-the-breakout-and-advance-to-the-lower-rhine-12-jun-30-

sep-1944/

9. Tatiana Metternich, *Purgatory of Fools*, p. 229.
10. Ibid., pp. 261-262.
11. Franz, p. 15.
12. Ibid.
13. Metternich, p. 265.
14. Ninel Ivanovna Podgornaja, *Mafalda di Savoia Assia*, p. 109.
15. Franz, p. 178.
16. Ibid., p. 54.
17. Ibid., pp. 42-43.
18. Ibid., p. 40.
19. Ibid., p. 56.
20. Ibid., pp. 41-42.
21. Ibid., p. 27.
22. Ibid., p. 26.
23. Ibid., p. 28.
24. Ibid., p. 48.
25. Ibid., p. 36.
26. Eurohistory Archive, *Hesse and by Rhine Folder, Obituary of Prince Ludwig of Hesse and by Rhine.*
27. Franz, p. 43.
28. Ibid.
29. Ibid., p. 163.
30. Ibid. pp. 17-18.
31. Ibid., p. 17
32. Ibid., 18.
33. Ibid., p. 29.
34. Ibid., p. 17.
35. Email from Archduchess Helen of Austria (née Törring-Jettenbach) to Arturo E. Beéche, April, 19, 2020.
36. Ibid.
37. Franz, p. 28.
38. https://www.independent.co.uk/news/obituaries/obituary-princess-margaret-of-hesse-and-the-rhine-1285869.html
39. Franz, pp. 9-10.
40. Ibid., pp. 162-166.
41. Ibid., p. 13.
42. Ibid., p. 179.
43. Ibid., p. 107.
44. Ibid., p. 18.
45. Marlene Eilers-Koenig "Landgraf Moritz of Hesse (1926-2013)" *The European Royal History Journal. Vol. 16.3, Issue XCIII, June 2013*, p.32.
46. LAD1, p. 240.
47. Jonathan Petropoulos, *Royals and the Reich*, p. 106.
48. Ibid., p. 126.
49. Ibid., p. 102.
50. Ibid., p. 318.
51. Ibid., p. 360.
52. Interview of Landgraf Moritz of Hesse with Arturo E. Beéche at Schloß Friedrichshof,

April 24, 2012 – Eurohistory Archive, Hesse Folder.
53. https://www.thetimes.co.uk/article/moritz-landgrave-of-hesse-lm6d9rswvfd
54. "German Princely Treasures Land on These Shores." *The New York Times*, November 2, 2005.
55. Ibid.
56. http://www.suedostschweiz.ch/leben/2016-03-30/der-neue-schlossherr-uebernimmt-die-schluessel
57. https://www.thetimes.co.uk/article/moritz-landgrave-of-hesse-lm6d9rswvfd
58. LAD1, p. 247.

Chapter XI

1. LAD1, p. 76.
2. *Haus Hessen*, p. 275.
3. Michel Huberty et al, *L'Allemagne Dynastique (LAD3), Tome III*, pp. 41-43.
4. LAD1, p. 95.
5. *Haus Hessen*, p. 275.
6. Michel Huberty et al, *L'Allemagne Dynastique (LAD4), Tome IV*, pp. XX-XX.
7. LAD1, p. 95.
8. Ibid., p. 409.
9. Ibid., p. 395.
10. *Haus Hessen*, p. 291.
11. LAD1, p. 111.
12. *Haus Hessen*, p. 292.
13. LAD1, p. 111.
14. Ibid.
15. *Haus Hessen*, 293.
16. LAD1, p. 111.
17. Ibid.
18. *Haus Hessen*, p. 294.
19. Ibid.
20. LAD1, p. 113.
21. *Haus Hessen*, p. 301.
22. LAD1, p. 113.
23. Ibid., p. 131.
24. Ibid.
25. *Haus Hessen*, p. 319.
26. Ibid., p. 318.
27. Ibid., p. 319.
28. LAD6, pp. 113-114.
29. Kathrin Ellwardt, *Das Haus Baden*, p. 27.
30. Ibid., p. 97.
31. LAD1, p. 164.
32. Ibid., p. 133.
33. Ibid., pp. 149-150.
34. *Haus Hessen*, p. 415.
35. Ibid.
36. LAD1, p. 133.
37. *Haus Hessen*, p. 414.

38. Ibid., p. 321.
39. G.P. Gooch, *Frederick the Great*, p. 142.
40. Ibid.
41. Robert B. Asprey, *Frederick the Great*, p. 43.
42. Michel Huberty et al, *L'Allemagne Dynastique (LAD5), Tome V*, pp. 197-205.
43. Ibid., p. 183.
44. Hedvig Elisabeth Charlottas of Sweden (ed. Cecilia Klercker), *Diaries*, VI (1797-1799), p. 122.
45. LAD5, p. 184.
46. LAD1, p. 167.
47. LAD6, p. 113.
48. LAD5, p. 127-128.
49. Alan Palmer, *Alexander I*, p. 49.
50. LAD6, p. 113.
51. *Haus Hessen*, p. 324.
52. Jeffrey Moussaieff Masson, *Lost Prince*, p. 76.
53. *Haus Hessen*, p. 326.
54. Henri Troyat, *Catherine the Great*, p. 131.
55. Ibid., p. 133.
56. Ibid., p. 134.
57. Ibid., p. 139.
58. Ibid.
59. Ibid., p. 154.
60. Almedingen, p. 42.
61. Ibid.
62. Ibid.
63. Ibid.
64. Ibid., p.43.
65. Ibid., pp. 43-44.
66. Troyat, 230.
67. Ibid.
68. Almedingen, p. 45.
69. Ibid.
70. Ibid.
71. Ibid., p. 50
72. Troyat, p. 262.
73. Ibid.
74. Almedingen, p. 51.
75. Ibid., 52.
76. Ibid.
77. *Haus Hessen*, p. 327.
78. LAD1, p. 481.
79. *Haus Hessen*, p. 328.
80. https://en.wikipedia.org/wiki/Karl_August,_Grand_Duke_of_Saxe-Weimar-Eisenach
81. Haus Hessen, p. 328.
82. LAD1, p. 169
83. Ibid.
84. LAD6, p. 211.
85. Ibid., pp. 223-224.
86. Ibid., p. 211.
87. Haus Hessen, p. 337.
88. RHB, p. 27.

89. Ibid.
90. *Haus Hessen*, p. 337.
91. LAD1, p. 206.
92. Charlotte Zeepvat, *Romanov Autumn*, pp. 31-32.
93. Edvard Radzinsky, *Alexander II*, pp. 66-67.
94. Galina Korneva & Tatiana Cheboksarova, *Russia & Europe*, p. 13.
95. Enache, p. 62.
96. Radzinsky, p. 49.
97. Stephen Graham, *Alexander II*, p. 18.
98. Ibid.
99. Korneva & Cheboksarova, p. 16.
100. Zeepvat, p. 33.
101. Ibid., p. 52.
102. Enache, pp. 69-71.
103. Radzinsky, p. 49.
104. Graham, p. 19.
105. Anna Tiutcheva, *At the Court of Two Emperors*, pp. 78-80.
106. Radzinsky, p. 97.
107. Enache, p. 45.
108. Radzinsky, p. 104.
109. Ibid., p. 128.
110. Zeepvat, p. 51.
111. Battenberg, p. 56.
112. Zeepvat, p. 56.
113. Radzinsky, p. 198.
114. Enache, 72.
115. Zeepvat, p. 57.
116. John van der Kiste, *The Romanovs: 1818-1859*, p. 55.
117. Battenberg, p. 175.
118. Roger Fulford, *Darling Child*, p. 163.
119. Battenberg, p. 180.
120. https://en.wikipedia.org/wiki/Catherine_Dolgorukov#cite_note-Tarsaidze_1970-8
121. Coryne Hall, *Little Mother of Russia*, p. 73.
122. Roger Fulford, *Beloved Mama*, p. 92.
123. Hall, p. 76.
124. Ibid., p. 77.
125. Radzinsky, p. 416.
126. Hall, 79.

Bibliography

Books:

*A*ckerman, Carl W. *Trailing the Bolsheviki.* (Charles Scribner, 1919)

Albert, Herzog zu Sachsen. *Die Wettiner in Lebensbildern.* (Styria: 1995)

Alexander, Grand Duke of Russia. *Once a Grand Duke.* (Cassell, 1932)

Alexandrov, Victor. *The End of the Romanovs.* (Hutchinson, 1966)

Alexander, John T. *Catherine the Great: Life and Legend.* Oxford University Press, 1989)

Alford, Kenneth D. *The Spoils of War III: The American Military's Role in Stealing Europe's Treasures.* (Birch Bird Lane Press, 1994)

Alice, Grand Duchess of Hesse. *Biographical Sketch and Letters.* Preface by Princess Christian. (John Murray, 1884)

Almedingen, E. M. *Alexander I.* (The Vanguard Press, 1964)

Almedingen, E. M. *Alexander II.* (The Bodley Head, 1962)

–– *An Unbroken Unity.* (The Bodley Head, 1964)

–– *So dark a Stream: A Study of the Emperor Paul I of Russia (1754-1801).* (Hutchinson, 1959)

–– *The Romanovs: Three Centuries of an Ill-Fated Dynasty.* (Bodley Head, 1966)

Anon. (Stopford) *The Russian Diary of an Englishman.* (McBride & Co, 1919)

Arapova, Dr Tatiana & others. *Nicholas and Alexandra. The Last Imperial Family of Tsarist Russia.* (Booth-Clibborn Editions, 1998)

Arkhanguelski, Alexandre. *Alexandre I, le feu follet.* (Fayard, 2000)

Aronson, Theo. *A Family of Kings: The Descendants of Christian IX of Denmark.* (Cassell & Company Lyd., 1976)

–– *Crowns in Conflict.* (John Murray, 1986)

–– *Grandmama of Europe.* (Cassel & Co., 1973)

*B*arkowez, Olga, Fedorov, Fyodor, and Krylov, Alexander. *"Geliebter Nicky."* (Edition q, 2002)

Asprey, Robert B. *Frederick the Great: The Magnificent Enigma.* (Ticknor & Fields, 1986)

Battenberg, Princess Marie of.

Reminiscences. (George Allen & Unwin Ltd., 1925)

Battiscombe, Georgina. *Queen Alexandra.* (Constable, 1969)

Beéche, Arturo. *Dear Ellen…* (Eurohistory, 2011)

–– *The Coburgs of Europe.* (Eurohistory 2013)

–– (editor). *The Grand Duchesses.* (Eurohistory, 2004)

–– (editor). *The Grand Dukes.* (Eurohistory, 2010)

–– (editor). *The Other Grand Dukes.* (Eurohistory, 2012)

–– & Coryne Hall. *The Royal House of Bavaria, Volume I: Royal Collections III.* (Eurohistory, 2019)

Benagh, Christine. *An Englishman at the Court of the Tsar.* (Conciliar Press, 2000)

Bergamini, John. *The Tragic Dynasty.* (Constable, 1970)

Bertin, Celia. *Marie Bonaparte: A Life.* (Harcourt, Brace, Jovanovich Publishers, 1982)

Bing, Edward J. *The Letters of Tsar Nicholas and Empress Marie.* (Ivor Nicholson & Watson, 1937)

Bokhanov, Alexander & others. *The Romanovs: Love, Power & Tragedy.* (Lippe Publications, 1993)

Botkin, Gleb. *The Real Romanovs.* (Putnam, 1932)

Brook-Shepherd, Gordon. *Iron Maze.* (Macmillan, 1998)

–– *Royal Sunset.* (Weidenfeld & Nicolson, 1987)

Boulay, Cyrille. *Les Romanov: De Saint-Petersbourg à Saint-Briac* (Exhibition Catalogue). (Couvente de la Sagesse, 2015)

Buchanan, Sir George. *My Mission to Russia. Volumes 1 & 2.* (Cassell, 1923)

Buchanan, Meriel. *Queen Victoria's Relations* (Cassel & Co., 1954)

Burke's Guide to the Royal Family. (Burke's Peerage Ltd, 1973)

Butenschön, Marianna. *Die Hessin auf dem Zarenthron: Maria, Kaiserin von Russland.* (Theiss, 2017)

Buxhoeveden, Baroness Sophie. *Left Behind.* (Longmans Green, 1929)

–– *The Life & Tragedy of Alexandra Feodorovna.* (Longmans, Green, 1928)

Bykov, Paul. *The Last Days of Tsardom.* (Martin Lawrence, 1934)

*C*adbury, Deborah. *Queen Victoria's Matchmaking.* (Bloomsbury, 2017)

Cate, Curtis. *The War of the Two Emperors.* (Random House, 1985)

Chaffanjon, Arnaud. *Histoires de Familles Royales.* (Editions Ramsay, 1980)

Channon, Sir Henry. Chips. *The Diaries of Sir Henry Channon.* Edited by Robert Rhodes James. (Weidenfeld & Nicolson, 1967)

Christopher, Prince of Greece. *Memoirs.* (Hurst & Blackett, 1938)

Clay, Catrine. *King, Kaiser, Tsar.* (John Murray, 2006)

Constant, Stephen. *Foxy Ferdinand, Tsar of Bulgaria.* Franklin Watts, 1980)

Corti, Count Egon. *Alexander von Battenberg.* (Cassell and Company, Ltd., 1954)

–– *The Downfall of Three Dynasties.* (Methuen, 1934)

Crankshaw, Edward. *The Shadow of the Winter Palace.* (Macmillan London Ltd., 1976)

Custine, Marquis de. *Empire of the Czar: A Journey Through Eternal Russia.* (Doubleday, 1971)

*D*ecker-Hauff, Hansmartin. *Frauen im Hause Württemberg.* (DRW-Verlag, 1998)

Dehn, Lili. *The Real Tsaritsa.* (Thornton Butterworth, 1922)

Diesbach, Ghislain de. *Secrets of the Gotha.* (Meredith press, 1964)

Duff, David. *Hessian Tapestry.* (Frederick Muller, 1967)

Dziewanowski, M. K. *Alexander I: Russia's Mysterious Tsar.* (Hippocrene Books, 1990)

*E*ade, Philip. *Prince Philip. The Turbulent Early Life of the Man Who Married Queen Elizabeth II.* (Henry Holt and Company, 2011)

Edwards, Anne. *Matriarch. Queen Mary and the House of Windsor.* (Hodder & Stoughton, 1984)

Eilers (Koenig), Marlene. *Queen Victoria's Descendants.* (Rosvall Royal Books, 1997)

Enache, Nicolas. *La Descendance de Pierre le Grand, Tsar de Russie.* (Sedopolis, 1983)

Ernst Ludwig, Großherzog von Hessen und bei Rhein. *Erinnertes.* (Eduard

Roether Verlag, 1983)

Eugenie, Princess of Greece. *Le Tsarevich, Enfant Martyr.* (Perrin, 1990)

Ferro, Marc. *Nicholas II: The Last of the Tsars.* (Viking, 1991)

Footprints of a Life: In Memory of the beloved Princess Alice of Great Britain and Ireland, Grand Duchess of Hesse-Darmstadt (Dedicated by Permission of HRH The Princess Mary Adelaide, Duchess of Teck). (JR Borwn Printer, 1879)

Franz, Eckhart G (ed). *Haus Hessen – Biografisches Lexikon.* (Hessische Historische Kommission, 2012)

Franz, Eckhart and Karl Eugen Schlapp. *Margaret Prinzessin von Hessen und bei Rhein.* (Verlag H.L. Schlapp, 1997)

Fuhrmann, Joseph T. (ed). *The Complete Wartime Correspondence of Tsar Nicholas II and the Empress Alexandra: April 1914 – March 1917.* (Greenwood Press, 1999)

Fulford, Roger (ed). *Dearest Child.* (Evans Brothers, 1965)

–– *Dearest Mama.* (Evans Brothers, 1968)

–– *Your Dear Letter.* (Evans Brothers, 1971)

–– *Darling Child.* (Evans Brothers, 1976)

–– *Beloved Mama.* (Evans Brothers, 1981)

Gabriel Constantinovich, Grand Duke. *Memories in the Marble Palace.* (Gilbert's Books, 2009)

Gehrlein, Thomas. *Daus Haus Sachsen-Altenburg.* (Borde Verlag, 2014)

–– *Daus Haus Sachsen-Meiningen.* (Borde Verlag, 2014)

Gerhardi, William. *The Romanovs: Autocrats of All the Russias.* (G. P. Putnam's Sons,1939)

Gerladi, Julia. *Born to Rule.* (Headline Press, 2005)

Gerladi, Julia. *From Splendour to Revolution.* (New York: St Martin's Press, 2011)

Gelardi, Julia. *Pageant of Kings: The Nine Sovereigns at Edward VII's Funeral.* (2019)

Gerard, Noel. *Princess Alice.* (Constable, 1974)

Gilliard, Pierre. *Thirteen Years at the Russian Court.* (Hutchinson, 1921)

Gooch, G. P. *Frederick the Great: The Ruler, the Writer, the Man.* (Dorset press, 1947)

Graham, Stephen. *The Life and Reign of Alexander II.* (Ivor Nicholson & Watson, 1935)

Hall, Coryne. *Little Mother of Russia. A Biography of the Empress Marie Feodorovna, 1847-1928.* (Shepheard-

Walwyn, 1999)

–– *Queen Victoria and the Romanovs: Sixty years of Mutual Distrust.* (Amberley Publishing, 2020)

–– *To Free the Romanovs: Royal Kinship and Betrayal in Europe 1917-1919.* (Amberley, 2018)

–– *Princesses on the Wards. Royal Women in Nursing Through Wars and Revolutions.* (The History Press, 2014)

–– & Beéche, Arturo. *The Romanovs: An imperial Tragedy – (Royal Collections II).* (Eurohistory, 2017)

–– & Beéche, Arturo. *APAPA: The Descendants of King Christian IX.* (Eurohistory, 2013)

Haarmann, Torsten. *Das Haus Hessen: Eine europäische Familie des Hochadels.* (Borde Verlag, 2014)

–– *Das Haus Sachsen-Coburg und Gotha: Eine europäische Familie des Hochadels.* (Borde Verlag, 2014)

Hesse – Exhibition Catalogue. (Marquand Books, Inc., 2006)

Hicks (Mountbatten), Pamela. *Daughter of Empire: Life as a Mountbatten.* (Weidenfeld & Nicolson, 2012)

Hohenlohe-Langenburg, Feodora, Fürstin zu. *Letters from 1828-1872.* (Spottiswoode & Co., 1874)

Hohenlohe-Schillingsfürst, Fürst Franz Josef zu. *Monarchen, Edelleute, Burger.* (Verlag Degener & Co., Inhaber Herhards Gessner, 1952)

Horn, Joachim, et al. *Die Battenbergs: Eine europäische Familie.* (Waldemar Kramer, 2019)

Hough, Richard. *Advice to a Granddaughter.* (Heinemann, 1975)

–– *Louis & Victoria.* (Weidenfeld & Nicolson, 1974)

–– *Mountbatten: A Biography* (Random House, 1981)

Huberty, Michael, Alain Giraud, F. et B. Madeleine. *L'Allemagne Dynastique, Tome I: Hesse, Reuss, Sachsen.*

–– *L'Allemagne Dynastique, Tome II: Anhalt, Lippe, Württemberg.* (1979)

–– *L'Allemagne Dynastique, Tome III: Brunswick, Nassau, Schwarzbourg.* (1981)

–– *L'Allemagne Dynastique, Tome IV: Wittelsbach.* (1985)

–– *L'Allemagne Dynastique, Tome V: Hohenzollern, Waldeck, Familles alliées A-B.* (1988)

–– *L'Allemagne Dynastique, Tome VI: Bade, Mecklenbourg, Famille alliées C-G.* (1991)

–– *L'Allemagne Dynastique, Tome*

VII: Oldenbourg, Familles alliées H-L. (1994)

Ignasiak, Detlef. *Regenten-Tafeln Thüringischer Fürstenhäuser.* (quartus-Verlag, 1996)

Kejserinde Dagmar. *Exhibition Catalogue.* (The Royal Silver Room, 1997)

Knodt, Manfred. *Die regenten von Hessen-Darmstadt.* (Verlag H.L. Schlapp, 1989)

–– *Ernst Ludwig Großherzog von Hessen und bei Rhein.* (Verlag H.L. Schlapp, 1997)

Jackman, S. W. (wed). *Romanov Relations.* (Macmillan, 1969)

King, Greg. *The Last Empress.* (Birch Lane Press, 1994)

–– *Twilight of Splendour.* (John Wiley, 2007)

–– and Wilson, Penny. *The Fate of the Romanovs.* (John Wiley, 2003)

–– and Wilson, Penny. *Romanovs Adrift.* (Eurohistory, 2019)

Klein, Sven-Michael. *Das Haus Sachsen-Weimar-Eisenach.* (Borde Verlag, 2016)

Kleinpenning, Petra H. *The Correspondence of the Empress Alexandra of Russia with Ernst Ludwig and Eleonore Grand Duke and Duchess of Hesse: 1878-1916.* (Books on Demand, 2010).

Knatchbull, Timothy. *From a Clear Blue Sky: Surviving the Mountbatten Bomb.* (Hutchinson, 2009)

Knoß, Carsten. *Zur Erinnerung an Großherzog Ernst Ludwig von Hessen und bei Rhein und seine Familie.* (WK/Mediensdesign Verlag, 2017)

Koch, A. *Prince Alexander of Battenberg: Reminiscences of His Reign in Bulgaria.* (Whittaker & Co., 1887)

Korneva, Galina & Cheboksarova, Tatiana (Arturo Beéche, ed). *Russia and Europe. Dynastic Ties.* (Eurohistory, 2013)

Kozlov, Vladimir A, & Khrustalev, Vladimir M (ed). *The Last Diary of Tsaritsa Alexandra.* (Yale University Press, 1997)

Lambton, Anthony. *The Mountbattens.* (Constable, 1989)

Lee, A. G. (ed). *The Empress Frederick Writes to Sophie.* (Faber & Faber, 1955)

Lerche, Anna & Mandal, Marcus. *A Royal Family.* (Aschehoug, 2003)

Lincoln, W. Bruce. *Nicholas I. Emperor and Autocrat of All the Russias.* (Allen Lane, 1978)

–– *The Romanovs.* (The Dial Press, 1981)

Longford, Elizabeth. *Victoria: Born to Succeed.* (Harper & Row, 1964)

Lorenz, Sönke et al. *Das Haus Württemberg: Ein biographisches Lexikon.*

(Kohlhammer, 1997)

*M*andache, Diana. *Later Chapters of My Life*. (Sutton Publishing, 2004)

Marie, Grand Duchess of Russia. *Education of a Princess*. (Viking Press, 1930)

–– *A Princess in Exile*. (Viking Press, 1932)

Marie, Queen of Romania. *The Story of My Life. Volumes I, II & III*. (Cassel, 1935)

Marie Louise, Princess. *My Memories of Six Reigns*. (Evans Brothers, 1956)

Massie, Robert. *Nicholas & Alexandra*. (Victor Gollancz, 1968)

Massie, Suzanne. *Pavlovsk: The Life of a Russian Palace*. (Hodder & Stoughton, 1990)

Maylunas, Andrei and Mironenko, Sergei. *A Lifelong Passion*. (Weidenfeld & Nicolson, 1996)

Metternich, Tatiana. *Purgatory of Fools: A Memoir of the Aristocrats' War in Nazi Germany*. (Quadrangle/The New York Times Book Co., 1976)

Millar, Lubov. *Grand Duchess Elizabeth of Russia. New Martyr of the Communist Yoke*. (Nikodemos Orthodox Publication Society, 1991)

Miller, Ilana D. *The Four Graces*. (Eurohistory, 2011).

Montefiore, Simon Sebag. *The Romanovs:1613-1918*. (Weidenfeld & Nicolson, 2016).

Montgomery-Massingberd, Hugh. *Burke's Royal Families of the World, Volume I: Europe & Latin America*. (Burke's Peerage Ltd, 1977)

Morgan, Janet. *Edwina Mountbatten: A Life of Her Own*. (Charles Scribner's Sons, 1991)

Morrow, Ann. *Cousins Divided*. (Sutton Publishing, 2006)

Mossolov, A.A. *At the Court of the Last Tsar*. (Methuen, 1935)

Mountbatten of Burma, Earl (Louis). *The Mountbatten Lineage: The Direct Descent of the Family of Mountbatten from the House of Brabant and the Rulers of Hesse*. (Private circulation, 1958)

Mountbatten, Pamela (Lady Pamela Hicks). *India Remembered*. (Pavillion Books, 2007)

Museum Jagdschloß Kranichstein Wiedereröffnung 1998. (Stiftung Hessischer Jägerhof, 1998)

*N*arishkin-Kurakin, Elizabeth. *Under Three Tsars*. (E. P. Dutton & Co., Inc., 1931)

Nelipa, Margarita. *Alexei: Russia's Last Imperial Heir: A Chronicle of Tragedy*. (Gilbert's Books, 2015)

Nicholas II, Tsar of Russia. *Journal Intime de Nicolas II*. (Payot, 1923)

Nicholas, Prince of Greece. *My Fifty Years: The Memoirs of Prince Nicholas of Greece* (annotated and expanded by Arturo Beéche). (Eurohistory, 2006)

Nicolson, Harold. *King George V*. (Constable, 1952)

Norwich, John Julius (ed). *The Duff Cooper Diaries*. (Weidenfeld & Nicolson, 2005)

Notovitch, Nicolas. *L'Empereur Alexandre III et Son Entourage*. (1893)

*P*akula, Hannah. *The Last Romantic. A Biography of Queen Marie of Romania*. (Weidenfeld paperbacks, 1984)

Paley, Princess. *Memories of Russia, 1916-1919*. (Herbert Jenkins Ltd, 1924)

Palmer, Alan. *Alexander I – Tsar of War and Peace*. (Harper & Row Publishers, 1974)

Palmer, Alan. *Crowned Cousins: The Anglo-German Royal Connection*. (Weidenfeld and Nicolson, 1985)

Perry, John Curtis & Pleshakov, Constantine. *The Flight of the Romanovs*. (Basic Books,1999)

Pares, Bernard. *The Fall of the Russian Monarchy*. (Jonathan Cape, 1939)

Petropoulos, Jonathan. *Royals and the Reich: The Princes von Hessen in Nazi Germany*. (Oxford University Press, 2006)

Podgornaja, Ninel Ivanovna. *Mafalda di Savoia Assia: Facile essere una principessa…* (Solfanelli, 2009)

Poliakoff, V. *When Lovers Ruled Russia*. (D. Appleton and Company, 1928)

Ponsonby, Sir Frederick (ed). *Letters of the Empress Frederick*. (Macmillan, 1929)

–– *Recollections of Three Reigns*. (Eyre & Spottiswoode, 1951)

Poore, Judith. *The Memoirs of Emily Loch*. (Kinloss: Librario Publishing Ltd, 2007)

Pope-Hennessy, James. *Queen Mary*. (George Allen & Unwin Ltd, 1959)

Posse, Otto. *Die Wettiner 1897*. (Zentralantiquariat Leipzig, 1994)

Preston, Sir Thomas. *Before the Curtain*. (John Murray, 1950)

*R*adzinsky, Edvard. *Alexander II. The Last Great Tsar*. (N.Y.: Free Press, 2005)

Radzinsky, Edvard. *The Last Tsar*. (Doubleday, 1992)

Ramm, Agatha. *Beloved & Darling Child*. (Alan Sutton, 1990)

Rappaport, Helen. *Ekaterinburg*.

(Hutchinson, 2008)

–– *Four Sisters*. (Macmillan, 2014)

Riehl, Hans. *Als die deutschen Fürsten fielen*. (Schneekluth, 1979)

Rimius, Henry. *Memoirs of the House of Brunswick*. (J. Haberkorn, 1750)

Romanow, Prince Roman. *Am Hof des Letzten Zaren: 1896-1919*. (Piper, 1995)

Rose, Kenneth. *George V*. (Weidenfeld & Nicolson, 1983)

Rosenthal, Norman (ed). *The Misfortunate Margravine: The Early Memoirs of Wilhelmina Margravine of Bayreuth*. (Macmillan St Martin's Press, 1970)

*S*aénz, Jorge F. *A Poet Among the Romanovs. Prince Vladimir Paley*. (Eurohistory, 2004)

Service, Robert. *The Last of the Tsars*. (Macmillan, 2017)

Shoberl, Frederic. *A Historical Account of the House of Saxony*. (R. Ackerman, 1816)

Smith, Douglas. *Rasputin*. (Macmillan, 2016)

St Aubyn, Giles. *Queen Victoria. A Portrait*. (Sinclair-Stevenson, 1991)

Steinberg, Mark D. & Khrustalev, Vladimir M. *The Fall of the Romanovs*. (Yale University Press, 1995)

Stoeckl, Baroness Agnes de. *Not All Vanity*. (John Murray, 1950)

Stravlo, Marie. *Mi amigo el Príncipe: Biografía de Alfredo de Prusia*. (REA, 2014)

*T*arsaidze, Alexandre. *Katia, Wife Before God*. (Macmillan, 1970)

The Romanovs. Documents & Photographs relating to the Russian Imperial House. (Sotheby's Auction Catalogue, London, 1990)

Trevelyan, Raleigh. *Grand Dukes and Diamonds*. (Martin Secker & Warburg, 1991)

Troyat, Henri. *Alexander of Russia*. (Sevenoaks: New English Library, 1984)

–– *Alexandre III: Le tsar des Neiges*. (Grasset, 2004)

–– *Catherine the Great*. E. P. Dutton, 1980)

*V*alynseele, Joseph. *Les Prétendants aux Trones d'Europe*. (1967)

*U*rbach, Karina. *Go Betweens for Hitler*. (Oxford University Press, 2015)

Van der Kiste, John. *Alfred. Queen Victoria's Second Son*. (Fonthill Media, 2013)

–– *A Divided Kingdom*. (Sutton Publishing, 2007)

–– *Crowns in a Changing World*. (Alan Sutton, 1993)

–– *Edward VII's Children*. (Alan Sutton, 1989)

–– *Frederick III: German Emperor 1888*. (Alan Sutton, 1981).

–– *Princess Victoria Melita*. (Alan Sutton, 1991)

–– *The End of German Monarchy: The Decline and Fall of the Hohenzollerns*. (Fonthill, 2017)

–– *The Romanovs, 1818-1959*. (Stroud: Sutton Publishing, 1998)

Vickers, Hugo. *Alice Princess Andrew of Greece*. Hamish Hamilton 2000)

Vorres, Ian. *The Last Grand Duchess*. (Hutchinson, 1964)

Vovk, Justin C. *Imperial Requiem: Four Royal Women – The Fall of the Age of Empires*. (iUniverse Inc, 2012)

Vyrubova, Anna. *Memories of the Russian Court*. (MacMillan, 1923)

Waliszewski, K. *Paul the First of Russia, the Son of Catherine the Great*. (William Heinemann, 1913)

Warwick, Christopher. *Ella: Princess, Saint & Martyr*. (John Wiley, 2006)

Welch, Frances. *Imperial Tea Party*. (Short Books, 2018)

–– *The Russian Court at Sea*. (Short Books, 2011)

Wrangel, Count F.U. *Les Maisons Souveraines de l'Europe, Volume I & II*. (Hasse-W. Tullberg, 1898)

Wright, Constance. *Beautiful Enemy: A Biography of Queen Luise of Prussia*. (Dodd, Mead and Company, 1969)

Zeepvat, Charlotte. *Prince Leopold: The Untold Story of Queen Victoria's Youngest Son*. (Sutton Publishing, 1998)

–– *Queen Victoria's Family: A Century of Photographs*. (Sutton Publishing, 2001)

–– *Romanov Autumn*. (Sutton Publishing, 2000)

–– *The Camera and the Tsars: A Romanov Family Album*. (Sutton, 2004)

Magazine Articles:

Abrash, Merritt. 'A Curious Royal Romance. The Queen's Son and the Tsar's Daughter.' *In The Slavonic and East European Review, No. 109. July 1969*, pp. 389-400.

Brady, Kevin, "His Grand Ducal Highness Prince Friedrich Wilhelm of Hesse and by Rhine." *The European Royal History Journal (Eurohistory), Issue XIV, November-December 1999*.

Eilers-Koenig, Marlene, "Hessian Endings," *The European Royal History Journal (Eurohistory), Vol. 21.2, Issue CXVIII, Summer 2018*.

–– "Landgraf Moritz of Hesse (1926-2013)" *The European Royal History Journal (Eurohistory), Vol. 16.3, Issue XCIII, June 2013*.

Eilers-Koenig, Marlene, "Windsor or Mountbatten-Windsor" Royal Musings, March 24, 2009. *http://royalmusingsblogspotcom.blogspot.com/2009/03/windsor-or-mountbatten-windsor.html*

Hall, Coryne, "Princess Alice of Battenberg", *EUROHISTORY, Issue CXXIV, Volume 22.4 – Winter 2019*.

Hicks, India, "What Lady Pamela Hicks, Queen Elizabeth's Lady-in-Waiting, Thinks of The Crown". *http://www.townandcountrymag.com/society/tradition/news/a8741/the-crown-india-hicks/*

King, Greg. "A Fragment of Hellas in the North:" The Wedding of Princess Alice of Battenberg to Prince Andrew of Greece in Darmstadt, 1903". *Atlantis Magazine, vol. 2, no.2*.

King, Greg, "The Battenberg Family" *Atlantis Magazine vol.2 no.2*

King, Greg, "The Hessian Royal Family", *Atlantis Magazine: In the Courts of Memory, vol.2, no.2*.

Timms, Elizabeth Jane, "Princess Marie of Hesse, 1874-1878." *Royalty Digest Quarterly, no. 1, 2014*.

Katrina Warne, "Royal Associations with Jerusalem," *EUROHISTORY, Issue CXXI, Volume 22.1 – Spring 2019*.

Zeepvat, Charlotte, "Dear Marie Erbach." *Royalty Digest, vol. XIV, No. 9, March 2005*.

Zeepvat , Charlotte, "One October in Darmstadt…" *Royalty Digest: A Journal of Record vol. XIII, No. 4, October 2003*.

Zeepvat, Charlotte, H.R.H Prince Moritz, Landgraf of Hesse 1926-2013. *Royalty Digest Quarterly no. 2, 2013, p. 61-62*.

Zeepvat, Charlotte, "Riding to Russia: The First Grand Dukes of Hesse-Darmstadt," *Royalty Digest, vol. VII, No. 2, August 1997*.

Newspapers and Journals

Los Angeles Times
Notizen zur Ortsgeschichte.
The Daily Telegraph.
The European Royal History Journal (Eurohistory).
The Times.
Royal Russia.
Royalty Digest.
Royalty Digest Quarterly.
Sotheby's auction catalogue. Russian sale, June 2018.
The Daily Telegraph.
The European Royal History Journal (Eurohistory).
The Illustrated London News.
The New York Times.
The Sphere
The Telegraph.
The Times.

Archives:

Eurohistory Royal Archive
Eurohistory Royal Photo Collection
Hemmelmark Archives
The Hohenlohe-Langenburg Archive
The Royal Archive
The William M. Lalor Photo Collection at the Eurohistory Archive

Unpublished Memoirs:

Victoria, Marchioness of Milford Haven, *Recollections*. Hessische Staatsarchiv, Darmstadt.

Websites:

http://heinbruins.nl
https://www.rct.uk
https://www.npg.org.uk
http://www.angelfire.com/realm/gotha/gotha.htm
http://www.alexanderpalace.org
https://www.nobiliana.de
http://www.townandcountrymag.com
https://www.youtube.com

Index

Bassus, Baron Maximilian von 62
Baumbach, Baron von 40
Bavaria
Adelgunde, Princess of (Duchess of Modena) 47
Albrecht, Duke of 222
Amalie, Princess of 281
Augusta (née Hesse-Darmstadt), Countess and Duchess of Palatinate Zweibrücken 27, 280, 281, 282
Auguste Amalie, princess of (married Duke of Leuchtenberg) 281
Franz, Duke of 282
Karl, Prince of 281
Karoline, Princess of 281
Karoline (née Baden), Queen of 266, 282
Ludwig I, King of 47, 281
Ludwig II, King of 57, 261, 289
Luitpold, Prince Regent of 47
Marie (née Prussia), Queen of 57, 261, 264
Maximilian Heinrich, Elector Archbishop of Cologne 248
Maximilian I Joseph, King of 24, 27, 266, 267, 268, 280, 281, 282
Maximilian II, King of 47, 57, 261
Otto, King of 57, 261
Therese (née Saxe-Hildburghausen), Queen of 47
Beéche, Rafael 176
Belgium
Albert I, King of the Belgians 142
Leopold I, King of the Belgians 59
Leopold III, King of the Belgians 222
Bender, Josephine (Frau von Lichtenberg) 63
Bernadotte, Jean-Baptiste 32
Bernhold, Barbara Christine von 255
Binswanger, Dr. 197
Bismarck, Prince Otto von (German Chancellor) 52, 53, 54, 74, 75, 115, 123
Blomberg, General Field Marshal Werner von 189
Blücher, Gebhard Leberecht von (Fürst von Wahlstatt) 57
Bonaparte
Josephine (née Tascher de la Pagerie), Empress 40, 267
Marie Louise (née Austria), Empress Consort 36
Napoleon I, Emperor of the French 32, 33, 34, 35, 36, 40, 112, 243, 262, 267, 267, 277, 280, 282
Napoleon (II) 36
Napoleon III, Emperor of the French 54, 60, 114
Borivikova, Vera 292, 294
Brachetti Peretti, Ferdinando dei conti 243

Brandenburg
Albrecht V, Margrave of 20, 254
Elisabeth (née Anhalt-Zerbst), Electress of 6
Johan Georg, Elector of 6
Sophia Margaretha (née Oettingen-Oettingen), Margravine of 20
Brazil
Amélie (née Leuchtenberg), Empress of 47
Pedro I, Emperor of 47
Bream, Julian 227
Briegel, Carl Wolfgang 15, 20

Britten, Benjamin 227, 233, 235
Browne, John Ulick, 6th Marquess of Sligo 168
Brunswick
Anne, Princess of 247
Benedikta Henriette (née Palatinate-Simmern) 247
Christian, Duke of 9
Christian Ludwig, Duke of Brunswick-Lüneburg 247
Dorothea (née Schleswig-Holstein-Sonderburg-Glücksburg) 247
Dorothea Magdalena 247
Ernst August, Elector of Hannover 247
Friedrich Wilhelm, Duke of Brunswick-Wolfenbüttel 266
Georg, Duke of Brunswick-Lüneburg 7, 247
Georg Wilhelm, Duke of Brunswick-Celler 247
Johann Friedrich, Duke of Hannover 247
Magdalena, Duchess of Brunswick-Lüneburg 247
Marie (née Baden), Duchess of Brunswick-Wolfenbüttel 266, 267, 268
Sophia (née Palatinate), Duchess of Brunswick 247
Sophia Amalie 247
Brudenell, Jeremy 174
Bryce, Major Francis 217
Bryce, Mrs. Francis 217
Buccleuch and Queensberry, Duke of 214
Buchanan, Sir George 107
Bulgaria
Alexander, Prince of (see Battenberg, Alexander ("Sandro"), Prince of)
Ferdinand I, King of 124, 142
Simeon, King of 245

C
Call, Peter 14
Cassel, Sir Ernest 160
Charlemagne, Holy Roman Emperor 159
Chaplin, Charlie 160, 200
Chavchavadze, Prince David 149
Cheirouze, Marie Adelaide (Countess of Lemberg) 27
Churchill, Winston 146, 199, 200
Clarkson, Adrienne 170
Courland, Jakob Ketteler, Duke of 255
Coutois, Maurice 192
Cowan, Atalanta 171
Coward, Noel 199
Coyne, James Joseph 219
Custine, General Count Adam de 31
Custine, Marquis de 284

D
Dalwigk, Baron Reinhard von 52, 53, 54
D'Alembert, Jean le Rond 29
De la Fosse, Louis Remy 18, 19

H

V

Vanderbilt, Consuelo 129
Vanderbilt, Mrs. Cornelius 168
Vanderbilt, Gloria 150
Vanderbilt, Gloria Morgan 150
Verbeck, Salomon 14
Vetsera, Baroness Marie 122
Vital, Not 245
Voltaire (François-Marie Arouet) 259

W

Wagner, Winifred 189
Waldeck u. Pyrmont
Albertina, Countess of 16
Johann II, Count of 11
Wamboldt, Mayor Otto 190
Waldus, Petrus 51
Walker, George 218
Walker, Sarah Georgina 218
Wellington, Arthur Wellesley, Duke of 57
Werner von Langenstein, Countess Katharina 268
Wernher, Alex 215
Wernher, Georgina ("Gina") 197, 215, 217
Wernher, Sir Harold 215
Widmann, Pastor Friedrich 189
Wieland, Christoph Martin 259
Willich gennant von Pöllnitz, Caroline (Baroness von Nidda) 62
Windisch-Grätz
Friedrich Karl, Prince of 162
Wood, David Flint 175
Württemberg
Anna Catharina (née Salm-Kyrburg), Duchess of 250
Anna Maria (née Brandenburg)-Ansbach), Duchess of 6
Carl, Duke of 251
Christoph, Duke of 6
Eberhard III, Duke of 250, 251
Eberhard Ludwig, Duke of 250, 251
Eberhardine Louise, Duchess of 250
Eleonora Dorothea, Duchess of 250
Friedrich Ludwig, Hereditary Prince of 251
Johanna Elisabeth (née Baden-Durlach), Duchess of 251
Karl, King of 112
Karl Alexander, Duke of 251
Ludwig Friedrich, Duke of (Montbéliard) 6
Magdalena Sophie, Duchess of 251
Olga (née Russia), Queen of 112
Wilhelm Ludwig, Duke of 13, 250
Wyclif, John 51

Y

Yeltsin, Boris 155

Yourievsky

Ekaterina (née Dolgoruky), Princess 289, 291, 292, 294
Ekaterina Alexandrovna, Princess 291
George Alexandrovich, Prince 291, 292
Olga Alexandrovna, Princess 291, 292Marie Ale
Yugoslavia
Andrej, Prince of 161
Olga (née Greece), Princess of 188
Paul, Prince Regent of 188
Tomislav, Prince of 166

Z

Zeepvat, Charlotte 114, 291
Zeyher, Johann Michael 41, 63
Ziegler, Philip 199
Zimmermann, Dr. Ernst 46
Zhukovsky, Vassili 286
Zuckerman, Ariel 171